Portuguese

FOR

DUMMIES®

BESTSELLING BOOK SERIES

Portuguese For Dummies®

Your Portuguese ABCs

Here's a handy guide to help you get a handle on how to pronounce letters in Portuguese:

a (ah)	**h** (ah-*gah*)	**o** (awe)	**v** (veh)
b (beh)	**i** (ee)	**p** (peh)	**w** (*dah*-boo yoo)
c (seh)	**j** (*zhoh*-tah)	**q** (keh)	**x** (sheez)
d (deh)	**k** (kah)	**r** (*eh*-hee)	**y** (*eep*-see-loh)
e (eh)	**l** (*eh*-lee)	**s** (*eh*-see)	**z** (zeh)
f (*eh*-fee)	**m** (*eh*-mee)	**t** (teh)	
g (zheh)	**n** (*eh*-nee)	**u** (ooh)	

Standard Greetings

How are you? Tudo bem? (*too*-doh *bang*)

How are things? Como vai? (*koh*-moh *vah*-ee)

Bye! Tchau! (*chah*-ooh)

See you later! Até logo! (ah-*teh loh*-goo)

See you tomorrow! Até amanhã! (ah-*teh* ah-mang-*yah*)

Exclamations in Portuguese

Cool! Legal! (lay-*gah*-ooh)

Great! Ótimo! (*oh*-chee-moh)

How beautiful! Que bonito! (kee boo-*nee*-too)

I love it! Adoro! (ah-*doh*-doo)

How delicious! Que gostoso! (kee goh-*stoh*-zoo)

Key Questions in Portuguese

Who? Quem? (kang)

When? Quando? (*kwahn*-doh)

Where? Onde? (*ohn*-jee)

Why? Por quê? (poh *keh*)

How? Como? (*koh*-moo)

What? O que? (ooh *kee*)

Which? Qual? (*kwah*-ooh)

How much? Quanto? (*kwahn*-too)

Portuguese Numbers

1 um (oong)

2 dois (*doh*-eez)

3 três (tdehz)

4 quatro (*kwah*-tdoo)

5 cinco (*sing*-koh)

6 seis (*say*-eez)

7 sete (*seh*-chee)

8 oito (*oh*-ee-toh)

9 nove (*noh*-vee)

10 dez (dez)

Portuguese For Dummies®

Cheat Sheet

Making Friends

Knowing the right questions to ask in Portuguese goes a long way toward helping you make friends in Brazil. Here are some common questions:

What's your name? Qual é seu nome? (*kwah*-ooh *eh* seh-ooh *noh*-mee)

Where are you from? De onde é? (jee *ohn*-jee *eh*)

Do you speak English? Fala inglês? (*fah*-lah eeng-*glehz*)

What's your e-mail address? Qual é seu e-mail? (*kwah*-ooh *eh* seh-ooh ee-*meh*-ooh)

What do you like to do? O que gosta de fazer? (ooh *kee goh*-stah jee fah-*zeh*)

Tricky Pronunciations

Some common words in Portuguese are tricky for non-native speakers to pronounce. This list contains a few of them and their correct pronunciations so you can speak them like a pro.

João (zhoo-*ah*-ooh) a man's name

Roberta (hoh-*beh*-tah) a woman's name

Rio de Janeiro (*hee*-ooh dee zhah-*nay*-doo) the Brazilian city of Rio

Brasil (bdah-*zeeh*-ooh) Brazil

Carnaval (kah-nah-*vah*-ooh) Carnival

samba (*sahm*-bah) a type of Brazilian dance

festa (*feh*-stah) party

amigo (ah-*mee*-goo) friend

praia (*pdah*-ee-ah) beach

música (*moo*-zee-kah) music

Speaking Formally

If you're talking to an authority figure or you want to show respect to an elderly person, be sure to call him or her:

Sir (*Literally:* the gentleman) o senhor (ooh seen-*yoh*)

Ma'am (*Literally:* the lady) a senhora (ah seen-*yoh*-dah)

Conjugating Regular Verbs

Regular verbs in Portuguese end in **-ar, -er,** and **-ir**. Here's an **-ar** verb: **falar** (fah-*lah*; to speak). For the present tense of the verb, just take off the ending and add **-o, -a, -amos** or **-am**:

Eu falo. I speak.

Você fala. You speak.

Ele/ela fala. He/she speaks.

Nós falamos. We speak.

Eles falam. They speak.

For Dummies: Bestselling Book Series for Beginners

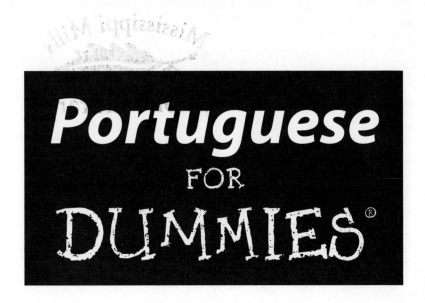

by Karen Keller

WILEY

Wiley Publishing, Inc.

Portuguese For Dummies®

Published by
Wiley Publishing, Inc.
111 River St.
Hoboken, NJ 07030-5774
www.wiley.com

About the Author

Karen Keller is a journalist who lived and worked in São Paulo, Brazil, for three years. Before moving to Brazil, the California native taught Spanish at a New York City–based foreign language education Web site. Keller is also a published travel guide writer. She currently lives in New Jersey, where she is a local newspaper reporter.

Dedication

To my dear non-Brazilian friends from the São Paulo days, for our chuckles over the **maravilha** that is Brazilian Portuguese.

Author's Acknowledgments

I'd like to extend my profound thanks to all editors I became involved with during the writing process: Natalie Harris, Stacy Kennedy, Danielle Voirol, Jennifer Bingham, and Peter Musson. It's been an absolute kick.

I must also thank my Columbia University Graduate School of Journalism professor Tim Harper for putting me in touch with my literary agent for the book, Jessica Faust. Jessica, thanks for putting good faith in me.

Next, my warmest gratitude goes out to my editor and co-worker in Brazil, Matt Cowley. Your job offer made my Brazilian adventure possible, and you gave me my first Portuguese lessons. I still remember your directive that "Rodrigo has an 'h' sound at the beginning" as my first glimpse of the language I would soon be mesmerized by.

Now for those non-Brazilian friends: Ivan, Mario, Ainhoa, Anna, Diego, Andrea, Juan, Sophia, Marisol. The sharing of our perspectives on life in Brazil and on that **lingua esquisita** are the stuff of my best memories.

And to the Brazilian who always helped set us straight. You became my closest Brazilian confidante, Dayanne Mikevis.

Chloe — thanks for all the sensible advice you've ever given me and for inspiring my first trips abroad. Jenny — you're my soul mate and the best person ever for last-minute queries on Portuguese. Yolanda — **si no fuera por ti y tu obsesión sobre Brasil, jamás hubiera ido.**

Finally, to my family: Mom, Dad, Chris, Jerry, Diane. I'm not that crazy, after all. After having melted away into the Southern Hemisphere, I'm back! And Mom: My open mind, curiosity, and word-wonder all stem from you.

Publisher's Acknowledgments

We're proud of this book; please send us your comments through our Dummies online registration form located at www.dummies.com/register/.

Some of the people who helped bring this book to market include the following:

Acquisitions, Editorial, and Media Development

Project Editor: Natalie Faye Harris

Acquisitions Editor: Stacy Kennedy

Assistant Editor: Courtney Allen

Copy Editors: Danielle Voirol, Jennifer Bingham

Editorial Program Coordinator: Hanna K. Scott

Technical Editor: Peter Musson

Media Development Specialist: Constance Lewis

Editorial Manager: Christine Beck

Media Development Manager: Laura VanWinkle

Editorial Assistants: Erin Calligan, Nadine Bell, David Lutton

Cartoons: Rich Tennant (www.the5thwave.com)

Composition Services

Project Coordinator: Adrienne Martinez

Layout and Graphics: Jonelle Burns, Denny Hager, Stephanie D. Jumper, Lynsey Osborn, Julie Trippetti

Proofreaders: Laura Albert, Betty Kish, Jessica Kramer

Indexer: Joan Griffitts

Publishing and Editorial for Consumer Dummies

    Diane Graves Steele, Vice President and Publisher, Consumer Dummies

    Joyce Pepple, Acquisitions Director, Consumer Dummies

    Kristin A. Cocks, Product Development Director, Consumer Dummies

    Michael Spring, Vice President and Publisher, Travel

    Kelly Regan, Editorial Director, Travel

Publishing for Technology Dummies

    Andy Cummings, Vice President and Publisher, Dummies Technology/General User

Composition Services

    Gerry Fahey, Vice President of Production Services

    Debbie Stailey, Director of Composition Services

Contents at a Glance

Table of Contents

Introduction

The world is shrinking. Communication technology is getting faster and faster, making it easier to contact people in what used to be exotic, far-away lands. Air travel has gotten a lot cheaper, too, so visiting these places has never been simpler. Experiencing **um pouco** (oong *poh*-koo; a little) of a new language is a great way to familiarize yourself with a region of the world or specific country. Not only does it allow you to communicate verbally, but learning new words opens the door to understanding the specific culture itself.

If you're curious about language and want to learn how to ask someone's name, ask for directions in a city, or talk about what your interests are, you've come to the right place. I'm not promising fluency here, but this book provides a great start.

This book tells you about the language spoken in Brazil. Thanks to Brazil's huge population — around 170 million or so — Portuguese is the fifth-most spoken language in the world. Flip ahead to Chapter 1 to read about which other countries in the world speak Portuguese.

Brazilian Portuguese is specific because the accent and some basic words are unique to Brazil. And the country itself is a pretty popular destination these days, with its earned reputation as a land of fun-loving, generous people.

A bonus to learning Brazilian Portuguese is that it can help you to understand a little French, Spanish, and Italian, too. They're all Romance languages, which means many words among these languages sound similar.

Brazilian Portuguese is very lyrical. The sounds can be difficult to make for non native speakers, but speaking Portuguese is fun after you get into it. I advise you to treat yourself while you're reading the book: Buy some Brazilian music. You'll fall in love with the sounds, and the background music adds great ambience.

About This Book

Here's the good news: This book isn't a class you have to drag yourself to. It's a reference book, so use it at your leisure. You're the boss. You may choose to just leaf through, glancing only at chapters and pages that grab your attention. Or you can read the whole thing from start to finish. (From finish to start is okay, too — no one's looking.)

The first few chapters may be helpful to read first, though, because they explain some basic information about pronunciation and explain words that appear throughout the book.

Conventions Used in This Book

To make the book easy to read and understand, I've set up a few stylistic rules:

- ✔ Web addresses appear in `monofont`.

- ✔ Portuguese terms are set in **boldface** to make them stand out.

- ✔ Pronunciations and definitions, which are shown in parentheses, follow the terms the first time they appear in a section.

- ✔ Within the pronunciation, the part of the word that's stressed is shown in *italics*.

- ✔ Verb conjugations (lists that show you the forms of a verb) are given in tables in this order: the *I* form, the *you* form, the *he/she* form, the *we* form, and the *they* form. Pronunciations follow in a second column. (You can also find conjugation charts in Appendix A.)

Here's an example of a conjugation chart for the word **ser** (seh; to be). Because the subjects always come in the same order, you can see that words in this chart mean *I am, you are, he/she is, we are,* and *they are:*

Conjugation	*Pronunciation*
eu sou	*eh*-ooh *soh*
você é	voh-*seh eh*
ele/ela	*eh*-lee/*eh*-la *eh*
nós somos	*nohz soh*-mooz
eles/elas são	*eh*-leez/*eh*-lahz *sah*-ooh

In each chapter, you can also find the following:

- ✔ **Talkin' the Talk dialogues:** The best way to learn a language (and the most fun way) is to be exposed to real-life dialogues, so I include little conversations throughout the book. The dialogues come under the

heading "Talkin' the Talk" and show you the Portuguese words, the pronunciation, and the English translations. These conversations are on
the CD that came with this book, so when you see a CD icon, be sure to
listen along.

✔ **Words to Know blackboards:** Knowing key words and phrases is also
important in the quest to speak a new language. I collect important
words that appear in the Talkin' the Talk dialogues (and perhaps add a
few related terms) and put them in a special blackboard-shaped box that
follows the dialogues.

✔ **Fun & Games activities:** At the end of each chapter, I give you an activity to help you practice some of the words and concepts I tell you in that
chapter. I try to pick the most basic words for this section to ensure you
know the essentials.

Assumptions, Foolish and Otherwise

To write this book, I had to imagine who my readers would be. Yes, you! I
think if you've picked up this book, you're probably a pretty open-minded
person who enjoys learning. That's excellent. Because the first step to
absorbing new information is wanting to absorb it.

Here are some other things I'm imagining about you:

✔ You don't want to memorize long lists of vocabulary to learn Portuguese.

✔ You want to get your feet wet in Portuguese while having fun at the
same time.

✔ You're interested in learning about Brazilian culture as well as its
language.

✔ You're not looking for a book to make you fluent in Portuguese but one
that instead gives you bite-sized information that provides a solid base
to understanding the language.

The only thing I ask of you is to leave any foolish assumptions behind that
you may have that would prevent you from getting the most out of this book!
For example, it's nonsense that only younger people can learn languages. The
desire to learn is all you need. And it doesn't matter how well you did in high
school French or German, or whichever language classes you've taken before.
This book is designed to take a fresh approach to learning languages, and I
won't grade you.

How This Book Is Organized

This book is divided by topic into parts and then into chapters. Chapters are further divided into sections. The following sections tell you what types of information you can find in each part.

Part 1: Getting Started

This part lets you get your feet wet by giving you some Portuguese basics — how to pronounce words, how sentences are constructed, and so on. I also give you an ego boost by showing you Portuguese words that are so close to English that you already know their meanings.

Part 11: Portuguese in Action

In this part, you begin discovering the language and practicing Portuguese. Instead of focusing on grammar points and philosophizing about why the language is structured the way it is, I jump right in. I *show* you how it works instead of *telling* you how it works. This section in particular highlights how to talk to new Brazilian friends.

Part 111: Portuguese on the Go

This part gives you the tools you need to take your Portuguese on the road, whether you're going to a local restaurant, checking out a museum, or getting help planning a trip with a Brazilian travel agent. This section's devoted to the traveler in you, the one who checks into hotels, hails a cab, and studies bus schedules. This information is all, of course, to help you get to places where you can have a good time — whether that means going out on a Saturday night in Rio or enjoying yourself during Brazil's famous Carnaval season.

Part 1V: The Part of Tens

If you're looking for small, easily digestible pieces of information about Portuguese, this part is for you. Here, you can find ten ways to speak Portuguese quickly, ten useful Portuguese expressions to know, and ten common slang expressions.

Part V: Appendixes

This part of the book is a great reference guide. I lay out verb conjugation tables for the most common Brazilian Portuguese verbs. I also include two mini-dictionaries here — one from English to Portuguese and the other from Portuguese to English. Another appendix lets you check out the answers to the "Fun & Games" activities. Finally, I provide a listing of the tracks that appear on the audio CD that comes with this book (the disc's on the inside part of the last page). That's so you can listen and follow along while you're reading the dialogues.

Icons Used in This Book

Drawings and symbols always liven things up a bit, don't they? Here are some icons that point you to important information:

This icon shows you where you can find some fascinating tidbits that highlight either a linguistic aspect or give travel tips. Tips can save you time and frustration.

This handy icon pops up whenever you run across a bit of information that you really should remember after you close the book, whether it's about the Portuguese language or Brazil in general.

Pay attention when this icon appears, because it's probably pointing out information that can keep you out of trouble or from making embarrassing boo-boos.

The "Cultural Wisdom" snippets help give insight into Brazilian culture.

The audio CD lets you listen to native Brazilian speakers. The icon marks some "Talkin' the Talk" sections and reminds you that you can listen to the dialogue while you read it.

Where to Go from Here

When you have a spare moment, pop open the book. All you need is a curious mind and the openness to learn about Brazil. Above all, don't think of reading the book as a chore. It's meant to be relaxing and enjoyable.

Feel free to complement this book with other activities that enhance your knowledge of Portuguese, like entering a Portuguese-language chat room on the Internet or having Brazilian music on in the background so you can hear the sounds of the language.

Oh, and **boa sorte** (*boh*-ah *soh*-chee; good luck)!

Part I
Getting Started

The 5th Wave   By Rich Tennant

BRAZILIAN
DIPHTHONGS

"Whoa, hold on. I came here to learn how to
speak Portuguese, not what to wear on the
beaches of Brazil."

In this part . . .

This part introduces you to Brazilian Portuguese. It lets you get your feet wet by giving you some Portuguese basics — how to pronounce words, how sentences are constructed, and so on. I also give you an ego boost by showing you Portuguese words that are so close to English, you already know their meanings.

Chapter 1

You Already Know a Little Portuguese!

*B*elieve it or not, the Portuguese language comes in different versions. Pronunciation of Brazilian Portuguese and Portuguese from Portugal, say, is totally different. Some Brazilian tourists in Portugal report that they didn't understand a word! I think it's a little more of a stretch than the differences between American and British English, just to give you an idea. But if a group of people from Texas, South Africa, and Scotland got together, they'd probably scratch their heads when trying to understand each other, too!

Written Portuguese, on the other hand, is very standard, especially when it's in a newspaper or some formal publication that doesn't use slang. A Brazilian can understand a Portuguese newspaper or read the works of Portugal's Nobel prize–winning author José Saramago, no problem.

In this book, I focus on Brazilian Portuguese, as opposed to the Portuguese spoken in Portugal and countries in Africa — Cape Verde (islands off northwestern Africa), Mozambique (on the coast of southeast Africa), Guinea-Bissau (in western Africa), Angola (in southwestern Africa), and Sao Tome and Principe (islands off western Africa).

Exploring the Roots of Portuguese

The beautiful Portuguese language belongs to a linguistic family known as the Romance languages. Back when the Roman Empire was around, Rome was in the center of a wide swath of Europe, northern Africa, and parts of Asia. With Rome's influence came its language — Latin.

And the closer a place was to Rome, the more likely it was to absorb Latin into its language. This was the case with Portugal — where the Portuguese language originates — as well as with places like France, Spain, and even Romania.

So how did Portuguese get all the way to Brazil? A Portuguese conquistador named Pedro Álvares Cabral landed in modern-day Brazil on April 22, 1500, and is the person credited for having "discovered" Brazil. Many indigenous people were already living in the area, of course, many of whom spoke a language that's part of a language family today called **Tupi-Guarani** (too-*pee* gwah-dah-*nee*).

Brazilian Portuguese uses some Tupi-Guarani words. Mostly the words appear as names of towns in Brazil — for example, **Uba-Tuba** (*ooh*-bah-*too*-bah) is a pretty beach town in Sao Paulo state (it's nicknamed **Uba-Chuva** because **chuva** [*shoo*-vah] means *rain* and it rains there a lot!). Tupi-Guarani words also name native plants and animals. *Armadillo,* for example, is **tatu** (tah-*too*). After you get used to speaking Portuguese, telling whether a word is Latin-based or Tupi-Guarani–based is pretty easy.

Still other words in Brazilian Portuguese are based on African languages, from the vast influence African slaves had on creating modern-day Brazil and its culture.

What you may not realize is that the English language has a lot of Latin influence. Linguists consider English to be a Germanic language, and it technically is. But due to the on-and-off French occupations of the British Isles, some of those French (Latin-based) words rubbed off on English. Some people say as much as 40 percent of English is Latin-based.

That's great news for you. It means many Portuguese words have the same root as English words. The *root* of a word is usually the middle of the word — those few sounds that really define what the word means. Some examples of Portuguese words that resemble English include **experimento** (eh-speh-dee-*men*-toh; experiment), **presidente** (pdeh-zee-*dang*-chee; president), **economía** (eh-koh-noh-*mee*-ah; economy), **decisão** (ah deh-see-*zah*-ooh; decision), **computadora** (kom-*poo*-tah-*doh*-dah; computer), **liberdade** (lee-beh-*dah*-jee; liberty), and **banana** (bah-*nah*-nah). And that's only to name a few!

Another benefit: **O português** (ooh poh-too-*gehz;* Portuguese), like all Latin languages, uses the English alphabet. Some funny accent marks appear on some of the vowels, but they just add to the mystique of Portuguese. Learning Portuguese isn't the same as learning Japanese or Arabic, which use totally different alphabets.

Finally, due to the influence the U.S. has had on the world recently — in some ways greater than Rome's ancient influence — many English words are used commonly in Portuguese, with no adaptation in the way they're written. These words include modern technology words like **e-mail** (ee-*may*-oh) and also basic words like **shopping** (*shoh*-ping) or **show** (shoh; show/performance).

Reciting Your ABCs

Brazilian Portuguese sounds very strange at first. I myself thought it sounded Russian, back when I didn't understand a **palavra** (pah-*lahv*-dah; word)! A few of the sounds are a little hard to imitate, because people don't use them in English. But Brazilians often understand you even if you don't say words perfectly. Many think a foreign **sotaque** (soh-*tah*-kee; accent) is charming, so don't worry about it.

But the way the sounds correspond to the written letters is very systematic in Brazilian Portuguese — more so than in English. After you get used to the way a letter or combination of letters sounds, you get the hang of pronunciations pretty quickly. There are few surprises in **a pronúncia** (ah pdoh-*noon*-see-ah; pronunciation) after you get the basics down.

 Track 2 of the audio CD that accompanies this book also contains a pronunciation guide to help you get a better feel for the Portuguese laungage.

At the beginning of this chapter, did you notice how the pronunciation is shown in parentheses after the Portuguese word? That's how this book shows the pronunciation of all new words. The italicized part is where you put the emphasis on the word. On "Words to Know" lists, the part you emphasize is underlined rather than italicized.

Are you ready to learn the basics of **o português?** You can start with the alphabet. Practice spelling your name out:

- ✔ **a** (ah)
- ✔ **b** (beh)
- ✔ **c** (seh)
- ✔ **d** (deh)
- ✔ **e** (eh)

- ✔ **f** (*eh*-fee)
- ✔ **g** (zheh)
- ✔ **h** (ah-*gah*)
- ✔ **i** (ee)
- ✔ **j** (*zhoh*-tah)

- **k** (kah)
- **l** (*eh*-lee)
- **m** (*eh*-mee)
- **n** (*eh*-nee)
- **o** (awe)
- **p** (peh)
- **q** (keh)
- **r** (*eh*-hee)

- **s** (*eh*-see)
- **t** (teh)
- **u** (ooh)
- **v** (veh)
- **w** (*dah*-boo yoo)
- **x** (sheez)
- **y** (*eep*-see-loh)
- **z** (zeh)

When the book uses the sound *zh* as part of the phonetic transcription (the pronunciation guide in parenthesis), think of the sound in Hungarian actress Zsa-Zsa Gabor's name. That's the *zh* sound I'm talking about.

Conquering Consonants

Getting through this book will hopefully be a cinch after you go through the basic pronunciation guide in this section. Skipping the guide is okay, too — you can get the gist by listening to the CD and reading the pronunciations of words in other chapters aloud. But if you want to get a general idea of how to pronounce words that don't show up in this book, this is a great place to begin. I start with the consonants first — you know, all those letters in the alphabet that aren't vowels.

The most hilarious aspect of Brazilian Portuguese pronunciation occurs when a word ends in a consonant. In most cases, these are foreign (and mostly English) words that Brazilians have adopted. They add an *ee* sound to the end of the word when there isn't one. Here are some examples: **club** (*kloo*-bee); **laptop** (lahp-ee-*top*-ee); **hip-hop** (heep-ee-*hoh*-pee); **rap** (*hah*-pee); and **rock** (*hoh*-kee).

Most consonants in Brazilian Portuguese have the same sound as in English. In the following sections, I go over the exceptions.

The letter C

A *c* that begins a word sounds usually like a *k*.

- **casa** (*kah*-zah; house)
- **café** (kah-*feh;* coffee)

If the *c* has a hook-shaped mark under it, like this — *ç* — it makes an *s* sound.

- **serviço** (seh-*vee*-soo; service)
- **França** (*fdahn*-sah; France)

The most common appearance of what Brazilians call the **c-cedilha** (*seh* seh-*deel*-yah; ç/cedilla) is at the end of a word, followed by **-ão.** It's the Brazilian equivalent of the English *-tion* ending.

- **promoção** (pdoh-moh-*sah*-ooh; sale/discount/sales promotion)
- **evolução** (eh-voh-loo-*sah*-ooh; evolution)

The letter D

If the word begins with a *d*, the sound is usually a hard *d,* like in English.

- **dançar** (dahn-*sah;* to dance)
- **data** (*dah*-tah; date)

The word **de** (jee), which means *of,* is an exception.

If the *d* comes in the middle of a word, before a vowel, it can have either a hard *d* sound or a *j* sound — like in the English word *jelly.*

- **modelo** (moh-*deh*-loo; model)
- **estado** (eh-*stah*-doh; state)
- **advogado** (ahj-voh-*gah*-doh; lawyer)
- **pedir** (peh-*jee;* to ask for)
- **liberdade** (lee-beh-*dah*-jee; freedom)

The letter G

The *g* in Portuguese usually is a hard *g,* like in the English word *go.*

- **gato** (*gah*-too; cat)
- **governo** (goh-*veh*-noo; government)
- **segundo** (seh-*goon*-doh; second)

But it takes a *zh* sound, as in the famous Zsa-Zsa Gabor, when followed by an *e* or an *i*.

- ✔ **gente** (*zhang*-chee; people)
- ✔ **biologia** (bee-oh-loh-*zhee*-ah; biology)

The letter H

The Brazilian Portuguese *h* is one of the most versatile consonants around. If the word begins with an *h*, the letter's silent.

- ✔ **honesto** (oh-*neh*-stoh; honest)
- ✔ **hora** (*oh*-dah; hour)

If the *h* follows an *l (lh)* or an *n (nh)*, *h* sounds like a *y*.

- ✔ **maravilhoso** (mah-dah-veel-*yoh*-zoo; marvellous/amazing)
- ✔ **palhaço** (pahl-*yah*-soh; clown)
- ✔ **companhia** (kohm-pahn-*yee*-ah; company)
- ✔ **Espanha** (eh-*spahn*-yah; Spain)

The letter J

The *j* in Portuguese sounds like the *zh* in Zsa-Zsa.

- ✔ **julho** (*zhool*-yoh; July)
- ✔ **Jorge** (*zhoh*-zhee; George)
- ✔ **loja** (*loh*-zhah; store)
- ✔ **joelho** (zhoh-*el*-yoh; knee)

The letter L

The *l* in Portuguese normally sounds like the *l* in English.

- ✔ **líder** (*lee*-deh; leader)
- ✔ **gelo** (*zheh*-loo; ice)

But if it comes at the end of a word, the *l* sounds like *ooh*.

  ✔ **mil** (mee-*ooh;* one thousand)

  ✔ **Natal** (nah-*tah*-ooh; Christmas)

The letters M and N

The *m* and *n* in Portuguese generally sound like *m* and *n* in English.

  ✔ **mel** (*meh*-ooh; honey)

  ✔ **medo** (*meh*-doo; fear)

  ✔ **janela** (zhah-*neh*-lah; window)

  ✔ **não** (*nah*-ooh; no)

But at the end of a word, an *m* or *n* takes on an *ng* sound.

  ✔ **homem** (*oh*-mang; man)

  ✔ **cem** (sang; one hundred)

The letter Q

The *q* in Portuguese has a *k* sound.

  ✔ **quilo** (kee-*loo;* kilo)

  ✔ **quilômetro** (kee-*loh*-meh-tdoh; kilometer)

The letter R

If the word begins or ends with an *r,* the *r* sounds like an *h.*

  ✔ **Roberto** (hoh-*beh*-too; Robert)

  ✔ **rosa** (*hoh*-zah; pink)

If the *r* comes in the middle of a word, on the accented syllable, it sounds like an even stronger *h.* In the words **porta** and **carta** that follow, push air out of your mouth as you say the *h.* It's a breathy *h,* not a gutteral sound like you'd hear in Hebrew or German.

  ✔ **porta** (*poh*-tah; door)

  ✔ **carta** (*kah*-tah; letter)

If the *r* comes in the middle of a word, on an unaccented syllable, it sounds like a soft *d*. Feel what your mouth does when you read the pronunciation for **Brasil.** The way you say the *d* in *bdah* is how you should say it in the *dah* of koh-dah-*sah*-ooh, too. It's not a hard *d* like in English.

- **Brasil** (bdah-*zeeh*-ooh; Brazil)
- **coração** (koh-dah-*sah*-ooh; heart)

If a word has two *r*'s *(rr),* they make an *h* sound, as in **burro** (*boo*-hoh; dumb).

If the *r* comes at the end of a word, it's silent.

- **caminhar** (kah-ming-*yah;* to walk)
- **gostar** (goh-*stah;* to like)

The letter S

The *s* is the same as the English *s,* except it becomes a *z* sound at the end of a word.

- **olhos** (*ohl*-yooz; eyes)
- **dedos** (*deh*-dooz; fingers)

The letter T

The *t* in Portuguese has a soft *t* sound in general. In English, you don't use the soft *t* sound very often. Say *ta, ta, ta* in a quiet voice, as if you're marking a rhythm. That's the soft *t* of Portuguese.

- **motocicleta** (moh-too-see-*kleh*-tah; motorcycle)
- **atuar** (ah-too-*ah;* to act)
- **Tailândia** (tah-ee-*lahn*-jee-ah; Thailand)

But *t* sounds like *ch* when followed by an *e* or an *i.*

- **passaporte** (pah-sah-*poh*-chee; passport)
- **forte** (*foh*-chee; strong)
- **noticia** (noh-*chee*-see-ah; news)
- **time** (*chee*-mee; team)

The letter W

The *w* doesn't naturally occur in Portuguese, but when it does, it sounds like a *v*. The only places you really see a *w* is in someone's name.

- **Wanderlei** (*vahn*-deh-lay)
- **Wanessa** (vah-*neh*-sah)

The letter X

The *x* generally has a *sh* sound in Portuguese.

- **axé** (ah-*sheh;* a popular Brazililan type of dance)
- **lixo** (*lee*-shoo; garbage)
- **taxa** (*tah*-shah; rate)
- **bruxa** (*bdoo*-shah; witch)

But it can also have a *ks* sound, like in English: **tóxico** (*tohk*-see-koh; toxic).

Exercising Your Jowls with Vowels

In this section, I go over all five vowels in Portuguese, including the ones with the weird accents on top of them.

The letters A and Ã

The *a* normally has an *ah* sound.

- **amigo** (ah-*mee*-goo; friend)
- **ajuda** (ah-*zhoo*-dah; help)
- **Tatiana** (tah-chee-*ah*-nah)

If the *a* has a squiggly mark, or **til** (*chee*-ooh; ~/tilde*)*, on top of it (*ã*), the letter makes a nasal sound. Instead of opening your mouth to say *a,* as in the English word *at,* try closing your mouth almost completely while you make the same sound. Do you hear that? It becomes more of an *uh* than an *ah.* Then try to open your mouth (making the same sound) without bringing your lips farther apart. And voilá! You have the *ã* sound!

The *ã* is a very common sound in Brazilian Portuguese. But to be honest, I took more than a year to be able to say it like a Brazilian. Don't sweat it — most Brazilians will probably understand you either way.

The *ã* occasionally comes at the end of a word.

- **maçã** (mah-*sah;* apple)
- **Maracanã** (mah-dah-kah-*nah;* a soccer stadium in Rio)

However, *ã* is usually followed by an *o (ão)*. Together, these letters make an *ah-ooh* sound. But say it fast, and you say *Ow!* like you've hurt yourself. Brazilians say the *ã* like the English *ow,* only with the nasal sound you just practiced.

- **não** (*nah*-ooh; no)
- **informação** (een-foh-mah-*sah*-ooh; information)

The letters E and Ê

In general, the *e* sounds like *eh,* as in *egg* or *ten.*

- **elefante** (eh-leh-*fahn*-chee; elephant)
- **dedo** (*deh*-doo; finger)

If it comes at the end of a word, though, *e* usually has an *ee* sound.

- **dificuldade** (jee-fee-kool-*dah*-jee; difficulty)
- **boate** (boh-*ah*-chee; nightclub)

If the *e* has a hat on it *(ê)*, don't worry. It has the same *eh* sound as normal.

- **três** (tdehz; three)

The letter I

The *i* has an *ee* sound, pretty much without exception.

- **inglês** (eeng-*glehz;* English)
- **livro** (*leev*-doh; book)

The letters O and Ô

The *o* by itself has an easy-to-make *oh* sound.

- ✓ **ontem** (*ohn*-tang; yesterday)
- ✓ **onda** (*ohn*-dah; wave)

At the end of a word, though, it usually sounds like *ooh*.

- ✓ **tudo** (*too*-doo; everything/all)
- ✓ **Gramado** (gdah-*mah*-doo; a city in Rio Grande do Sul, famous for its film festival)

The *o* also comes with a hat on it *(ô)*. Don't fear the weirdness — it takes an *oh* sound, like normal.

- ✓ **ônibus** (*oh*-nee-boos; bus)

The letter U

The *u* has an *ooh* sound.

- ✓ **urso** (*ooh*-soo; bear)
- ✓ **útil** (*ooh*-chee-ooh; useful)
- ✓ **ou** (ooh; or)

Regional Differences in Accent

The Portuguese pronunciation I give you in this book works for most of Brazil, and it's certainly perfectly understandable to nearly any Brazilian. There are distinctive differences in accent depending on the region in Brazil. Usually the difference isn't an entire way people speak, just how they say a certain sound.

Following are a few classic accent hallmarks that can help you tell which region of Brazil your conversation partner is from. You don't have to memorize anything — this info's just for your amusement!

Rio de Janeiro

Cariocas (kah-dee-*oh*-kahz; people from the city of Rio) are famous for saying *sh* instead of *s*.

Word	Rio Pronunciation	Standard Pronunciation	Meaning
mulheres	mool-*yeh*-deesh	mool-*yeh*-deez	women
esquina	eh-*shkee*-nah	eh-*skee*-nah	corner

Interior of São Paulo state

People from inland São Paulo state (not the city of São Paulo) are famous for sounding like Americans speaking bad Portuguese, believe it or not! That's because they say the Portuguese *r* in an accented syllable like a hard English *r* instead of a strong *h*.

Word	Interior of São Paulo Pronunciation	Standard Pronunciation	Meaning
interior	een-teh-dee-*or*	een-teh-dee-*oh*	inland
porta	*por*-tah	*poh*-tah	door

Northeastern Brazil

In this part of the country, most people (except for those in Bahia state) say a hard *d* for *d* instead of *j* as in *jelly*. And their *t* is a snappy *t* like in English, instead of the *ch* sound made in the rest of the country.

Word	Northeastern Pronunciation	Standard Pronunciation	Meaning
bom dia	boh-oong *dee*-ah	boh-oong *jee*-ah	good morning
forte	*foh*-tee	*foh*-chee	strong

Rio Grande do Sul

Gaúchos (gah-*ooh*-shohz; people from Rio Grande do Sul state) are famous for talking in a sing-song voice that goes up and down a lot. These people live near the border with Argentina and Uruguay, which means their accents are more Spanish-sounding than those in the rest of Brazil.

Fun & Games

Try to match these Portuguese letters with the sound they generally make in English. Then give a Portuguese word that uses the sound. See Appendix C for the answer key.

1. **a**   a. s

2. **u**   b. ch

3. **t**   c. ooh

4. **ç**   d. v

5. **w**   e. ah

Chapter 2

The Nitty-Gritty: Basic Portuguese Grammar and Numbers

. . . .

In This Chapter

▶ Nouns and adjectives: Describing people, places, and things

▶ Including articles: *A, the,* and *some*

▶ Practicing using pronouns: *I, you, he, she, we, they*

▶ Forming simple sentences

▶ Understanding regular and irregular verb conjugations

▶ Combining words with contractions

▶ Indirect objects: When something happens *to you* and *me*

▶ Practicing the numbers 1-100 (and up)

. . . .

*I*ck. Grammar. Remember that word from high school? The way grammar is usually taught, you feel like you're doing math problems, not exploring fun cultural stuff. Well, in this chapter, I don't talk about grammar as a set of rules to memorize. (Though if you really want to do some math, I introduce some Portuguese numbers at the end.)

Figuring out how to categorize types of words and understanding where they go in a sentence is like putting together a puzzle. And here's some good news: Portuguese and English use only several pieces, and they're the same. Each piece refers to a category of word that's used to put together the sentence — the parts of speech.

Agreeing with Nouns and Adjectives

Like in English, nouns are one of the main parts of Portuguese speech — the most important pieces of the puzzle. They're used to name people, places, and things, like **casa** (*kah*-zah; house), **amigo** (ah-*mee*-goo; friend), **Maria** (mah-*dee*-ah; the name of a woman), **caneta** (kah-*neh*-tah; pen), and **Brasil** (bdah-*zee*-ooh; Brazil).

Portuguese nouns come in two types: masculine and feminine. Masculine nouns usually end in an **-o,** and feminine nouns usually end in an **-a.** If a noun ends in a different letter, you can look up the word's gender in a Portuguese-English dictionary. At first, imagining that a door, a key, a chair and other "things" can be masculine or feminine can be very weird.

Keep the gender of the thing you're talking about in mind: In Portuguese, every time you describe the noun with an adjective — like **bonita** (boo-*nee*-tah; pretty), **simpático** (seem-*pah*-chee-koo; nice), or **grande** (*gdahn*-jee; big) — you change the end of the adjective to make it either masculine or feminine. The adjective's gender should match the gender of the noun. Like nouns, masculine adjectives normally end in **-o,** and feminine adjectives end in **-a.**

Another little trick: In Portuguese, the adjective normally comes after the noun. This word order is the opposite of what it is in English, in which people first say the adjective and then the noun (red dress; beautiful sunset). It's one of the few differences in word order between Portuguese and English.

Here's how the nouns and adjectives get paired off. In the first couple examples, notice how the ending of **lindo** (*leen*-doo; good-looking) changes, depending on the gender of the noun it follows:

- ✔ **homem lindo** (*oh*-mang *leen*-doo; good-looking/handsome man)
- ✔ **mulher linda** (mool-*yeh leen*-dah; good-looking/beautiful woman)
- ✔ **quarto limpo** (*kwah*-too *leem*-poo; clean room)
- ✔ **casa suja** (*kah*-zah *soo*-zhah; dirty house)
- ✔ **comida gostosa** (koh-*mee*-dah goh-*stoh*-zah; delicious food)

Some adjectives are neutral and stay the same for both masculine and feminine nouns. These adjectives often end in **-e** rather than **-o** or **-a.** Adjectives in this group include **inteligente** (een-*teh*-lee-*zhang*-chee; intelligent) and **grande** (*gdahn*-jee; big).

Notice how the word **inteligente** stays the same, whether the noun is male or female:

- ✔ **Ela é muito inteligente.** (*eh*-lah *eh* moh-*ee*-toh een-*teh*-lee-*zhang*-chee; She is very intelligent.)
- ✔ **Ele é muito inteligente.** (*eh*-lee *eh* moh-*ee*-toh een-*teh*-lee-*zhang*-chee; He is very intelligent.)

If the noun is plural, just add an s to the end of the adjective: **cachorros pequenos** (kah-*shoh*-hooz peh-*keh*-nooz; small dogs).

Looking at Some Articles

Just like with Portuguese nouns and adjectives, the gender game is also at play when it comes to articles, the words like *the, a, an,* and *some.*

Now's the time to *ooh* and *ah* over grammar — **o** (ooh) means *the* for masculine nouns, and **a** (ah) means *the* for feminine nouns. In the following phrases, check out how the first and last letters match:

- ✔ **o homem lindo** (ooh *oh*-mang *leen*-doo; the handsome man)
- ✔ **a mulher linda** (ah mool-*yeh leen*-dah; the beautiful woman)
- ✔ **o quarto limpo** (ooh *kwah*-too *leem*-poo; the clean room)
- ✔ **a casa suja** (ah *kah*-zah *soo*-zhah; the dirty house)

Brazilians use the word *the* in front of nouns much more often than people do in English. When you'd say *Books are fun,* they'd say **Os livros são divertidos** (oohz *leev*-dooz *sah*-ooh jee-veh-*chee*-dooz; *Literally:* The books are fun). *Brazil is big* would be **O Brasil é grande** (ooh bdah-*zee*-ooh eh *gdahn*-jee; *Literally:* The Brazil is big).

Brazilians always use **o** or **a** before a person's name: **A Mónica** (ah *moh*-nee-kah), **a Cláudia** (ah *klah*-ooh-jee-ah), **o Nicolas** (ooh nee-koh-*lahs*), **o Roberto** (ooh hoh-*beh*-too). It's like saying *the Steve, the Diane.*

If a noun is plural, use **os** (ooz) if the noun's masculine and **as** (ahz) if it's feminine:

- ✔ **os barcos grandes** (ooz *bah*-kooz *gdahn*-jeez; the big boats)
- ✔ **as flores amarelas** (ahz *floh*-deez ah-mah-*deh*-lahz; the yellow flowers)

To say *a,* as in *a hat* or *a table,* say **um** (oong) for masculine nouns and **uma** (*ooh*-mah) for feminine nouns:

- ✔ **um banheiro** (oong bahn-*yay*-doh; a bathroom)
- ✔ **uma pessoa** (*ooh*-mah peh-*soh*-ah; a person)
- ✔ **um livro** (oong *leev*-doh; a book)
- ✔ **uma mesa** (*ooh*-mah *meh*-zah; a table)

To say *some,* use **uns** (*oonz*) if the noun's masculine or **umas** (*ooh*-mahz) if it's feminine:

> ✔ **uns sapatos** (*oonz* sah-*pah*-tooz; some shoes)
>
> ✔ **umas garotas** (*ooh*-mahz gah-*doh*-tahz; some girls)
>
> ✔ **umas praias** (*ooh*-mahz *pdah*-ee-ahz; some beaches)

When you make the plural of a word ending in *m,* such as **um,** the *m* always changes to an *n:* **Um homem** (*oong oh*-mang; a man) becomes **uns homens** (*oonz oh*-mangz).

Introducing Pronouns: You and I Both

You use pronouns to refer to people when you don't say their names. Here's the way Brazilians do it:

> ✔ **eu** (*eh*-ooh; I)
>
> ✔ **você** (voh-*seh;* you)
>
> ✔ **ele** (*eh*-lee; he/him)
>
> ✔ **ela** (*eh*-lah; she/her)
>
> ✔ **nós** (nohz; we/us)
>
> ✔ **eles** (*eh*-leez; they/them — all males or males and females)
>
> ✔ **elas** (*eh*-lahz; they/them — all females)

Brazilians don't have an equivalent of the English word *it.* Because "things" are either masculine or feminine in Portuguese, Brazilians refer to the thing or things as **ele/ela/eles/elas** when the thing isn't named. You don't hear this too often, because more often than not, Brazilians use the name of what they're talking about. But **a mala** (ah *mah*-lah; the suitcase) can become **ela** (*Literally:* she) if both speakers understand the context. **Eu perdi ela** (*eh*-ooh peh-*jee eh*-ah; I lost it) can mean *I lost the suitcase.*

If you're talking to a person who's a lot older than you (especially the elderly) or to an important person like a boss or a politician, instead of using **você,** use **o senhor** (ooh seen-*yoh; Literally:* the gentleman) or **a senhora** (ah seen-*yoh*-dah; *Literally:* the lady) to show respect.

Here are some sentences using pronouns:

> ✔ **Eu falo português.** (*eh*-ooh *fah*-loh poh-too-*gez;* I speak Portuguese.)

> ✔ **Você escreve.** (voh-*seh* ehs-*kdeh*-vee; You write.)

> ✔ **A senhora é brasileira?** (ah seen-*yoh*-dah eh bdah-zee-*lay*-dah; Are you Brazilian? — to an older woman)

Examining Verbs and Simple Sentence Construction

To really make a sentence come alive, you need verbs. Along with nouns, verbs make up the main parts of a sentence. Verbs can link a describing word to what it describes. The most basic linking-verb words in Portuguese are **é** (eh; is) and **são** (*sah*-ooh; are). The following sentences simply use nouns, verbs, and adjectives in the same order you'd use them in English:

> ✔ **A casa é bonita.** (ah *kah*-zah *eh* boo-*nee*-tah; The house is pretty.)

> ✔ **O amigo é simpático.** (ooh ah-*mee*-goo *eh* seem-*pah*-chee-koo; The friend is nice.)

> ✔ **As rosas são vermelhas.** (ahz *hoh*-zahz *sah*-ooh veh-*mel*-yahz; The roses are red.)

Of course, all you need to create a sentence is a noun followed by a verb. When the person, place, or thing is doing something, a verb signals the action. Action verbs include **estuda** (eh-*stoo*-dah; studies), **vai** (*vah*-ee; goes), and **canta** (*kahn*-tah; sings). Here are some complete sentences:

> ✔ **Os amigos falam.** (oohz ah-*mee*-gooz *fah*-lah-ooh; The friends talk.)

> ✔ **O gato dorme.** (ooh *gah*-too *doh*-mee; The cat sleeps.)

> ✔ **A mãe cozinha.** (ah *mah*-ee koh-*zing*-yah; The mom cooks.)

When you want to ask a question, you don't have to change the order of the words. Just say the same thing, but raise the pitch of your voice at the end of the sentence. Use the voice you use to ask questions in English; it's that easy.

> ✔ **A casa é bonita?** (ah *kah*-zah *eh* boo-*nee*-tah; Is the house pretty?)

> ✔ **As rosas são vermelhas?** (ahz *hoh*-zahz *sah*-ooh veh-*mel*-yahz; Are the roses red?)

The verb can change a bit depending on who's doing the action. The next section tells you how to know which verb form to use.

Introducing Verb Conjugations

Conjugation is basically a matter of matching a verb to a subject. Portuguese verbs come in three varieties: those that end in **-ar, -er,** and **-ir.** The **-ar** ending is your best friend; with a few exceptions, **-ar** verbs tend to be conjugated the same way, all the time. The **-ir** and **-er** verbs can be a little trickier. There are general rules for their conjugation, but not all verbs ending in **-ir** or **-er** follow the rules. Appendix A gives you a list of verb conjugations, including some of the rule-breakers.

To conjugate a verb, you snip off the ending (**-ar, -er, -ir**) and add a new one, depending on who's doing the action. The following sections explain which endings to use.

In this book, I separate **você** (you) and **ele/ela** (him/her) into different lines even though they use the same conjugation. I also don't show in the conjugation charts the formal version of *you:* **o senhor/a senhora** (ooh seen-*yoh*/ah seen-*yoh*-dah). This form of address uses the same conjugation as **você** and **ele/ela.** So whenever you want to say *you* — whether you're being formal or not — you can always use the same form of the verb.

If the noun is not a person but rather a thing or place, first check out whether it's singular or plural. If it's singular, use the **ele/ela** conjugation; if it's plural, use the **eles/elas** conjugation.

Sometimes, you don't have to conjugate the verb at all. This often happens when you'd use an *-ing* ending in English: **Dançar é divertido** (dahn-*sah* eh jee-veh-*chee*-doo; Dancing is fun). **Falar português não é difícil** (fah-*lah* poh-too-*gez nah*-ooh eh jee-*fee*-see-ooh; Speaking Portuguese is not hard).

Using the -ar verbs

To use a verb that ends in **-ar,** replace the **-ar** with one of the new verb endings: **-o, -a, -a, -amos,** and **-am;** which ending you choose depends on the subject of the sentence. Table 2-1 shows you how the endings match up with the pronouns.

Table 2-1	Verb Endings to Use with -ar Verbs	
English Pronoun	*Portuguese Pronoun*	*Verb Ending*
I	eu	-o
you	você	-a
he/she	ele/ela	-a
we	nós	-amos
they	eles/elas	-am

Take, for example, the verb **falar** (fah-*lah;* to talk/speak). First remove the **-ar** ending. You now have **fal,** which is the *root* or *stem* of the word. Now just add the proper verb endings:

Conjugation	*Pronunciation*
eu falo	*eh*-ooh *fah*-loo
você fala	voh-*seh fah*-lah
ele/ela fala	*eh*-lee/*eh*-lah *fah*-lah
nós falamos	nohz fah-*lah*-mooz
eles/elas falam	*eh*-leez/*eh*-lahz *fah*-lam

Here's how to use the **-ar** verbs **adorar** (ah-doh-*dah;* to love [something]), **fechar** (feh-*shah;* to close), and **começar** (koh-meh-*sah;* to begin). Some of the nouns in the following examples are not people, but they're all singular like the English word *it,* so you use the **ele/ela** conjugation:

- **Eu adoro viajar.** (*eh*-ooh ah-*doh*-doo vee-ah-*zhah;* I love to travel.)

- **A loja fecha cedo hoje.** (ah *loh*-zhah *feh*-shah *seh*-doo *oh*-zhee; The store closes early today.)

- **O concerto começa agora.** (ooh kohn-*seh*-too koh-*meh*-sah ah-*goh*-dah; The concert begins now.)

Talkin' the Talk

Vitor (*vee*-toh) and **Danilo** (dah-*nee*-loo) have just met at the gym. The two guys chat about physical activities they like to do besides lifting weights. Notice the verb conjugations. The verbs all originally end in **-ar: gostar** (goh-*stah;* to like), **caminhar** (kah-ming-*yah;* to walk), **fazer** (fah-*zeh;* to do), and **jogar** (zhoh-*gah;* to play).

Danilo: **O quê tipo de esporte você gosta de fazer?**
ooh *kee chee*-poh jee eh-*spoh*-chee voh-*seh goh*-stah jee fah-*zeh?*
What type of sports do you like to do?

Vitor: **Eu caminho muito, e faço aula de Tai Chi.**
eh-ooh kah-*ming*-yoh moh-*ee*-toh, ee *fah*-soh ah-ooh-lah jee *tah*-ee-*chee.*
I walk a lot, and I do Tai Chi classes.

Danilo: **Você não joga futebol?**
voh-*seh* nah-ooh *zhoh*-gah foo-chee-*bah*-ooh?
You don't play soccer?

Vitor: **Só as vezes.**
soh ahz *veh*-zeez.
Only sometimes.

Words to Know

quê	kee	what
tipo	chee-poo	type
esporte	eh-spoh-chee	sport
gosta	goh-stah	you like
caminho	kah-ming-yoh	I walk
muito	moh-ee-toh	a lot
e	ee	and
aula	ah-ooh-lah	class
não	nah-ooh	no/not
joga	zhoh-gah	play
futebol	foo-chee-bah-ooh	soccer
só	soh	only
as vezes	ahz veh-zeez	sometimes

Using the -er and -ir verbs

Conjugating regular **-er** and **-ir** verbs isn't difficult. For most **-er** and **-ir** verbs, just replace the **-er** or **-ir** with **-o, -e, -e, -emos/-imos,** or **-em.** Table 2-2 shows you which endings to use.

Table 2-2	Verb Endings to Use with Regular -er and -ir Verbs	
English Pronoun	**Portuguese Pronoun**	**Verb Ending**
I	eu	-o
you	você	-e
he/she	ele/ela	-e
we	nós	-emos (for -er verbs) -imos (for -ir verbs)
they	eles/elas	-em

A simple **-er** verb you can practice is **comer** (koh-*meh;* to eat). Remove the **-er** ending and add the new endings to the stem:

Conjugation	*Pronunciation*
eu como	*eh*-ooh *koh*-moo
você come	voh-*seh koh*-mee
ele/ela come	*eh*-lee/*eh*-lah *koh*-mee
nós comemos	nohz koh-*meh*-mooz
eles/elas comem	*eh*-leez/*eh*-lahz *koh*-mang

Many **-er** and **-ir** verbs have special endings. With verbs that end in **-zer,** for example, like **fazer** (fah-*zeh;* to do) and **trazer** (tdah-*zeh;* to bring), you remove **-zer** to get the stem; the verbs then take the following endings: **-ço, -z, -z, -zemos,** and **-zem.** The last two endings are similar to the **-er** verb endings (for *we* and *they*), but the first few endings (for *I* and *you/he/she*) are indeed bizarre. Here are some examples, using the *I* and *you* forms:

- ✔ **Eu faço muitas coisas.** (*eh*-ooh *fah*-soo moh-*ee*-tahz *koy*-zahz; I do many things.)

- ✔ **Você traz um presente.** (voh-*seh tdah*-eez oong pdeh-*zang*-chee; You bring a present.)

Making Contractions: It's a Cinch!

When you make contractions in English — in words like *can't* and *don't* — you use an apostrophe to show that a letter's missing. Brazilians likewise combine words so they're shorter or easier to pronounce, but Portuguese doesn't use apostrophes. This section helps you recognize these weird Portuguese contractions and tells you what they mean.

Remembering to use contractions can be hard, but don't worry. Contractions are just those little words in a sentence that glue things together. They're not the noun, verb, or adjective — which are the real **estrelas** (eh-*stdeh*-lahz; stars) of the sentence. If you skip contractions altogether when you speak, people will still understand you.

Take a look at what happens in Portuguese when you combine **em** and **o. Em** (ang) means *in/on,* and **o** (oh) means *the.* But **em o** (*in the*) doesn't exist in Portuguese, because Brazilians use the contraction **no** (noo):

- ✔ **no banheiro** (noo bahn-*yay*-doh; in the bathroom)
- ✔ **no quarto** (noo *kwah*-too; in the room)
- ✔ **no teto** (noo *teh*-too; on the roof)

The previous examples are for singular, masculine nouns. Take a look at what happens with feminine and plural nouns. Instead of **no,** you now have **na** (feminine and singular), **nos** (masculine and plural) and **nas** (feminine and plural):

- ✔ **na mesa** (nah *meh*-zah; on the table)
- ✔ **na cozinha** (nah koh-*zing*-yah; in the kitchen)
- ✔ **na rua** (nah *hoo*-ah; on the street)
- ✔ **nos livros** (nooz *leev*-dooz; in books)
- ✔ **nas praias** (nahz *pdah*-ee-ahz; on beaches)

Contractions with **o** also happen with **de** (deh; of) and **por** (poh; through/on/around). For example, when you want to say *of the,* you combine **de** and **o** to form **do/da/dos/das.** To say *through/on/around the,* use **pelo/pela/pelos/pelas.** (If you're confused about which form to use, just remember that *o* goes with masculine nouns, *a* goes with feminine, and *s* makes words plural.)

Here are some examples:

- ✔ **do computador** (doo kom-*poo*-tah-*doh;* of the computer)
- ✔ **das professoras** (dahz pdoh-feh-*soh*-dahz; of the teachers)

✔ **pelo telefone** (*peh*-loo teh-leh-*foh*-nee; on the phone)

✔ **pelas ruas** (*peh*-lahz *hooh*-ahz; through the streets)

✔ **dos pais** (dooz *pah*-eez; of the parents)

Brazilians also use contractions specifically to say *of him, of her,* or *of them.* (See Chapter 4 for more on how to use these contractions to say *his, her,* or *their.*)

✔ **dela** (*deh*-lah; of her)

✔ **dele** (*deh*-lee; of him)

✔ **delas** (*deh*-lahz; of them — females)

✔ **deles** (*deh*-leez; of them — males or males and females)

Here are some examples of sentences using the contractions I just introduced:

✔ **Gosto de viagar pelo mundo.** (*goh*-stoo jee vee-ah-*zhah* peh-loo *moon*-doh; I like to travel around the world.)

✔ **Ele mora no Brasil.** (*eh*-lee *moh*-dah noo bdah-*zee*-ooh; He lives in Brazil.)

✔ **Nos Estados Unidos, há cinqüenta estados.** (nooz eh-*stah*-dooz ooh-*nee*-dooz, ah sing-*kwen*-tah eh-*stah*-dooz; In the United States, there are 50 states.)

✔ **As chaves estão em cima da mesa.** (ahz *shah*-veez eh-*stah*-ooh ang *see*-mah dah *meh*-zah; The keys are on the table.)

To Me, to You: Indirect Objects

One of my favorite aspects of Portuguese grammar is the way they talk about *me* and *you* being on the receiving end. In grammar books, these words are called *indirect objects;* the words *me* and *you* are in the sentence, but they're not the ones doing the action.

Te (teh) means *you,* and **me** (meh) means *me* (that one's easy to remember). Put these indirect objects right before the verb. Take a look at some examples:

✔ **Eu te dou dinheiro.** (*eh*-ooh chee *doh* jing-*yay*-doh; I give you money.)

✔ **Me diga o seu nome.** (mee *jee*-gah ooh *seh*-ooh *noh*-mee; Tell me your name.)

In the first sentence, **eu** is the subject. In the second sentence, the subject isn't even stated. You can tell that the verb **diga** is in the **voce/ele/ela** form. If someone looks at you and says **Me diga o seu nome,** it's no mystery that he or she is asking *you,* not *him* or *her* or some other person. Brazilians leave out the subject of the sentence sometimes when it's obvious who they're talking about. Just like in English, you can drop the *you* at the beginning of a sentence when you're telling someone to do something. Brazilians love to use the formula **Me** plus a verb:

- ✔ **Me faz um recibo, por favor?** (mee *fah*-eez oong heh-*see*-boo poh fah-*voh;* Can you write a receipt for me, please?)

- ✔ **Me traz uma agua, por favor.** (mee *tdah*-eez ooh-mah *ah*-gwah, poh fah-*voh;* Bring me a water, please.)

- ✔ **Me explica o que aconteceu.** (mee eh-*splee*-kah ooh *kee* ah-kohn-teh-*seh*-ooh; Explain to me what happened.)

- ✔ **Me leva até a rodoviária?** (mee *leh*-vah ah-*teh* ah hoh-doh-vee-*ah*-dee-ah; Can you take me to the bus station?)

- ✔ **Me da o seu passaporte, por favor.** (mee *dah* ooh seh-ooh pah-sah-*poh*-chee poh fah-*voh;* Give me your passport, please.)

Numbers to Know: When Everything Counts

Good news! Numerals are the same in Portuguese as in English, so inside a Brazilian store, you can understand the price of something — even if you don't remember a word of Portuguese. This may sound obvious, but the point is that a little familiarity in new surroundings can give you the reassurance and courage to have a little chat with the store clerk.

If you need to actually talk about the price tag, you have to delve into the world of numbers. They will be in **reais** (hay-*eyes*), by the way — that's the name for Brazilian currency. (See Chapter 11 for more on money. Chapters 5 and 6 can tell you a bit about buying food and going shopping.)

Whether you're telling the time, asking about street numbers, or discussing prices, you need to know how to say numbers. Here are numbers one through ten:

- ✔ **um** (oong; 1)
- ✔ **dois** (*doh*-eez; 2)
- ✔ **três** (tdehz; 3)
- ✔ **quatro** (*kwah*-tdoo; 4)
- ✔ **cinco** (*sing*-koo; 5)
- ✔ **seis** (*say*-eez; 6)
- ✔ **sete** (*seh*-chee; 7)
- ✔ **oito** (*oh*-ee-toh; 8)
- ✔ **nove** (*noh*-vee; 9)
- ✔ **dez** (dez; 10)

Now check out how to say 11 to 19:

- ✔ **onze** (*ohn*-zee; 11)
- ✔ **doze** (*doh*-zee; 12)
- ✔ **treze** (*tdeh*-zee; 13)
- ✔ **quatorze** (kah-*toh*-zee; 14)
- ✔ **quinze** (*keen*-zee; 15)
- ✔ **dezeseis** (dez-ee-*say*-eez; 16)
- ✔ **dezesete** (dez-ee-*seh*-chee; 17)
- ✔ **dezoito** (dez-*oh*-ee-toh; 18)
- ✔ **dezenove** (dez-ee-*noh*-vee; 19)

And these are numbers 20 to 100, counting by tens:

- ✔ **vinte** (*ving*-chee; 20)
- ✔ **trinta** (*tdeen*-tah; 30)
- ✔ **quarenta** (kwah-*dang*-tah; 40)
- ✔ **cinqüenta** (sing-*kwen*-tah; 50)
- ✔ **sessenta** (seh-*sen*-tah; 60)
- ✔ **setenta** (seh-*ten*-tah; 70)
- ✔ **oitenta** (oh-ee-*ten*-tah; 80)
- ✔ **noventa** (noh-*ven*-tah; 90)
- ✔ **cem** (sang; 100)

To say a double-digit number that doesn't end in zero, you just put the word **e** (ee; and) in between your tens and ones digits. If you want to say *34,* for example, say **trinta e quatro** (*tdeen*-tah ee *kwah*-tdoh; *Literally:* 30 and 4).

To say 101–199, use **cento e** (*sehn*-too ee) plus the rest of number: **Cento e trinta e quatro** (*sehn*-too ee *tdeen*-tah ee *kwah*-tdoh) is 134, and **cento e oitenta e sete** (*sehn*-too ee oh-ee-*ten*-tah ee *seh*-chee) is 187.

For 201–999, replace the **cento** with the following hundreds terms:

- **duzentos** (doo-*zen*-tooz; 200)
- **trezentos** (tdeh-*zen*-tooz; 300)
- **quatrocentos** (kwah-tdoo-*sen*-tooz; 400)
- **quinhentos** (keen-*yen*-tooz; 500)
- **seiscentos** (say-*sen*-tooz; 600)
- **setecentos** (*seh*-chee-*sen*-tooz; 700)
- **oitocentos** (*oh*-ee-too-*sen*-tooz; 800)
- **novecentos** (*noh*-vee-*sen*-tooz; 900)

One thousand is **mil** (*mee*-ooh), and *one million* is **um milhão** (oong meel-*yah*-ooh). For numbers in those ranges, just add an **e** and then the rest of the number.

Fun & Games

Carolina (kah-doh-*lee*-nah) and **Mauricio** (mah-ooh-*dee*-see-oh) are husband and wife. Match each adjective given below with him or her. Some adjectives can be used with both of them! Answers are in Appendix C.

1. **inteligente**
2. **simpático**
3. **honesta**
4. **linda**

5. **alto**
6. **jovem**
7. **médica**
8. **organizado**

Chapter 3

Oi! Hello! Greetings and Introductions

Saying *hello* and *goodbye* are the nuts and bolts of any **lingua** (*ling*-gwah; language). If you visit Brazil, you'll have plenty of chances to **praticar** (pdah-chee-*kah;* practice) these basic **palavras** (pah-*lah*-vdahz; words). Walking in and out of **lojas** (*loh*-zhahz; shops), **restaurantes** (heh-stah-oo-*dahn*-cheez; restaurants), and **hotéis** (oh-*tay*-eez; hotels), you'll hear **Tudo bom?** (too-doh *boh*-oong; How are you?) and **Tchau!** (*chah*-ooh; Bye! — from the Italian word *ciao,* which also means *bye*) several times a day.

The **próximo passo** (*pdoh*-see-moh *pah*-soh; next step) is introducing yourself to people and introducing the people you're with. You'll want to tell people your **nome** (*noh*-mee; name), maybe even your **apelido** (ah-peh-*lee*-doh; nickname).

After you establish names and where you're from, the next step in a **conversa** (kohn-*veh*-sah; conversation) sometimes involves explaining what you do and even what kind of a person you are. You can use these description techniques to help talk about what kind of a person someone else is, too. What are they like **fisicamente** (*fee*-zee-kah-*men*-chee; physically) — **alto** (*ah*-ooh-toh; tall) or **baixo** (*bah*-ee-shoh; short)? Are they **simpático** (seem-*pah*-chee-koo; nice)?

Finally, you'll also want to figure out how to talk about how you are or someone else is in a particular **momento** (moh-*men*-toh; moment). Are you **cansado** (kahn-*sah*-doo; tired)? **Contente** (kohn-*ten*-chee; happy)? **Pronto** (*pdohn*-toh; ready) to learn some basic Portuguese?

A Few Ways to Say Hello

Saying *hello* is the bare necessity whether you're at home or in Brazil. After you communicate a friendly greeting, the scene is set for social interaction. That's the fun part! What comes after the hello is unpredictable, and that's the beauty of **a vida** (*ah vee*-dah; life).

Here are the most common ways of saying *hello* in Brazil:

> ✔ **Oi.** (*oh*-ee; Hi.)
>
> ✔ **Olá.** (oh-*lah;* Hello.)

If you're walking into a shop, restaurant, or hotel, it's more common to use *Good morning* or *Good afternoon* — just like in English:

> ✔ **Bom dia.** (*boh*-oong *jee*-ah; Good morning.)
>
> ✔ **Boa tarde.** (*boh*-ah *tah*-jee; Good afternoon/Good evening.)
>
> ✔ **Boa noite.** (*boh*-ah *noh*-ee-chee; Good evening/Good night.)

In Brazil, **a tarde** (ah *tah*-jee; the afternoon) starts and ends a little bit later than you may be used to. The afternoon **começa** (koh-*meh*-sah; starts) around 2 p.m. and ends at about 8 p.m. Noon to 2 p.m. is **meio-dia** (may-oh-*jee*-ah; midday). But **ninguém** (ning-*gang;* no one) ever says **Bom meio-dia!** Go figure. They usually just say **Boa tarde.**

Another way of saying *hello* in Brazil is by asking directly *How are you?* There are two ways of saying it:

> ✔ **Tudo bem?** (*too*-doh *bang;* How are you? *Literally:* Everything well?)
>
> ✔ **Tudo bom?** (*too*-doh *boh*-oong; How are you? *Literally:* Everything good?)

Here's how you answer:

> ✔ **Tudo bem.** (*too*-doh *bang;* I'm good. *Literally:* Everything well.)
>
> ✔ **Tudo bom.** (*too*-doh *boh*-oong; I'm good. *Literally:* Everything good.)

So what's the difference between **Tudo bem** and **Tudo bom,** you ask? Here's the big answer: There is none! They mean the same thing. But here's a great trick: If someone asks you **Tudo bem?** say **Tudo bom.** If it's **Tudo bom?** answer back **Tudo bem.** Just use the opposite expression that he or she used. It took me many, many months to figure out that Brazilians prefer not to use matching phrases here. I had randomly used one expression or the other until I finally got around to asking someone about the **bom/bem** dilemma. Brazilians are such nice people, they never bothered correcting me.

People commonly combine some of these phrases, like **Olá, tudo bom?** (oh-lah, too-doh *bong;* Hello, how are you?) or **Oi, tudo bem?** (*oh*-ee, too-doh bong; Hi, how are you?).

Introducing Yourself

Introducing yourself is easy as **torta de morango** (*toh*-tah jee moh-*dahng*-goh; strawberry pie). Here are a couple different ways to do it:

▶ **O meu nome é . . .** (ooh *meh*-ooh *noh*-mee eh; My name is . . .)

▶ **Eu sou o/a . . .** (*eh*-ooh *soh* ooh/ah; I'm . . .)

Use the *o* in front of your name if you're male and the *a* if you're female. Because *o* is the masculine way of saying *the* and *a* is the feminine *the,* saying **Eu sou a Karen** is like saying, "I'm the Karen." It sounds **estranho** (eh-*stdahn*-yoh; weird) in English. But that's the fun of learning another language — you get to be **estranho** and say **coisas divertidas** (*koy*-zahz jee-veh-*chee*-dahz; fun stuff).

To ask someone his or her name, say **Cual é seu nome?** (*kwah*-ooh *eh seh*-ooh *noh*-mee; What's your name?).

After someone asks you for your name, you can say **E o seu?** (ee ooh *seh*-ooh; And yours?).

If you want to **apresentar** (ah-pdeh-zen-*tah;* introduce) friends or family members after you introduce yourself, say:

Este é . . .	*es*-chee *eh*	This is . . . (name of man)
Esta é . . .	*eh*-stah *eh*	This is . . . (name of woman)
Estes são . . .	*es*-jeez *sah*-ooh	These are . . . (names of multiple people)
Estas são . . .	*eh*-stahz *sah*-ooh	These are . . . (names of women)

Here are some common introductions:

▶ **Este é o meu amigo.** (*es*-chee *eh* ooh *meh*-ooh ah-*mee*-goo; This is my friend. — male)

▶ **Esta é a minha amiga.** (*eh*-stah *eh* ah *ming*-yah ah-*mee*-gah; This is my friend. — female)

✔ **Estes são os meus amigos.** (*es*-cheez *sah*-ooh ooz *meh*-ooz ah-*mee*-gooz; These are my friends. — group of all men or men and women)

✔ **Estas são as minhas amigas.** (*eh*-stahz *sah*-ooh ahz *ming*-yahz ah-*mee*-gahz; These are my friends. — group of all women)

To introduce specific family members, like your sister, brother, cousin, mom, and so on, flip to Chapter 4. The whole **árvore geneológica** (*ah*-voh-dee geh-nee-ah-*lah*-jee-kah; family tree) is there!

First Names, Last Names, and Nicknames, Brazilian-Style

First names are **primeiros nomes** (pdee-*may*-dohz *noh*-meez; names), and last names are **sobrenomes** (*soh*-bdee *nah*-meez; surnames. *Literally:* over-names).

So when someone says **Qual é seu nome?** she's after your first name. If she says **Qual é seu nome completo?** (*kwah*-ooh *eh* seh-ooh *nah*-mee kohm-*pleh*-too; What's your full name? *Literally:* What's your complete name?), then she's after both your **primerio nome** and **sobrenome.**

Most Brazilians just have one plain old first and last name. But a few use two last names — one from their dad and one from their mom. The longer the name, the more likely the person is from a **familia rica** (fah-*mee*-lee-ah *hee*-kah; rich family) that enjoys preserving **tradicão** (tdah-dee-*sah*-ooh; tradition).

If the name does include two last names, the mom's last name goes before the dad's last name. Some people even use a first name, a middle name, and two last names. Check out this mouthful: **Henrique Alfredo Gonçalves de Almeida** (ang-*hee*-kee ah-ooh-*fdeh*-doh gohn-*sah*-ooh-veez jee ahl-*may*-dah).

Sometimes names come with a **de** (jee; of — before a masculine name) or **da** (dah; of — before a feminine name): **Vinicius de Moraes** (vee-*nee*-see-oohz jee moh-*dah*-eez; one of the composers of the famous song "Girl From Ipanema").

Do you know what the Brazilian version of *Smith* is? The most common last name in Brazil is **da Silva** (dah *see*-ooh-vah). In fact, there are way more **da Silvas** in Brazil than there are *Smiths* in English-speaking countries.

The President of Brazil (as of 2005) himself has a very strange name. It's **Luiz Inácio Lula da Silva** (loo-*eez* ee-*nah*-see-oh *loo*-lah dah *see*-ooh-vah). He has two first names, but the third name, Lula, is an **apelido** (ah-peh-*lee*-doh; nickname) for Luiz. It's like saying *John Scott Johnny Smith*. It's not common for a nickname to be part of a full name like this. But then again, Brazilians are very down-to-earth, and anything goes!

Os brasileiros (oohz bdah-zee-*lay*-dohz; Brazilians) are pretty **informal** (een-foh-*mah*-ooh; informal), too. They call their president just **Lula.** And the previous president, **Fernando Henrique Cardoso** (feh-*nahn*-doh ang-*hee*-kee kah-*doh*-zoo), was simply called **Fernando Henrique.** No one — not even on news shows — calls them **Senhor da Silva** or **Senhor Cardoso.** If people want to be formal, they'd say **o Presidente Lula** (ooh pdeh-zee-*dang*-chee *loo*-lah) — that's like saying *President George* for George Bush.

Brazilians have an obsession with **apelidos** (ah-peh-*lee*-dooz; nicknames). I recently learned that the real name of Brazil's biggest soccer star of all time, **Pelé,** is **Edson Arantes Nascimento** (*eh*-jee-soh ah-*dahn*-cheez nah-see-*men*-toh). But I learned that in the U.S. — in Brazil I only heard him referred to as **Pelé** — about a thousand times!

Brazilians also prefer to stick to **primeiros nomes** (first names) in general. I have friends who say they don't even know many of their friends' **sobrenomes** (last names), after a while of knowing them!

Dividing the World between Formal and Informal

You can sort of divide the world into people you call *Mr.* or *Mrs.* and people you call by their first names.

Brazilians use the terms **Senhor** (seen-*yoh;* Mr.) and **Senhora** (seen-*yoh*-dah; Mrs.) pretty much just like you use *Mr.* and *Mrs.* in English. When you're talking to your elderly **vizinho** (vee-*zeen*-yoh; neighbor), he's **Senhora** so-and-so. When a **casal** (kah-*zah*-ooh; couple) walks in to a real estate agency, they're called **Senhor e Senhora** (seen-*yoh* ee seen-*yoh*-dah; Mr. and Mrs.) so-and-so.

Brazilians always use **o/a** (the) before saying Mr. or Mrs. It's like saying "the Mr. Oliveira." Weird, right? Well, here goes:

- **o Senhor Oliveira** (ooh seen-*yoh* oh-lee-*vay*-dah; Mr. Oliveira)
- **o Senhor da Silva** (ooh seen-*yoh* dah *see*-ooh-vah; Mr. da Silva)
- **a Senhora Tavares** (ah seen-*yoh*-dah tah-*vah*-deez; Mrs. Tavares)
- **a Senhora Gimenes** (ah seen-*yoh*-dah zhee-*men*-ez; Mrs. Gimenes)

Another strange difference is that in Brazil, it's common to use **Senhor** and **Senhora** for young people — even teenagers. There's no term like *Miss* for younger women. And it's also normal for people to say **Senhor David** or **Senhora Luciana** — using the first name instead of the last name.

I was always **Senhora Karen** (seen-yoh-dah *kahd*-eeng), whether I was at the **cabelereiro** (kah-beh-leh-*day*-doh; hairdresser's), talking to an **agente de viagens** (ah-*jehn*-chee jee vee-*ah*-jehnz; travel agent), or at my favorite **padaria** (pah-dah-*dee*-ah; bakery). At first I wondered whether people thought I was older than my age (I was under 30). Then I noticed the same treatment for teenagers. Whew — so I didn't look 55. That was nice to know!

Imagine you're talking to the concierge of your hotel. He treats you with respect because it's his job to serve you. He asks you the following questions if you're a man:

> ✔ **O senhor mora aqui?** (ooh seen-*yoh moh*-dah ah-*kee;* Do you live here?)

> ✔ **O senhor está cansado?** (ooh seen-*yoh* eh-*stah* kahn-*sah*-doo; Are you tired?)

> ✔ **O senhor é brasileiro?** (ooh seen-*yoh* eh bdah-zee-*lay*-doh; Are you Brazilian?)

> ✔ **O senhor gosta do restaurante?** (ooh seen-*yoh goh*-stah doo heh-stah-oo-*dahn*-chee; Do you like the restaurant?)

And he asks you these questions if you're a woman:

> ✔ **A senhora gosta de dançar?** (ah seen-*yoh*-dah *goh*-stah jee dahn-*sah;* Do you like to dance?)

> ✔ **A senhora é americana?** (ah seen-*yoh*-dah eh ah-meh-dee-*kah*-nah; Are you American?)

> ✔ **A senhora vai para praia?** (ah seen-*yoh*-dah vah-ee pah-dah *pdah*-ee-ah; Are you going to the beach?)

> ✔ **A senhora está de férias?** (ah seen-*yoh*-dah eh-*stah* jee *feh*-dee-ahz; Are you on vacation?)

Now imagine that the speaker who asked you all these questions is just another fellow traveler — a Brazilian one. All the **o senhor's** and the **a senhora's** become **você** (voh-*seh;* you — informal). **Você** is what you call people when you don't need to be formal.

If you vacation to Brazil, most people you come into contact with will be people in the tourism industry, who will be calling you **o Senhor** or **a Senhora.** For practical purposes, the only time you should really try to **lembrar** (lehm-*bdah;* remember) to use **o Senhor** or **o Senhora** is if you meet **um idoso** (oong ee-*doh*-soh; an elderly person). It's nice to show respect.

Talkin' the Talk

Tatiana (*tah*-chee-*ah*-nah) is deep in the Amazon, getting settled at her jungle lodge. She's meeting her tour guide, **Lucas** (*loo*-kahs), for the first time. He's a young guy from the area. Notice how Tatiana calls Lucas **você** and he calls her **a Senhora**.

Tatiana:	**Olá, você é o guia?** oh-*lah*, voh-*seh* eh ooh *gee*-ah? Hello, are you the guide?
Lucas:	**Olá. Sim, sou.** oh-*lah*. sing, *soh*. Hello. Yes, I am.
Tatiana:	**Qual é seu nome?** *kwah*-ooh eh *seh*-ooh *noh*-mee? What's your name?
Lucas:	**Lucas. E o nome da Senhora?** *loo*-kahs. ee ooh *noh*-mee dah seen-*yoh*-dah? Lucas. And your name?
Tatiana:	**Tatiana.** tah-chee-*ah*-nah. Tatiana.
Lucas:	**A senhora é de onde?** ah seen-*yoh*-dah eh jee *ohn*-jee? Where are you from?
Tatiana:	**Sou do Rio. E você, é daqui?** *soh* doo *hee*-ooh. ee voh-*seh*, eh dah-*kee*? I'm from Rio. And you, are you from here?
Lucas:	**Sim, sou. A senhora quer uma caipirinha?** sing, *soh*. ah seen-*yoh*-dah *keh* ooh-mah kah-ee-pee-*ding*-yah? Yes, I am. Would you like a caipirinha?
Tatiana:	**Eu quero! Obrigada!** *eh*-ooh *keh*-doo! oh-bdee-*gah*-dah! Yes (*Literally:* I want)! Thanks!

Words to Know

guia	<u>gee</u>-ah	guide
daqui	dah-<u>kee</u>	from here
quer	keh	want
uma caipirinha	<u>ooh</u>-mah kah-ee-pee-<u>ding</u>-yah	a caipirinha (Brazilian national drink, made from sugarcane liquor, lime and sugar)

Describing Permanent Qualities: Ser

The verb **ser** (seh; to be) is the way to describe what someone or something is like. Use this verb when you would say *is* or *are* in English.

Brazilians use **ser** for permanent qualities of a thing or person. I'm talking about qualities of places and people that don't change much: *New York is an island. New York is big. New York is pretty. She is married. He is from New York. He is rich and nice.* The verb **estar** (eh-*stah;* to be) is also used to mean *is* and *are.* But only in situations where the quality being described is temporary, like being tired. You may be tired right now, but after a nap, you'll be energized and ready to go. **Estar** is a linguistic tag that denotes a temporary state. For example, say **Eu estou cansada** (*eh*-ooh eh-*stoh* kahn-*sah*-dah; I am tired), not **Eu sou cansada** (no pronunciation, because this phrase doesn't exist).

Say you're talking about your friend Ana, who has a rich husband. Don't worry yourself over questions like *What if Ana's husband goes bankrupt tomorrow?* or *What if Ana gets divorced tomorrow?* Just remember the decade rule: If the quality you're talking about seems like it will last another ten years, then use **ser.**

And if you make a mistake, don't sweat it. That's how you learn. And Brazilians are nice. They won't laugh at you.

Using an example

I'm going to use the **exemplo** (eh-*zehm*-ploh; example) of **Gisele Bundchen** (zhee-*zeh*-ooh *boon*-chang), Brazil's most famous fashion **modelo** (moh-*deh*-loh; model) — and perhaps the best-paid supermodel in the world **hoje** (*oh*-zhee; today). If you don't know what she looks like, Google her name and then come back to this text.

Did you do it? Okay. What are Gisele's permanent qualities? These are qualities about her that last for **um longo periodo** (oong *lohn*-goo peh-*dee*-ooh-doh; a long time) — think decades. When talking about these qualities, use the verb **ser** (seh; to be). When conjugated for *she,* the verb **ser** is **é** (eh).

Ela é (eh-lah *eh;* She is):

- ✔ **alta** (*ah*-ooh-tah; tall)
- ✔ **bonita** (boo-*nee*-tah; pretty)
- ✔ **loira** (*loy*-dah; blonde)
- ✔ **rica** (*hee*-kah; rich)
- ✔ **uma modelo** (*ooh*-mah moh-*deh*-loh; a model)
- ✔ **do Rio Grande do Sul** (doo *hee*-ooh *gdahn*-jee doo *soo;* from Rio Grande do Sul state)

I talked about what she looks like (physical characteristics), what her profession is, and where she's from. These are a few things that probably won't **mudar** (moo-*dah;* change) about Gisele for another **dez anos** (dez *ah*-nohz; ten years). She certainly won't get **baixa ou feia** (*bah*-ee-shah ooh *fay*-ah; short or ugly) any time **logo** (*loh*-goo; soon).

The verb **ser** (seh) is the one most often used in Portuguese. It's an irregular verb (look at Chapter 2 for a quickie lesson on verbs). But it's the easiest irregular verb there is in Portuguese. Check it out:

Conjugation	Pronunciation
Eu sou	*eh*-ooh *soh*
Você é	voh-seh *eh*
Ele/ela é	*eh*-lah/*eh*-lee *eh*
Nós somos	nohz *soh*-mooz
Eles/elas são	*eh*-leez/*eh*-lahz *sah*-ooh

Warming up to ser

Entendeu? (en-ten-*deh*-ooh; Did you get it?). **Ser** is just the plain old *is* and *are* and *am*. How basic is that?

Now that you know the verb **ser,** you can say a ton of things:

- ✔ **Eu sou homem.** (*eh*-ooh *soh oh*-mang; I am a man.)

- ✔ **Eu sou de California.** (*eh*-ooh *soh* jee kah-lee-*foh*-nee-ah; I am from California.)

- ✔ **Ele é muito alto.** (eh-lee *eh* moo-*ee*-toh *ah*-ooh-toh; He is very tall.)

- ✔ **Nós somos amigos.** (nohz *soh*-mooz ah-*mee*-gooz; We are friends.)

- ✔ **Elas são simpáticas.** (eh-lahz *sah*-ooh seem-*pah*-chee-kahz; Those women are nice.)

- ✔ **Ela é jovem.** (eh-lah *eh zhoh*-vang; She is young.)

- ✔ **Nós somos da Australia.** (nohz *soh*-mooz dah ah-ooh-*stah*-lee-ah; We are from Australia.)

- ✔ **Eles são intelligentes.** (eh-leez *sah*-ooh een-teh-lee-*zhang*-cheez; They are smart.)

Some adjectives describing permanent states

As you can see, **ser** goes perfectly with descriptions of things and people. Now glance at some basic description words you can use with **ser;** take a look at Table 8-1. These words are sure to come in handy.

Table 8-1	Adjectives Describing Permanent States	
Adjective	**Pronunciation**	**Translation**
alto	*ah*-ooh-toh	tall
baixo	*bah*-ee-shoh	short (height)
caro	*kah*-doh	expensive
barato	bah-*dah*-toh	cheap
bom	*boh*-oong	good
mau	*mah*-ooh;	bad
curto	*kooh*-toh	short (length)
comprido	koom-*pdee*-doh	long
pequeno	peh-*keh*-noh	small
grande	*gdahn*-jee	big

Adjective	Pronunciation	Translation
fácil	*fah*-see-ooh	easy
difícil	jee-*fee*-see-ooh	difficult
divertido	jee-veh-*chee*-doo	fun
chato	*shah*-toh	boring/annoying
gordo	*goh*-doh	fat
magro	*mah*-gdoh	thin
jovem	*zhoh*-vang	young
velho	*vehl*-yoh	old

Talkin' the Talk

You're at a charming cafe in the old part of Rio and overhear the following conversation. Note all the uses of **ser** to describe New York.

Marco: **E como é a Nova Iorque?**
ee *koh*-moh *eh* ah *noh*-vah *yoh*-kee?
And what's New York like?

Ana: **É muito grande. Também é muito bonita.**
eh moh-*ee* toh *gdahn*-jee. tahm-*bang* eh moh-ee-toh boo-*nee*-tah.
It's really big. It's also really pretty.

Marco: **É uma ilha, né?**
eh ooh-mah *eel*-yah, neh?
It's an island, right?

Ana: **Manhattan é uma ilha.**
Mahn-*hah*-tahn *eh* ooh-mah *eel*-yah.
Manhattan is an island.

Marco: **E foi para visitar a sua irmã, né?**
ee *foh*-ee pah-dah vee-see-*tah* ah soo-ah ee-*mah*, neh?
And you went to visit your sister, right?

Ana: **É. Ela é muito legal.**
eh. eh-lah *eh* moh-ee-toh leh-*gow*.
Yeah. She's really cool.

Marco: **Ela é casada?**
eh-lah *eh* kah-*zah*-dah?
Is she married?

Ana: **É. O marido dela é de Nova Iorque.**
eh. ooh mah-*dee*-doh *deh*-lah *eh* dah noh-vah *yoh*-kee.
Yeah. Her husband is from New York.

Marco: **Como ele é?**
koh-moh *eh*-lee *eh*?
What is he like?

Ana: **É rico e simpático!**
eh *hee*-koo ee seem-*pah*-chee-koh!
He's rich and nice!

Words to Know

Como é . . . ?	koh-moh eh	What is . . . like?
Nova Iorque	noh-vah yoh-kee	New York
muito	moh-ee-toh	really/very
grande	gdahn-jee	big
também	tahm-bang	too/also
ilha	eel-yah	island
foi	foh-ee	you went
para	pah-dah	in order to
visitar	vee-zee-tah	to visit
irmã	ee-mah	sister
legal	leh-gow	cool
casada	kah-zah-dah	married
marido	mah-dee-doh	husband

For those of you who want to sound a little more sophisticated, use **né** at the end of a sentence to mean **Right?** Né is the contraction of **não é** (*nah*-ooh *eh;* Literally: is not), which can be used to mean the same thing as well. And use **É** at the beginning of a sentence to affirm a question someone just asked you. These words aren't necessary for you to learn, but they're fun, and Brazilians use them all the time!

Describing Temporary Qualities: Estar

The verb **estar** (eh-*stah*) is used to describe the temporary qualities of a thing or person. Is the state of the person or thing going to change? Then use **estar.** In terms of people, **estar** is used most often to describe mood or physical state or physical location.

Use **estar** to say you're **nervoso** (neh-*voh*-zoo; nervous) about something, that you're **doente** (doh-*en*-chee; sick), or that you're at the **banco** (*bahn*-koh; bank). Tomorrow, you may be *happy*, *well*, and *at work*! If you were to use **ser** with these adjectives, it would be like you're saying you'll be *nervous* or *sick* or *at the bank* for many years. Hopefully that isn't the case!

But again, just a reminder: If you mix up the verbs, Brazilians will still perfectly understand you. They won't expect you to speak perfectly.

Using an example

I'm going to use the example of model Gisele Bunchen. But now I'll talk about **Gisele's** *temporary qualities.* If it helps you, you can think about temporary qualities as someone's *state of being.* These are often things that can change from minute-to-minute or from one day to the next.

All use the verb **estar.** When conjugated for *she,* the verb **estar** is **está** (eh-*stah*).

Imagine Gisele on a photo shoot on a bad day. **Ela está** (eh-lah eh-*stah;* She is):

- **com fome** (kong *foh*-mee; hungry)
- **triste** (*tdees*-chee; sad)
- **gordinha** (goh-*jing*-yah; a little chubby)
- **com os sapatos vermelhos** (kohng *ooz* sah-*pah*-tooz veh-*mel*-yooz; wearing red shoes)
- **em Roma** (ang *hoh*-mah; in Rome)

I talked about how she is (emotions, daily physical needs), temporary aspects of her appearance, and her physical location.

Tomorrow, **Gisele** will be back to New York, where she lives, and where she'll start to do extra exercises — so that next week she'll be **magra** (*mah*-gdah; thin) again.

Estar, remember, is for qualities of a person, place, or thing that are temporary. Both **ser** and **estar** are used to say *am, is,* and *are.* To find out the different forms of **estar,** take a look:

Conjugation	*Pronunciation*
Eu estou	*eh*-ooh eh-*stoh*
Você está	voh-*seh* eh-*stah*
Ele/ela está	*eh*-lee/*eh*-lah eh-*stah*
Nós estamos	nohz eh-*stah*-mohz
Eles/elas estão	*eh*-leez/*eh*-lahz eh-*stah*-ooh

Warming up to estar

Here are some common phrases that use **estar:**

- ✔ **Ela está de férias.** (*eh*-lah eh-*stah* jee *feh*-dee-ahz; She is on vacation.)
- ✔ **Nós estamos com fome.** (nohz eh-*stah*-mohz kohng *foh*-mee; We are hungry.)
- ✔ **Eu estou triste.** (*eh*-ooh eh-*stoh* t*dees*-chee; I am sad.)
- ✔ **Ela está no carro.** (*eh*-lah eh-*stah* noh *kah*-hoh; She is in the car.)
- ✔ **Eu estou em casa.** (*eh*-ooh eh-*stoh* ang *kah*-zah; I am at home.)
- ✔ **Eles estão no Brasil.** (*eh*-leez eh-*stah*-ooh noh bdah-*zee*-ooh; They are in Brazil.)

With **estar,** you're talking about people's emotional states, their physical states, and where they're located. All are examples of what people are doing or are like or where they're located right now. No one should be hungry or on vacation permanently.

Speaking about Speaking: Falar

Now onto a really easy, fun verb: **falar** (fah-*lah;* to speak/to talk). Talking is, after all, how to really learn a language! This book is a good primer for learning Portuguese, but if you can spend some time in Brazil or can find a Brazilian where you live who will **falar** with you, your learning curve will go up exponentially.

And Brazilians love to **falar**, so you're in luck! They're the perfect conversation partners.

To find out the different forms of **falar**, take a look at the following conjugation:

Conjugation	*Pronunciation*
Eu falo	*eh*-ooh *fah*-loh
Você fala	voh-*seh fah*-lah
Ele/ela fala	*eh*-lee/*eh*-lah *fah*-lah
Nós falamos	*nohz* fah-*lah*-mohz
Eles/elas falam	eh-leez/eh-lahz *fah*-lah-ooh

Falar is the **verbo perfeito** (*veh*-boh peh-*fay*-toh; perfect verb) to use to talk about speaking Portuguese — or about any language at all. Take a look at Table 8-2 for a rundown of how to say the names of some of the world's major languages.

Table 8-2	Some of the World's Major Languages	
Language	*Pronunciation*	*Translation*
inglês	eeng-*glehz*	English
português	poh-too-*gez*	Portuguese
português de Portugal	poh-too-*gez* jee poh-too-*gah*-ooh	Portuguese from Portugal
português do Brasil	poh-too-*gez* doh bdah-*zee*-ooh	Brazilian Portuguese
espanhol	eh-spahn-*yoh*-ooh	Spanish
russo	*hoo*-soh	Russian
chinês	shee-*nehz*	Chinese
francês	fdahn-*sehz*	French
italiano	ee-tah-lee-*ah*-noh	Italian
alemão	ah-leh-*mah*-ooh	German
árabe	*ah*-dah-bee	Arabic
hebréu	eh-*bdeh*-ooh	Hebrew

Some Brazilians prefer to say they speak **brasileiro** (bdah-zee-*lay*-doh; Brazilian) instead of **português** or **português do Brasil.**

And hey — did you notice that they don't capitalize the **primeira letra** (pdee-*may*-dah *let*-drah; first letter) of names of languages in Portuguese? This is the opposite of English, where you **sempre** (*sem*-pdee; always) capitalize the first letter of **linguas estrangeiras** (*ling*-gwahz eh-stdahn-*jay*-dahz; foreign languages).

Here are some easy ways to use **falar:**

- ✔ **Eu falo inglês.** (*eh*-ooh *fah*-loh eeng-*glehz;* I speak English.)

- ✔ **Eu gostaria de falar chinês.** (*eh*-ooh goh-stah-*dee*-ah jee fah-*lah* shee-*nehz;* I would like to speak Chinese.)

- ✔ **Você fala muito rápido!** (voh-seh *fah*-lah moh-*ee*-toh *hah*-pee-doh; You talk really fast!)

- ✔ **Na reunião, nós falamos durante cinco horas!** (*nah* hay-*ooh*-nee-*ah*-ooh nohz fah-*lah*-mohz doo-*dahn*-chee *sing*-koh *oh*-dahz; During the meeting, we talked for five hours!)

- ✔ **Elas falam muito bem.** (eh-lahz *fah*-lah-ooh moh-*ee*-toh *bang;* They speak really well.)

- ✔ **Você fala quantas linguas?** (voh-seh *fah*-lah *kwahn*-tuz *ling*-gwahz; How many languages do you speak?)

I'll bet this will be one of your favorite phrases of the whole book: **Como se fala . . . ?** (*koh*-moo see *fah*-lah; How do you say . . . ?). This great phrase got me out of many linguistic jams.

Talkin' the Talk

You're back at that cafe in the old part of Rio. You overhear a waiter talking to a woman who's alone at a table. He mistakes the woman for a tourist; she's actually Brazilian.

Waiter: **A senhora fala português?**
ah seen-*yoh*-dah *fah*-lah poh-too-*gez?*
Do you speak Portuguese?

Woman: **Sou brasileira. Você fala quantas linguas?**
soh bdah-zee-*lay*-dah. voh-*seh* fah-lah *kwahn*-tahz *ling*-gwahz?
I'm Brazilian. How many languages do you speak?

Waiter:	**Eu falo o inglês e o francês — e o português, é claro!** *eh*-ooh *fah*-loh ooh eeng-*glehz* ee ooh fdahn-*sehz* — ee ooh poh-too-*gez*, eh *klah*-doh! I speak English and French — and Portuguese, of course!
Woman:	**É difícil falar o francês?** eh jee-*fee*-see-ooh fah-*lah* ooh fdahn-*sehz*? Is it hard to speak French?
Waiter:	**Não, é fácil.** *nah*-ooh, eh *fah*-see-ooh. No, it's easy.
Woman:	**E é difícil falar o inglês?** ee *eh* jee-*fee*-see-ooh fah-*lah* ooh eeng-*glehz*? And is it hard to speak English?
Waiter:	**Inglês é mais difícil para mim.** eeng-*glehz* eh *mah*-eez jee-*fee*-see-ooh pah-dah *ming.* English is harder for me.
Woman:	**Bom, eu só falo o português!** *Boh*-oong, *eh*-ooh *soh fah*-loh ooh poh-too-*gez*! Well, I only speak Portuguese!
Waiter:	**Mas é a melhor língua do mundo . . .** Mah-eez *eh* ah mehl-*yoh ling*-gwah doo *moon*-doh . . . But it's the best language in the world . . .
Maria Lucia:	**É. Eu adoro falar o português.** *Eh. eh*-ooh ah-*doh*-doo fah-*lah* ooh poh-too-*gez*. Yeah. I love speaking Portuguese.

Does it seem weird that **alguém** (ah-ooh-*gang;* someone) would say he loves speaking his **língua nativa** (*ling*-gwah nah-*chee*-vah; native language)? It's like saying you love to speak English (if you're a native speaker). Well, for Brazilians, it's different. When famous Brazilians are interviewed and the interviewer asks what they miss most about Brazil when **fora do pais** (*foh*-dah doo pah-*eez;* out of the country), they often say they miss **falando em português** (fah-*lahn*-doh ang poh-too-*gez;* speaking in Portuguese). Aw, how sweet! The truth is, I miss speaking Portuguese now that I'm not living in Brazil anymore, too.

Words to Know

quantas	kwahn-tahs	which
É claro!	eh klah-doh	Of course!
mais difícil	mah-eez jee-fee-see-ooh	harder
para mim	pah-dah ming	for me
Bom,	boh-oong	Well,
só	soh	only
mas	mah-eez	but
melhor	mehl-yoh	better
mundo	moon-doh	world
eu adoro	eh-ooh ah-doh-doo	I love

Goodbyes Aren't Hard to Do

Saying goodbye to a Brazilian is easy! Well, the expression is **fácil** (*fah*-see-ooh; easy), at least. When you've made **um bom amigo** (oong *boh*-oong ah-*mee*-goo; a good friend) and you realize you won't see them for a while, it's **difícil** (jee-*fee*-see-ooh; difficult) to say goodbye in any language.

The quick way to say goobye is simply to say **Tchau!** (chow; Ciao!)

Todo mundo (*toh*-doo *moon*-doh; everyone. *Literally:* all world) in Brazil uses **Tchau**, in almost all situations. It's not like in English, where *Ciao!* can sound a little snobby sometimes. In Brazil, **Tchau** is used by everyone from the guy selling **abacaxi** (ah-bah-kah-*shee*; pineapple) on the street to the **dono** (*doh*-noo; owner) of the restaurant where you're eating.

It's also very common in Brazil to say **Até** (ah-*teh;* until) plus another word when you think you'll see the person **de novo** (jee *noh*-voh; again). If you only **memorizar** (meh-moh-dee-*zah;* memorize) one of the following phrases, pick **Até logo.** It never fails.

✔ **Até logo.** (ah-teh *loh*-goo; See you later.)

✔ **Até mais.** (ah-teh *mah*-eez; See you.)

✔ **Até amanhã.** (ah-*teh* ah-mahn-*yah;* See you tomorrow.)

✔ **Até a semana que vem.** (ah-*teh* ah seh-*mah*-nah kee *vang;* See you next week.)

Some people like to say religious phrases, too:

✔ **Fique com Deus.** (*fee*-kee kohng *deh*-ooz; Take care. *Literally:* Be with God.)

✔ **Adeus.** (ah-*deh*-oohz; Goodbye. *Literally:* To God.)

A gente se vê (ah *zhang*-chee see *veh;* See you around) is a common slang-sounding of way of saying *bye* in a casual situation.

Fun & Games

Now you can play Choose Your Own Dialogue. You're in Brasilia, Brazil's capital, and a friendly Brazilian woman befriends you during breakfast at your hotel. Her name is **Simone** (see-*moh*-nee). She's leaving the hotel tomorrow.

Pick eight phrases from the following list of ten phrases:

Tchau!

Oi, tudo bem?

Qual é seu nome?

Obrigado/a!

Adeus!

Até a semana que vem.

Tudo bom.

Boa noite.

Você fala bem o português!

O meu nome é . . .

Now, write them into the appropriate the dialogue slots. Watch out, or you may get tricked by the couple of phrases that don't belong . . . Flip to Appendix C for the answers.

1. Simone:

2. You:

3. Simone:

4. You:

5. Simone:

6. You:

7. Simone:

8. You:

Part II
Portuguese in Action

"I'm so proud of Ted. He ordered our entire meal in Portuguese and everything came out perfect—from the sushi appetizers to the noodle and won ton soup with shrimp tempura."

In this part . . .

In this part, you begin to really put Brazilian Portuguese to use. Instead of focusing on grammar points and philosophizing about why the language is structured the way it is, here you jump right in. I *show* you how the language works instead of *telling* you how it works. This section in particular highlights how to talk to your new Brazilian friends.

Chapter 4

Getting to Know You: Making Small Talk

*W*hen you're just learning a language, talking to people — even about the most basic things — can be a little stressful. But if you think about it, the first few minutes of talking to anybody new usually involves the same old questions. This chapter covers the questions that people who speak Portuguese are most likely to ask you, as well as the questions you'll probably want to ask them!

"Where Are You From?"

The first question you're likely to be asked in Brazil is **De onde você é?** (jee *ohng*-jee voh-seh *eh;* Where are you from?). Brazilians are very proud that people from all over the **mundo** (*moon*-doh; world) come to visit their country. They're always curious to imagine how **longe** (*lohn*-zhee; far) you came. They may also ask **De que pais você é?** (jee kee pah-*eez* voh-seh *eh;* Which country are you from?).

Here's how you can answer:

- ✔ **Eu sou inglês** (*eh*-ooh *soh* eeng-*glehz;* I'm English.)
- ✔ **Eu sou da Inglaterra** (*eh*-ooh *soh* dah *eeng*-glah-*teh*-hah; I'm from England.)

Here are some countries and nationalities that you may find useful:

- ✔ **Estados Unidos** (ehs-*tah*-dooz ooh-*nee*-dooz; United States)
- ✔ **americano/a** (ah-meh-dee-*kahn*-oh/ah; American)
- ✔ **Canadá** (kah-nah-*dah;* Canada)
- ✔ **canadense** (kah-nah-*dehn*-see; Canadian)
- ✔ **Inglaterra** (eeng-glah-*teh*-hah; England)
- ✔ **inglês/inglesa** (eeng-*glehz*/*gleh*-sah; English)
- ✔ **Australia** (ah-oo-*stdah*-lee-ah; Australia)
- ✔ **australiano/a** (ah-oo-stdah-lee-*ah*-noh/nah; Australian)
- ✔ **Alemanha** (ah-leh-*mahn*-yah; Germany)
- ✔ **alemão/ã** (ah-leh-*mah*-ooh/*mah;* German)
- ✔ **França** (*fdahn*-sah; France)
- ✔ **francês/francesa** (fdahn-*sehz*/fdahn-*seh*-zah; French)
- ✔ **China** (*shee*-nah; China)
- ✔ **chinês/chinesa** (shee-*nehz*/shee-*neh*-zah; Chinese)
- ✔ **Japão** (zhah-*pah*-ooh; Japan)
- ✔ **japonês/japonesa** (zhah-poh-*nez*/zhah-poh-*nes*-ah; Japanese)

Don't be surprised if a Brazilian from a touristy place like Rio responds **Eu já sabia** (*eh*-ooh jah sah-*bee*-ah; I knew it) when you say which country you're from. With so many tourists around, Brazilians get plenty of practice at pinpointing nationalities.

Did you notice that in Portuguese, they don't capitalize the first letter of nationalities? In English, people write American. In Portuguese, it's **americano.**

And another tip, while I'm talking about Americans: A few Brazilians get offended by the term **americano.** They say, "We're Americans too!" These folks prefer the term **norteamericano** (*noh*-chee-ah-meh-dee-*kah*-noh).

Brazilians often tell you where they're from by using the nickname for people from their city or state. Here are the most common ones:

- **gaucho/a** (gah-*ooh-sh*oh/ah; someone from Rio Grande do Sul state)
- **paulistano/a** (pow-lee-*stahn*-oh/ah; someone from the city of São Paulo)
- **paulista** (pow-*lee*-stah; someone from São Paulo state)
- **carioca** (kah-dee-*oh*-kah; someone from the city of Rio)
- **bahiano/a** (bah-ee-*ah*-noh/ah; someone from Bahia state)
- **mineiro/a** (mee-*nay*-doh/ah; someone from Minas Gerais state)

After telling you where they're from, Brazilians often try to tell you that their part of Brazil is the best. Their food and beaches are the best. And of course, the people are the nicest where they're from.

The truth is, Brazilians are nice in all parts of the country. But **mineiros** take the cake. They even have a reputation among Brazilians as being particularly nice. The common phrase is **Mineiros, gente boa** (mee-*nay*-dohz *zhang*-chee *boh*-ah; people from Minas state are really nice, cool people).

Gente boa is a very common phrase in Brazil. It's used to describe people who are laid-back and down-to-earth. It literally means *good people,* but you can use it to describe one person or a group of people. Here are a couple phrases you can use to win Brazilian friends:

- **Você é gente boa.** (voh-*seh* eh *zhang*-chee *boh*-ah; You're a really cool person.)
- **Os seus amigos são muito gente boa.** (oohz *say*-oohz ah-*mee*-gohz sah-ooh moo-*ee*-toh *zhang*-chee *boh*-ah; Your friends are really great.)

Talkin' the Talk

Juliana is a waitress at a **churrasqueria** (shoo-*hahs*-keh-*dee*-ah; Brazilian barbeque restaurant) in Rio Grande do Sul state, where **churrasco** (shoo-*hah*-skoh; all-you-can-eat grilled cuts of meat and salad) food originates. Samir, from Ohio, has just sat down.

Juliana: **Tudo bem? De onde você é?**
             too-doh *bang?* jee *ohn*-jee voh-*seh* eh?
             How are you? Where are you from?

Samir: **Sou americano.**
             soh ah-meh-dee-*kahn*-oh.
             I'm American.

Juliana: **De que lugar?**
             jee kee loo-*gah?*
             From whereabouts?

Samir: **De Ohio. E você, e daqui?**
             jee oh-*hah*-ee-oh. ee voh-*seh,* eh dah-*kee?*
             From Ohio. And you, are you from here?

Juliana: **Sim, sou gaucha. De onde vem?**
             sing, *soh* gah-*ooh*-shah. jee *ohn*-jee *vang?*
             Yes, I'm Gaucha (from Rio Grande do Sul state).
             Where are you coming from?

Samir: **Do Rio. Vou passar uma semana aqui no Rio Grande do Sul.**
             Doo *hee*-ooh. voh pah-*sah* ooh-mah seh-*mah*-nah
             ah-*kee* noh hee-ooh *gdahn*-jee doo *soo.*
             From Rio. I'm going to stay here in Rio Grande do Sul
             for a week.

Juliana: **Ótimo. Está gostando o Brasil?**
             ah-chee-moh. ehs-*tah* goh-*stahn*-doh ooh bdah-*zee*-
             ooh?
             Great. Are you liking Brazil?

Samir: **É claro! Estou adorando esse pais.**
             eh *klah*-doh! ehs-*toh* ah-doh-*dahn*-doh eh-see
             pah-*eez.*
             Of course! I'm loving this country.

Words to Know

De que lugar?	jee kee loo-_gah_	From whereabouts?
De onde vem?	jee ohn-jee _vang_	Which part of Brazil have you just been to?
Está gostando o Brasil?	eh-_stah_ gohs-_tahn_-doh ooh bdah-_zee_-ooh	Are you liking Brazil?
Estou adorando esse pais.	ehs-_toh_ ah-doh-_dahn_-doh eh-see pah-_eez_	I'm loving this country.

The Good, the Bad, and the Humid: Weather

Though the **clima** (_klee_-mah; weather) in some parts of Brazil is nearly the same year-round, you'll find that Brazilians talk about the weather just as much as people from countries with more dramatic weather.

In southern Brazil, and as far north as São Paulo, the **inverno** (een-_veh_-noo; winter) can get very **frio** (_fdee_-ooh; chilly). It even **neva** (_neh_-vah; snows) some years in Rio Grande do Sul state, the southernmost part of the country. In Rio, which is five hours by car up the coast from São Paulo, no one even owns a **casaco** (kah-_zah_-koh; coat). I met a young, rich guy from Rio in New York once in the winter. He told me that all his brothers, his dad, and his uncles shared the same coat, and anytime one went to visit a cold country, he'd borrow it.

In northern and northeastern Brazil, the concept of having **quatro estações** (_kwah_-tdoh eh-stah-_soh_-eez; four seasons) seems very foreign to locals. For them, there are just two seasons: **temporada de chuva** (temp-oh-_dah_-dah jee _shoo_-vah; rainy season) and **temporada seca** (temp-oh-_dah_-dah _seh_-kah; dry season). At many schools across Brazil, instructors teach children only about **verão** (veh-_dah_-ooh; summer) and **inverno.**

Here are a few more seasonal terms:

- ✔ **otono** (oh-*toh*-noo; autumn)
- ✔ **primavera** (pdee-mah-*veh*-dah; spring)
- ✔ **estacão** (ehs-tah-*sah*-ooh; season)

Talkin' the Talk

 Vinicius (vee-*nee*-see-ooz) is from **Florianópolis** (floh-dee-ah-*noh*-poh-lees), a beautiful island in southern Brazil. It's July, and he's just arrived in **Manaus** (mah-*nah*-ooz)— the biggest city in Brazil's share of the Amazon. During breakfast, he chats with a hotel worker about local weather.

Vinicius: **Que calor! Estava esperando chuva.**
kee kah-*loh*! ehs-*dah*-vah ehs-peh-*dahn*-doh *shoo*-vah.
It's so hot! I was expecting rain.

Worker: **Não e só chuva aqui como todo mundo pensa.**
nah-ooh *eh* soh *shoo*-vah ah-*kee* koh-moh toh-doo moon-doh *pen*-sah.
It's not all rain here like everyone thinks.

Vinicius: **Porque estamos em temporada de chuva, né?**
poh-keh ehs-*tahm*-ohz ang tem-poh-*dah*-dah jee *shoo*-vah, neh?
Because we're in the rainy season, right?

Worker: **Estamos. Na verdade, não e tipico ter sol em julho.**
ehs-*tah*-mohz. nah veh-*dah*-jee *nah*-ooh *eh* *chee*-pee-koh *teh* *soh*-ooh ang *joo*-lee-oh.
We are. Actually, it's not normal to have sun in July.

Vinicius: **Tenho sorte, então.**
tang-yoh *soh*-chee, en-*tah*-ooh.
I'm lucky, then.

Worker: **Sim, mas quem sabe — pela tarde pode precisar um guarda-chuva.**
sing, mah-eez kang *sah*-bee — peh-lah *tah*-jee poh-jee pdeh-see-*zah* oong goo-*ah*-dah *shoo*-vah.
Yeah, but who knows — in the afternoon you may need an umbrella.

Vinicius:	**Obrigado pela dica. Vou lever um.**
	ohb-dee-*gah*-doh peh-lah *jee*-kah. *voh* leh-*vah* oong.
	Thanks for the tip. I'll bring one along.

Words to Know

sol	<u>soh</u>-ooh	sun
quente	<u>kang</u>-chee	hot
calor	kah-<u>loh</u>	heat
frio	<u>fdee</u>-ooh	cold
chuva	<u>shoo</u>-vah	rain
chover	shoh-<u>veh</u>	to rain
guarda-chuva	goo-<u>ah</u>-dah <u>shoo</u>-vah	umbrella
nuvens	<u>noo</u>-vangz	clouds
úmido	<u>ooh</u>-mee-doh	humid
a umidade	ah ooh-mee-<u>dah</u>-jee	humidity

Figuring Out Family Connections

Brazilian families are very tight-knit; they tend to live in the same cities as their **pais** (*pah*-eez; parents) and **irmões** (ee-*moy*-eez; siblings/brothers and sisters) and to see each other at least once a week.

Brazilians like to ask new friends how many siblings they have and where their **mãe** (*mah*-ee; mom) and **pãe** (*pah*-ee; dad) live, right off the bat. This is opposed to some countries, where asking about **familiares** (fah-*mee*-lee-*ah*-deez; family members) can seem too intimate — or even too boring — within the first few minutes of a conversation.

Take a look at Table 4-1 for more words to express family **relações** (heh-lah-*soh*-eez; relationships).

Table 4-1	Relatives	
Portugese Word	*Pronunciation*	*English word*
irmão	ee-*mah*-ooh	brother
irmã	ee-*mah*	sister
primo	*pdee*-moh	male cousin
prima	*pdee*-mah	female cousin
primos	*pdee*-mooz	cousins
avô	ah-*vah*	grandfather
avó	ah-*voh*	grandmother
avós	ah-*vohz*	grandparents
filho	*feel*-yoo	son
filha	*feel*-yah	daughter
filhos	*feel*-yooz	children
marido	mah-*dee*-doh	husband
mulher	mool-*yeh*	wife
neto	*neh*-toh	grandson
neta	*neh*-tah	granddaughter

 In Brazil, street kids often call any adult **tia** (*chee*-ah; aunt) or **tio** (*chee*-ooh; uncle) — especially when they're asking for money or for help. If you find yourself in this situation, it's okay to give the child a small amount of money. Otherwise, just say, **Não posso** (*nah*-ooh *poh*-soo; I can't).

Using Posessives: "My . . ."

In Portuguese, it's easy to identify whether the sister you're talking about is **a sua irmã** (*ah soo*-ah ee-*mah*; your sister), **a irmã do seu amigo** (ah ee-*mah* doo *seh*-ooh ah-*mee*-goo; your friend's sister), or **a irmã dela** (ah ee-*mah* *deh*-lah; her sister).

The **exemplos** (eh-*zem*-plooz; examples) below use family relationships to **mostrar** (moh-*stdah*; show) how to say *my, your, his, her, their* in Portuguese. But these **palavras** (pah-*lahv*-dahz; words) come up in tons of situations that don't have anything to do with family, **é claro** (*eh klah*-doh; of course).

Possessives come up in day-to-day conversation all the time. You may want to talk about **a minha idéia** (*ah ming*-yah ee-*day*-ah; my idea), **os meus amigos** (*ooz meh*-ooz ah-*mee*-gooz; my friends), **a sua profissão** (ah *soo*-ah *pdoh*-fee-*sah*-ooh; your profession), **o apartamento dela** (*ooh* ah-*pah*-tah-*men*-toh *deh*-lah; her apartment) or **os preços da loja** (*ooz pdeh*-sooz dah *loh*-zhah; the store's prices).

To express *my,* say the phrases in Table 4-2:

Table 4-2		Phrases That Mean "My"	
Phrase	*Pronunciation*	*Type of Relative*	*Example*
a minha	ah *ming*-ya	one female	a minha irmã (my sister)
o meu	ooh *meh*-oo	one male	o meu irmão (my brother)
as minhas	ahz *ming*-yahs	multiple females	as minhas irmãs (my sisters)
os meus	oohz *meh*-ooz	multiple males or males and females	os meus irmãos (my brothers)

To express *your* in an informal setting (that is, when the person you're addressing is not an older person or an authority figure), say the phrases in Table 4-3. In formal settings, see Table 4-5. (You can read more about that in a little bit.)

Table 4-3		Phrases That Mean "Your"	
Phrase	*Pronunciation*	*Type of Relative*	*Example*
a sua	ah *soo*-ah	one female	a sua irmã (your sister)
o seu	ooh *seh*-oo	one male	o seu irmão (your brother)
as suas	ahz *soo*-ahz	multiple females	as suas irmãs (your sisters)
os seus	oohz *seh*-ooz	multiple males	os seus irmãos (your brothers)

To express *our,* say the phrases in Table 4-4:

Table 4-4		Phrases That Mean "Our"	
Phrase	*Pronunciation*	*Type of Relative*	*Example*
a nossa	ah *noh*-sah	one female	a nossa irmã (our sister)
o nosso	ooh *noh*-soo	one male	o nosso irmão (our brother)
as nossas	ahz *noh*-sahz	multiple females	as nossas irmãs (our sisters)
os nossos	oohz *noh*-sooz	multiple males	os nossos irmãos (our brothers)

To express *his* or *her* or *their,* say the phrases in Table 4-5. When talking about the possessions of other people, Brazilians reverse the order of *who* has *what.* Instead of mentioning the owner first, and then what's theirs, like with *my* and *our,* the owned thing is mentioned before the owner.

For example, with **os nossos irmãos** (*oohz noh*-sooz ee-*mah*-ooz), the literal translation is *our brothers. Our* comes first, then *brothers* — just like in English. But if you want to talk about *Tatiana's brother,* the correct translation is **o irmão da Tatiana** (*oo* ee-*mah*-ooh dah *tah*-chee-*ah*-nah; the brother of Tatiana). Say first what the owner owns, then name the owner. Another example is **as casas deles** (*ahz kah*-zahz *deh*-leez; their houses).

Sometimes, the owner isn't a person but rather a thing or even a place: **os resultados financeiros da empresa** (*ooz heh*-zool-*tah*-dooz fee-nahn-*say*-dooz dah em-*pdeh*-zah; the company's financial results) or **as praias do Rio** (*ahz pdah*-ee-ahz doo *hee*-ooh; Rio's beaches).

In English, you could technically say the beaches of Rio as well as Rio's beaches. But in Portuguese, you can only say the beaches of Rio.

That said (and complicated as it is), if you make a mistake in the word order, a Brazilian will most likely still understand you! So don't sweat it.

Table 4-5	Phrases That Mean "'s," "Her," "His," and "Their"		
Phrase	*Pronunciation*	*Translation*	*Example*
de (name)	jee	(name)'s (*Literally:* of [name])	irmã de José (José's sister *Literally:* sister of José)
dela	*deh*-lah	her (*Literally:* of her)	irmã dela (her sister *Literally:* sister of her)

Phrase	Pronunciation	Translation	Example
dele	*deh*-lee	his (*Literally:* of him)	irmã dele (his sister *Literally:* sister of him)
deles	*deh*-lahz	their (*Literally:* of them)	irmã deles (their sister *Literally:* sister of them)

The word **de** *(of)* in Portuguese often gets attached to the next word, in what people sometimes call a contraction. In the case of *his* and *hers,* Brazilians have found it easier to say **dela** instead of **de ela** and **dele** instead of **de ele,** and so on. It's sort of fun to pronounce! Try it.

Knowing Who, What, and Where

As a tourist in Brazil, you may want to ask locals about the best events and beaches around. You'll want to know **onde** (*ohn*-jee; where), **quando** (*kwahn*-doh; when), and **quanto** (*kwahn*-toh; how much).

If you want to ask someone what something means, say **O quê quer dizer . . . ?** (ooh *keh* keh jee-*zeh*). It literally means *What does . . . mean to say?* For example, say you're at one of Brazil's millions of drink stands on the street and you see the word **vitamina.** It looks like the word *vitamin* in English. But surely they're not selling vitamins? So you ask **O quê quer dizer vitamina? Vitamina** (vee-tah-*mee*-nah), by the way, means *milkshake.* **Vitaminas** come in more than 20 flavors in Brazil! You'll be glad to know what the word means, because your favorite flavor is waiting for you to discover it.

Here are some other basic words to help you find information:

- **o quê?** (ooh *kee;* what?)
- **quem?** (kang; who?)
- **por quê?** (poo-*keh;* why?)
- **como?** (*koh*-moo; how?)
- **qual?** (*kwah*-ooh; which?)

The following are examples of how to use these words:

- **O que é isso?** (ooh *kee* eh *ee*-soh; What is that?)
- **Onde fica a praia?** (*ohn*-jee *fee*-kah ah *pdah*-ee-ah; Where is the beach?)
- **Quando é o concerto?** (*kwahn*-doh *eh* ooh kohn-*seh*-toh; When is the concert?)

- ✔ **Quem é ele?** (kang eh *eh*-lee; Who is he?)
- ✔ **Por quê é assim?** (poh *keh* eh ah-*sing;* Why is it like that?)
- ✔ **Como é ela?** (*koh*-moo eh eh-lah; What is she like?)
- ✔ **Quanto que é?** (*kwahn*-toh kee *eh;* How much does it cost?)
- ✔ **Qual carro é seu?** (*kwah*-ooh *kah*-hoh eh *seh*-ooh; Which car is yours?)

Three "Save Me!" Phrases

A few months after arriving in Brazil, I was sent as a reporter to cover a business conference. I still didn't understand much of the language, and I felt helpless. **De repente** (deh heh-*pen*-chee; Suddenly), a speaker got up to the podium, and I could **compreender** (kohm-pdee-en-*deh;* understand) a lot more Portuguese than normal. I thought, is this guy from some region of Brazil that's easier to understand? **Talvez** (*tah*-ooh *vehz;* Maybe) he's Portuguese.

It turned out that the guy was American! He spoke Portuguese very well but still had an American **sotaque** (soh-*tah*-kee; accent).

The Brazilian accent is hard to understand at first, and sometimes you'll just want to tell the person you're speaking with: *Slow down!*

When you're feeling frustrated, pull these phrases out of your pocket:

- ✔ **Não entendi.** (*nah*-ooh ehn-ten-*jee;* I didn't understand.)
- ✔ **Oi?** (*oh*-ee; What did you say? — informal)
- ✔ **Poderia repetir por favor?** (poh-deh-*dee*-ah heh-peh-*chee* poh fah-*voh;* Could you repeat that, please?)

Giving Out Your Contact Information

After your first conversation with some people who speak Portuguese, you may decide you'd like to keep in contact with them. Or they may ask you **Qual o seu número de telefone?** (*kwah*-oo ooh seh-oo *noo*-meh-doh jee teh-leh-*fohn*-ee; What's your phone number?) You respond **O meu número de telefone é . . .** (ooh *meh*-oo *noo*-meh-doh jee teh-leh-*foh*-nee eh; My phone number is . . .).

Here are some other questions you can ask them. Notice the use of **seu** (your) and **meu** (my), which I talk about earlier in this chapter:

- **Qual é o seu sobrenome?** (*kwah*-ooh *eh* ooh *seh*-oo soh-bdee-*noh*-mee; What's your last name?)

- **Onde mora?** (ohn-jee *moh*-dah; Where do you live?)

- **Qual é o seu e-mail?** (*kwah*-ooh *eh* ooh *seh*-oo ee-*may*-oh; What's your e-mail?)

And here's how you can respond if you're asked these questions:

- **O meu sobrenome é . . .** (ooh *meh*-oo soh-bdee-*noh*-mee *eh*; My last name is . . .)

- **Eu moro . . .** (eh-ooh *moh*-doo; I live . . .)

- **O meu e-mail é . . .** (ooh *meh*-oo ee-*may*-oh *eh*; My e-mail is . . .)

Talkin' the Talk

Diogo (jee-*oh*-goo) and **Zeca** (*zeh*-kah) are samba music fanatics. They like an old type of samba called **chorinho** (shoh-*deen*-yoh). They just met each other in the audience of a **chorinho** show.

Zeca is telling **Diogo** about a **chorinho** concert next week. Notice that even Brazilians themselves have trouble understanding each other (it's a loud concert):

Zeca: **Tem um concerto de chorinho na semana que vem, sabia?**
tang oong kohn-*seh*-toh jee shoh-*deen*-yoh nah seh-*mahn*-ah kee *vang*, sah-*bee*-ah?
There's a concert next week, did you know?

Diogo: **Ah é? Quando e onde?**
ah *eh*? *kwahn*-doh ee *ohn*-jee?
Really? When and where?

Zeca: **Na noite da quarta-feira, no bairro da Laranjeiras.**
nah *noh*-ee-chee dah *kwah*-tah *fay*-dah, noh *bah*-ee-hoo dah lahd-ang-*zhay*-dahz.
On Wednesday night, in the neighborhood of Laranjeiras.

Diogo: **Poderia me mandar um e-mail com os dados?**
poh-deh-*dee*-ah mee mahn-*dah* oong ee-*may*-oh kohng ooz *dah*-dooz?
Could you send me an e-mail with the details?

Zeca:	**Claro. Qual é o seu e-mail?**
	klah-doh. *kwah*-ooh *eh* ooh *seh*-ooh ee-*may*-oh?
	Sure. What's your e-mail?
Diogo:	**É diogo.conrado@uol.com.br.**
	eh jee-*oh*-goh *pohn*-toh kohng-*hah*-doh ah-*hoh*-bah
	ooh-*oh*-ooh *pohn*-toh kohng *pohn*-toh beh *eh*-hee.
	It's diogo.conrado@uol.com.br.
Zeca:	**Não entendi.**
	nah-ooh en-ten-*jee*.
	I didn't understand.
Diogo:	**É diogo.conrado@uol.com.br.**
	eh jee-*oh*-goh pohn-toh kohng-*hah*-doh ah-*hoh*-bah
	ooh-*oh*-ooh *pohn*-toh kohng *pohn*-toh beh *eh*-hee.
	It's diogo.conrado@uol.com.br.

The symbol @ in Portuguese is called the **arroba** and is pronounced ah-*hoh*-bah. If you have a period in your e-mail, you may want to remember that's called a **ponto** (*pohn*-toh).

Fun & Games

Match the English sentences below with their translation in Brazilian Portuguese. All the main words are based on information in this chapter. Remember that learning a new language is all about meeting new people. Sit back, relax, and enjoy! Check Appendix C for the answers.

1. Where are you from?

2. I didn't understand.

3. Where do your parents live?

4. Are you enjoying Brazil?

5. How many siblings do you have?

6. What's your last name?

7. Could you repeat that, please?

8. What's your e-mail?

9. Where do you live?

a. **Onde moram os seus pais?**

b. **Quantos irmãos tem?**

c. **Qual o seu sobrenome?**

d. **Qual o seu e-mail?**

e. **Onde mora?**

f. **De onde você é?**

g. **Poderia repetir por favor?**

h. **Está gostando o Brasil?**

i. **Não entendi.**

Chapter 5

Dining Out and Going to Market

Está com fome? (eh-*stah koh*-oong *foh*-mee; Are you hungry?). **Quer comer?** (*keh* koh-meh; Do you want to eat?). Well, **se fala** (see *fah*-lah; they say) that you can't really get to know a **cultura estrangeira** (kool-*too*-dah ehs-tdahn-*zhey*-dah; foreign culture) until you've eaten its **comida** (koh-*mee*-dah; food). This chapter helps you become acquainted with Brazilian cuisine and how to order it, talk about it, and enhance your enjoyment of it.

Bom Appetite! Enjoy Your Meal!

Eating is something you'll definitely have to do in Brazil — and you're in for a treat. Brazilian cuisine uses exotic fruits and combines foods you're already familiar with in new and exciting ways. This section gives you some dining basics. But before you take a seat at the **mesa** (*meh*-zah; table), check out some of these place-setting terms:

  ✔ **garfo** (*gah*-foh; fork)

  ✔ **faca** (*fah*-kah; knife)

  ✔ **colher** (kool-*yeh;* spoon)

  ✔ **prato** (*pdah*-toh; plate)

  ✔ **prato fundo** (*pdah*-toh *foon*-doh; bowl)

- **copo** (*koh*-poo; cup/glass)
- **guardanapo** (gwah-dah-*nah*-poh; napkin)

Following are some basic items that you may want to **pedir** (peh-*jee;* ask for) at a **restaurante** (heh-stah-ooh-*dahn*-chee; restaurant) or someone's **casa** (*kah*-zah; house):

- **sal** (*sah*-ooh; salt)
- **pimenta do reino** (pee-*mehn*-tah doo *hay*-noo; black pepper)
- **pimenta** (pee-*mehn*-tah; Brazilian hot sauce — hot red peppers soaking in oil. *Literally:* pepper)
- **limão** (lee-*mah*-ooh; lime — Brazilians squeeze **limão** on everything!)
- **pão** (*pah*-ooh; bread)
- **gelo** (*zheh*-loh; ice)

Here are some useful phrases that you can use to talk about food:

- **Eu adoro chocolate!** (*eh*-ooh ah-*doh*-doo shoh-koh-*lah*-chee; I love chocolate! *Literally:* I adore chocolate!)
- **Eu detesto ovos.** (*eh*-ooh deh-*teh*-stoh *oh*-vooz; I hate eggs. *Literally:* I detest eggs.)
- **Qual a sua comida favorita?** (*kwah*-ooh ah *soo*-ah koh-*mee*-dah fah-voh-*dee*-tah; What's your favorite food?)
- **Que tipo de comida gosta?** (kee *chee*-poh jee koh-*mee*-dah *goh*-stah; What type of food do you like?)
- **Qual prefere — a comida hindu ou a comida chinesa?** (*kwah*-ooh pdeh-*feh*-dee — ah koh-*mee*-dah een-*doo* ooh ah koh-*mee*-dah shee-*neh*-sah; Which do you prefer — Indian or Chinese food?)
- **Você gosta de cozinhar?** (voh-*seh goh*-stah jee koh-zing-*yah;* Do you like to cook?)
- **Pode recomendar um bom restaurante por aqui?** (*poh*-jee heh-koh-mehn-*dah* oong *boh-oong* heh-stah-ooh-*dahn*-chee poh ah-*kee;* Can you recommend a good restaurant around here?)

Take a look at how to say the basic meals and parts of meals:

- **café da manhã** (kah-*feh* dah mahn-*yah;* breakfast; *Literally:* morning's coffee)
- **almoço** (*ah*-ooh-*moh*-soo; lunch)

> ✔ **jantar** (zhahn-*tah;* dinner)
>
> ✔ **entrada** (ehn-*tdah*-dah; appetizer. *Literally:* entry)
>
> ✔ **sobremesa** (soh-bdee-*meh*-zah; dessert)

And these are some phrases you can say at the table:

> ✔ **Que gostoso!** (kee gohs-*toh*-zoo; How amazingly delicious!)
>
> ✔ **É delicioso.** (eh deh-lee-see-*oh*-zoo; It's delicious.)
>
> ✔ **Está quente.** (eh-*stah kang*-chee; It's hot.)
>
> ✔ **Está frio.** (es-*stah fdee*-oh; It's cold.)
>
> ✔ **Bom appetite!** (boh-oong ah-peh-*tee*-chee; Bon appetite!)
>
> ✔ **Saúde!** (sah-*oo*-jee; Cheers! *Literally:* Health!)

At the Restaurant: Trying Local Foods

The classic Brazilian **comida** (koh-*mee*-dah; meal/food) is **simples** (*seem*-pleez; basic). It's a piece of **carne** (*kah*-nee; beef) served with **feijão** (fay-*zhow;* beans), **arroz** (ah-*hohz;* rice), and **salada** (sah-*lah*-dah; salad). In this section, I explore the restaurant experience and the food you can find there.

You can get a **refeição** (heh-fay-*sah*-ooh; meal) at five basic places in Brazil:

> ✔ **boteco** (boo-*teh*-koo; cheap restaurant where people also go to drink beer or take shots of liquor)
>
> ✔ **padaria** (pah-dah-*dee*-ah; bakery — at Brazilian **padarias** you can also sit down for a meal)
>
> ✔ **lanchonete** (lahn-shoh-*neh*-chee; restaurant that specializes in hamburgers, sandwiches, and fruit juices)
>
> ✔ **restaurante por quilo** (heh-stah-ooh-*dahn*-chee poh *kee*-loh; self-serve buffet, pay per kilo — these are delicious, healthy, and cheap in Brazil)
>
> ✔ **restaurante** (heh-stah-ooh-*dahn*-chee; restaurant)

The first four options are for quick meals. They generally offer **sanduíches** (sahn-*dwee*-sheez; sandwiches), **hamburgers** (ahm-*booh*-gehz; hamburgers), **salgados** (sah-ooh-*gah*-dohz; savory pastries), and **pratos feitos** (pdah-tohz *fay*-tohz; a combo plate, usually rice, beans, meat, and salad). Another option, the **restaurante,** is covered in this section.

Brazilians generally don't leave a **gorjeta** (goh-*zheh*-tah; American-type tip) at restaurants. If service is exceptional, you can leave a **gorjeta** of 10 percent. Sometimes a 10 percent or 15 percent tip is required and included in the **conta** (*kohn*-tah; bill). You can tell because it says **serviço incluido** (seh-*vee*-soh een-kloo-*ee*-doh; tip included). *Sales tax* on a **conta** shows up as **I.V.A.** (*ee*-vah).

In addition to Brazilian **restaurantes,** you can also find a lot of **italiano** (ee-tah-lee-*ah*-noh; Italian) and **japonês** (zhah-poh-*nehz*; Japanese) restaurants in Brazil.

If you need to go to the bathroom in a **restaurante,** you can just say **O banheiro?** (ooh bahn-*yay*-doh; The bathroom?). To be fancier, you can say **Por favor, onde fica o banheiro?** (poh fah-*voh* ohn-jee *fee*-kah ooh bahn-*yay*-doh; Where is the bathroom, please?)

Ordering at a restaurant

When you arrive at a **restaurante** (heh-stah-ooh-*dahn*-chee; restaurant), the **garçon** (gah-*sohng;* waiter) or **garconete** (gah-soh-*neh*-chee; waitress) leads you to a **mesa** (*meh*-zah; table). He or she may ask you whether you want to **sentar** (sehn-*tah;* sit) **fora** (*foh*-dah; outside) or **dentro** (*dehn*-tdoh; inside).

Then the waiter or waitress gives you the **cardápio** (kah-*dah*-pee-oh; menu). You may see these sections:

- ✔ **entradas** (ehn-*tdah*-dahz; starters)
- ✔ **pratos principais** (*pdah*-tohz pdeen-see-*pah*-eez; main dishes)
- ✔ **bebidas** (beh-*bee*-dahz; drinks)
- ✔ **sobremesas** (soh-bdee-*meh*-zahz; desserts)

You may also see the heading **especialidades da casa** (eh-speh-see-ah-lee-*dah*-jeez dah *kah*-zah; house specialties).

When you're **pronto** (*pdohn*-toh; ready) to **pedir** (peh-*jeeh;* order. *Literally:* to ask for), you can just say **Quero . . . por favor** (*keh*-doo . . . poh-fah-*voh;* I want . . . please).

Brazilians generally say **Vou querer** (*voh* keh-*deh;* I will have. *Literally:* I will want) instead of **Quero.** But **Quero** is easier to memorize, and it's a useful word for many other situations. I get back to **querer** later in this chapter.

If the **cardápio** is too confusing, you may just want the **garçon** to recommend something for you. Say **O quê recomenda?** (ooh *keh* heh-koh-*mehn*-dah; What do you recommend?).

If you want to go with what is recommended, say **OK, tá bom** (oh-*kay* tah *boh-*oong; Okay, I'll go with that. *Literally:* That's good).

If you want to ask for something specific, say **Têm . . . ?** (tang; Do you have . . . ?). You can fill in the blank with one of the following words or phrases:

- **sopa** (*soh*-pah; soup)
- **salada** (sah-*lah*-dah; salad)
- **sanduíches** (sahn-doo-*ee*-sheez; sandwiches)
- **algo para crianças** (*ah*-ooh-goh *pah*-dah kdee-*ahn*-sahz; something for kids)
- **pratos vegetarianos** (*pdah*-tohz veh-zheh-teh-dee-*ah*-nohz; vegetarian dishes)

You can also use **Têm . . . ?** to ask whether a **prato** (*pdah*-toh; dish) contains a specific **ingrediente** (eeng-gdeh-jee-*ehn*-chee; ingredient) that you may or may not want:

- **Têm carne?** (tang *kah*-nee; Does it have meat in it?)
- **Têm frutos do mar?** (tang *fdoo*-tohz doo *mah*; Does it have any seafood in it?)
- **Têm azeite de dendê?** (tang ah-*zay*-chee jee dehn-*deh*; Does it have palm oil?)

Beware the **azeite de dendê,** found in Bahia state. It's very strong and can cause stomachaches for those who've never tried it before. It's used most famously to make **acarajé** (ah-kah-dah-*zheh*; typical Bahian food item sold on the street — read the "On to the main course" section for more).

If you know a **prato** has a specific **ingrediente** that you want **retirado** (heh-chee-*dah*-doh; taken out), say **sem . . .** (sang; without . . .). You can fill in the blank with one of the following words:

- **queijo** (*kay*-zhoh; cheese)
- **manteiga** (mahn-*tay*-gah; butter)
- **maionese** (mah-ee-oh-*neh*-zee; mayonnaise)
- **leite** (*lay*-chee; milk)
- **açucar** (ah-*soo*-kah; sugar)
- **cebola** (seh-*boh*-lah; onion)
- **molho** (*mohl*-yoh; sauce)

✔ **óleo** (oh-*lay*-oh; vegetable oil)

✔ **alho** (*ahl*-yoh; garlic)

And **a carne** (ah *kah*-nee; meat) can be **grelhada** (gdeh-ooh-*yah*-dah; grilled), **cozida** (koh-*zee*-dah; boiled), **frito** (*fdee*-toh; fried), or **assado** (ah-*sah*-doh; sautéed), so you may want to specify how you want it prepared.

Brazilian food is not **picante** (pee-*kahn*-chee; spicy). But you can ask for **pimenta** (pee-*mehn*-tah; hot chilies soaked in oil) or **molho de pimenta** (*mohl*-yoh jee pee-*mehn*-tah; hot sauce).

Ordering a drink

Sucos (*soo*-kohz; fruit juices) and the incredible **variedade** (vah-dee-eh-*dah*-jee; variety) they come in was my favorite aspect of eating or drinking in Brazil. The average **restaurante** (heh-stah-ooh-*dahn*-chee; restaurant) has between 10 and 20 types of **sucos** to choose from, and the selection varies depending on the region. Brazilians love their **sucos** and **vitaminas** (vee-tah-*mee*-nahz; fruity milkshakes). Juice bars are everywhere; Rio seems to have one on every block.

Here are the most common **frutas** (*fdoo*-tahz; fruits) in Brazil. If you want to ask for the fruit in **suco** form, say **suco de . . .** (soo-koh *jee;* juice of . . .). Just plug one of these fruits into the blank:

✔ **laranja** (lah-*dahn*-zhah; orange)

✔ **abacaxi** (ah-bah-kah-*shee;* pineapple)

✔ **mamão** (mah-*mah*-ooh; papaya)

✔ **melancia** (meh-lahn-*see*-ah; watermelon)

✔ **goiaba** (goy-*ah*-bah; guava)

✔ **maracujá** (mah-dah-koo-*zhah;* passionfruit)

✔ **manga** (*mahn*-gah; mango)

My favorite **suco** is **cupuaçu** (koo-poo-ah-*soo;* milky white Amazonian fruit with a tangy taste).

To help you wash down all the wonderful Brazilian food, you may want one of the following **bebidas** (beh-*bee*-dahz; drinks):

✔ **água sem gas** (*ah*-gwah *sang* gahz; still mineral water)

✔ **água com gas** (*ah*-gwah *koh*-oong *gahz;* sparkling mineral water)

- **Guaraná Antartica** (gwah-dah-*nah* ahn-*tah*-chee-kah; Brazil's most popular brand-name soda, made from the Amazonian berry **guaraná** — **Antártica** is the brand name)

- **Guaraná diet** (gwah-dah-*nah dah*-ee-chee; diet Guaraná)

- **Coca-Cola** (koh-kah *koh*-lah; Coke)

- **Coca light** (koh-kah *lah*-ee-chee; Diet Coke)

- **cerveja** (seh-*veh*-zhah; can of beer)

- **chope** (*shoh*-pee; light draft beer)

- **vinho** (*ving*-yoo; wine)

- **café** (kah-*feh;* coffee)

- **chá** (shah; tea)

- **leite** (*lay*-chee; milk)

If you go to a bar in Brazil, you may notice people saying **Mais um.** (*mah*-eez oong) or **Mais uma.** (*mah*-eez *ooh*-mah) a lot. The phrases mean *I'll have another* (*Literally:* More one).

A note about Brazilian **cerveja:** Brazilians often joke that beer has to be **estupidamente gelada** (eh-*stoo*-pee-dah-*mehn*-chee zheh-*lah*-dah; stupidly cold). A Brazilian sends back a beer that's not ice cold. And the only place you can possibly get good **cerveja escura** (seh-*veh*-zhah ehs-*koo*-dah; dark beer) in Brazil is during the German beer festival Oktoberfest, held each year in **Blumenau** (*bloo*-meh-*now*), which is in Santa Catarina state (southern Brazil, where there are many descendants of German immigrants).

Then, of course, there's the national drink of Brazil, the **caipirinha** (*kah*-ee-pee-*deen*-yah). It's made with **cachaça** (kah-*shah*-sah; sugar cane liquor), **gelo** (*zheh*-loh; ice), **limão** (lee-*mah*-ooh; lime) and **açucar** (ah-*soo*-kah; sugar). You can also order a **caipifruta** (*kah*-ee-pee-*fdoo*-tah) — a caipirinha made from a fruit of your choice, instead of lime.

First foods up: Salads and condiments

Saladas (sah-*lah*-dahz; salads) in Brazil are very basic if they come with your meal. But the salad bars, on the other hand, are stocked full of interesting items. Brazilians tend not to mix salad ingredients like they do in the U.S. Instead, they usually put the items side by side and then drizzle olive oil and red wine vinegar on top.

Here are some typical Brazilian items that you can expect to see at the salad bar:

- **alface** (ah-ooh-*fah*-see; lettuce)
- **rúcula** (*hoo*-koo-lah; arugula)
- **tomate** (toh-*mah*-chee; tomato)
- **tomate seco** (toh-*mah*-chee *seh*-koh; sun-dried tomato)
- **milho** (*meew*-yoh; corn)
- **palmito** (*pah*-ooh-*mee*-toh; heart of palm)
- **cenoura** (seh-*noh*-dah; carrots)
- **cebola** (seh-*boh*-lah; onion)
- **beterraba** (beh-teh-*hah*-bah; beets)
- **abobrinha** (ah-boh-*bdeeng*-yah; zucchini)
- **mozzarella de búfalo** (moh-tzah-*deh*-lah jee *boo*-fah-loh; fresh mozzarella)
- **queijo** (*kay*-zhoh; cheese)
- **azeite de oliva** (ah-*zay*-chee jee oh-*lee*-vah; olive oil)
- **vinagre** (vee-*nah*-gdee; red wine vinegar)
- **vinagrete** (vee-nah-*gdeh*-chee; chopped tomato, onion, and green bell pepper, with vinegar. *Literally:* vinaigrette — Brazilians put **vinagrete** on barbecued meat)

A note about **alface:** Brazilians call iceberg lettuce **alface americano** (ah-ooh-*fah*-see ah-meh-dee-*kah*-noh; American lettuce)! That's because iceberg lettuce is more popular in the U.S. than it is in Brazil.

On to the main course

The most famous Brazilian dish is called **feijoada** (fay-zhoh-*ah*-dah; bean/pig parts stew). It has **orelha de porco** (oh-*dehl*-yah jee *poh*-koo; pig's ears) and even **joelho de porco** (zhoh-*ehl*-yoh jee *poh*-koo; pig's knees), in addition to the more **nobre** (*noh*-bdee; good quality. *Literally:* noble) parts of the pig.

Feijoada was first whipped up in **cozinhas** (koh-*zeen*-yahz; kitchens) by **escravos** (ehs-*kdah*-vohz; slaves) brought from Africa hundreds of years ago. The slaves were **pobres** (*poh*-bdeez; poor), and they made sure they ate almost all parts of every animal. **Feijoada** is usually served in restaurants on **quarta-feira** (*kwah*-tah *fay*-dah; Wednesday) and on **sábado** (*sah*-bah-*doh;* Saturday).

Here's an index of classic Brazilian food items and dishes — besides **churrasco** (choo-*hah*-skoo; Brazilian barbecue), which I cover in the "Basking in Brazilian barbecue" section, and **feijoada:**

- ✔ **limão** (lee-*mah*-ooh): Brazilians squeeze *lime* on just about anything, especially the classic meal combo of rice, beans, and skirt beef steak. It's also used in juices and desserts. Don't try to ask for a lemon in Brazil — they don't have any.

- ✔ **coco** (*koh*-koh): Brazilians love *coconut.* They drink coconut juice out of a whole green coconut, through a straw. Men chop off a top slice of the coconut with a machete and then sell it for 1 real (about 30 cents) on the beach and on the street. **Coco** is also used in lots of main dishes from Bahia state.

- ✔ **pão de queijo** (*pah*-ooh jee *kay*-zhoh): **Pão de queijo** is *cheese bread —* sold either as little balls or in pieces the size of a biscuit. It's unbelievably delicious.

- ✔ **moqueca** (moh-*keh*-kah): This *thick fish stew from Bahia state* is made with **azeite de dendê** (ah-*zay*-chee jee dehn-*deh;* palm oil), which is hard on some tourists' stomachs, and **leite de coco** (*lay*-chee jee *koh*-koo; coconut milk).

- ✔ **acarajé** (ah-*kah*-dah-*zheh*): This popular dish from Bahia state is sold on beaches and on the street. It's *deep-fried black-eyed-pea cakes, filled with tiny unpeeled shrimp, raw onions, tomato, green pepper, and peanut sauce.* It's also made with **azeite de dendê.**

- ✔ **coxinha** (koh-*sheeng*-yah): **Coxinhas** are *mashed potatoes, fried, shaped into a teardrop, with shredded chicken inside.* You can find them at most corner **botecos** (boo-*teh*-kooz; cheap restaurants) or bakeries in Brazil.

- ✔ **açai na tigela com granola** (ah-sah-*ee* nah tee-*zheh*-lah *koh*-oong gdah-*noh*-lah): *Amazonian fruit sorbet in a large bowl, topped with granola and sometimes honey:* This is the favored beach food of Brazilian surfers. **Açai** is a small eggplant-colored berry.

- ✔ **farofa** (fah-*doh*-fah): This is toasted manioc flour mixed in with bits of fried pork and scrambled eggs. It's served with **feijoada** or on the side with your steak. Mmmm. A not-to-miss!

- ✔ **mandioca frita** (mahn-jee-*ah*-kah *fdee*-tah): *Fried yucca* is my favorite Brazilian food item. It's way better than French fries!

- ✔ **X-salada** (*sheez* sah-*lah*-dah): This is a *cheeseburger with lettuce and tomato* (*Literally:* cheese with salad). The letter *x* is pronounced *sheez* in Portuguese, which sounds like the English word *cheese,* so they just write the letter *x*. Brazilians always have a sense of humor.

Basking in Brazilian barbeque

You can't talk about Brazilian food without mentioning the beloved **churrascaria** (choo-*hah*-skeh-*dee*-ahz; Brazilian-style barbeque joint). It's a **comer à vontade** (koh-*meh* ah vohn-*tah*-jee; all-you-can-eat) affair.

Waiters come by your **mesa** (*meh*-zah; table) with about ten different **cortes** (*koh*-cheez; cuts) of meat every five minutes or so. Sometimes they give you a round card that's **verde** (*veh*-jee; green) on one side and **vermelho** (veh-*mehl*-yoh; red) on the other. When you want to **comer mais** (koh-*meh mah*-eez; eat more), place the card with the **verde** side up. And when you're **satisfeito** (sah-tees-*fay*-toh; full), be sure to have the **vermelho** side showing. Otherwise, it'll be hard to fend off the **garçons** (gah-*soh*-oongz; waiters)!

The only thing the **garçon** won't bring by your **mesa** is **peixe** (*pay*-shee; fish). Here are the typical **cortes** the **garçons** may bring by your **mesa:**

- **picanha** (pee-*kahn*-yah; rumpsteak)
- **alcatra** (ow-*kah*-tdah; top sirloin)
- **fraldinha** (fdah-ooh-*jeen*-yah; flank steak)
- **linguiça** (ling-*gwee*-sah; Brazilian chorizo-style sausage)
- **lombo** (*lohm*-boh; pork loin)
- **coxa de frango** (*koh*-shah jee *fdahn*-goh; chicken thighs)
- **peito de frango** (*pay*-toh jee *fdahn*-goh; chicken breast)
- **coração de frango** (koh-dah-*sah*-ooh jee *fdahn*-goh; chicken hearts)
- **cordeiro** (koh-*day*-doh; lamb)

Farinha (fah-*ding*-yah; manioc flour) is simply **esquisito** (ehs-kee-*zee*-toh; bizarre) the first time you encounter it. Flour you dip your meat into? I personally didn't like **farinha** for about a year. But now when I eat a steak here in the States, I miss it. It's an acquired taste. And once acquired, it's impossible to **vivir sem** (vee-*vee sang;* live without).

Vegetarianos (veh-zheh-teh-dee-*ah*-nohz; vegetarians), never fear: **Churrascarias** always have a wonderful salad buffet.

Talkin' the Talk

Paying the bill isn't the most fun part of eating out, but this dialogue can help you practice what to say when the time comes. **Alberto** (ah-ooh-*beh*-too) and **Marina** (mah-*dee*-nah) are surprised when their tasty seafood meal ends in an expensive bill.

Alberto:	(To the waiter) **A conta, por favor.** ah *kohn*-tah, poh fah-*voh*. The check, please.
Waiter:	**Vou trazé-la agora.** voh tdah-*zeh*-lah ah-*goh*-dah. I'll bring it now.
Alberto:	**Aceita cartão?** ah-*say*-tah kah-*tah*-ooh? Do you accept credit cards?
Waiter:	**Aceitamos.** ah-say-*tah*-mohz. Yes, we do (*Literally:* we accept).
Alberto:	(After he sees the bill) **Que caro. Noventa e sete reais?** kee *kah*-doh. noh-*vehn*-tah ee *seh*-chee hay-eyes? How expensive. Ninety-seven reais (about US$30)?
Marina:	**O serviço está incluido?** ooh seh-*vee*-soh eh-*stah* eeng-kloo-*ee*-doo? Is the tip included?
Alberto:	**Ah — foi por isto. É taxa de quinze por cento.** ah — *foh*-ee poh *ees*-toh. eh *tah*-shah jee *keen*-zee poh *sehn*-toh. Ah — that's why. It's 15 percent.
Marina:	(To the waiter, after the credit card receipt comes back) **Tem caneta?** *tang* kah-*neh*-tah? Do you have a pen?
Waiter:	**Aqui tem.** ah-*kee tang*. Here you go (*Literally:* Here you have).

Words to Know

a conta	ah <u>kohn</u>-tah	the bill
vou	<u>voh</u>	I will
trazé-lo	tdah-<u>zeh</u>-loh	bring it
aceita	ah-<u>say</u>-tah	do you accept/he or she accepts
cartão	kah-<u>tah</u>-ooh	credit card (*Literally:* card)
aceitamos	ah-say-<u>tah</u>-mohz	we accept
uma porção	<u>ooh</u>-mah poh-<u>sah</u>-ooh	an order (one portion of food)
cada	<u>kah</u>-dah	each
caro	<u>kah</u>-doh	expensive
o serviço	ooh seh-<u>vee</u>-soh	obligatory tip (*Literally:* service)
incluido	eeng kloo-<u>ee</u>-doo	included
foi por isto	<u>foh</u>-ee poh <u>dee</u>-stoh	that's why
caneta	kah-<u>neh</u>-tah	pen

Doing Dessert

To end the section, I talk **sobremesa** (soh-bdee-*meh*-zah; dessert). Here are some of my favorites:

- **bolo de laranja** (boh-loo jee lah-*dahn*-zhah; orange-flavored pound cake)
- **bolo de limão** (boh-loo jee lee-*mah*-ooh; lime-flavored pound cake)
- **flan** (fluhn; flan custard)
- **mousse de maracujá** (mooz jee mah-dah-koo-*jah;* passionfruit mousse)

- **mousse de chocolate** (mooz jee sho-koh-*lah*-chee; chocolate mousse)

- **sorvete** (soh-*veh*-chee; ice cream)

- **iogurte** (ee-oh-*goo*-chee; yogurt)

- **Romeo e Julieta** (*hoh*-mee-oh ee zhoo-lee-*eh*-tah; guava paste with a piece of hard cheese. *Literally:* Romeo and Juliet)

- **pizza doce** (*pee*-tzah *doh*-see; sweet pizza)

In Brazil it's common for pizza joints to offer several dessert pizzas. **Chocolate e morango** (sho-koh-*lah*-chee ee; chocolate and strawberry) is an experience not to be missed.

You may want a **cafezinho** (kah-feh-*zeen*-yoh; shot of Brazilian coffee, served in a tiny cup or glass and sweetened with a lot of sugar) to go with your **sobremesa.** In good restaurants, you can ask for your coffee to be **sem açúcar** (sang ah-*soo*-kah; unsweetened). And if you're really in a decadent mood, you can ask for **chantily** (shan-chee-*lee;* whipped cream) with your coffee.

Mastering the Eating and Drinking Verbs

I've included the word **comida** (koh-*mee*-dah; food) in this chapter already. It comes from the verb **comer** (koh-*meh;* to eat/to have lunch). Here's how to conjugate **comer:**

Conjugation	*Pronunciation*
eu como	*eh*-ooh *koh*-moo
você come	voh-*seh koh*-mee
ele/ela come	*eh*-lee/*eh*-lah *koh*-mee
nós comemos	*nohz* koh-*meh*-mohz
eles/elas comem	*eh*-leez/*eh*-lahz *koh*-mang

These are some basic sentences that use **comer:**

- **Vamos comer.** (*vah*-mohz koh-*meh;* Let's eat.)

- **O meu cachorro come cenoura.** (ooh *meh*-ooh kah-*shoh*-hoo *koh*-mee seh-*noh*-dah; My dog eats carrots.)

- **Como muito.** (*koh*-moo moh-*ee*-toh; I eat a lot.)

- **Ela come pouco.** (*eh*-lah *koh*-mee poh-ooh-koh; She doesn't eat much. *Literally:* She eats little.)

Next, glance at the verb **beber** (beh-*beh;* to drink). Depending on the context, **beber** can also specifically mean *to drink alcohol* — like in English when people say "He drinks a lot" to mean *He drinks a lot of alcohol.* The Portuguese equivalent is **Ele bebe muito** (*eh*-lee *beh*-bee moh-*ee*-toh). Here's how to conjugate **beber:**

Conjugation	*Pronunciation*
eu bebo	*eh*-ooh *beh*-boh
você bebe	voh-*seh beh*-bee
ele/ela bebe	*eh*-lee/*eh*-lah *beh*-bee
nós bebemos	*nohz* beh-*beh*-mohz
eles/elas bebem	*eh*-leez/*eh*-lahz *beh*-bang

Here are some basic phrases that use **beber:**

✔ **É preciso beber muita água todos os dias.** (eh pdeh-*see*-zoh beh-*beh* moh-*ee*-tah *ah*-gwah *toh*-dooz ooz *jee*-ahz; It's necessary to drink a lot of water every day.)

✔ **O quê quer para beber?** (ooh kee *keh* pah-dah beh-*beh;* What do you want to drink?)

Brazilians often also use the verb **tomar** (toh-*mah*) to mean *to drink.* It's okay to use **tomar** when you'd say in English *to have a drink.*

✔ **Gostaria de tomar uma Coca-Cola?** (gohs-tah-*dee*-ah jee toh-*mah* ooh-mah koh-kah *koh*-lah; Would you like to have a Coke?)

✔ **Vamos tomar um drinque.** (*vah*-mohz toh-*mah* oong *dreeng*-kee; Let's have a drink/cocktail.)

Tomar also means *to take.* Brazilians and English-speakers use some of the same expressions that use *take:*

✔ **tomar a iniciativa** (toh-*mah* ah ee-*nee*-see-ah-*chee*-vah; to take the initiative)

✔ **tomar conta de** (toh-*mah* kohn-tah *jee;* to take care of)

✔ **tomar remédios** (toh-*mah* heh-*meh*-jee-ooz; to take medicine)

Saying What You Want: The Verb Querer

You say **quero** (*keh*-doo; I want) when you're at a **restaurante** (heh-stah-ooh-*dahn*-chee; restaraunt) and are ready to **pedir** (peh-*jee;* order). **Quero** comes from the verb **querer** (keh-*deh;* to want), which comes in handy in lots of **situações** (see-too-ah-*soh*-eez; situations), not just when **tem fome** (tang *foh*-mee; you're hungry).

You can use **querer** at a store to tell the clerk what you want, to tell an **amigo** (ah-*mee*-goh; friend) while at his **casa** (*kah*-zah; house) what kind of **bebida** (beh-*bee*-dah; drink) you'd like, or even to tell someone about your job or life aspirations. Take a look to see how to conjugate **querer:**

Conjugation	Pronunciation
eu quero	*eh*-ooh *keh*-dooh
você quer	voh-*seh keh*
ele/ela quer	*eh*-lee/*eh*-lah *keh*
nós queremos	*nohz* keh-*deh*-mohz
eles/elas querem	*eh*-leez/*eh*-lahz *keh*-dang

You can practice **querer** with some mini-dialogues:

- ✔ **Quer um Guaraná?** (*keh* oong *gwah*-dah-*nah;* Do you want a Guaraná?)
- ✔ **Sim, quero.** (*sing keh*-dooh; Yes, please. *Literally:* Yes, I want.)

- ✔ **Quer ir à praia comigo?** (*keh* ee ah *pdah*-ee-ah koh-*mee*-goo; Do you want to go to the beach with me?)
- ✔ **Não, não quero, obrigada.** (*nah*-ooh, nah-ooh *keh*-dooh, oh-bdee-*gah*-dah; No thanks.)

- ✔ **O quê quer fazer na vida?** (ooh *kee keh* fah-*zeh* nah *vee*-dah; What do you want to do in life?)
- ✔ **Quero ter filhos e ser um bom amigo.** (*keh*-dooh *teh feel*-yohz ee *seh* oong *boh*-oong ah-*mee*-goo; I want to have children and to be a good friend.)

Brazilians often just say **Quer?** (keh; Do you want?) to ask whether you want something. They may offer you a bite of their food by pointing to it and saying **Quer?**

Having (or Not Having) Specific Items

When you're at a **restaurante** (heh-stah-ooh-*dahn*-chee; restaurant) and want to ask if they serve a specific **prato** (*pdah*-toh; dish), say **Têm . . . ?** (tang; Do you have . . . ?).

Têm comes from the verb **ter** (teh; to have). To see how to conjugate **ter,** take a look:

Conjugation	*Pronunciation*
eu tenho	*eh*-ooh *tang*-yoh
você tem	voh-*seh tang*
ele/ela tem	*eh*-lee/*eh*-lah *tang*
nós temos	*nohz teh*-mohz
eles/elas têm	*eh*-leez/*eh*-lahz tang

And here are some ways to use **ter:**

- ✔ **Eu tenho um gato.** (*eh*-ooh *tang*-yoh oong *gah*-toh; I have a cat.)

- ✔ **Eu tenho muitos amigos brasileiros.** (*eh*-ooh *tang*-yoh moo-*ee*-tohz ah-*mee*-gohz bdah-zee-*lay*-dohz; I have a lot of Brazilian friends.)

- ✔ **Eu tenho uma casa na Bahia.** (*eh*-ooh *tang*-yoh ooh-mah *kah*-zah nah bah-*ee*-ah; I have a house in Bahia.)

- ✔ **Eles têm muito dinheiro.** (eh-leez *tang* moo-*ee*-toh jing-*yay*-doh; They have a lot of money.)

- ✔ **Você tem olhos muito bonitos.** (voh-*seh* tang *ohl*-yooz moo-*ee*-toh boo-*nee*-tohz; You have really pretty eyes).

- ✔ **Nós temos um carro.** (nohz *teh*-mohz oong *kah*-hoh; We have a car.)

- ✔ **A empresa tem um novo diretor.** (ah ehm-*pdeh*-zah tang oong *noh*-voo jee-deh-*toh;* The company has a new director.)

Check out these common expressions that use **ter:**

- ✔ **ter razão** (*teh* hah-*zah*-ooh; to be right)

- ✔ **ter sorte** (teh *soh*-chee; to be lucky. *Literally:* to have luck)

And here's how to use them:

- ✔ **Ah, você tem razão.** (ah voh-*seh* tang hah-*zah*-ooh; Ah, you're right.)

- ✔ **Ela sempre tem muita sorte.** (eh-lah *sehm*-pdee *tang* moh-*ee*-tah *soh*-chee; She's always really lucky.)

Shopping at the Market

Brazilians shop at **supermercados** (*soo*-peh-meh-*kah*-dooz; supermarkets), but they also love to buy **frutas** (*fdoo*-tahz; fruits) and **legumes e verduras** (leh-*goo*-meez ee veh-*doo*-dahz; vegetables) at **feirinhas** (fay-*deen*-yahz; outdoor markets), where the food is usually **mais barato** (may-eez bah-*dah*-toh; cheaper) and **melhor** (mehl-*yoh;* better). (Check out Chapter 11 to find out about Brazilian money.)

The biggest supermarket chain in Brazil is called **Pão de Acucar** (*pah*-ooh jee ah-*soo*-kah; The Sugarloaf), named after the famous rock that distinguishes Rio's skyline.

Getting some practical items

Here are some items you can buy at a **supermercado** (*soo*-peh-meh-*kah*-doo; supermarket), besides **comida** (koh-*mee*-dah; food):

- **papel higiênico** (pah-*peh*-ooh ee-*zheh*-nee-koh; toilet paper)
- **produtos de limpeza** (pdoh-*doo*-tohz jee leem-*peh*-zah; cleaning products)
- **latas de legumes** (*lah*-tahz jee leh-*goo*-meez; cans of vegetables)
- **coisas congeladas** (*koy*-zahz kohn-zhe-*lah*-dahz; frozen things)
- **adoçante** (ah-doh-*sahn*-chee; sugar substitute in liquid form — it's very popular in Brazil)
- **revistas** (heh-*vee*-stahz; magazines)
- **massas** (*mah*-sahz; pasta)
- **temperos** (tehm-*peh*-dooz; herbs and spices)
- **creme dental** (*kdeh*-mee dehn-*tah*-ooh; toothpaste)
- **escova dental** (eh-*skoh*-vah dehn-*tah*-ooh; toothbrush)
- **sabonete** (sah-boh-*neh*-chee; soap)
- **xampu** (shahm-*poo;* shampoo)
- **fralda** (*fdah*-ooh-dah; diapers)
- **aparelho de barbear** (ah-pah-*dehl*-yoh jee bah-bee-*ah;* shaving razor)

Check out www.paodeacucar.com.br to learn the names of more supermarket items in Portuguese.

Shopping at the outdoor market

Now check out the **feirinha** (fay-*deen*-yah; outdoor market). Here are some typical **verduras** (veh-*dooh*-dahz; leafy veggies) and **legumes** (leh-*goo*-meez; veggies that grow underground) you can find:

- **batatas** (bah-*tah*-tahz; potatoes)
- **couve** (*koh*-ooh-vee; bitter greens — necessary to make **feijoada** [fay-zhoh-*ah*-dah; bean/pig parts stew]; the **couve** is fried with garlic and eaten on the side)
- **coentro** (koh-*ehn*-tdoh; cilantro)
- **salsinha** (sah-ooh-*seen*-yah; parsley)
- **feijão** (fay-*zhow;* beans)
- **pepino** (peh-*pee*-noh; cucumber)
- **brócolis** (*bdoh*-koh-leez; broccoli)
- **espinafre** (ehs-pee-*nah*-fdee; spinach)
- **repolho** (heh-*pol*-yoh; cabbage)
- **berinjela** (beh-dang-*zheh*-lah; eggplant)
- **abóbora** (ah-*boh*-boh-dah; pumpkin)

Here are some types of fish and meat:

- **peixe** (*pay*-shee; fish)
- **frutos do mar** (*fdoo*-tohz doo *mah;* shellfish. *Literally:* fruits of the sea)
- **atum** (ah-*toong;* tuna)
- **salmão** (sah-ooh-*mah*-ooh; salmon)
- **camarões** (kah-mah-*doh*-eez; shrimp)
- **caranguejo** (kahn-*gdeh*-zhoh; crab)
- **lula** (*loo*-lah; squid)
- **polvo** (*pohl*-voh; octopus)
- **cortes de carne** (*koh*-cheez jee *kah*-nee; cuts of meat)
- **carne moída** (*kah*-nee moh-*ee*-dah; ground beef)
- **aves** (*ah*-veez; poultry)
- **frango sem osso** (*fdahn*-goh sang *oh*-soo; boneless chicken)
- **frango com osso** (*fdahn*-goh koh-oong *oh*-soo; boned chicken)

Sometimes the butcher asks whether you want your meat **de primeira ou de segunda** (jee pdee-*may*-dah ooh jee seh-*goon*-dah; Grade A or Grade B).

Talkin' the Talk

Luiza (loo-*ee*-zah) and **Susana** (soo-*zah*-nah) are friends. They decide to visit the local **feirinha** (fay-*deen*-yah; outdoor market) together to do their shopping. All around them, vendors are shouting out what they're selling.

Luiza: **O que você precisa?**
ooh *keh* voh-*seh* pdeh-*see*-zah?
What do you need?

Susana: **Preciso uns tomates e muita fruta.**
pdeh-*see*-zoo oonz toh-*mah*-cheez ee moh-ee-tah
fdoo-tah.
I need some tomatoes and a lot of fruit.

Luiza: **Vamos lá.**
vah-mooz *lah.*
Let's get to it.

Susana: (To the vendor) **Os tomates, quanto custam?**
oohz toh-*mah*-cheez, *kwahn*-toh *koos*-tah-oong?
How much for the tomatoes?

Vendor: **Dois e cinquenta o quilo.**
doh-eez ee sing-*kwehn*-tah ooh *kee*-loh.
Two-fifty a kilo.

Susana: **Dois quilos, por favor.**
doh-eez *kee*-looz, poh fah-*voh.*
Two kilos, please.

Vendor: **Quer eles numa sacola ou duas?**
keh eh-leez nooh-mah sah-*koh*-lah ooh *doo*-ahz?
Do you want them in one or two bags?

Susana: **Duas, por favor. Vai ser pesado demais senão.**
doo-ahz, poh fah-*voh. vah*-ee *seh* peh-*zah*-doh jee-
mah-eez seh-*nah*-ooh.
Two, please. It'll be too heavy otherwise.

Luiza: **Agora as frutas . . .**
ah-*goh*-dah ahz *fdoo*-tahz . . .
Now the fruit . . .

Another seller: **Pêssego docinho, quatro por um real! Pêssego bem docinho!**
peh-seh-goh doh-*seen*-yoh, *kwah*-tdoh poh oong hay-*ow*! *peh*-seh-goh bang doh-*seen*-yoh!
Sweet peaches, four for one real! Really sweet peaches!

Words to Know

precisa	pdeh-<u>see</u>-zah	you need
preciso	pdeh-<u>see</u>-zoo	I need
Vamos lá.	vah-mooz <u>lah</u>	Let's get to it.
Quanto custam?	<u>kwahn</u>-toh <u>koos</u>-tah-ooh	How much do they cost?
quilo	<u>kee</u>-loh	kilogram
sacola	sah-<u>koh</u>-lah	bag
pesado	peh-<u>zah</u>-doh	heavy
demais	jee-<u>mah</u>-eez	too much
senão	see-<u>nah</u>-ooh	otherwise
pêssego	<u>peh</u>-seh-goh	peach
docinho	doh-<u>sing</u>-yoh	sweet
bem	bang	very (Literally: well)

Fun & Games

A Brazilian friend has come to visit. You take him to a fancy restaurant. Of course, the menu is in English, and he asks you to translate for him. Write the Portuguese words following each menu item:

1. chicken:

2. beer:

3. water:

4. onions:

5. rice:

6. beans:

7. meat:

After translating the menu, your friend chooses what he wants to eat. Translate his choices to English. Flip to Appendix C for the answers:

8. **um chope:**

9. **uma água com gas:**

10. **um sanduíche de carne assada e queijo, sem tomate:**

Chapter 6
Shopping Made Easy

. . . .

In This Chapter

▶ Telling the vendor what you want

▶ Trying things on

▶ Buying and wearing clothes

▶ Expressing opinions: Good, better, best

▶ Checking out Brazilian handicrafts

▶ Bargaining

. . . .

*I*n Brazil or anywhere, you can shop for **prazer** (pdah-*zeh;* pleasure) or out of **necessidade** (neh-seh-see-*dah*-jee; necessity).

And you can **fazer compras** (fah-*zeh kohm*-pdahz; shop) in three main ways in most countries: Go to **um shopping** (*oong shoh*-ping; a shopping mall), to **uma loja na rua** (*ooh*-mah *loh*-zhah nah *hoo*-ah; a store on the street), or to **uma feira** (*ooh*-mah *fay*-dah; an outdoor market).

Brazil's **shoppings** are very similar to the malls you've been to wherever you're from. They have **lojas de roupas** (*loh*-zhahz jee *hoh*-pahz; clothing stores), **livrarias** (lee-vdah-*dee*-ahz; bookstores), **farmácias** (fah-*mah*-see-ahz; drugstores), **lojas de CDs** (*loh*-zhahz jee seh-*dehz;* CD stores), **salas de cinema** (*sah*-lahz jee see-*neh*-mah; movie theaters), and a **praça de alimentação** (*pdah*-sah jee ah-lee-mehn-tah-*sah*-ooh; food court). One thing's a little different, though — in Brazil, **shoppings** are more associated with the middle and upper classes. Those people with less **dinheiro** (jeen-*yay*-doh; money) prefer **lojas na rua** or **feiras** — where **coisas** (*koy*-zahz; things) are **mais barato** (*mah*-eez bah-*dah*-toh; cheaper).

At Brazil's **feiras,** you can **comprar** (kohm-*pdah;* buy) locally made **artesanato** (ah-teh-zah-*nah*-toh; handicrafts), which vary according to region. You can find **bonecos feitos à mão** (boo-*neh*-kooz *fay*-tohz ah *mah*-ooh; handmade dolls) in Pernambuco state, lots of items made from **pedra** (*peh*-drah; stone) in Minas Gerais state, and excellent **redes** (*heh*-jeez; hammocks) in practically any Brazilian **povoado** (poh-voh-*ah*-doh; town).

Saying What You're Looking For

In this section, I start with shopping for **roupas** (*hoh*-pahz; clothes). When you enter a Brazilian **loja** (*loh*-zhah; store), expect to hear **Posso ajudar?** (*poh*-soo ah-zhoo-*dah;* Can I help you?). After **Posso ajudar?** the **atendente** (ah-tehn-*dehn*-chee; salesperson) may say

- ✔ **Está procurando algo em especifico?** (eh-*stah* pdoh-koo-*dahn*-doh *ah*-ooh-goh ang eh-speh-*see*-fee-koh; Are you looking for something in particular?)

- ✔ **Já conhece a nossa loja?** (zhah kohn-*yeh*-see ah *noh*-sah *loh*-zhah; Are you already familiar with our store?)

- ✔ **Temos uma promoção.** (*teh*-mohz *ooh*-mah pdoh-moh-*sah*-ooh; We're having a sale.)

And here are some things you can say to the **atendente:**

- ✔ **Estou só olhando.** (eh-*stoh* soh ohl-*yahn*-doh; I'm just looking.)

- ✔ **Estou procurando . . .** (eh-*stoh* pdoh-koo-*dahn*-doh; I'm looking for . . .)

- ✔ **Tem . . . ?** (tang; Do you have . . . ?)

Now for the goods. **O que precisa?** (ooh *keh* pdeh-*see*-zah; What do you need?). You can tell the salesperson **Estou procurando** (eh-*stoh* pdoh-koo-*dahn*-doh; I'm looking for) one of the following items:

- ✔ **calças** (*cow*-sahz; pants)
- ✔ **calça jeans** (*cow*-sah *jeenz;* jeans)
- ✔ **blusa** (*bloo*-zah; woman's shirt)
- ✔ **camisa** (kah-*mee*-zah; man's shirt)
- ✔ **camiseta** (kah-mee-*zeh*-tah; T-shirt)
- ✔ **saia** (*sah*-ee-ah; skirt)
- ✔ **vestido** (ves-*chee*-doo; dress)
- ✔ **cinto** (*seen*-too; belt)
- ✔ **meias** (*may*-ahz; socks)

- **sapatos** (sah-*pah*-tohz; shoes)
- **relógio** (heh-*law*-zhee-oh; watch)
- **chapéu** (shah-*peh*-ooh; hat)

You may want to specify a **tamanho** (tah-*mahn*-yoh; size). In Brazil, **os taman-hos** are either European (when they're in numbers — both clothing and shoes) or generic, from small to extra large:

- **pequeno (P)** (peh-*keh*-noh; small)
- **médio (M)** (*meh*-jee-oh; medium)
- **grande (G)** (*gdahn*-jee; large)
- **extra grande (GG)** (*ehz*-tdah *gdahn*-jee; extra large)
- **tamanho único** (tah-*mahn*-yoh *oo*-nee-koh; one size fits all)

Brazilian sizes are smaller than in North America and in some European countries. The same size shirt will be a medium, say, in the U.S. but a large in Brazil. I'm a semi-tall gal who tries to exercise regularly, and sadly, I most often had to buy the **grande** or **extra grande** sizes. So don't feel like you suddenly go on a **regime** (heh-*zhee*-mee; diet) after you hit the Brazilian stores!

You can also request a certain **cor** (koh; color):

- **branco** (*bdahn*-koh; white)
- **preto** (*pdeh*-toh; black)
- **vermelho** (veh-*meh*-ooh-yoh; red)
- **verde** (*veh*-jee; green)
- **amarelo** (ah-mah-*deh*-loo; yellow)
- **azul** (ah-*zoo;* blue)
- **marrom** (mah-*hoh*-oong; brown)
- **rosa** (*hoh*-zah; pink)
- **lilás** (lee-*lahz;* purple)
- **laranja** (lah-*dahn*-zhah; orange)

If you want a different shade, just add **claro** (*klah*-doh; light) or **escuro** (eh-*skoo*-doh; dark) after the name of the color:

- **azul claro** (ah-*zoo klah*-doh; light blue)
- **vermelho escuro** (veh-*meh*-ooh-yoh eh-*skoo*-doh; dark red)

Brazilian **atendentes** can actually be annoying on your first encounter. They never seem to leave you alone. But remember that they're just being friendly and trying to be helpful.

So what happens if your **cinto** or **camiseta** is too small? Or too big? You could say:

> ✓ **É pequeno demais.** (eh peh-*keh*-noh jee-*my*-eez; It's too small.)
>
> ✓ **É grande demais.** (eh *gdahn*-jee jee-*my*-eez; It's too big.)

Putting the word **demais** after a word is like adding the word *too* or *really* in front of an English word. Check it out:

> ✓ **É caro demais.** (eh *kah*-doh jee-*my*-eez; It's too expensive.)
>
> ✓ **É bonito demais.** (*eh* boo-*nee*-too jee-*my*-eez; It's really beautiful.)

É bom demais! (eh *boh-oong* jee-*my*-eez; It's fantastic!) is a common phrase that literally means *It's too good!*

Trying and Trying On: The Verb Experimentar

The verb for trying on clothes is **experimentar** (eh-*speh*-dee-mehn-*tah*). It's easy to remember — what does the word look like? **Tá certo** (tah *seh*-toh; That's right) — *experiment*. In Portuguese, you "experiment" with new **cores** (*koh*-deez; colors) and new looks by **experimentando** (eh-speh-dee-mehn-*tahn*-doh; trying on) **artigos de roupa** (ah-*chee*-gohz jee *hoh*-pah; articles of clothing).

Experimentar has a second meaning that's useful to know as well — *to try,* as in to try **uma comida nova** (*ooh*-mah koh-*mee*-dah *noh*-vah; a new food). Here are some common phrases using **experimentar**:

> ✓ **Quer experimentar . . . ?** (*keh* eh-*speh*-dee-mehn-*tah*; Would you like to try/try on . . . ?)
>
> ✓ **Posso experimentar . . . ?** (*poh*-soo eh-*speh*-dee-mehn-*tah*; Can I try/ try on . . . ?)
>
> ✓ **Tem que experimentar . . .** (*tang* kee eh-*speh*-dee-mehn-*tah*; You've got to try/try on . . .)
>
> ✓ **Experimenta!** (eh-*speh*-dee-*mehn*-tah; Try it!)

And here's how to conjugate **experimentar:**

Conjugation	Pronunciation
eu experimento	*eh*-ooh eh-*speh*-dee-*mehn*-too
você experimenta	voh-*seh* eh-*speh*-dee-*mehn*-tah
ele/ela experimenta	*eh*-lee/*eh*-lah eh-*speh*-dee-*mehn*-tah
nós experimentamos	*nohz* eh-*speh*-dee-mehn-*tah*-mohz
eles/elas experimentam	*eh*-leez/*eh*-lahz eh-*speh*-dee-mehn-*tah*-ooh

Here are some uses for **experimentar:**

- ✔ **Posso experimentar essa blusa?** (*pah*-soo eh-*speh*-dee-mehn-*tah* eh-sah *bloo*-zah; Can I try on this [women's] shirt?)

- ✔ **Gostaria de experimentá-lo?** (goh-stah-*dee*-ah jee eh-*speh*-dee-mehn-*tah*-loh; Would you like to try it on?)

- ✔ **É só experimentar.** (eh *soh* eh-*speh*-dee-mehn-*tah;* It won't hurt just to try it/try it on. *Literally:* It's just trying.)

After you leave the **provedor** (pdoh-veh-*doh;* dressing room), you need to decide whether you want to **comprar ou não** (kohm-*pdah* ooh *nah*-ooh; buy or not).

Wearing and Taking: The Verb Levar

Quer levar? (keh leh-*vah;* Would you like to get it?). After you've tried on the item, the salesperson may use the verb **levar** (leh-*vah;* to get/to take, as in to buy something) to ask whether you want to buy it.

Here are some common phrases using **levar:**

- ✔ **Vou levar.** (voh leh-*vah;* I'll take it.)
- ✔ **Não, não vou levar, mas obrigado/a.** (*nah*-ooh, *nah*-ooh voh leh-*vah,* mah-eez oh-bdee-*gah*-doh/ah; No, I'm not going to get it, but thanks.)

Levar is another **-ar** verb (the easiest kind of verb to conjugate — see Chapter 2). Here's what **levar** looks like conjugated:

Conjugation	Pronunciation
eu levo	*eh*-ooh *leh*-voh
você leva	voh-*seh leh*-vah

ele/ela leva	*eh*-lee/*eh*-lah *leh*-vah
nós levamos	*nohz* leh-*vah*-mohz
eles/elas levam	*eh*-leez/*eh*-lahz leh-*vah*-ooh

Levar also means *to take* in the general sense, just like in English. Here are some usage examples of **levar** — both as in *to buy* and *to take:*

- ✔ **Vai levar tudo, ou só as calças?** (*vah*-ee leh-*vah too*-doh, ooh *soh* ahz *kah*-ooh-sahz; Are you going to get everything, or just the pants?)

- ✔ **Levou aqueles sapatos?** (leh-*voh* ah-*keh*-leez sah-*pah*-dohz; Did you get those shoes?)

- ✔ **Leva uma toalha.** (*leh*-vah *ooh*-mah toe-*ahl*-yah; Take a towel.)

- ✔ **Leva ela para a escola, por favor.** (*leh*-vah *eh*-lah *pah*-dah ah eh-*skoh*-lah, poh fah-*voh*; Take her to school, please.)

Talkin' the Talk

 Dudu (doo-*doo*; the nickname for Eduardo — like saying Eddy for Edward) is looking for a new pair of **óculos de sol** (*oh*-koo-lohz jee *soh*-ooh; sunglasses). He stops at a stall on the street on Copacabana beach and picks up a pair.

Dudu:	**Gosto muito desses.** *goh*-stoo moh-*ee*-too *deh*-seez. I really like these.
Salesperson:	**São bonitos. Quer experimentar?** *sah*-ooh boo-*nee*-tooz. *keh* eh-*speh*-dee-mehn-*tah*? They're nice. Do you want to try them on?
Dudu:	**Posso?** *poh*-soo? Can I?
Salesperson:	**Claro.** *klah*-doo. Of course.
Dudu:	**Obrigado. São muito legais.** oh-bdee-*gah*-doh. *sah*-ooh moh-ee-toh lay-*gah*-eez. Thanks. They're really cool.

Salesperson:	**Estou vendendo muito desse modelo.** eh-stoh vehn-*dehn*-doh moh-ee-too *deh*-see moh-*deh*-loo. I'm selling a lot of that type.
Dudu:	**Quanto custam?** *kwahn*-toh *koo*-stah-ooh? How much do they cost?
Salesperson:	**São oito reais. Quer levar?** *sah*-ooh *oh*-ee-toh hay-*eyes*. *keh* leh-*vah*? Eight reais. You wanna take them?
Dudu:	**Vou sim. Tem troco para dez reais?** voh *sing*. tang *tdoh*-koo pah-dah *dehz* hay-*eyes*? Yeah. Do you have change for ten reais?

Words to Know

gosto	goh-stoo	I like
desses	deh-seez	of these
estou	eh-stoh	I am
vendendo	vehn-dehn-doh	selling
troco	tdoh-koo	change (for money)

The verb **gostar** (goh-*stah;* to like) is always followed by **de** (jee), which means *of.* But in English, saying something like "I like of these" just sounds weird, so when you translate **Gostar desses** (I like these) to English, just leave out the *of.*

Making Comparisons and Expressing Opinions

If you're shopping with an **amigo** (ah-*mee*-goh; friend), you may want to share your **opinião** (oh-pee-nee-*ah*-ooh; opinion) about the things in the **loja** (*loh*-zhah; shop).

If you think something is so-so, you can say:

- ✔ **Gosto.** (*gohs*-doo; I like it.)
- ✔ **Está bem.** (eh-*stah bang;* It's okay.)
- ✔ **Nao está mau.** (*nah*-ooh eh-*stah mah*-ooh; It's not bad.)

Then if you see something that you like even more, you can say:

- ✔ **Esse é melhor.** (*ehs*-ee *eh* meh-ooh-*yoh;* This one's better.)
- ✔ **Esse eu gosto mais.** (*eh*-see ee-ooh *goh*-stoo *mah*-eez; I like this one more.)
- ✔ **É bem bonito esse.** (eh *bang* boo-*nee*-too *eh*-see; This one's really nice.)

When you see the best one, you can say:

- ✔ **Esse é o melhor.** (*eh*-see *eh* ooh meh-ooh-*yoh;* This one's the best.)
- ✔ **É perfeito esse.** (eh peh-*fay*-toh *eh*-see; This one's perfect.)

Better is **melhor** (meh-ooh-*yoh*), and *the best* is **o melhor** (ooh meh-ooh-*yoh*).

Now comes the fun part. In Portuguese, adding the ending **-íssimo/a** or **-érrimo/a** to the end of some adjectives exaggerates whatever's being said.

Brazilians love to **exagerar** (eh-zah-zheh-*dah;* exaggerate). Something that's nice but not really **caro** (*kah*-doh; expensive) is suddenly **chiquérrimo** (shee-*keh*-hee-moh; really glamorous). This exaggeration is all about Brazilians' great quality of making the most of **a vida** (ah *vee*-dah; life). Whatever's in front of them is **o melhor.**

Here are some common expressions you can use while shopping:

- ✔ **Chiquérrimo!** (shee-*keh*-hee-moh! Really glamorous/expensive-looking! — from the word **chique**)
- ✔ **Caríssimo!** (kah-*dee*-see-moh; So expensive! — from the word **caro**)

And here are exaggerating expressions you can use in other situations:

- ✔ **Divertidíssimo!** (jee-*veh*-chee-*jee*-see-moh; Incredibly fun! — from **divertido**)
- ✔ **Gostosérrimo!** (goh-stoh-*zeh*-hee-moh; Delicious! — from **gostoso**)

Talkin' the Talk

 Luis (loo-*eez*) and **Fabiano** (fah-bee-*ah*-noh) are checking out a used CD store.

Luis:	**Legal. Eles têm muito do Caetano.** lay-*gow*. eh-leez *tang* moh-ee-too doo kah-eh-*tah*-noh. Cool. They have a lot of Caetano (Caetano Veloso, one of Brazil's most famous singers).
Fabiano:	**Tem *Outras Palavras*?** tang *oh*-tdahz pah-*lahv*-dahz? Do they have (the album) *In Other Words?*
Luis:	**Têm. Mas acho melhor os CDs mais recentes dele.** *tang*. mah-eez *ah*-shoo mel-*yoh* oohz say-*dayz* mah-eez heh-*sehn*-cheez *deh*-lee. They have it. But I think his more recent albums are better.
Fabiano:	**Bom, o melhor de todos é *Fina Estampa*.** *boh*-oong, ooh mel-*yoh* jee *too*-dooz eh *fee*-nah eh-*stahm*-pah. Well, the best of all is *Fina Estampa*.
Luis:	**Cada qual têm a sua opinião.** kah-dah *kwah*-ooh *tang* ah *soo*-ah oh-pee-nee-*ah*-ooh. Each to his own opinion.
Fabiano:	**Nossa, esse da Metállica é baratíssimo! Dois reais!** *noh*-sah, *eh*-see dah meh-*tah*-lee-kah eh bah-dah-*chee*-see-moh! *doh*-eez hay-*eyes*! Wow, this Metallica one is so cheap! Two reais!
Luis:	**Que bom.** kee *boh*-oong. Great.
Fabiano:	**Esqueça o Caetano!** eh-*skeh*-sah ooh kah-ee-*tah*-noh! Forget Caetano!

Words to Know

legal	lay-*gow*	cool
Caetano Veloso	kah-eh-*tah*-noh veh-*loh*-zoo	Caetano Veloso
acho melhor	*ah*-shoo mel-*yoh*	I prefer
recentes	heh-*sehn*-cheez	recent
melhor de todos	meh-ooh-*yoh* jee *too*-dooz	the best of all
baratíssimo	bah-dah-*chee*-see-moh	really cheap
esqueça	eh-*skeh*-sah	(you) forget

Exploring the Treasure Trove of Typical Brazilian Items

Brazilian **mercados** (meh-*kah*-dooz; markets) have plenty of **artesanato** (*ah*-teh-zah-*nah*-toh; handicrafts) that you may want to **levar** (leh-*vah;* take) with you. The type of **objetos** (ohb-*zheh*-tohz; objects) depends on the **região** (hey-zhee-*ow;* region) of Brazil.

The two most popular **lembranças** (lehm-*bdahn*-sahz; souvenirs) from Brazil are **redes** (*heh*-jeez; hammocks) and **berimbaus** (beh-deem-*bah*-ooz; musical instruments from the state of Bahia).

Berimbaus look like the bow from a bow and arrow, with a semi-open wooden gourd at the bottom. To play it, you pluck the bow with your finger. The sound isn't particularly charming, and the instrument is only capable of veering a note or two up or down. But the **berimbau** is beautiful, with striped colors on the gourd. And beginners, delight! It's impossible to make a bad sound on the thing.

Also in Bahia are the famous colorful **fitas de Bomfim** (*fee*-tahz jee *boh*-oong-*feeng;* ribbons of Bomfin). These ribbons, which have religious sayings on them, come from a church called Bomfim in the city of Salvador. When you buy a **fita,** the seller ties it around your wrist and tells you to make a wish. The vendor then warns you **nunca** (*noon*-kah; never) to take it off; otherwise, you'll be cursed with **má sorte** (*mah soh*-chee; bad luck). On the upside, if you let it disintegrate naturally, they say the wish you made will come true!

Havaianas (ah-vah-ee-*ah*-nahz; Hawaiians) brand beach flip-flops are also popular tourist items.

Many women enjoy the inexpensive **bijouteria** (bee-*zhoo*-teh-*dee*-ah; jewelery) sold in outdoor markets. You can find handmade **anéis** (ah-*nay*-eez; rings), **brincos** (*bdeeng*-kohz; earrings), and **colares** (koh-*lah*-deez; necklaces).

Check out some other classic Brazilian souvenirs:

- ✔ **uma pintura** (*ooh*-mah peen-*too*-dah; a painting)
- ✔ **um biquini** (oohng bee-*kee*-nee; a bikini)
- ✔ **uma canga com a bandeira brasileira** (*ooh*-mah *kahn*-gah kohng ah bahn-*day*-dah bdah-zee-*lay*-dah; a beach sarong used as a towel or skirt, printed with the Brazilian flag)
- ✔ **música brasileira** (*moo*-zee-kah bdah-zee-*lay*-dah; music)
- ✔ **produtos dos índios** (pdoh-*doo*-tohz dohz *een*-jee-ohz; products made by native Brazilian tribes)
- ✔ **po de guaraná** (*poh* jee gwah-dah-*nah;* guarana berry powder used to make a traditional natural energy drink)
- ✔ **uma camiseta de um time de futebol** (*ooh*-mah kah-mee-*zeh*-tah jee oong *chee*-mee jee foo-chee-*bah*-ooh; a T-shirt with a Brazilian soccer team logo)

Soccer T-shirts with the team's name are sold all over Brazil. On the street, the shirts are probably knockoffs (which makes a great bargain in terms of price). The official team shirts are very expensive — so buy the fake!

In Brazil, you may find tons of knickknacks made from

- ✔ **barro** (*bah*-hoh; clay)
- ✔ **madeira** (mah-*day*-dah; wood)
- ✔ **pedra** (*peh*-drah; stone)
- ✔ **palha** (pahl-*yah;* straw)

✔ **cerámica** (seh-*dah*-mee-kah; ceramics)

✔ **vidro** (*vee*-droh; glass)

✔ **semente** (seh-*mehn*-chee; seeds)

✔ **renda** (*hehn*-dah; crocheted yarn)

If you want to know whether the item is *handmade,* ask whether it's **feito á mão** (*fay*-toh ah *mah*-ooh). If it's food, the term for *homemade* is **caseiro** (kah-*zay*-doh) — which comes from the word **casa** (*kah*-zah; house).

Bargaining in Outdoor Markets

As a rule of thumb, you can bargain in Brazil in outdoor **mercados** (meh-*kah*-dooz; markets) but not inside **lojas** (*loh*-zhahz; stores). At **feirinhas** (fay-*deen*-yahz; outdoor food markets), most locals don't bargain, though you can always try; it won't be considered offensive.

Start out by asking how much something costs, and then offer a lower price (see Chapter 2 for more on numbers or Chapter 11 to find out about money) or tell the vendor you have only a certain amount of money:

✔ **Quanto custa?** (*kwahn*-toh *koo*-stah; How much does it cost?)

✔ **Quanto que é?** (*kwahn*-toh kee *eh;* How much is it?)

✔ **Posso pagar . . . reais?** (*pah*-sooh pah-*gah* . . . hay-*eyez;* Can I pay . . . [number] reais?)

✔ **Só tenho vinte reais.** (*soh tang*-yoh *veen*-chee hay-*eyez;* I have only twenty reais.)

You can then accept the price the vendor gives you or make a final offer.

Of course, if you tell the vendor you only have 15 reais, you probably don't want to pay with a 20-real bill. Separate the bills you'd use to pay for the item before approaching the stall.

When bargaining, keep your cool. If you make the first move, your first offer should be about half what you're prepared to pay; you can then accept the vendor's counteroffer or state your final price. Be firm but polite. Few vendors will give you their best price if they feel you're disrespecting them.

Fun & Games

Go ahead — you can pretend you're a kid, learning to say colors. Match the name of the color of the object with its Portuguese equivalent. Then flip to Appendix C for the answers.

1. tomato   a. **verde**

2. watermelon   b. **azul**

3. the sun   c. **rosa**

4. a plant   d. **amarelo**

5. the sky   e. **vermelho**

Now imagine that you want to surprise each of your amigos with a pair of Havianas sandals, and you're trying to decide what colors to buy. Translate to Portuguese the colors you think your friends like best:

6. Marina (light blue):

7. Sarah (purple):

8. Jim (black):

9. Carlos (dark red):

10. Kim (white):

Chapter 7

At the Beach

Most of Brazil's population is concentrated near its **litoral** (lee-toh-*dah*-oo; coastline), making **praias** (*pdah*-ee-ahz; beaches) a focus of daily life for many locals. It's an opportunity to sip **água de coco** (ah-gwah jee *koh*-koh; coconut water, sipped through a straw, out of a green coconut) or drink a **cerveja** (seh-*veh*-zhah; beer) with old friends and a chance to make new acquaintances, too. At urban beaches, you may see many people **fazendo cooper** (fah-*zen*-doh *koo*-peh; jogging) on the beachfront avenue and some **surfistas** (soo-*fee*-stahs; surfers).

Most visitors to Brazil choose to stay for a few days in **Rio** (*hee*-ooh) and/or **Salvador** (*sah*-oo-vah-*doh*) — Brazil's two most famous beach cities. Almost all of Brazil's beaches are really lovely — except for those in Brazil's south-ernmost region, in **Rio Grande do Sul** (hee-ooh gdahn-jee doo *soo*) state.

There are interesting places to visit in Brazil that aren't on the beach, like the **Amazonas** (ah-mah-*soh*-nahz; Amazon rainforest) or the **Pantanal** (pahn-tah-*nah-ooh;* safari-like landscape with rare animal species, in Brazil's central-west region). But beaches are best for practicing your Portuguese. There are tons of people on them, and you'll be catching them when they're **de bem humor** (jee *bang* ooh-*moh;* in a good mood. *Literally:* of good humor).

In Rio, the two main beaches are named **Copacabana** (koh-pah-kah-*bah*-nah) and **Ipanema** (ee-pah-*neh*-mah). Copacabana draws many types of people, while Ipanema is favored by the **jovens** (*joh*-vangs; young) and **gente de moda** (zhang-chee jee *moh*-dah; hip people). There are wooden post markers on Ipanema beach, each with a different number, to help situate people. **Posto 9** (*poh*-stoh *noh*-vee; post number 9) is considered the trendiest. But whatever part of Ipanema beach you're on, be sure to see the unforgettable **pôr do sol** (*poh* doo *soh*-oo; sunset).

To get away from the tourists and **ladrões** (lah-*droh*-eez; pickpockets), head to **Barra da Tijuca** (*bah*-hah *dah* tee-*zhoo*-kah), which is just a few beaches over from Ipanema. It's now one of the most popular beaches and is known for having the cleanest water. This beach is also in front of the latest high-rise developments in Rio's **Zona Sul** (*soh*-nah *soo;* South Zone — Rio's most touristy area, with nice apartment buildings and hotels).

Beachwear: A Topic Brazilians Take Very Seriously

It's a myth that all Brazilian **mulheres** (moo-*yeh*-deez; women) wear itsy bitsy teeny weeny thong bikini bottoms. In Portuguese, thong bikini bottoms are called **fio dental** (*fee*-oh dang-*tah*-ooh; dental floss) — Brazilians always have a sense of humor. You may see this type of bathing suit on many Rio de Janeiro state beaches but only in isolated cases on other Brazilian beaches. It is true, however, that the average top and bottom parts of a Brazilian **biquini** (bee-*kee*-nee; bikini) is **menor** (meh-*noh;* smaller) than the average American or European bikini.

Most Brazilian men wear **sungas** (*soong*-gahz; Speedo-style swim trunks), and young male surfers tend to wear **bermudas** (beh-*moo*-dahz; longer, American-style swimming shorts — Bermuda shorts).

Everyone should feel **confortável** (kong-foh-*tah*-veh-ooh; comfortable) on a Brazilian beach. Though locals are known for being **vaidosos** (*vah*-ee-*doh*-zooz; vain) and for wearing skimpy bathing suits (both men and women), locals are also incredibly **de mente aberta** (jee *mehn*-chee ah-*beh*-tah; open-minded). You can see people of all shapes and sizes enjoying themselves on many Brazilian beaches.

There's no need for you to buy a Brazilian bathing suit if you end up on a beach there, if you don't want to. Brazilians are plenty used to **turistas** (too-*dees*-tahz; tourists) having a different **estilo** (ehs-*chee*-loh; style) and cultural background than themselves. Brazilians are in fact **curiosos** (koo-dee-*oh*-zooz; curious) about these differences and may be eager to discuss them with you.

Here are some items that you're sure to see people wearing or using on a beach:

- ✔ **chinelos** (shee-*neh*-looz; flip-flops)
- ✔ **toalha** (toe-*ahl*-yah; towel)
- ✔ **canga** (*kang*-gah; sarong to sit down on)
- ✔ **óculos de sol** (oh-koo-lohz jee *soh*-oo; sunglasses)
- ✔ **protetor solar** (pdoh-teh-*toh* soh-*lah;* sunblock)
- ✔ **prancha de surf** (*pdahn*-shah jee *sooh*-ee; surfboard)

Brazilians tend to use **cangas** (*kang*-gahz; sarongs) more often than actual **toalhas** (toe-*ahl*-yahz; towels) on beaches. **Camelôs** (kahm-eh-*lohs;* street vendors) often sell **cangas** directly on the beach. Or you can find one at a nearby **loja** (*loh*-zhah; store).

Brazil's most popular flip-flop company, **Havaianas** (ah-vah-ee-*ah*-nahz), has become hugely successful worldwide. You can see thousands of pairs of the famous brand on Brazilian beaches, as well as on the streets of New York and Paris. The name **Havaianas** means *Hawaiians,* oddly enough. That's because to Brazilians, Hawaii is the most exotic beach location they can think of. Never mind that to Americans, Brazil itself is pretty exotic.

What Else Is On a Brazilian Beach?

On most major beaches, you can rent a **cadeira de praia** (kah-*deh*-dah jee *pdah*-ee-ah; beach chair) and **sombrinha** (sohm-*bdeen*-yah; beach umbrella. *Literally:* little shade) from people selling them right on the beach.

You can also buy snacks, which generally cost **um real** (oong hay-*ah*-ooh; one Brazilian real, or about 35 cents). People walk by, shouting **Um real! Um real!** with the name of the food they're selling. Typical beach snack food includes **queijo coalho** (*kay*-zhoh koh-*ahl*-yoh; barbequed cheese cubes), **um espeto de carne** (oong eh-*speh*-toh jee *kah*-nee; a beef shish kabob), **amendoim** (ah-*mang*-doh-*eeng;* peanuts), and **picolé** (pee-koh-*leh;* fruity popsicles). See Chapter 5 for more about food.

Here are a few more things you can expect to see on a Brazilian beach:

- ✔ **barraca** (bah-*hah*-kah; beach shack that serves food/drinks)
- ✔ **areia** (ah-*day*-ah; sand)

✔ **frescobol** (*fdeh*-skoo-*bah*-ooh; beach ping-pong)

✔ **crianças** (kdee-*ahn*-sahz; kids)

✔ **livros** (*leev*-dohz; books)

✔ **pescadores** (pehs-kah-*doh*-deez; fishermen)

✔ **futebol** (foo-chee-*bah*-ooh; soccer)

✔ **vôlei** (*voh*-lay; volleyball)

Talkin' the Talk

Paula (*pah*-ooh-lah) and **Rogério** (hoh-*zheh*-dee-ooh) are heading to Posto 9 on Ipanema beach, in Rio. Did they remember to bring everything they need from home for a day at the beach?

Paula: **Temos protetor solar?**
           teh-mohz pdoh-teh-*toh* soh-*lah?*
           Do we have sunblock?

Rogério: **Sim, mas só fator oito. Tá bom para ti?**
           sing, *maz soh* fah-*toh* oh-ee-toh. tah *boh-oong* pah-
           dah *chee?*
           Yeah, but it's just SPF 8. Is that okay for you?

Paula: **Sim, tá bom. Eu estou com uma canga, mas acho sufi-
           ciente para os dois.**
           sing, tah *boh-oong. eh*-ooh ehs-*toh* kohng ooh-mah
           kahng-gah, maz *ah*-shoo soo-fee-see-*ehn*-chee pah-
           dah ooze *doh*-eez.
           Yeah, that's fine. I have one sarong (to lay down on),
           but I think it's enough for the two of us.

Rogério: **Ótimo. Agora só quero uma cerveja.**
           oh-chee-moh. ah-*goh*-dah soh keh-doo ooh-mah seh-
           veh-zhah.
           Great. Now I just want a beer.

Paula: **Eu estou de regime. Vou tomar uma água de coco.**
           eh-ooh ehs-*toh* jee heh-*zhee*-mee. voh toh-*mah* oo-
           mah ah-gwah jee *koh*-koo.
           I'm on a diet. I'm going to have coconut water.

Words to Know

Temos . . . ?	<u>teh</u>-mohz	Do we have . . . ?
fator . . .	fah-<u>toh</u>	SPF . . . number
para ti	pah-dah <u>chee</u>	for you
Tá bom.	tah <u>boh-oong</u>	That's fine.
acho	<u>ah</u>-shoo	I think
Ótimo	<u>oh</u>-chee-moh	Great.
agora	ah-<u>goh</u>-dah	now
regime	heh-<u>zhee</u>-mee	diet

Expressing Beauty: "It's So Beautiful! Amazing!"

It's a matter of opinion which regions of Brazil have the best beaches. If you like lush-green mountain landscapes and **turquesa** (too-*keh*-zah; turquoise) water, head for southeast Brazil (Rio or São Paulo states). If it's **água quente** (ah-gwah *kang*-chee; warm water) and lots of **coqueiros** (koh-*kay*-dohz; coconut trees) you're after, head for the northeast — Bahia state and up — or north — Rio Grande do Norte state and west.

Brazilians themselves tend to glorify beaches in the northeast, where the beaches are gorgeous and the local culture is particularly **relaxado** (heh-lah-*shah*-doo; relaxed). Bahia state would probably win the prize as the favorite beach **férias** (*feh*-dee-ahz; vacation) destination of Brazilians themselves.

Other famous places known for their beaches include **Florianópolis** (floh-dee-ah-*noh*-poh-lees), an island off the coast of **Santa Catarina** (*sahn*-tah kah-tah-*dee*-nah) state (in the south), **Ceará** (say-ah-*dah*) state (in the north), and **Fernando de Noronha** (feh-*nahn*-doh jee noh-*dohn*-yah), an island about an hour by **avião** (ah-vee-*ah*-oo; plane) from the northeast.

All beaches have a unique beauty, of course. Check out some phrases you can use to talk about how pretty a beach is:

- ✔ **Que bonita!** (kee boh-*nee*-tah; How pretty!)
- ✔ **É maravilhosa!** (eh mah-dah-vee-lee-*oh*-zah; It's amazing!)
- ✔ **Incrível!** (eeng-*kdee*-veh-ooh; Unbelievable!)
- ✔ **Nossa senhora!** (noh-sah seen-*yoh*-dah; Wow!)
- ✔ **Que legal!** (kee leh-*gah*-ooh; How cool!)
- ✔ **Meu deus!** (meh-oo *deh*-ooz; Oh my God!)
- ✔ **Não acredito!** (*nah*-ooh ah-kdeh-*jee*-toh; I can't believe it!)

Nossa senhora! literally means *Our lady* and would be the English equivalent of saying *Holy Mary, mother of God!* It's very common in Brazil, and people often just say **Nossa!**

Talkin' the Talk

Marta and Fabiana have just reached Ilha Grande, a beautiful island off the coast of Rio de Janeiro state.

Marta:	**Nossa, que bonita!** *noh*-sah, kee boo-*nee*-tah! Wow, how pretty!
Fabiana:	**Incrível!** eeng-kdee-*veh*-ooh! Unbelievable!
Marta:	**É a praia mais bonita que eu já vi.** eh ah *pday*-ee-ah mah-eez boo-*nee*-tah kee eh-ooh zhah *vee*. It's the prettiest beach I've ever seen.
Fabiana:	**Não sei disso, mas acho super legal.** *nah*-ooh say *jee*-soh, maz ah-shoh *soo*-peh lay-*gah*-ooh I don't know about that, but I think it's really cool.
Marta:	**A água é cor de turquesa mesmo.** ah *ah*-gwah eh koh jee too-*keh*-zah *mez*-moh. The water is really turquoise.

Walking Along the Beach

Taking **uma caminhada** (ooh-mah kah-meen-*yah*-dah) along the **beira-mar** (bay-dah-*mah;* seashore) is one of life's simple pleasures. In Brazil, you'll see many people walking along the beach — in order to **se divertir** (see jee-veh-*chee;* enjoy themselves), to **observer as pessoas** (ohb-seh-*vah* ahz peh-*soh*-az; people-watch), and for **exercício** (eh-seh-*see*-see-ooh; exercise).

On **praias urbanas** (*pdah*-ee-ahz ooh-*bahn*-az; urban beaches), people especially like to walk on the **calcadão** (cow-sah-*dah*-ooh; broad beachfront sidewalk). In Rio, the sidewalks have a famous black-and-white pattern that look like **ondas** (*ohn*-dahz; waves).

In Brazil's rain forests and **mata atlântica** (mah-tah aht-*lahn*-chee-kah; jungle regions near the coast, in southeast Brazil) people like to **fazer trilha** (fah-*zeh* *tdeel*-yah; to hike).

Caminhar (kah-meen-*yah*) is an **–ar** verb, and it's easy to use:

Conjugation	*Pronunciation*
eu caminho	eh-ooh kah-*mee*-yoh
você caminha	voh-seh kah-*mee*-yah
ele/ela caminha	eh-lee/eh-lah kah-*mee*-yah
nós caminhamos	nahs kah-mee-*yah*-mohz
eles/elas caminhan	eh-leez/eh-lahz kah-*mee*-yah-ooh

These phrases can help you talk about walking:

- ✔ **Eu adoro caminhar pela praia.** (eh-ooh ah-*doh*-doo kah-mee-*yah* peh-lah *pdah*-ee-ah; I love to walk on the beach.)

- ✔ **Nós caminhamos pela cidade sempre.** (nohz kah-mee-*yah*-mohz peh-lah see-*dah*-jee *same*-pdee; We always walk around the city.)

- ✔ **Ela caminha muito devagar.** (eh-lah kah-*mee*-yah moh-*ee*-toh deh-vah-*gah;* She walks really slowly.)

- ✔ **Ele caminha muito rápido.** (eh-lee kah-*mee*-yah moh-*ee*-toh *hah*-pee-doh; He walks very fast.)

- ✔ **Eles tem que caminhar até o estacionamento.** (eh-leez *tang* kee kah-mee-*yah* ah-*teh* ooh ehs-*tah*-see-ohn-ah-*mehn*-toh; They have to walk to the parking lot.)

Here are some words associated with hiking and walking:

- **trilha** (*tdee*-ooh-yah; trail)
- **fazer trilha** (fah-*zeh* *tdee*-ooh-yah; to hike)
- **correr** (koh-*heh;* to run/jog)
- **rápido** (*hah*-pee-doh; fast)
- **devagar** (deh-vah-*gah;* slow)
- **caminho** (kah-*mee*-yo; road)
- **conversar** (kohn-veh-*sah;* to chat)
- **pensar** (pehn-*sah;* to think)
- **relaxar** (heh-lah-*shah;* to relax)

Talkin' the Talk

Beto runs into a workmate, Márcia, on Itacaré beach, in Bahia state. They decide to go for a walk together.

Beto:	**Vamos fazer uma caminhada na praia?** vah-mohz fah-*zeh* ooh-mah kah-mee-*yah*-dah nah *pdah*-ee-ah? Shall we go for a walk on the beach?
Márcia:	**Tudo bem. Mas vamos rápido. Eu preciso fazer exerciso.** too-doh *bang*. maz vah-mohz *hah*-pee-doh. eh-ooh pdeh-*see*-zoo fah-*zeh* eh-seh-*see*-soo. All right. But let's go fast. I need to do exercise.
Beto:	**Eu também. Ajuda para relaxar.** eh-ooh tahm-*bang*. ah-*zhoo*-dah pah-dah heh-lah-*shah*. Me, too. It helps to relax.
Márcia:	**Conhece a trilha para a próxima praia?** kohn-*yeh*-see ah *tdee*-ooh-yah pah-dah ah *pdoh*-see-mah *pdah*-ee-ah? Do you know the trail to the next beach?
Beto:	**Sim, deixa comigo.** *sing*. *day*-shah koh-*mee*-goo. Yeah, leave it to me.

Words to Know

Deixa comigo.	<u>day</u>-shah koh-<u>mee</u>-goo	Leave it to me.
próximo/a	<u>pdoh</u>-see-moh/ah	next
Tudo bem.	too-doh <u>bang</u>	All right.
Eu também.	<u>eh</u>-oo tahm-<u>bang</u>	Me, too.

Talking about Beach Safety

Beaches are for relaxing. But before settling into your chair and making grooves into the sand, it's always best to ask some basic **perguntas** (peh-*goon*-tahz; questions) that concern your **segurança** (seh-goo-*dahn*-sah; safety).

Petty robbery is probably the biggest concern in Brazil, though the problem is not so widespread that you should **evitar** (eh-vee-*tah;* avoid) certain beaches. Keep all your belongings close to you, and never leave all your stuff **sozinho** (soh-*zee*-yoo; alone) when you go into the water.

The tide from the Atlantic Ocean is strong along all parts of Brazil's coast. There are **salva-vidas** (*sah*-ooh-vah-vee-dahz; lifeguards) on the most touristy beaches, and they wear yellow tank tops with a red cross.

Even Brazil's most famous urban beaches, like Ipanema in Rio, often have strong currents that cause powerful, **gigante** (zhee-*gahn*-chee; gigantic) waves that break right at the beach.

Tubarões (too-bah-*doy*-eez; sharks) are not generally a problem in Brazil. The place with the most reported shark attacks every year is the northeastern city of Recife. The waters just off the main coast — where the famous **Boa Viagem** beach is — have been fished to exhaustion, causing the hungry sharks to be tempted by **nadadores** (nah-dah-*doh*-deez; swimmers).

And don't forget the most common beach safety concern — **o sol** (ooh *soh*-ooh; the sun)! Beaches especially in the north of Brazil are very hot because they're close to the equator.

Check out some useful phrases about beach safety:

- ✔ **Tem ladrão aqui?** (tang lah-*drah*-ooh ah-*kee;* Are there pickpockets around here?)

- ✔ **É perigoso a ressaca aqui?** (eh peh-dee-*goh*-zoo ah heh-*sah*-kah ah-*kee;* Is the undercurrent strong here?)

- ✔ **Tem salva-vida aqui?** (tang *sah*-oo-vah *vee*-dah ah-*kee;* Are there any life-guards here?)

- ✔ **Tem tubarão aqui?** (tang too-bah-*dah*-ooh ah-*kee;* Are there sharks here?)

- ✔ **A praia tem pedras?** (ah *pdah*-ee-ah tang *peh*-drahz; Is the beach rocky?)

And here are some responses you may get:

- ✔ **Sim, é perigoso.** (*sing* eh peh-dee-*goh*-zoo; Yes, it's dangerous.)

- ✔ **Sim, cuidado.** (sing, kwee-*dah*-doh; Yes, be careful/watch out.)

- ✔ **Não se preocupe.** (nah-ooh see pdeh-oh-*koo*-pee; Don't worry.)

- ✔ **Não, é tranquilo.** (nah-ooh eh tdahn-*kwee*-loo; No, it's safe.)

Yell **Socorro!** (soh-*koh*-hoo; Help!) if you're in immediate danger.

On urban beaches, flags stuck in the sand often say **Perigoso** (peh-dee-*goh*-zoo; Dangerous) to alert you that entering the water is unsafe.

Playing Soccer — Brazil's National Pastime

Futebol (foo-chee-*bah*-ooh; soccer) is an activity that you may see more often on Brazil's **nordeste** (noh-*dehs*-chee; northeast) beaches than in beaches in Rio or São Paulo state. The farther south you go, the richer Brazil gets. The richer you are, the more money you have to build soccer fields. And Brazilians value soccer fields a lot.

I don't think I had ever heard of **Pelé** (peh-*leh;* 1960s soccer star), perhaps the world's most famous soccer player of all time, until I moved to South America.

Like most of my fellow Americans, soccer brings back memories of third grade. Many Americans don't exactly dig **futebol.** And in my case, the thought of the **esporte** (eh-*spoh*-chee; sport) conjures a memory of an adrenaline rush to the goal post, only to realize after making the **gol** (*goh*-oo; goal) that it was for the wrong team.

Within a few months in Brazil, though, I suddenly knew the names of several regional soccer **times** (*chee*-meez; teams — from the word teams) and how to associate specific friends with specific teams. People get upset if you peg them as a **torcedor** (toh-seh-*doh;* fan) of the wrong team.

If you catch my drift, soccer is a very important topic in Brazil — probably even more important than **religião** (heh-lee-zhee-*ah*-ooh; religion). The fastest way to make an **amigo** (ah-*mee*-goo; friend) — whether it be a Brazilian man or a woman — is to share the same favorite Brazilian soccer team.

Most of Brazil's famous soccer teams are in Rio or São Paulo. Here's a quick rundown:

- **Flamengo** (flah-*mang*-goh): city of Rio
- **Botafogo** (boh-tah-*foh*-goh): city of Rio
- **São Paulo** (sah-ooh *pah*-oo-loh): city of São Paulo
- **Corinthians** (koh-*deen*-chee-ahnz): city of São Paulo
- **Santos** (*sahn*-tohz): beach city in São Paulo state — claim to fame is being Pelé's first professional team

So what do the millions of Brazilians who don't live in São Paulo or Rio do? They either vote for the best team near them, or, in many cases, they just pick either **Flamengo** or **Corinthians** as their favorite team. These two teams always seem to have it in for each other.

It's also **comum** (koh-*moong;* common) for people to root for the team of their parents' home team, which is usually the place where the rest of their extended family comes from.

Besides soccer, there are a few other sports that Brazilians like as well:

- **basquete** (bahs-*keh*-chee; basketball)
- **tênis** (*teh*-neez; tennis)
- **vôlei** (*voh*-lay; volleyball)
- **surfar** (soo-*fah;* to surf)
- **nadar** (nah-*dah;* to swim)
- **fazer cooper** (fah-*zeh koo*-peh; to jog)

Check out some words that relate to all forms of exercise and recreation. All lead to **boa saúde** (*boh*-ah sah-*ooh*-jee; good health):

- **academia** (ah-kah-deh-*mee*-ah; gym)
- **levantar pesos** (leh-vahn-*tah peh*-zohz; to lift weights)

- **buggy** (*boo*-gee; sand dune buggy — common in northeastern Brazil)

- **jangada** (zhahng-*gah*-dah; tiny sailboat — common in northeastern Brazil)

- **ir de barco** (ee jee *bah*-koh; to take a boat ride)

- **fazer snorkeling** (fah-*zeh snoh*-keh-ooh-leeng; to snorkel)

- **fazer mergulho** (fah-*zeh* meh-*gool*-yoh; to scuba dive)

- **escalada em rocha** (ehs-kah-*lah*-dah ang *hoh*-shah; rock climbing)

- **ir de bicicleta** (eed jee bee-see-*kleh*-tah; to go bicycling)

There are a number of places to do **esportes radicais** (eh-*spoh*-cheez hah-jee-*kah*-eez; extreme sports) in Brazil. You can **voar de asa delta** (voh-*ah* jee ah-zah *deh*-ooh-tah; go hang gliding) in Rio, over Ipanema beach.

Asking People What They Like to Do

As you're on the beach making friends with Brazilians, you'll probably want to figure out what you have in common. An easy thing to ask, especially in a beach environment, is what sports or forms of recreation people enjoy.

It's simple. Just say **Você gosta de . . . ?** (voh-seh *goh*-stah jee; Do you like . . . ?) and then add in the activity, like this:

- **Você gosta de surfar?** (voh-seh *goh*-stah jee soo-*fah;* Do you like to surf?)

- **Você gosta de ir á academia?** (voh-*seh goh*-stah jee ee ah ah-kah-deh-*mee*-ah; Do you like to go to the gym?)

- **Você gosta de correr?** (voh-*seh goh*-stah jee koh-*heh;* Do you like to go running?)

- **Você gosta de jogar futebol?** (voh-*seh goh*-stah jee zhoh-*gah* foo-chee-*bah*-ooh; Do you like to play soccer?)

If someone asks you one of these questions, you can answer **Sim, gosto** (*sing goh*-stoo; Yeah, I like it) or **Não, não gosto** (*nah*-ooh, *nah*-ooh *goh*-stoo; No, I don't like it).

You can use the **você gosta de . . .** formula for a ton of fun activities, like these:

- **Você gosta de viajar?** (voh-seh *goh*-stah jee vee-ah-*zhah;* Do you like to travel?)

- **Você gosta de ir ao cinema?** (voh-*seh goh*-stah jee ee ah-ooh see-*neh*-mah; Do you like to go to the movies?)

✔ **Você gosta de praticar o seu inglês?** (voh-*seh goh*-stah jee pdah-chee-*kah* ooh seh-ooh eeng-*glehz;* Do you like practicing your English?)

✔ **Você gosta de cozinhar?** (voh-*seh goh*-stah jee koh-zeeng-*yah;* Do you like to cook?)

It's always difficult to express your most passionate feelings in another language. But here are a couple of easy tricks: To say you love doing something, use **Eu adoro . . .** (eh-ooh ah-*doh*-doo; I love . . .). If you hate it, say **Eu detesto . . .** (eh-ooh deh-*tehs*-toh; I hate . . .). Can you guess what the root of the Portuguese words are? That's right, to *adore* and to *detest*. People are people, and passions are passions!

Fun & Games

You've just arrived to the fabled island Fernando de Noronha, which lies an hour by plane from Brazil's northeast. It's known locally as **o Havaí brasileiro** (ooh ah-vah-*ee* bdah-zee-*lay*-doh; the Brazilian Hawaii).

You head for the beach, an hour before sunset, to take a dip. On your way, you see strange birds and trees. But on the beach, you see the same things you've already seen on other Brazilian beaches.

Match the Portuguese words with their English translation. Then see Appendix C for the answers.

1. **chinelos**   a. sunglasses
2. **água de coco**   b. sand
3. **toalha**   c. beach chairs
4. **óculos de sol**   d. surfers
5. **cadeiras de praia**   e. bikini
6. **areia**   f. towel
7. **biquini**   g. coconut water
8. **surfistas**   h. sunscreen
9. **protetor solar**   i. safe/calm
10. **tranquilo**   j. flip-flops

Chapter 8

Going Out on the Town

Brazil is probably most famous for its **praias** (*pdah*-ee-ahz; beaches) (check out Chapter 7) and **Carnaval** (kah-nah-*vah*-ooh) (see Chapter 17). But that's not all that Brazilian culture is. The country has fabulous **museus** (moo-*zay*-ooz; museums) and a vibrant arts scene, as well as lots of domestic **filmes** (*fee*-ooh-meez; films).

Brazilians are also good at enjoying themselves. Listening to **música ao vivo** (*moo*-zee-*kah* ah-ooh *vee*-voo; live music) and taking in the atmosphere at a bar — or even jiving to local DJs at a **boate** (boh-*ah*-chee; nightclub) — are great cultural classrooms, too. This chapter tells you what you need to know to explore and appreciate the art and culture of Brazil and to enjoy yourself as much as any Brazilian.

Talking about Going Out

Tem vontade de sair? (tang vohn-*tah*-jee jee sah-*eeh;* Are you in the mood to go out?).

Whether you're itching for **música ao vivo** (*moo*-zee-*kah* ah-ooh *vee*-voo; live music) or something else, you can use the following phrase to ask locals what you can do around town: **O que recomenda para fazer hoje á noite?** (ooh *keh* heh-koh-*mehn*-dah pah-dah fah-*zeh* oh-zhee ah *noh*-ee-chee; What do you recommend doing tonight?)

The locals will probably then ask you **O que você gosta?** (ooh *keh* voh-*seh goh*-stah; What do you like?). You can respond **Gosto de . . .** (*goh*-stoh *jee;* I like . . .)

- ✔ **bares** (*bah*-deez; bars)
- ✔ **boates** (boh-*ah*-cheez; nightclubs)
- ✔ **espectáculos** (eh-spehk-*tah*-koo-lohz; shows)
- ✔ **eventos culturais** (eh-*vehn*-tohz kool-too-*dah*-eez; cultural events)
- ✔ **o cinema** (ooh see-*neh*-mah; cinema)
- ✔ **o teatro** (ooh chee-*ah*-tdoh; theater)
- ✔ **as festas** (ahz *fehs*-tahz; parties)

If you're ever in Rio, try a night out at **Carioca da Gema** (*kah*-dee-*oh*-kah dah *zheh*-mah). It's a small place where you can eat, drink, and listen to **música ao vivo. Carioca** means *someone from Rio,* and **gema** means *egg yolk.* The translation is something like *Rio Native to the Core* — someone who's from Rio and proud of it. Though the place isn't so different from many others in Brazil, it enjoys a special popularity among locals and tourists alike.

If you're new in town and just want to ask how to get to the **centro** (*sehn*-tdoh; downtown), say **Onde fica o centro?** (*ohn*-jee *fee*-kah ooh *sehn*-tdoh; Where's the downtown area?).

Inviting someone and being invited

Of course, the best scenario happens not when you have to ask a local about things around town but when a local **te convida** (chee kohn-*vee*-dah; invites you) to some event. He or she may say

- ✔ **Estou te convidando!** (eh-*stoh* chee kohn-vee-*dahn*-doh; I'm inviting you!)
- ✔ **Vem conosco!** (*vang* koh-*noh*-skoh; Come with us!)
- ✔ **Vem comigo!** (*vang* koh-*mee*-goh; Come with me!)

If you're the one who's doing the inviting, you can say one of the preceding expressions or one of the following:

- ✔ **Quer ir comigo?** (*keh ee* koh-*mee*-goh; Do you want to go with me?)
- ✔ **Quer vir conosco?** (*keh vee* koh-*noh*-skoh; Do you want to come with us?)
- ✔ **Quero te convidar.** (*keh*-doo chee kohn-vee-*dah;* I want to invite you.)

Here are some more-specific examples of common expressions using **convidar** (kohn-vee-*dah;* to invite):

- ✔ **Quero convidar a todos para a minha casa.** (*keh*-doo kohn-vee-*dah* ah *toh*-dooz *pah*-dah ah *meen*-yah *kah*-zah; I want to invite everyone to my house.)

- ✔ **Estão convidando a gente para a praia.** (eh-*stah*-ooh kohn-vee-*dahn*-doh ah *zhang*-chee pah-dah ah *pdah*-ee-ah; They're inviting us to go to the beach.)

Brazilians often say **a gente** (ah *zhang*-chee) rather than **nós** (nohz) to mean *we* or *us*. **A gente** literally means *the people*. Strange but true, and fun to say.

Asking what the place or event is like

After you have an idea about the **evento** (eh-*vehn*-toh; event) or **lugar** (loo-*gah;* place) that a person from the area is recommending, you may want to ask for **mais detalhes** (*mah*-eez deh-*tahl*-yeez; more details).

Here are the what, when, how, where, and why questions:

- ✔ **Como é o lugar?** (koh-moh *eh* ooh loo-*gah;* What's the place like?)

- ✔ **Quando começa?** (*kwahn*-doh koh-*meh*-sah; When does it start?)

- ✔ **Onde fica?** (*ohn*-jee *fee*-kah; Where is it?)

- ✔ **Tem algum motivo?** (*tang* ah-ooh-goong moh-*chee*-voh; Why is it being put on?)

- ✔ **O que é, exatamente?** (ooh *kee eh,* eh-zah-tah-*mehn*-chee; What is it, exactly?)

And check out some additional phrases that can give you even more clues about what to do:

- ✔ **Custa caro?** (*koo*-stah *kah*-doh; Is it expensive?)

- ✔ **Vai ter muitas pessoas?** (*vah*-ee *teh* moh-*ee*-tahz peh-*soh*-ahz; Will there be a lot of people?)

- ✔ **Que tipo de música vai ter?** (kee *chee*-poh jee *moo*-zee-kah vah-ee *teh;* What type of music will there be?)

- ✔ **Que tipo de gente?** (kee *chee*-poh jee *zhang*-chee; What type of people?)

> ✔ **É informal ou formal?** (eh een-foh-*mah*-ooh ooh foh-*mah*-ooh; Is it informal or formal?)
>
> ✔ **Vale a pena ir?** (*vah*-lee ah *peh*-nah *ee;* Is it worth going to?)

Here are some answers you're likely to get about an event:

> ✔ **Não custa caro.** (*nah*-ooh *koo*-stah *kah*-doh; It's not expensive.)
>
> ✔ **Vai ser muito bom.** (*vah*-ee *seh* moh-*ee*-toh *boh*-oong; It's going to be really good.)
>
> ✔ **Vale a pena.** (*vah*-lee ah *peh*-nah; It's worth going to.)
>
> ✔ **Deve ter bastante gente.** (deh-vee *teh* bah-*stahn*-chee *zhang*-chee; There should be a lot of people.)
>
> ✔ **O lugar é pequeno.** (ooh loo-*gah* eh peh-*keh*-noh; The place is small.)
>
> ✔ **É muito jovem.** (*eh* moh-*ee*-toh *zhoh*-vang; It's really young.)
>
> ✔ **É para todas as idades.** (*eh* *pah*-dah *toh*-dahz ahz ee-*dah*-jeez; It's for all ages.)
>
> ✔ **É um bar gay.** (*eh* oong *bah* gay; It's a gay bar.)

You will also hear a "gay" place described as **GLS** (zeh *eh*-lee *eh*-see), or **gay, lésbicas e simpatizantes** (gay, lehz-bee-kahs ee seem-pah-chee-zahn-cheez; gay, lesbian, and those sympathetic). Brazilians say both **"gay"** and **GLS.**

Two other important questions to ask in Brazil about bars or events is whether there's an **entrada** (ehn-*tdah*-dah; cover charge) and whether the place has a **consumição minima** (kohn-soo-mee-*sah*-ooh *mee*-nee-mah; dollar-amount minimum), meaning you'd perhaps have to consume at least $10, say, in drinks or food. Ask **Tem entrada?** (*tang* ehn-*tdah*-dah; Does it have a cover charge?) or **Tem consumação mínima?** (*tang* kohn-soo-mah-*sah*-ooh *mee*-nee-mah; Is there a minimum?).

At most bars in Brazil, you receive a paper card called a **comanda** (koh-*mahn*-dah) when you walk in. Instead of paying for food and drinks when you order them, the bartender or waiter marks your orders on the card (each person gets a card; they aren't for groups). When you're ready to leave, you wait in line by the cashier and pay for everything at once.

Using time references: Time of day and days of the week

When you make social plans, the most important thing to ask may be **quando** (*kwahn*-doh; when) an event will take place. This section tells you how to say what day and time you want to meet. (Check out Chapter 2 to brush up on Portuguese numbers; Chapter 15 gives you months of the year.)

Time

Saying the time of **dia** (*jee*-ah; day) is easy in Portuguese. With a little practice, you can have it memorized in no time. Just say **São as . . .** (the number of hours) **e . . .** (the number of minutes) **horas: São as cinco e quinze horas** (*sah*-ooh ahz *sing*-koh ee *keen*-zee *oh*-dahz; It's 5:15).

Always use **as** (ahz; the) before the number of the hour because it matches **horas** (feminine, plural) — even if the number, like **cinco,** is masculine and singular.

Most of the time, people don't even say the word **horas.** Using the word **horas** is similar to saying *o'clock,* which is optional: **São as sete** (*sah*-ooh ahz *seh*-chee; It's seven) and **São as sete horas** (*sah*-ooh ahz *seh*-chee *oh*-dahz; It's seven o'clock) both mean the same thing. If it's half past the hour, say **e meia** (ee *may*-ah; and a half). Here are some examples:

✔ **São as duas horas.** (*sah*-ooh ahz *doo*-ahz *oh*-dahz; It's two o'clock.)

✔ **São as duas e meia.** (*sah*-ooh ahz *doo*-ahz ee *may*-ah; It's 2:30.)

✔ **São quinze para as três.** (*sah*-ooh *keen*-zee pah-dah ahz *tdehz;* It's 15 to 3:00 [2:45].)

✔ **São as onze e quinze.** (*sah*-ooh ahz *ohn*-zee ee *keen*-zee; It's 11:15.)

✔ **São as oito e dez.** (*sah*-ooh ahz *oh*-ee-toh ee *dez;* It's 8:10.)

In English, people sometimes give the time as *quarter after* or *five till* a certain hour. Brazilians sometimes use similar phrases and constructions. For times 15 minutes after the hour, you have the option of saying **e quinze** (ee *keen*-zee; and 15) or **e quarto** (ee *kwah*-too; and a quarter) when you give the minutes. For times ending in 45, you can say either **quinze para** (*keen*-zee pah-dah; 15 to) before you give the hour or **e quarenta e cinco** (*ee* kwah-*den*-tah ee *sing*-koh; and 45) after you give the hour.

Midnight is **meia-noite** (*may*-ah *noh*-ee-chee), and *noon* is **meio-dia** (*may*-oh *jee*-ah; midday). In these cases — and when you say *it's one o'clock* — use **É** instead of **São,** because the number one and the words *midnight* and *noon* are singular:

✔ **É meia-noite.** (eh *may*-ah *noh*-ee-chee; It's midnight.)

✔ **É meio-dia.** (eh *may*-oh *jee*-ah; It's noon.)

✔ **É a uma.** (eh ah *ooh*-mah; It's one.)

✔ **É a uma e vinte.** (eh ah *ooh*-mah ee *veen*-chee; It's 1:20.)

Brazilians often use military time, especially in formal situations, like checking transportation schedules.

Here are some other words and phrases that indicate time:

- ✔ **hoje à noite** (*oh*-zhee ah *noh*-ee-chee; tonight)
- ✔ **noite** (*noh*-ee-chee; night)
- ✔ **cedo** (*seh*-doo; early)
- ✔ **tarde** (*tah*-jee; late)

If you're meeting up with someone, you may want to ask **A que horas?** (ah kee *oh*-dahz; At what time?) you'll be meeting. If you're responding to the question, you can leave out the **são** and just give the time: **As nove e meia** (*noh*-vee ee *may*-ah; 9:30).

Days of the week

Dias da semana (*jee*-ahz dah seh-*mah*-nah; days of the week) in Portuguese seem bizarre at first. According to legend, the Portuguese were obsessed with **feiras** (*fay*-dahz; outdoor food markets), and they sold different goods on each day of the **semana. Feiras** were so important to the Portuguese that they talked about the weekdays in reference to which **feira** was happening that day. Here are the days of the week:

- ✔ **domingo** (doh-*ming*-goo; Sunday)
- ✔ **segunda-feira** (seh-*goon*-dah-*fay*-dah; Monday)
- ✔ **terça-feira** (*teh*-sah-*fay*-dah; Tuesday)
- ✔ **quarta-feira** (*kwah*-tah-*fay*-dah; Wednesday)
- ✔ **quinta-feira** (*keen*-tah-*fay*-dah; Thursday)
- ✔ **sexta-feira** (*seh*-stah-*fay*-dah; Friday)
- ✔ **sábado** (*sah*-bah-doh; Saturday)

Brazilians also sometimes refer to the weekdays by their name without the word **feira. Segunda** is technically **segunda-feira** (*Literally:* second market — Monday is the second day of the week and a *market* or business day). But people often just say **segunda** or **quarta** or **sexta** — instead of **segunda-feira, quarta-feira,** and **sexta-feira.**

To say *on* a certain day of week, like *on Sunday,* say **no** (noh) or **na** (nah) before the day of the week — **no** if the day is a masculine word, **na** if it's feminine:

- ✔ **no domingo** (noh doh-*meeng*-goh; on Sunday)
- ✔ **na segunda** (nah seh-*goon*-dah; on Monday)
- ✔ **na terça** (nah *teh*-sah; on Tuesday)

✔ **na quarta** (nah *kwah*-tah; on Wednesday)

✔ **na quinta** (nah *keen*-tah; on Thursday)

✔ **na sexta** (nah *seh*-stah; on Friday)

✔ **no sábado** (noh *sah*-bah-doh; on Saturday)

Here are some examples:

✔ **Tem um show na quarta.** (tang oong *shoh* nah *kwah*-tah; There's a show on Wednesday.)

✔ **Na segunda, eu preciso trabalhar.** (nah seh-*goon*-dah eh-ooh pdeh-*see*-zoo tdah-bal-*yah;* On Monday, I need to work.)

✔ **Vamos sair na sexta?** (vah-mooz sah-*eeh* nah *seh*-stah; Should we go out on Friday?)

The following phrases are related to days:

✔ **hoje** (*oh*-zhee; today)

✔ **amanhã** (ah-mahn-*yah;* tomorrow)

✔ **na semana que vem** (nah seh-*mah*-nah kee *vang;* next week)

✔ **no fim de semana** (noh *feeng* jee seh-*mah*-nah; on the weekend)

✔ **no mês que vem** (noh *mehz* kee *vang;* next month)

Brazilians love to use the verb **combinar** (kohm-bee-*nah*), which means *to plan to get together.* It literally means *to combine.* Weird, huh? They say **Vamos combinar para sair logo** (*vah*-mohz kohm-bee-*nah* pah-dah sah-*eeh loh*-goo; Let's plan to get together to go out soon). Or **Já combinou com ela?** (*zhah* kohm-bee-*noh* kohng *eh*-lah; Did you already make plans with her?) **Combinado!** (kohm-bee-*nah*-doh) is a common expression that people use after deciding on a time and place to meet. It means *Agreed!*

Talkin' the Talk

 Valéria (vah-*leh*-dee-ah) is into the arts. She asks her hotel concierge what sorts of events are happening in town that she might like.

Concierge: **Tem um espetáculo de dança moderna na semana que vem.**
tang oong eh-speh-*tah*-koo-loh jee *dahn*-sah moh-*deh*-nah nah seh-*mah*-nah kee *vang.*
There's a modern dance show next week.

Valéria: **Ah é? Vale a pena ir?**
             ah *eh? vah*-lee ah *peh*-nah *ee?*
             Really? Is it worth going to?

Concierge: **Sim, é uma companhia muito boa.**
             sing, eh ooh-mah kohm-pahn-*yee*-ah moh-*ee*-toh
             boh-ah.
             Yes, it's a very good company.

Valéria: **Que dia, e a que horas?**
             kee *jee*-ah, ee ah kee *oh*-dahz?
             What day, and what time?

Concierge: **Na sexta, às oito da noite.**
             nah *seh*-stah, ahz *oh*-ee-toh dah *noh*-ee-chee.
             On Friday, at 8:00 at night.

Valéria: **Quando acaba?**
             kwahn-doh ah-*kah*-bah?
             When does it end?

Concierge: **Às dez horas, mais ou menos.**
             ahz dehz *oh*-dahz, *mah*-eez ooh *meh*-nohz.
             At around 10:00.

Valéria: **Tá. Posso comprar um ingresso antes do show?**
             tah. *poh*-soo kohm-*pdah* oong eeng-*gdeh*-soo
             ahn-cheez doo *shoh?*
             Okay. Can I buy a ticket before the show?

Concierge: **Pode. Mas tenta chegar meia-hora antes.**
             poh-jee. maz *tehn*-tah sheh-*gah may*-ah *oh*-dah *ahn*-
             cheez.
             You can. But try to get there half an hour beforehand.

Words to Know

dança moderna	<u>dahn</u>-sah moh-<u>deh</u>-nah	modern dance
companhia	kohm-pahn-<u>yee</u>-ah	company
Que dia?	kee <u>jee</u>-ah	What day?
Quando acaba?	<u>kwahn</u>-doh ah-<u>kah</u>-bah	When does it end?
mais ou menos	<u>mah</u>-eez ooh <u>meh</u>-nohz	around (Literally: more or less)
Tá.	tah	Okay.
Posso . . . ?	<u>poh</u>-soh	Can I . . . ?
um ingresso	oong eeng-<u>gdeh</u>-soo	a ticket
antes	<u>ahn</u>-cheez	before
show	<u>shoh</u>-ooh	show

Taking in Brazil's Musical Culture

The one thing you shouldn't miss doing in Brazil **de noite** (*jee noh*-ee-chee; at night) is listening to **música ao vivo** (*moo*-zee-kah ah-ooh *vee*-voh; live music). Normally this involves going to a restaurant or bar where there's a **cantante** (kahn-*tahn*-chee; singer). Most often, the **cantante** plays the **violão** (vee-oh-*lah*-ooh; acoustic guitar) while singing, and a **baterista** (bah-teh-*dees*-tah; drummer) and a guy who plays the **baixo** (*bah*-ee-shoh; bass guitar) accompany.

There are about 40 Brazilian top hits that live music singers in Brazil repeat ad infinitum. The **platéia** (plah-*tay*-ah; crowd) always loves them and often sings along. For a long time after I first moved to Brazil, I recognized only a few **canções** (kahn-*soh*-eez; songs). But just before I left, I suddenly realized in a bar one night that I knew all the songs! I could now leave the country in peace, I thought to myself. Okay, the top hits are drummed into your brain over the years (you even hear them in the supermarkets), but it was still a small victory for me.

Using the musical verb: Tocar

Você toca algum instrumento? (voh-*seh toh*-kah ah-ooh-*goong een*-stdoo-*mehn*-toh; Do you play an instrument?). In Brazil, the **violão** (vee-ooh-*lah*-ooh; guitar) is by far the most common instrument played. But Brazilians appreciate all kinds of music, and anything having to do with music is a great conversation starter.

Here's how you conjugate **tocar** (toh-*kah;* to play [an instrument]):

Conjugation	*Pronunciation*
eu toco	*eh*-ooh *toh*-koo
você toca	voh-*seh toh*-kah
ele/ela toca	*eh*-lee/*eh*-lah *toh*-kah
nós tocamos	nohz toh-*kah*-mohz
eles/elas tocam	*eh*-leez/*eh*-lahz *toh*-kah-ooh

Take a glance at some names of instruments in Portuguese:

- ✔ **o violão** (ooh vee-ooh-*lah*-ooh; acoustic guitar)
- ✔ **a guitarra** (ah gee-tah-hah; electric guitar)
- ✔ **a bateria** (ah *bah*-teh-*dee*-ah; drums)
- ✔ **o baixo** (ooh *bah*-ee-shoh; bass guitar)
- ✔ **a flauta** (ah *flah*-ooh-tah; flute)
- ✔ **o piano** (ooh pee-*ah*-noh; piano)
- ✔ **o violino** (ooh vee-oh-*lee*-noh; violin)

And here are some phrases about playing these instruments:

- ✔ **Eu toco o piano.** (*eh*-ooh *toh*-koo ooh pee-*ah*-noh; I play the piano.)
- ✔ **Ela toca a bateria.** (*eh*-lah *toh*-kah ah bah-teh-*dee*-ah; She plays the drums.)
- ✔ **Eles tocam o violão.** (*eh*-leez *toh*-kah-ooh ooh vee-oh-*lah*-ooh; They play the guitar.)

Brazilians use the guitar as the model of the ideal woman's body. English-speakers say *hourglass figure;* Brazilians say **corpo de violão** (*koh*-poo jee vee-ooh-*lah*-ooh; guitar-shaped body).

Now for the Brazilian instruments. Perhaps hundreds of instruments are specific to Brazil and Brazilian music. Music is Brazilians' artistic specialty, after all. Here are some of the most famous ones:

- **a cuica** (ah *kwee*-kah; a stick that's rubbed through what looks like a small drum — it makes a donkey hee-haw or whine, depending on how it's moved)

- **o berimbau** (ooh *beh*-deem-*bah*-ooh; a large bow that's played with a wooden stick — it's used to accompany the Brazilian martial arts form **capoeira** [kay-poh-*ay*-dah])

- **o paxixi** (ooh pah-shee-*shee;* a woven rattle)

- **o cavaquinho** (ooh kah-vah-*keen*-yoh; an instrument similar to a ukulele — it's used in bands that play **forró** music, which originates in the northeast and sounds similar to country)

- **o pandeiro** (ooh pahn-*day*-doh; a tambourine)

- **a sanfona** (ah sahn-*foh*-nah; an accordion — used for **forró** music)

If you want to talk about children (or adults!) *playing,* avoid the verb **tocar,** which is only for playing instruments. Instead, use the verb **brincar** (bdeeng-*kah*): **As crianças gostam de brincar** (ahz kdee-*ahn*-sahz goh-stah-ooh jee bdeeng-*kah;* Children like to play). **Brincar** also means *to kid around:* **Está brincando?** (eh-*stah* bdeeng-*kahn*-doh) is a popular phrase that means *Are you kidding?*

Using the dancing verb: Dançar

Especially if you're **solteiro** (sohl-*tay*-doh; a single person), you'll probably want to learn how to ask someone to **dançar** (dahn-*sah;* dance) and how you'll be asked to **dançar.**

Couple-dancing is very common in Brazil. The most popular form is probably **forró** (foh-*hah*), a fast-paced country-sounding music and accompanying dance form that originates in the northeast. **Samba** (*sahm*-bah), the best-known music and dance from Brazil, is generally not for **casais** (kah-*zah*-eez; couples), at least during festivals. You dance **sozinho** (soh-*zeen*-yoh; alone).

Take a peek at the conjugations for **dançar:**

Conjugation	*Pronunciation*
eu danço	*eh*-ooh *dahn*-soh
você dança	voh-*seh dahn*-sah

ele/ela dança	*eh*-lee/*eh*-lah *dahn*-sah
nós dançamos	*nohz* dahn-*sah*-mohz
eles/elas dançam	*eh*-leez/*eh*-lahz *dahn*-sah-ooh

And here are some common expressions that use **dançar:**

- ✔ **Vamos dançar?** (*vah*-mohz dahn-*sah;* Shall we dance?)

- ✔ **Quer dançar comigo?** (keh dahn-*sah* koh-*mee*-goh; Do you want to dance with me?)

- ✔ **Não sei dançar.** (*nah*-ooh *say* dahn-*sah;* I don't know how to dance.)

Using the singing verb: Cantar

Você gosta de cantar? (voh-*seh goh*-stah jee kahn-*tah;* Do you like to sing?). The verb **cantar** (kahn-tah; to sing) is a great, basic verb to practice. Its ending is **–ar**, so the conjugations are a piece of cake (check out Chapter 2 for more on conjugations):

Pronunciation	*Conjugation*
eu canto	*eh*-ooh *kahn*-toh
você canta	voh-*seh kahn*-tah
ele/ela canta	*eh*-lee/*eh*-lah *kahn*-tah
nós cantamos	nohz kahn-*tah*-mohz
eles/elas cantam	*eh*-leez/*eh*-lahz *kahn*-tah-ooh

Here are some ways you can use **cantar:**

- ✔ **Ela canta super bem.** (eh-lah *kahn*-tah *soo*-peh *bang;* She sings really well.)

- ✔ **Eu não canto muito bem.** (*eh*-ooh *nah*-ooh *kahn*-toh moh-*ee*-toh *bang;* I don't sing very well.)

- ✔ **Você canta? Não sabia.** (voh-*seh kahn*-tah *nah*-ooh sah-*bee*-ah; You sing? I didn't know.)

- ✔ **Nós cantamos no chuveiro.** (nohz kahn-*tah*-mohz noh shoo-*vay*-doh; We sing in the shower.)

Exploring Art Galleries and Museums

Brazil has plenty of **galerias de arte** (gah-leh-*dee*-ahz jee *ah*-chee; art galleries) and **museus** (moo-*zeh*-oohz; museums). The biggest and most famous ones are in some of the country's largest cities: São Paulo, Brasilia, and Rio.

São Paulo has the most of all, and the best-known ones there are the **Museu de Arte de São Paulo,** known as **o MASP** (ooh *mah*-spee), and the **Oca** (*oh*-kah), which is located in the city's main park, **o Parque do Ibirapuera** (ooh *pah*-kee doo ee-*bee*-dah-poo-*eh*-dah). Both have excellent **exibições temporárias** (*eggs*-ee-bee-*soy*-eez temp-oh-*dah*-dee-ahz; temporary exhibitions).

Intriguing smaller museums are in all nooks and crannies in Brazil. I can't even remember the name of this great one I found in the city of **Maceió** (mah-say-*oh*), state of **Alagoas** (ah-lah-*goh*-ahz), at the back of a semi-outdoor **feira** (*fay*-dah; market). It had photos of Brazil's equivalent of Robin Hood, **o Lampião** (ooh lahm-pee-*ah*-ooh). He was a cowboy of sorts who ruled parts of the northeast region in the 1930s. His girlfriend was named **Maria Bonita** (mah-*dee*-ah boo-*nee*-tah; Pretty Maria). The powerful couple was finally killed by their enemies, and the museum shows an old photograph of their heads gruesomely on display, back in the day.

Brazil also has great **centros culturais** (*sehn*-tdohz kool-too-*dah*-eez; cultural centers), which put on their own art exhibitions. Often, they're funded by big Brazilian companies, like banks. **Banco do Brasil** (*bahn*-koh doo bdah-*zee*-ooh; Bank of Brazil) and **Banco Itaú** (*bahn*-koh ee-tah-*ooh;* Itaú Bank) are important patrons of the local arts.

Inside Brazil's galleries and museums, you can find **quadros** (*kwah*-drohz; paintings), **esculturas** (eh-skool-*too*-dahz; sculptures), **fotografias** (foh-toh-gdah-*fee*-ahz; photographs), and **objetos históricos** (ohb-*zheh*-tohz ee-*stoh*-dee-kohz; historic objects) — just like in any place in the world.

Check out some phrases that deal with **a arte** (ah *ah*-chee; art):

- ✔ **Você gosta de arte?** (voh-*seh* goh-stah jee *ah*-chee; Do you like art?)

- ✔ **Tem uma exibicão muito boa no Itaú Cultural.** (*tang ooh*-mah eggs-ee-bee-*sah*-ooh moh-ee-toh *boh*-ah noh ee-tah-*ooh* kool-too-*dah*-ooh; There's a really good exhibition at Itaú Cultural Center.)

- ✔ **Tem uns quadros famosos do Picasso naquele muséu.** (*tang* oonz *kwah*-drohz fah-*moh*-zooz doo pee-*kah*-soh nah-*keh*-lee moo-*zeh*-ooh; There are some famous Picasso paintings in that museum.)

- ✔ **Eu adoro as vernissages.** (*ee*-ooh ah-*doh*-doo ahz veh-nee-*sah*-zhehz; I love art exhibition opening nights.)

Going to the Movies

What type of **filmes** (*fee*-ooh-meez; movies) do you like? Have you ever seen **um filme brasileiro** (oong *fee*-ooh-mee bdah-zee-*lay*-doh; a Brazilian movie)? You may be surprised to find out that the Brazilian **indústria de filmes** (een-*doo*-stee-ah jee *fee*-ooh-meez; film industry) is very large and of high quality. (Check out Chapter 18 for a list of some Brazilian movies you can rent.)

At most **salas de cinema** (*sah*-lahz jee see-*neh*-mah; movie theaters) in Brazil, about half of the **filmes** playing are Brazilian — there are several **filmes novos** (*fee*-ooh-meez *noh*-vooz; new films) that come out every month. In addition to domestic films, you can also see **filmes americanos** (*fee*-ooh-meez ah-meh-dee-*kah*-nohz; American movies) and **filmes europeus** (*fee*-ooh-meez eh-ooh-doh-*peh*-ooz; European flicks).

You may want to ask whether the movie is **legendado** (leh-zhang-*dah*-doo; subtitled) or **dublado** (doo-*blah*-doo; dubbed over). Subtitled films are also sometimes referred to as **versão original** (veh-*sah*-ooh oh-*dee*-zhee-*nah*-ooh; original version).

Here are some handy phrases you can use to talk about **filmes:**

- ✔ **Vamos no cinema?** (*vah*-mohz noh see-*neh*-mah; Do you want to go to the movies?)

- ✔ **Quer assistir um filme?** (*keh* ah-sees-*chee* oong *fee*-ooh-mee; Do you want to see a movie?)

- ✔ **Que tipo de filmes gosta?** (kee *chee*-poh jee *fee*-ooh-meez *goh*-stah; What type of movies do you like?)

- ✔ **Qual filme gostaria de ver?** (*kwah*-ooh *fee*-ooh-mee gohs-tah-*dee*-ah jee *veh;* Which movie would you like to see?)

Talkin' the Talk

Diogo (jee-*oh*-goh) and **Catarina** (kah-tah-*dee*-nah) talk about going to the movies together.

Diogo: **Vamos ao cinema?**
           vah-mohz ah-ooh see-*neh*-mah?
           Should we go to the movies?

Catarina: **Vamos. Qual filme gostaria de assistir?**
           vah-mohz. *kwah*-ooh *fee*-ooh-mee gohs-tah-*dee*-ah
           jee ah-sees-*chee?*
           Let's go. What movie do you want to see?

Diogo: **Estou com vontade de assistir uma comédia.**
eh-*stoh koh*-oong vohn-*tah*-jee jee ah-sees-*chee* ooh-mah koh-*meh*-jah.
I feel like seeing a comedy.

Catarina: **Para mim, qualquer filme que não tem fila tá bom.**
pah-dah *ming*, *kwah*-keh *fee*-ooh-mee kee nah-ooh tang *fee*-lah tah *boh*-oong.
For me, any movie that doesn't have a line is good.

Diogo: **É verdade. Hoje é sábado.**
eh veh-*dah*-jee. *oh*-zhee eh *sah*-bah-doh.
That's right. Today is Saturday.

Catarina: **Bom, vamos para a Sala UOL, para ver?**
boh-oong, *vah*-mohz pah-dah ah *sah*-lah ooh-oh-*eh*-lee, pah-dah *veh?*
Well, should we go to the UOL (name of movie theater), to see?

Diogo: **Tá bom. Você espera na fila, e eu compro a pipoca.**
tah *boh*-oong. voh-*seh* eh-*speh*-dah nah *fee*-lah, ee *eh*-ooh *kohm*-pdoh ah pee-*poh*-kah.
Okay. You wait in the line, and I'll buy the popcorn.

Catarina: **Acha justo isso?**
ah-shah *zhoo*-stoh *ee*-soh?
Do you think that's fair?

Diogo: (With a laugh) **Acho.**
ah-shoo.
Yes, I do (*Literally:* I think).

Words to Know

Estou com vontade . . .	eh-_stoh_ kohng vohn-_tah_-jee	I feel like . . . (what you feel like doing)
assistir	ah-sees-_chee_	to see (a movie, a show, TV)
uma comédia	_ooh_-mah koh-_meh_-jah	a comedy
para mim	_pah_-dah _ming_	for me
qualquer	_kwah_-ooh _keh_	any/whichever
fila	_fee_-lah	line (of people)
verdade	veh-_dah_-jee	true/truth
bom	_boh_-oong	so/well
vamos	_vah_-mohz	let's go/should we go?
ver	veh	to see
espera	eh-_speh_-dah	wait
pipoca	pee-_poh_-kah	popcorn
Acha . . . ?	_ah_-shah	Do you think . . . ?
justo	_zhoo_-stoh	fair
isso	_ee_-soh	this/that

Names of non-Brazilian **filmes,** like American or European ones, are often translated slightly differently into Portuguese — and often with a funny result. My favorite is the movie *O Brother, Where Art Thou?* (2000), which was translated as **E Aí, Irmão, Cadê Você?** (ee ah-_ee_ eeh-_mah_-ooh kah-_deh_ voh-*seh*; Hey, Dude, Where Are You?).

Fun & Games

You have five nights to spend in São Paulo. Order the following activities according to your preferences.

1. **bar**

2. **cinema**

3. **música ao vivo**

4. **exibição de arte moderna**

5. **show de música rock**

Try to guess the English movie titles of these classic films. The following related words may help: **poderoso** (powerful); **chefe** (boss); **vento** (wind); **chuva** (rain); **estrela** (star); **tubarão** (shark). Flip to Appendix C for the answers.

6. *O Poderoso Chefão*

7. *. . . E O Vento Levou*

8. *O Mágico de Oz*

9. *Cantando na Chuva*

10. *Guerra nas Estrelas*

11. *Tubarão*

Chapter 9

Talking on the Phone

*B*razilians are very social people, so talking on the phone comes naturally to them. The **telefone** (teh-leh-*foh*-nee; telephone) itself even holds an important place in Brazilian history. The very first samba tune ever recorded was titled **"Pelo Telefone"** (*peh*-loo teh-leh-*foh*-nee; On the Phone) (Rio, 1917). This chapter gives you the basics of navigating Brazil's telephone system and following Brazilian phone etiquette.

Not only are Brazilians intensely social but they're also very **carinhosos** (kah-deen-*yoh*-zooz; affectionate). When a **chamada** (shah-*mah*-dah; phone call) ends between two female friends, a male and a female friend, or two family members, Brazilians often say **Um beijo** (oong *bay*-zhoh; A kiss) or **Um abraço** (oong ah-*bdah*-soo; A hug).

Using Phones, Phone Cards, and Numbers

If you visit Brazil, you'll probably want to use a **telefone público** (teh-leh-*foh*-nee *poo*-blee-koh; public phone) at some point. All you have to do is **comprar** (kohm-*pdah*; buy) a **cartão telefônico** (kah-*tah*-ooh teh-leh-*foh*-nee-koh; phone card) from any **banca de jornal** (*bahn*-kah jee zhoh-*nah*-ooh; news kiosk) on the **rua** (*hoo*-ah; street). The card may work only in the part of Brazil where you're located, however, because local fixed line telephone **companhias** (kohm-pahn-*yee*-ahz; companies) each sell their own cards.

You can find plenty of **telefones públicos** on Brazilian **ruas.** Locals, always with a sense of humor, call public phones **orelhões** (oh-deh-ooh-*yoh*-eez. *Literally:* big ears) because the phones are housed in a semi-open booth that resembles a three-foot tall **orelha** (oh-*deh*-ooh-yah; ear). In touristy cities, the **orelhões** are designed to look like an object that's native to the region. In the city of Salvador, for example, many **orelhões** look like a **berimbau** (*beh*-deem-*bah*-ooh), a popular local instrument, or a green **coco** (*koh*-koo; coconut).

In Brazil, most phone numbers have a two-digit prefix for the **cidade** (see-*dah*-jee; city) or a **código regional** (*koh*-jee-goo heh-jee-oh-*nah*-ooh; regional code), which often has a zero in front. The phone number of a famous hotel in Rio called Copacabana Palace, for example, looks like this: (021) 2548-7070. Basic phone numbers have either seven or eight digits.

The country is gradually migrating to all eight-digit numbers, due to a fast-growing **população** (poh-poo-lah-*sah*-ooh; population). If a seven-digit number in your travel guide doesn't seem to work, this may be the **razão** (hah-*zah*-ooh; reason). In most cases, they've added a 3 to the front of the number.

The **código internacional** (*koh*-jee-goh een-teh-nah-see-oh-*nah*-ooh; international calling code) for Brazil is 55. The phone number two paragraphs back would be (55-21) 2548-7070 when the caller's outside Brazil.

Brazilians themselves mostly use **telefones celulares** (teh-leh-*foh*-neez sel-loo-*lah*-deez; cell phones). In 2003, the number of cell phone **linhas** (*leen*-yahz; lines/accounts) in the country exceeded the number of land lines for the first time. Because most Brazilians don't have much **dinheiro** (jeen-*yay*-doh; money), they buy a cell phone only to **receber chamadas** (heh-seh-*beh* shah-*mah*-dahz; receive calls) — in Brazil, the caller to a cell phone pays for the whole call.

Here are a few useful phrases Brazilians use when they're dealing with phone digits:

- ✔ **número de telefone** (*noo*-meh-doh jee teh-leh-*foh*-nee; phone number)
- ✔ **está errado** (ehs-*tah* eh-*hah*-doh; it's wrong)
- ✔ **está correto** (ehs-*tah* koh-*heh*-toh; it's right)
- ✔ **fazer uma telefonema** (fah-*zeh* ooh-mah teh-leh-foh-*neh*-mah; to make a phone call)
- ✔ **ligar para alguém** (lee-*gah* pah-dah ah-ooh-*gang*; to call someone)
- ✔ **atender o telefone** (ah-tehn-*deh* ooh teh-leh-*foh*-nee; to answer the phone)

✔ **deixar um recado** (day-*shah* oong heh-*kah*-doh; to leave a voice mail message)

✔ **uma cabina telefônica** (ooh-mah kah-*bee*-nah teh-leh-*foh*-nee-kah; public phone booth) or **orelhão**

Saying Hello and Goodbye

Your phone is ringing. **Não se preocupe** (*nah*-ooh see pdeh-oh-*koo*-pee; Don't sweat it). I'll start with the greeting and goodbye words — they're a cinch. What comes in between is a little harder, **é claro** (eh *klah*-doh; of course), so take the opportunity to show off some words you've mastered. Brazilians are **impressionados** (eem-pdeh-see-ooh-*nah*-dooz; impressed) when foreigners make even the smallest **esforço** (es-*foh*-soo; effort) to understand their cherished **lingua** (*leeng*-gwah; language).

Perhaps the hotel receptionist is the one calling you, telling you there's **alguém** (ah-ooh-*gang;* someone) to see you in the lobby. Or **talvez** (*tah*-ooh-*vehz;* maybe) it's your **agente de viagens** (ah-*zhang*-shee jee vee-*ah*-zhangs; travel agent), ready to book your **vôo** (*voh*-ooh; flight) to the Amazon. Either way, answering the call is **fácil** (*fah*-see-ooh; easy).

Here's what you say:

✔ **Alô?** (ah-*loh;* Hello? — formal)

✔ **Sim?** (sing; Yes?)

✔ **Oi.** (*oy*-ee; Hi. — informal)

Here's what you can say before you hang up the phone:

✔ **Tchau.** (chow; Bye. *Literally:* Ciao, like in Italian)

✔ **Até logo.** (ah-*teh* loh-goo; Bye. *Literally:* Until soon.)

✔ **Até mais.** (ah-*teh* mah-eez; Bye. *Literally:* Until more.)

✔ **Até amanhã.** (ah-*teh* ah-mahn-*yah;* Talk to/See you tomorrow. *Literally:* Until tomorrow.)

Making a Call

Making phone calls in a different language can be kind of intimidating, but **você está com sorte!** (voh-*seh* eh-*stah* kohng *soh*-chee; you're in luck!). You've picked a great learners' language, for a variety of reasons.

First, Brazilians typically talk reasonably **devagar** (deh-vah-*gah;* slowly), and they tend to clearly enunciate their syllables. Brazilians are also very used to talking with **estrangeiros** (ehs-tdahn-*zhay*-dohz; foreigners). Most locals slow their speech down automatically when their conversation partner isn't fluent in Brazilian Portuguese. Best of all, Brazilians typically *love* foreigners and will be **contente** (kohn-*tehn*-chee; happy) to talk to you.

So go native: Relax. **Fique tranquilo** (*fee*-kee tdahn-*kwee*-loh; Don't worry).

Talkin' the Talk

Learn a little phone talk from **Patricia,** who's calling a hotel near Ipanema beach, in Rio. She wants to meet up with her friend **Roberta.**

Operator: **Bom dia. Hotel do Sol Ipanema.**
boh-oong *jee*-ah. oh-*teh*-ooh doo *soh*-ooh eeh-pah-*neh*-mah.
Good morning. Sun Hotel, Ipanema.

Patricia: **Bom dia. Poderia me comunicar com a Roberta Fernandes, quarto número setecentos e oitenta e três, por gentileza?**
boh-oong *jee*-ah. poh-deh-*dee*-ah mee koh-moo-nee-*kah* koh-oong ah hoh-*beh*-tah feh-*nahn*-jeez, *kwah*-toh *noo*-meh-doh seh-chee oh-ee-toh *tdehz*, poh zhehn-chee-*leh*-zah.
Good morning. Could you connect me with Roberta Fernandes, room number 783, please?

Operator: **Quem fala?**
kang *fah*-lah?
Who's calling?

Patricia: **Sou a Patricia Assunção.**
soh ah pah-*tdee*-see-ah ah-soong-*sah*-ooh.
This is Patricia Assunção.

Operator: **Só um momento, por favor.**
soh oong moh-*mehn*-toh, poh-fah-*voh*.
Just a moment, please.

Words to Know

Poderia me comunicar com . . .	poh-deh-*dee*-ah mee koh-moo-nee-*kah* koh-oong	Could you connect me with . . .
por gentileza	poh zhehn-chee-*lay*-zah	please (formal)
Quem fala?	kang *fah*-lah	Who's calling?
Sou . . .	soh-ooh	It's . . . (name)
Só um momento.	soh oong moh-*mehn*-toh	Just a moment.

The calling verb: Ligar

In this section, you get to know the verb **ligar** (lee-*gah;* to call). It's a great **–ar** verb you can use to practice verb conjugation. You may recall from Chapter 2 that **–ar** verbs are a piece of cake.

Ligar is almost always packaged with **para** — as in **ligar para** (lee-*gah* pah-dah; to call) someone or someplace. To use this expression, use **ligar para** plus the name of the person or place.

First, here are the conjugations of **ligar**:

Conjugation	Pronunciation
eu ligo	eh-ooh *lee*-goh
você liga	voh-*seh lee*-gah
ele/ela liga	*eh*-lee/*eh*-lah *lee*-gah
nós ligamos	*nohz* lee-*gah*-mohz
eles/elas ligam	*eh*-leez/*eh*-lahz *lee*-gah-ooh

And here are some example sentences that use **ligar:**

- ✔ **Ligo para os Estados Unidos todos os dias.** (*lee*-goh pah-dah ooz eh-*stah*-dooz ooh-*nee*-dohz *toh*-dooz ooz *jee*-ahz; I call the U.S. every day.)

- ✔ **Ela liga para o namorado dela cinco vezes por dia.** (*eh*-lah *lee*-gah pah-dah ooh nah-moh-*dah*-doh *deh*-lah *seen*-koh *veh*-zeez poh *jee*-ah; She calls her boyfriend five times a day.)

- ✔ **Você liga para a sua mãe muito?** (voh-*seh* *lee*-gah *pah*-dah ah *soo*-ah *mah*-ee moh-*ee*-toh; Do you call your mom often?)

The expression **ligar para** (to call) someone has a slang meaning. It can also mean *to have a crush on* someone or *to pay attention to* someone or something. **Ele liga muito para ela** (*eh*-lee *lee*-gah moh-*ee*-toh pah-dah *eh*-lah) means *He has a crush on her.* **Eu não ligo para o futebol** (*eh*-ooh *nah*-ooh *lee*-goh pah-dah ooh foo-chee-*bah*-ooh) translates to *I don't follow soccer.*

The verb **ligar** also means *to plug in* something: **Liga o computador, por favor.** (*lee*-gah ooh kohm-*poo*-tah-*doh*, poh-fah-*voh;* Plug in the computer, please.)

There's even a Brazilian Internet service provider called **Ligo** (www.ligo.com.br).

Desligar means *to unplug* or *to turn off* something: **Desliga a tevê!** (deh-*slee*-gah ah teh-*veh;* Turn off the TV!)

Se liga (see *lee*-gah) is another popular slang expression that uses the verb **ligar.** It means *Get with it* or *Wake up to the facts.* Someone obsessed with celebrity gossip can say *You don't know about that [insert name of new hot nightclub]? **Se liga!*** The expression literally means *Plug yourself in.*

Dealing with verbal mush

The first phone **conversa** (kohn-*veh*-sah; conversation) in any new language is tough. You can't see the person's face as she's talking, or see her body language. You feel **nervoso** (neh-*voh*-zoo; nervous) that you're taking up her valuable time. The connection may be bad. Her **palavras** (pah-*lahv*-dahz; words) come out sounding like mush.

The Brazilian **sotaque** (soh-*tah*-kee; accent) is particularly strange-sounding in the beginning. Though natives tend to speak slowly, the abundance of nasal vowels throws off even people with a good knowledge of Portuguese words and grammar. All the talking through the **nariz** (nah-*deez;* nose) causes people to sometimes mistake Brazilian Portuguese for **o russo** (ooh *hoo*-soh; Russian)!

On top of all the weird vowels, you also experience the difficulty encountered by anyone listening to a new language: Where do the words **começam** (koh-*meh*-sah-ooh; begin), and where do they **acabam** (ah-*kah*-bah-ooh; end)? At first, words sound like they're all strung together, with no breaks. And on the phone, it's especially tough.

Be easy on yourself for the first few days you're in Brazil (if you're one of the lucky ones with plans to visit). Turn on the **televisão** (teh-leh-vee-*zah*-ooh; TV) while you're getting ready to go out, and pay attention to people speaking around you. Soak up the sounds of the language. Pay attention to body language, which often provides useful clues as to the content of what the person's saying.

Slowly, you can begin to recognize repeated **sons** (*soh*-oongz; sounds) and repeated words. With a little effort on the listening end, you may be surprised by how many words you recognize with ease after just **uma semana** (*ooh*-mah seh-*mah*-nah; one week). Then talking on the phone won't be so hard.

Se não entende (see nah-ooh ehn-*tehn*-jee; If you don't understand) what the person calling you is saying, you can try asking whether he or she speaks English. Say **Fala inglês?** (*fah*-lah eeng-*glehz;* Do you speak English?)

I remember hearing the word **teatro** (chee-*aht*-doh; theater) for the first time. I had seen it on paper **muitas vezes** (moo-*ee*-tahz *veh*-zeez; many times), and it seemed like one of the easier words to **aprender** (ah-pdehn-*deh;* learn) — it's not so different from the English equivalent. Yet my friend repeated the word probably four times, and I still didn't get it! She then translated to English, and I felt a little **avergonhada** (ah-veh-gohn-*yah*-dah; embarrassed). But it was worth it — I was able to recognize the word the very next time I heard it.

Talkin' the Talk

Flavia tries to call her co-worker **Carlos** about a work project. The phone line is bad, and the conversation turns to mush.

Flavia:	**Olá, está o Carlos?**
	oh-*lah*, ehs-*tah* ooh *kah*-lohz?
	Hello, is Carlos there?
Voice on other side:	**Krnha estrn galades.**
	(Unintelligible.)

Flavia:	**Poderia falar um pouco mais devagar, por favor?** poh-deh-*dee*-ah fah-*lah* oong *poh*-koh *mah*-eez deh-vah-*gah*, poh-fah-*voh*? Could you speak a little more slowly, please?
Voice on other side:	**Sod snod manjekof.** (Unintelligible.)
Flavia:	**Não estou te escutando. Está ruim a linha.** *nah*-ooh ehs-*toh* chee ehs-koo-*tahn*-doh. ehs-*tah* hoo-*eeng* ah *leen*-yah. I can't hear you. The connection is bad.
Voice on other side:	**No momento, não se encontra.** noh moh-*mehn*-toh, *nah*-ooh see ehn-*kohn*-tdah. He's not here right now.
Flavia:	**Ligo mais tarde, obrigada.** lee-goh mah-eez *tah*-jee, oh-bdee-*gah*-dah. I'll call later, thanks.

Words to Know

não se encontra	nah-ooh see ehn-kohn-tdah	he/she isn't here (formal)
não está	nah-ooh eh-stah	he/she isn't here (informal)
a linha	ah leen-yah	the phone line
devagar	deh-vah-gah	slowly
mais tarde	mah-eez tah-jee	later
no momento	noh moh-mehn-toh	right now (formal)

If you want to say *right now* and you're not talking on the phone, you can say **agora mesmo** (ah-*goh*-dah *mehs*-moh. *Literally:* right now). **No momento** is frequently used on the phone with strangers because it sounds more formal.

Spelling it out

When making hotel, plane, or restaurant **reservas** (heh-*zeh*-vahz; reservations), you may need to spell out your name over the phone. Or you may need to **pedir** (peh-*jee;* ask) someone to spell his name for you.

Spelling in Brazilian Portuguese is pretty **fácil** (*fah*-see-ooh; easy), and the vast majority of Brazilians have common Portuguese **nomes** (*noh*-meez; names). Be prepared: Some of the names you hear may surprise you. There are **bastantes** (bah-*stahn*-cheez; quite a few) Brazilian men with interesting names like *Givanildo* or *Washington,* alongside the more classic Portuguese names like *João* or *Roberto.*

Brazil is also home to many foreign immigrants, like the Japanese in São Paulo, who have non-Portuguese names. Don't let **a pronúncia** (ah pdoh-*noon*-see-ah; the pronunciation) throw you off. Ask someone to spell out the name.

Talking in the past tense

Not everything happens in the **aqui** (ah-*kee*; here) and **agora** (ah-*goh*-dah; now). Sometimes you want to say that you've *already called* the hotel or to ask your friend whether your mom *called you yesterday.* This is stuff that happened in the **passado** (pah-*sah*-doh; past), so you need to change the verb conjugation.

For **ar** verbs, the past tense conjugations go like this. Take off the **ar** from the verb, and add on these endings:

Subject pronoun	Past tense verb ending
eu	-ei
você	-ou
ele/ela	-ou
nós	-amos (same as in present tense)
eles/elas	-aram

Here are the conjugations for the past tense of **ligar**:

Conjugation	Pronunciation
eu liguei	eh-ooh *lee*-gay
você ligou	voh-*seh* lee-*goh*
ele/ela ligou	*eh*-lee/*eh*-lah lee-*goh*
nós ligamos	*nohz* lee-*gah*-mohz
eles/elas ligaram	*eh*-leez/*eh*-lahz lee-*gah*-dah-ooh

Don't worry that the **eu** (I) form uses the stem **ligu-** while the others use the simple **lig-** stem. This means the verb **ligar** is *irregular* for the **eu** form. But spoken out loud, you can't hear the *u*. So don't sweat it.

Check out some examples of **ligar** in the past tense:

✔ **Ligaram para você ontem.** (lee-*gah*-dah-ooh pah-dah voh-*seh ohn*-tang; They called you yesterday.)

✔ **Já liguei para ele.** (zhah lee-*gay* pah-dah *eh*-lee; I already called him.)

✔ **Você não me ligou.** (voh-*seh nah*-ooh mee lee-*goh;* You didn't call me.)

Now here's a bunch of examples of **-ar** verbs that you may have learned elsewhere in this book. See how these verbs look in the past tense:

✔ **escutar** (eh-skoo-*tah;* to listen)

Ela escutou um som estranho. (eh-lah eh-skoo-*toh* oong *sohng* eh-*stdahn*-yoh; She heard a strange sound.)

✔ **falar** (fah-*lah;* to talk/to tell)

Ele me falou que hoje vai ter festa. (*eh*-lee mee fah-*loh* kee *oh*-zhee vah-ee teh *feh*-stah; He told me that there will be a party today.)

✔ **deixar** (day-*shah;* to leave)

Deixou recado? (day-*shoh* heh-*kah*-doh; Did you leave a message?)

✔ **fechar** (feh-*shah;* to close)

Fecharam a porta. (feh-*shah*-dah-ooh ah *poh*-tah; They closed the door.)

✔ **encontrar** (ehn-kohn-*tdah;* to find/to meet)

Finalmente encontrei a rua certa. (fee-nah-ooh-*mehn*-chee ehn-kohnt-*day* ah *hoo*-ah *seh*-tah; I finally found the right street.)

✔ **achar** (ah-*shah;* to think/believe)

Achamos que ele estava doente. (ah-*shah*-mohz kee *eh*-lee eh-*stah*-vah doh-*ehn*-chee; We thought he was sick.)

And check out Table 9-1 for some common time references that signal the past tense:

Table 9-1	Past Tense Time References	
Term	*Pronunciation*	*Meaning*
ontem	*ohn*-tang	yesterday
na semana passada	nah seh-*mah*-mah pah-*sah*-dah	last week
hoje de manhã	*oh*-zhee jee mahn-*yah*	this morning
ontem à noite	*ohn*-tang ah *noh*-ee-chee	last night
faz alguns dias	fah-eez ah-ooh *goonz* jee-ahz	a few days ago
faz vinte minutos	fah-eez *veen*-chee mee-*noo*-tohz	twenty minutes ago
faz muito tempo	*fah*-eez moh-*ee*-toh *tehm*-poh	a long time ago
no ano passado	noh *ah*-noh pah-*sah*-doh	last year

Next, take a look at an important irregular verb in the past tense: **ir** (ee; to go). Talking about where you've been and what you've done is simple.

Here are the conjugations for the past tense of **ir:**

Conjugation	*Pronunciation*
eu fui	*eh*-ooh *fwee*
você foi	voh-*seh foh*-ee
ele/ela foi	*eh*-lee/*eh*-lah *foh*-ee
nós fomos	*nohz foh*-mooz
eles/elas foram	*eh*-leez/*eh*-lahz *foh*-dah-ooh

And here are some examples of usage of **ir** in the past tense:

- **Eu fui para o Brasil em abril.** (*eh*-ooh *fwee* pah-dah ooh bdah-*zee*-ooh ang ah-*bdee*-ooh; I went to Brazil in April.)

- **Nós fomos para praia no domingo.** (nohz *foh*-mooz pah-dah *pdah*-ee-ah noh doh-*ming*-goh; We went to the beach on Sunday.)

- **Para onde ela foi?** (pah-dah *ohn*-jee eh-lah *foh*-ee; Where did she go?)

- **Eles foram para jantar num restaurante.** (eh-leez *foh*-dah-ooh pah-dah zhahn-*tah* noong heh-stah-ooh-*dahn*-chee; They went to have dinner at a restaurant.)

Talkin' the Talk

Eliana and **Leila** are office co-workers. They just got back from separate vacations in **Bahia** (bah-*ee*-ah) state. Notice the past-tense uses of the verbs **gostar** (goh-*stah;* to like) and **ir** (ee; to go).

Eliana:	**Gostou da Bahia?** goh-*stoh* dah bah-*ee*-ah? Did you like Bahia?
Leila:	**Sim, gostei muito.** *sing*, goh-*stay* moh-ee-too. Yeah, I liked it a lot.
Eliana:	**A onde foi?** ah *ohn*-jee *foh*-ee? Where did you go?
Leila:	**Nós fomos para Itacaré e Trancoso, além de Salvador.** nohz *foh*-mooz pah-dah ee-tah-kah-*deh* ee tdahn-*koh*-zoo, ah-*lang* jee sah-ooh-vah-*doh.* We went to Itacaré and Trancoso, besides Salvador.
Eliana:	**Eu nunca fui para o sul da Bahia.** *eh*-ooh *noon*-kah *fwee pah*-dah ooh *soo* dah bah-*ee*-ah. I've never been to the south of Bahia.
Leila:	**Nunca foi? Vale a pena.** noon-kah *foh*-ee? *vah*-lee ah *peh*-nah. You've never been? It's well worth it.
Eliana:	**No ano passado fui para os Lençóis Maranhenses. Que delicia!** noo *ah*-noh pah-*sah*-doo *fwee pah*-dah oohz lehn-*soy*-eez mah-dah-oong-*yang*-seez. kee deh-*lee*-see-ah! Last year I went to Lençóis Maranhenses (a sand dune area with pools of water, in Maranhão state). What a treat!

Words to Know

Gostou . . . ?	goh-<u>stoh</u>	Did you like . . . ?
gostei	goh-<u>stay</u>	I liked
a onde	ah <u>ohn</u>-jee	to where
além de	ah-<u>lang</u> jee	in addition to/besides
nunca	<u>noon</u>-kah	never
sul	soo	south
Vale a pena.	<u>vah</u>-lee ah <u>peh</u>-nah	It's well worth it.
Que delicia!	<u>kee</u> deh-<u>lee</u>-see-ah	What a treat!

The connector words

Now that your speech is getting sophisticated — with the past tense of verbs — I'll talk about the little connector words that make the rest of the sentence fit together. You'll be set to say native-sounding sentences in no time.

You may recognize some of the words in the Table 9-2, because some appear many times in this book. These connector words are small but very important.

Table 9-2	Connector Words (Conjunctions and Prepositions)	
Term	*Pronunciation*	*Meaning*
e	ee	and
além de	ah-*lang* jee	in addition to
mas	*mah*-eez	but
para	*pah*-dah	to/in order to

Term	Pronunciation	Meaning
se	see	if
mesmo se	*mehz*-moh see	even if
embora	ehm-*boh*-dah	although
que	kee	that
só que	soh *kee*	except that
desde	*dehz*-jee	since
porque	poh-*keh*	because
até	ah-*teh*	until
com	koh-oong	with
por	poh	through/by
de	jee	of
sobre	*soh*-bdee	about/on top of

Here are a few phrases that use connectors:

- ✔ **Romeo e Julieta** (*hoh*-mee-oh ee zhoo-lee-*eh*-tah; Romeo and Juliet)
- ✔ **café com leite** (kah-*feh* koh-oong *lay*-chee; coffee with milk)
- ✔ **desde a primeira vez que eu te vi** (*dehz*-jee ah pdee-*may*-dah *vehz* kee *eh*-ooh chee *vee;* ever since I first saw you)
- ✔ **é para você** (eh *pah*-dah voh-*seh;* it's for you)

Do you know what **Rio de Janeiro** (*hee*-ooh jee zhah-*nay*-doo) means? The literal translation is *River of January.* The Portuguese discovered the area on January 1, 1552, and mistook Rio's Guanabara Bay for the mouth of a river.

Fun & Games

• •

Imagine you just got back from a fabulous trip to **Ilha do Mel** (*eel*-yah doo *meh-ooh*; Island of Honey), just off the coast of **Paraná** (pah-dah-*nah*) state.

Tell a Brazilian about your adventures by filling in the blanks with the past tense of the given verb. Check out Appendix C for the correct conjugations.

1. **Nadar** (to swim)
   Eu _____ **num rio.** (I swam in a river.)

2. **Tomar sol** (to lie out in the sun)
   Eu _____ **muito sol.** (I lay out in the sun a lot. *Literally:* I took a lot of sun.)

3. **Cantar** (to sing)
   Eu _____ **muitas canções.** (I sang a lot of songs).

4. **Falar** (to talk)
   Eu _____ **com os meus amigos.** (I talked with my friends.)

5. **Cozinhar** (to cook)
   Eu _____ **pratos gostosos.** (I cooked delicious meals.)

• •

Chapter 10

At the Office and around the House

As you get to know new friends in Brazil, they may want to talk about where you live and what sort of (*trabalha ou estuda* (tdah-*bahl*-yah ooh ehs-*too*-dah; work or study) you do. You may want to ask your new friends the same questions. This chapter shows you the ropes on how to go about talking business in Brazil and also guides you through proper Brazilian etiquette when discussing work. Also, if you're staying in Brazil for a while and need a place to stay, this chapter can give you some pointers on securing your living space.

Talking about Work

Brazilians generally don't ask you what you do within the first few minutes of meeting you. Some locals consider the question rude. Instead, they ask you where you're from or how long you're staying in Brazil, but they wait until they know you a little better to ask what line of work you're in. Part of the reasoning is that Brazilians don't like talking about money or their lack of it.

Aside from the Brazilian ettiquette about not immediately asking someone about his or her occupation, conversations about work and professions don't vary much from those in other countries. In fact, you may notice that many Portuguese words about work are similar to those in English.

Here are some questions you can ask your new friends when the time's right:

- **Estuda ou trabalha?** (ehs-*too*-dah ooh tdah-*bahl*-yah; Do you study or work?)

- **Qual a sua profissão?** (*kwah*-ooh ah soo-ah pdoh-fee-*sah*-ooh; What's your profession?)

- **Gosta do seu trabalho?** (*goh*-stah doo seh-ooh tdah-*bahl*-yoh; Do you like your work?)

- **Quanto tempo trabalha nisso?** (*kwan*-toh *tang*-poh tdah-*bahl*-yah *nee*-soh; How long have you been in this line of work?)

And here's how you can respond if someone asks you these questions:

- **Eu trabalho na área de . . .** (*eh*-ooh tdah-*bahl*-yoh nah *ah*-dee-ah jee; I work in the field of . . .)

- **Eu estudo . . .** (*eh*-ooh ehs-*too*-doh; I study . . .)

- **Eu sou . . .** (*eh*-ooh soh; I'm . . . [profession])

Check out Table 10-1 for some common occupations:

Table 10-1	Occupations	
Occupation	*Pronunciation*	*Translation*
estudante	es-too-*dahn*-chee	student
professor/a	pdoh-feh-*soh*-dah	teacher
médico	*meh*-jee-koh	doctor
advogado/a	ahj-voh-*gah*-doh	lawyer
journalista	zhoh-nah-*lee*-stah	journalist
banqueiro	bahng-*kay*-doh	banker
cozinheiro	koh-zeen-*yay*-doh	chef
executivo	eh-zeh-koo-*chee*-voh	executive
artista	ah-*chees*-tah	artist
diretor de . . .	jee-deh-*toh* jee	director of . . .
gerente de . . .	jeh-*dang*-chee jee	manager of . . .

Talkin' the Talk

A man and a woman have met in a bar Fortaleza, the capital of Ceará state. They've been talking for a while and want to get to know each other a little better.

Man: **O que você faz?**
oh *keh* voh-seh *faz?*
What do you do?

Woman: **Sou professora de inglês. E você?**
soh pdoh-feh-*soh*-dah jee een-*glehz*. ee voh-*seh*?
I'm an English teacher. And you?

Man: **Legal. Eu sou advogado.**
lay-*gah*-ooh. *eh*-ooh *soh*-ooh ahj-voh-*gah*-doo.
Cool. I'm a lawyer.

Woman: **Interessante. Você gosta do seu trabalho?**
een-teh-deh-*sahn*-chee. voh-say *goh*-stah doo seh-ooh
tdah-*bahl*-yoo?
Interesting. Do you like your job?

Man: **Sim, gosto. E você, durante quanto tempo é professora?**
sing, *goh*-stoo. ee voh-*say*, doo-*rahn*-chee *kwahn*-toh
tang-poh eh pdoh-feh-*soh*-dah?
Yeah, I like it. And what about you, how long have you been a teacher?

Woman: **Faz dez anos que eu sou professora de inglês.**
fah-eez day-eez *ah*-nohz kee *eh*-ooh soh pdoh-feh-
soh-dah jee een-*glehz*.
I've been an English teacher for ten years.

Words to Know

O que você faz?	oh <u>keh</u> voh-seh <u>faz</u>	What do you do?
durante quanto tempo é . . . ?	doo-<u>rahn</u>-chee <u>kwahn</u>-toh <u>tang</u>-poh eh	How long have you been a . . . (profession)?

Faz plus the number of years is a handy way of saying *It's been (number of years) since . . . :*

- ✔ **Faz dez anos que eu não falo inglês.** (fah-eez dehz *ah*-nohz kee *eh*-ooh *nah*-ooh fah-loh eeng-*glehz;* It's been ten years since I've spoken English.)

- ✔ **Faz um ano que eu estou sem trabalho.** (fah-eez oong *ah*-noh kee *eh*-ooh ehs-*toh* sang tdah-*bahl*-yoh; I've been out of work for a year.)

Or you can say **Faz muito tempo que . . .** to mean *It's been a long time since . . .* without mentioning the number of years.

- ✔ **Faz muito tempo que eu fui para o Rio de Janeiro.** (fah-eez moo-*ee*-toh *tang*-poh kee *eh*-ooh *nah*-ooh *voh* pah-dah ooh hee-ooh jee jah-*nay*-doh; It's been a long time since I've been to Rio.)

Fazer: The doing/making verb

Faz (fahz) comes from the verb **fazer** (fah-*zah;* to make or do), which is a good verb to become acquainted with. Brazilians use it a lot, in many ways. In terms of professions, some jobs are best expressed by **eu faço . . .** (pronunciation; *I do . . .*) plus the name of the profession.

Eu faço . . .

- ✔ **marketing** (*mah*-keh-cheeng; marketing)
- ✔ **desenho** (dee-*zehn*-yoh; design)
- ✔ **advertising** (*ahj*-veh-*ty*-zeeng; advertising)
- ✔ **relações públicas** (heh-lah-*soy*-eez *poob*-lee-kahz; public relations)

Here's how you can conjugate **fazer:**

Conjugation	*Pronunciation*
eu faço	*eh*-ooh *fah*-soh
você faz	voh-*say fah-eez*
ele/ela faz	*eh*-lee/*eh*-lah *fah-eez*
nós fazemos	nohz fah-*zeh*-mohz
eles/elas fazem	*eh*-leez/*eh*-lahz *fah*-zehm

Check out some common uses of **fazer:**

- ✔ **Eu faço ioga.** (*eh*-ooh *fah*-soh ee-*oh*-gah; I do yoga.)

- ✔ **Ela faz analise de contas.** (eh-lah *fah-eez* ah-*nah*-lah-zee jee *kohn*-tahz; She does account-analysis.)

- ✔ **Você faz uma pasta muito boa.** (voh-seh *fah-eez* ooh-mah *pahs*-tah moh-*ee*-toh *boh*-ah; That pasta dish you make is really good.)

- ✔ **Eles fazem produção de filmes.** (eh-leez *fah*-zang pdoh-doo-*sah*-ooh jee *fee*-ooh-meez; They do film production.)

And here are some everyday expressions and words that use **fazer:**

- ✔ **fazer fila** (fah-*zeh fee*-lah; to wait in line)

- ✔ **faz sentido** (fah-eez sang-*chee*-doo; it makes sense)

- ✔ **tanto faz** (tahn-toh *fahz;* whatever)

- ✔ **fazenda** (fah-*zang*-dah; ranch, large farm — common in rural Brazil)

- ✔ **fazer uma festa** (fah-*zeh* ooh-mah *fehs*-tah; to throw a party)

- ✔ **. . . mas fazer o quê?** (mah-eez fah-*zeh* ooh *keh;* . . . but what can you do?)

Trabalhar: The working verb

Brazilians know how to enjoy life, but they're also very hard-working people. Whether they're selling coconut water on the beach or wearing a tie in an office, Brazilians always offer great customer service.

Work itself is a sensitive issue for many Brazilians, because it's often hard to come by. When a person does manage to get a job, the job often doesn't pay much and doesn't come with benefits.

Within Brazil, Sao Paulo is known as the "work capital." That's where Brazil's hugely profitable banking industry is, and it's also the most common city that multinationals use as their Brazilian corporate headquarters. Brazilians often say **São Paulo é só trabalho** (sah-oo *pah*-ooh loh eh *soh* tdah-*bahl*-yoh; All they do is work in Sao Paulo).

Here's how to conjugate **trabalhar** (tdah-*bahl*-yah; to work):

Conjugation	*Pronunciation*
eu trabalho	*eh*-ooh tdah-*bahl*-yoh
você trabalha	voh-*seh* tdah-*bahl*-yah
ele/ela trabalha	*eh*-lee/*eh*-lah tdah-*bahl*-yah
nós trabalhamos	nohz tdah-bahl-*yah*-mohz
eles/elas trabalham	*eh*-leez/*eh*-lahz tdah-bahl-*yah*-ooh

Brazilians commonly express someone's occupation by saying **trabalha de** plus the name of the job. Someone may ask **Ele/ela faz o quê?** (eh-lee/eh-lah fah-eez ooh *keh;* What does he/she do?). You can respond:

- ✔ **Ela trabalha de faxineira.** (*eh*-lah tdah-*bahl*-yah jee fah-shee-*nay*-dah; She works as a cleaning lady.)

- ✔ **Ele trabalha de cozinheiro.** (eh-lee tdah-*bahl*-yah jee koh-zing-*yay*-doh; He works as a cook.)

- ✔ **Ele trabalha de condutor de ônibus.** (eh-lee tdah-*bahl*-yah jee kohn-doo-*toh* jee *oh*-nee-boos; He works as a bus driver.)

The Brazilians you meet in a corporate setting tend to speak English, and they speak it well. But even a Brazilian fluent in English can appreciate your attempts to speak some simple Portuguese.

Here are some typical office words:

- ✔ **escritório** (eh-skdee-*toh*-dee-oh; office)

- ✔ **caneta** (kah-*neh*-tah; pen)

- ✔ **computador** (kohm-poo-tah-*doh;* computer)

- ✔ **notebook** (notch-*book*-ee; laptop)

- ✔ **responder** (hehs-pohn-*deh;* to answer)

- ✔ **imprimir** (eemp-dee-*mee;* to print out)

Talkin' the Talk

 Ana and Carlos both work for a Brazilian advertising company. Anna is out sick for the day, but she is taking a few minutes to help her co-worker plan a meeting. They're instant messaging over the Internet:

Ana: **Bom dia Carlos. Vamos planejar a reunião?**
          boh-oong *jee*-ah *kah*-looz. *vah*-mohz plahn-eh-*zhah*
          ah heh-ooh-nee-*ah*-ooh?
          Good morning Carlos. Shall we plan the meeting?

Carlos: **Sim. Vai ser a que hora?**
          sing. vah-ee seh ah kee *oh*-dah?
          Yes. What time will it be?

Ana: **As quatorze horas. Convide todo mundo.**
          ahz kah-*toh*-zee *oh*-dahz. kohn-*vee*-jee toh-doo
          moon-doh.
          At two o'clock. Invite everyone.

Carlos: **OK. Vou enviar um e-mail agora para todos.**
          ah-*kay*-ee. voh en-vee-*ah* oong ee-*may*-oh ah-*goh*-
          dah pah-dah *toh*-dooz.
          Okay. I'm going to send an e-mail now to everyone.

Ana: **Perfeito. Depois me manda um e-mail com todos os
          nomes.**
          peh-*fay*-toh. deh-*poy*-eez mee *mahn*-dah oong ee-
          may-oh koh-oong toh-dohz oohz *noh*-meez.
          Perfect. Afterward, send me an e-mail with all the
          names.

Carlos: **Ta bom. Não se preocupe por isto, e eu espero que
          melhore.**
          tah *boh*-oong. *nah*-ooh see pdeh-oh-*koo*-pee poh
          ees-toh, eh *eh*-ooh eh-*sped*-oh kee mehl-*yoh*-dee.
          Okay. Don't worry, and I hope you get better.

Words to Know

planejar	plahn-eh-<u>zhah</u>	to plan
reunião	hay-oon-ee-<u>ah</u>-ooh	meeting
enviar	ang-vee-<u>ah</u>	to send
e-mail	ee-<u>may</u>-oh	e-mail
conferência	kohn-feh-<u>dehn</u>-see-ah	conference

Finding a Place to Live

Most Brazilians in cities live in apartments, and most Brazilians in rural areas live in houses — like most people in the world. If you're staying in Brazil for a while and need to rent a place to stay, you may find that renting an apartment in Brazil is a little different from renting an apartment in the U.S. Most come unfurnished, with no appliances. On the upside, appliances and furniture are inexpensive in Brazil. And all apartments have a nice patio area, with a tiled floor where you can put a washing machine and hang wet clothes out to dry. Brazilians do not use dryers.

In general, Brazilian stoves are gas-powered. Calling a propane tank vendor to refill your gas whenever you need it is a cinch.

Tap water is okay to use for cooking and cleaning, although most Brazilians keep five-gallon plastic jugs of drinking water in their apartments; these jugs sit on top of a plastic base with a spigot. You can call a company to come refill it every week or so.

Another thing that's different about Brazilian apartments and houses is the addition of one small room. Can you guess why? Because of the huge gap between the rich and poor in Brazil, labor is cheap, and live-in maids are common. Middle- and upper-class houses and apartments in Brazil have a room just for the **empregada doméstica** (em-pdeh-*gah*-dah doh-*mehs*-chee-kah; maid).

Most families with children pay for a woman to live with them. She cleans, cooks, and cares for the children. Other people hire women called **faxineiras** (fah-shee-*neh*-dahs; cleaning women), who come once a week to clean a house or apartment.

If you're serious about renting an apartment in Brazil, you'll probably need a **fiador** (fee-ah-*doh;* guarantor) — someone who owns property in the city — to back you financially. Apartment owners often ask new renters to name a **fiador.**

Here are some questions you may want to ask the landlord of an apartment you're interested in:

- ✔ **Fica em qual andar?** (*fee*-kah ang kwah-ooh ahn-*dah;* What floor is it on?)

- ✔ **Que tipo de vista tem?** (kee chee-poh jee *vee*-stah tang; What type of a view does it have?)

- ✔ **Quanto que é o aluguel?** (*kwahn*-toh kee eh ooh ah-loo-*geh*-ooh; How much is the rent?)

- ✔ **Tem ar condicionado?** (tang *ah* kohn-dee-see-ooh-*nah*-doo; Does it have air conditioning?)

- ✔ **Quantos metros quadrados?** (*kwahn*-toh *meht*-doh kwah-*drah*-doh; How many square meters?)

- ✔ **Vem incluído a luz?** (vang een-kloo-*ee*-doh ah *looz;* Is electricity included?)

- ✔ **Tem estacionamento?** (tang eh-stah-see-oh-nah-*mehn*-toh; Does it have a parking spot?)

Take a look at Table 10-2 for some basic words that you may want to use when you discuss accomodations or start to furnish your apartment:

Table 10-2	Living-Space Words	
Term	*Pronunciation*	*Translation*
casa	*kah*-zah	house
apartamento	ah-*pah*-tah-*mehn*-toh	apartment
porta	*poh*-tah	door
quarto	*kwah*-toh	room
banheiro	bahn-*yay*-doh	bathroom
terraça	teh-*hah*-sah	balcony
jardim	zhah-*jing*	garden
piscina	pee-*see*-nah	pool
cozinha	koh-*zing*-yah	kitchen

(continued)

Table 10-2 *(continued)*

Term	Pronunciation	Translation
luz	looz	light
janela	zhah-*neh*-lah	window
geladeira	zheh-lah-*day*-dah	refrigerator
fogão	foh-*gah*-ooh	stove
mesa	*meh*-zah	table
cadeira	kah-*day*-dah	chair
sofá	soh-*fah*	sofa
cama	*koo*-mah	bed
travesseiro	tdah-veh-*say*-dah	pillow
lençois	lehn-*soh*-eez	sheets
escrivaninha	ehs-kdee-vah-*nee*-ah	desk
televisão	teh-leh-vee-*zah*-ooh	television

There's a famous town in Bahia state called Lençois, which means *sheets*. It lies at the foothills of one of Brazil's most famous national parks, **Chapada Diamantina** (shah-*pah*-dah jee-ah-mahn-*chee*-nah), a beautiful terrain with magestic plateus. So why did they name the town *Sheets?* One theory is that the numerous miners' tents at one point in history made the land look like it was made of sheets.

Brazilians call the first floor of a building the **térreo** (*teh*-hee-oh; ground), and what people call in English the second floor, they call the **primer andar** (pdee-*meh* ahn-*dah;* first floor). A tad confusing at first, but fairly easy to get used to!

Unfortunately, poverty is a big problem in Brazil, making some locals' living situation a little bit different. Some people live in **favelas** (fah-*veh*-lahz; shantytowns). The worst shantytowns are on the fringes of Brazil's biggest cities: São Paulo, Rio, Recife, Salvador, and Brasilia. Not all shantytown-dwellers are miserable, though. In Rio, some of the poorest people in the city have the best views from the windows of their houses! They build houses on the sides of steep cliffs that overlook Rio's magical landscape. Brazil's biggest **favela** is named **Rocinha** (hoh-*seen*-yah), and it's in Rio. About 200,000 people live there, and most have magnificent views of the city and ocean.

E-mailing

If you can't make it to Brazil to practice your Portuguese, try making Brazilian friends over the Internet — whether they be in Brazil or in your country. If they live close to you, you can write a few e-mails to get acquainted and then meet in person.

Many Brazilians use the Internet. And because they're such social people, they spend a lot of time chatting online.

If you already have Brazilian friends, ask them whether they're registered on www.orkut.com. It was invented in the U.S., but the site creators were surprised to find out that Brazilians are using the service more than people from any other country! If you have a Brazilian friend, he or she can hook you into a network of friends.

There are also thousands of chat rooms these days on the Internet. That gives you plenty of opportunities to make new friends.

You can write the following words and abbreviations when you e-mail:

- **Greetings**

Oi	Hi
Olá	Hello
Prezado . . .	Dear . . . — formal

- **Abbreviations to use in the body of the e-mail**

vc	you — informal (short for você)
vcs	you guys — informal (short for vocês)

- **Closings**

Abs,	Hugs, — informal (short for abraços)
Bjs,	Kisses, — informal (short for beijos)
Saudações,	Greetings, — formal
Atensiosamente,	Attentively, — formal

Fun & Games

You've won the lottery in Brazil! You decide to buy a condo in Rio overlooking Copacabana beach (and invest the rest of your millions of reais Brazilian currency — just to be sensible).

Unscramble the words below to discover some of the parts of your new place. Flip to Appendix C for the answers.

1. orapt

2. acestionnemota

3. rajimd

4. zlu

5. csadaa

6. csipani

7. dgleaaeir

8. maca

9. sstarveaeir

Part III
Portuguese on the Go

The 5th Wave   By Rich Tennant

"I'd ask for directions in Portuguese, but I don't know how to form a question in the shape of an apology."

In this part . . .

This part gives you the tools you need to take your Portuguese on the road in Brazil, whether you're going to a local restaurant, checking out a museum, or getting help planning a trip with a Brazilian travel agent. This section is devoted to the traveler in you, the one who checks into hotels, hails a cab, and studies bus schedules. This information is all, of course, to help you get to places where you can have a good time, whether that means going out on a Saturday night in Rio or enjoying yourself during Brazil's famous Carnaval season.

Chapter 11

Money, Money, Money

· ·

In This Chapter
▶ Accessing and exchanging your money
▶ Buying things — using the paying verb: **Pagar**

· ·

O **dinheiro** (ooh jing-*yay*-doh; money) is the universal language. Or is that **o amor** (ooh ah-*moh;* love)?

In this chapter, I talk about the one that's more clear-cut. In Brazil, your best bet for getting **dinheiro** is by bringing your **cartão de banco** (kah-*tah*-ooh jee *bahn*-koh; ATM card) and your **cartão de crédito** (kah-*tah*-ooh jee *kdeh*-jee-toh). Unlike in Europe, **cheques de viagem** (*sheh*-keez jee vee-*ah*-zhang; traveler's checks) are be hard to **trocar** (tdoh-*kah;* change) to the national currency in Brazil. The **taxa de câmbio** (*tah*-shah jee *kahm*-bee-oh; exchange rate) is generally good at ATMs.

Using Brazilian Banks and ATMs

Most small towns in Brazil have a **banco** (*bahn*-koh; bank) and a **caixa automática** (*kah*-ee-shah ah-ooh-toh-*mah*-chee-koh; ATM) that takes **cartões internacionais** (kah-*toh*-eez *een*-teh-nah-see-ooh-*nah*-eez; international cards). Chances are, your ATM/debit card from home will work. If it has on the back a Cirrus or Star logo, and you're in a big city, you're okay. Citibank and HSBC are good to use, because they're international banks. Both have several branches in Rio and São Paulo. You can check with your bank to find out how much the service charge is per international transaction. Credit cards are harder to use to withdraw money from in Brazil, but they're great for paying for food and things in a shop.

Watch out for small beach towns, especially in the north and northeast of the country — many don't have any bank access, which means you have to **retirar** (heh-chee-*dah*; withdraw) as much **dinheiro** as you think you'll need before you get there. Also keep in mind that smaller branches of Brazilian banks often are not connected to the international system. Your best bet is to withdraw at least a few days' worth of money when you're in one of Brazil's larger cities.

The **moeda** (moh-*eh*-dah; currency) in Brazil is called **o real** (ooh hay-*ah*-ooh), and the plural is **reais** (hay-*eyez*). **Um real** (oong hay-*ah*-ooh; one real) is worth around $0.45 (2.22 reais per US$1), and things are generally more than **duas vezes** (*doo*-ahz *veh*-zeez; two times) **mais barato** (*mah*-eez bah-*dah*-toh; cheaper) than they are in the U.S. Rejoice!

Of course, how much of a deal you get all depends on the **taxa de câmbio** (*tah*-shah jee *kahm*-bee-oh; exchange rate), and you can do yourself a favor by checking before planning a visit to Brazil. Between 2001 and 2004, for example, the exchange rate fluctuated between about two **reais** per US$1 and nearly four **reais** per US$1. If you can plan your trip when the exchange rate is good (when you can get two or more **reais** per US$1), you can save a lot of money.

If you want to **trocar** (tdoh-kah; change) U.S. **dolares** (*doh*-lah-deez; dollars) or some other **moeda** to **reais,** you're likely to find the best rates at an **agência de viagens** (ah-*zhang*-see-ah jee vee-*ah*-zhangz; travel agency).

O real was created in 1994, after several years of financial instability in the country. During the 20 preceding years, Brazil changed **moedas** several times. **A piada** (ah pee-*ah*-dah; the joke) was that as soon as you got paid, you had to do your supermarket shopping — inflation was so quick that food was cheaper in the morning than in the afternoon.

Brazilian slang for **dinheiro** is **grana** (gdah-nah). **Estou sem grana** (eh-*stoh* sang gdah-nah) means *I don't have any dough* (Literally: I'm without dough).

Brazilian vendors always seem to be out of **trocado** (tdoh-*kah*-doh; change). Getting large bills changed at the **banco,** right after you get it out of the **caixa automática,** is best. Vendors often ask **Tem trocado?** (*tang* tdoh-*kah*-doh; Do you have change?) when you pay, meaning *Do you have exact change? That would help me out.*

To ask where the nearest **banco** or **caixa automática** is, say:

- ✔ **Por favor, sabe onde tem uma caixa automática?** (poh fah-*voh, sah*-bee ohn-jee *tang* ooh-mah *kah*-ee-shah ah-ooh-toh-*mah*-chee-kah; Excuse me, do you know where there's an ATM?)

- ✔ **Por favor, tem um banco perto daqui?** (poh fah-*voh, tang* oong *bahn*-koh *peh*-toh dah-*kee;* Excuse me, is there a bank near here?)

Following up by asking whether the area the bank or ATM is located is reasonably **seguro** (seh-*goo*-doh; safe) is a good idea. Say **O local é seguro?** (ooh loh-*kah*-ooh eh seh-*goo*-doh; Is the area safe?). If you avoid withdrawing money at night, you should be fine.

Agências de viagens are easy to find in big cities and touristy areas. There, you can ask these questions when you want to change money:

- ✔ **Trocam dólares por reais?** (*tdoh*-kah-ooh *doh*-lah-deez poh hay-*eyez*; Do you change dollars for reais?)

- ✔ **A quanto está o dólar?** (ah *kwahn*-toh eh-*stah* ooh *doh*-lah; What's the rate for the dollar?)

- ✔ **Cobram taxa de comissão?** (*koh*-bdah-ooh *tah*-shah jee koh-mee-*sah*-ooh; Do you charge a commission fee?)

Talkin' the Talk

Silvio just got back from a trip to New York, and he needs to change $100 to reais. He goes to an **agência de viagens.**

Silvio:	**Por favor, trocam dólares por reais aqui?** poh fah-*voh*, tdoh-kah-ooh *doh*-lah-deez poh hay-*eyez* ah-*kee?* Excuse me please, do you change dollars for reais here?
Worker:	**Trocamos.** tdoh-*kah*-mooz. Yes, we do (*Literally:* We change).
Silvio:	**Cobram taxa de comissão?** koh-bdah-ooh *tah*-shah deh *koh*-mee-*sah*-ooh? Do you charge a fee?
Worker:	**Sim, é de dois por cento. Quanto quer trocar?** *sing*, eh jee *doh*-eez poh-*sehn*-toh. *kwahn*-toh keh tdoh-*kah?* Yes, it's 2 percent. How much do you want to change?
Silvio:	**Cem dólares. A quanto está o dólar?** *sang* doh-lah-deez. ah *kwahn*-toh eh-*stah* ooh *doh*-lah? $100. What's the rate for the dollar?

Worker:	**Está a dois reais e trinta e quatro.**
	eh-*stah* ah *doh*-eez hay-*eyes* ee tdeen-tah ee *kwah*-tdoh.
	It's at 2.34 reais.
Silvio:	**Tá bom. Me da em notas de dez?**
	tah *boh*-oong. mee *dah* ang *noh*-tahz jee *dehz?*
	That's fine. Can you give it to me in bills of 10?
Worker:	**Tudo bem. Não tem problema.**
	too-doh *bang. nah*-ooh *tang* pdoh-*bleh*-mah.
	Okay. No problem.

Words to Know

Me da . . . ?	mee <u>dah</u>	Can you give me . . . ?
notas	<u>noh</u>-tahz	bills
Não tem problema.	<u>nah</u>-ooh <u>tang</u> pdoh-<u>bleh</u>-mah	No problem.

Checking Prices and Making Purchases

Talking about **o preço** (ooh *pdeh*-soo; the price) of **as coisas** (ahz *koy*-zahz; things) in Brazil is easy. To find the **preço,** just look on the price tag if you're in a store. If you're at an informal outdoor market, you will probably have to ask for the **preço** from the vendor.

Brazilian **reais** come in several bills, each with its own color and an animal found in Brazil on the back. The bills are as follows: R$1 (green/hummingbird), R$2 (blue/tortoise), R$5 (purple and blue/heron), R$10 (red/parrot), R$20 (yellow/golden-faced lion monkey), R$50 (brown/jaguar) and R$100 (blue/grouper fish).

Coins come in R$1, R$0.50, R$0.25, R$0.10, R$0.05 and R$0.01. The **um centavo** (*oong* sen-*tah*-voh; one-cent) coin is tiny and is hardly worth anything. Stores more often than not let you get away with paying to within R$0.05 of the price, to avoid having the one-cent pieces around. Remember, they're worth 1/100 of one real, or about 1/3 of a U.S. one-cent coin.

Here are the three most common ways of asking how much something is:

> ✔ **Quanto vale?** (*kwahn*-toh *vah*-lee; How much does it cost? *Literally:* How much is it worth?)
>
> ✔ **Quanto custa?** (*kwahn*-toh *koo*-stah; How much does it cost?)
>
> ✔ **Quanto que é?** (*kwahn*-toh kee *eh;* How much is it?)

Here's how the vendor usually answers (for a review of numbers in Portuguese, see Chapter 2):

> ✔ **Vale . . . reais.** (*vah*-lee . . . hay-*eyez;* It costs . . . [number] reais.)
>
> ✔ **Custa . . . reais.** (*koos*-tah . . . hay-*eyez;* It costs . . . [number] reais.)
>
> ✔ **São . . . reais.** (*sah*-ooh . . . hay-*eyez;* It costs . . . [number] reais.)

To say a **preço (price),** use the following formula: the number of **reais,** plus **e** (ee; and), plus the number of **centavos** (sehn-*tah*-vohz; cents):

> ✔ **R$12,30**
>
> **doze reais e trinta centavos** (doh-zee hay-*eyez* ee *tdeen*-tah sehn-*tah*-vohz; twelve reais and thirty cents)
>
> ✔ **R$4,60**
>
> **quatro reais e sessenta centavos** (*kwah*-tdoh hay-*eyez* ee seh-*sehn*-tah sehn-*tah*-vohz; four reais and sixty cents)
>
> ✔ **R$2,85**
>
> **dois reais e oitenta e cinco centavos** (*doh*-eez hay-*eyez* ee oh-ee-*tehn*-tah ee *sing*-koh sehn-*tah*-vohz; two reais and eighty-five cents)

Did you notice that instead of decimal points, Brazilians use commas? The decimal point is reserved in Portuguese for numbers beginning with one thousand — which looks like 1.000. So R$2.440 would be *two thousand, four hundred and forty reais.*

The paying verb: Pagar

Luckily, when you **pagar** (pah-*gah;* pay), visible **números** (*noo*-meh-dohz) are often involved. At a nice shop or supermarket, you'll be seeing the number pop up on a cash register. That makes communication a little easier. If you're having problems communicating at an informal, outdoor market (where you often won't find even a calculator), you can always pull out a pen and paper to clear things up.

Here's how to conjugate **pagar:**

Conjugation	*Pronunciation*
eu pago	*eh*-ooh *pah*-goh
você paga	voh-*seh pah*-gah
ele/ela paga	*eh*-lee/*eh*-lah *pah*-gah
nós pagamos	*nohz* pah-*gah*-mohz
eles/elas pagam	*eh*-leez/*eh*-lahz *pah*-gah-ooh

This is what **pagar** looks like in the past tense (for a review of the past tense, see Chapter 9):

Conjugation	*Pronunciation*
eu paguei	*eh*-ooh pah-*gay*
você pagou	voh-*seh* pah-*goh*
ele/ela pagou	*eh*-lee/*eh*-lah pah-*goh*
nós pagamos	*nohz* pah-*gah*-mohz
eles/elas pagaram	*eh*-leez/*eh*-lahz pah-*gah*-dah-oong

Here are some uses of **pagar:**

> ✔ **Quer pagar agora, ou depois?** (*keh* pah-*gah* ah-*goh*-dah ooh deh-*poh*-eez; Do you want to pay now or later?)
>
> ✔ **Já pagou?** (zhah pah-*goh;* Did you pay already?)
>
> ✔ **Paguei vinte reais.** (pah-*gay veen*-chee hay-*eyez;* I paid 20 reais.)
>
> ✔ **Essa empresa paga bem.** (*eh*-sah ehm-*pdeh*-sah *pah*-gah *bang;* This company pays well.)
>
> ✔ **Vão pagar a conta.** (*vah*-ooh pah-*gah* ah *kohn*-tah; They will pay the bill.)

Paying for items and services

You can relax when you're at a Brazilian cash register. The prices are often a great deal, and the process for paying is similar to what you're already used to. You can pay with cash or a credit card. The one thing to remember is to bring along an I.D. card, because that may be asked of you if you pay by credit card. Receipts are easy to get in an established store, and sometimes vendors at informal markets can give you an official receipt filled out by pen.

For bargaining tips, see Chapter 6.

These phrases may come in handy when you're at the **caixa** (*kah*-ee-shah; register):

- ✔ **Tem desconto para estudantes?** (*tang* dehs-*kohn*-toh *pah*-dah eh-stoo-*dahn*-cheez; Do you have a student discount?)

- ✔ **Tem caneta?** (*tang* kah-*neh*-tah; Do you have a pen?)

- ✔ **Me da um recibo, por favor?** (mee *dah* oong heh-*see*-boh poh fah-*voh;* Can you give me a receipt, please?)

The vendor may ask you:

- ✔ **Tem algum documento? Um passaporte?** (*tang* ah-ooh-*goong* doh-koo-*mehn*-toh oong pah-sah-*poh*-chee; Do you have some I.D.? A passport?)

- ✔ **Qual é a validade do cartão?** (*kwah*-ooh *eh* ah vah-lee-*dah*-jee doo kah-*tah*-ooh; What's the expiration on the card?)

Talkin' the Talk

Leila is a Portuguese woman on vacation in the state of **Minas Gerais**, Brazil. She stepped into a store to buy some beautiful stone sculptures.

Leila:	**Aceita cartão Visa?** ah-*say*-tah kah-*tah*-ooh *vee*-zah? Do you accept Visa?
Cashier:	**Aceitamos.** ah-say-*tah*-mooz. Yes (*Literally:* We accept).
Leila:	(Hands her the credit card) **Aqui tem.** ah-*kee tang.* Here you go.
Cashier:	**Tem algum documento? Um passaporte?** tang ah-ooh-*goong* doh-koo-*mehn*-toh? oong pah-sah-*poh*-chee? Do you have some I.D.? A passport?
Leila:	(Shows her the passport) **Sim, tenho.** sing, *tang*-yoh. Yes (*Literally:* Yes, I have).
Cashier:	**OK, assine aqui, por favor.** oh-*keh*-ee, ah-*see*-nee ah-*kee, poh* fah-*voh.* Okay, sign here, please.

Leila: **Me da um recibo, por favor?**
           mee *dah* oong heh-*see*-boh, poh fah-*voh?*
           Can you give me a receipt, please?

Cashier: **É claro.**
           eh klah-doo.
           Of course.

Have you noticed that Brazilians often repeat a word in a question they're being asked? With **Tem . . . ?** (tang; Do you have . . . ?), the answer is **Tenho** (*tang*-yoh; I have) rather than just **Sim** (sing; Yes). **Você é americano?** (voh-*seh eh* ah-meh-dee-*kah*-noh; Are you American?). If you are, the answer is what? **Sou** (soh; I am), not **Sim.**

Words to Know

Aceita cartão?	ah-<u>say</u>-tah kah-<u>tah</u>-ooh	Do you accept credit cards?
cartão Visa	kah-<u>tah</u>-ooh <u>vee</u>-zah	Visa
cartão American Express	kah-<u>tah</u>-ooh ah-<u>meh</u>-dee-ken eh-<u>spdehz</u>	American Express
cartão Mastercard	kah-<u>tah</u>-ooh mahs-teh-<u>kah</u>-jee	Mastercard
algum documento	ah-ooh-<u>goong</u> doh-koo-<u>mehn</u>-toh	some I.D.
um passaporte	oong pah-sah-<u>poh</u>-chee	a passport
Assine aqui, por favo	ah-<u>see-nee</u> ah-<u>kee.</u> poh fah-<u>voh</u>	Sign here, please.
um recibo	oong heh-<u>see</u>-boh	a receipt

Fun & Games

Imagine your friend Samantha has asked you to pick up a trendy Brazilian top for her while you're on vacation in Rio. She said she'll pay you back when you return. What do you do?

Fill in the blanks with the Portuguese translation of the English words in parentheses to find out. See Appendix C for the answers.

First, you go to a local **1.** _____ (bank) to **2.** _____ (withdraw) **3.** _____ (money). Your **4.** _____ (account) has plenty of **5.** _____ (dough)! You punch into the **6.** _____ (ATM) that you want R$200. The machine dispenses **7.** _____ (two bills) of R$100 reais. Then, you head to the local mall, where you find the perfect top. It's colorful, and a couple of the saleswomen are wearing it. It costs R$50 (what a bargain, you think). You then **8.** _____ (pay) for it and ask for a **9.** _____ (receipt). Finally, you head to the beach, happy that you've gotten a practical matter done with and can relax for the rest of the day.

Chapter 12

Onde Fica? (Where Is It?) Asking for Directions

. . . .

In This Chapter

▶ Asking **onde:** Where things are

▶ Interpreting directions

▶ Mapping out a new city

▶ The verbs that take you up and down: **Subir** and **descer**

▶ Going from here to there

▶ First, second, third: Ordinal numbers

▶ Measuring distances and other stuff: The metric system

. . . .

*G*etting directions is one of the most important topics to get a handle on in any new language. In a **país estrangeiro** (pah-*eez* eh-stahn-*zhay*-doh; foreign country), you're not familiar with the **cidades** (see-*dah*-jeez; cities) or **bairros** (*bah*-ee-hooz; neighborhoods), and you need to know **para onde** (*pah*-dah *ohn*-jee; to where) you should **ir** (eeh; go).

As soon as you get to a place, getting yourself **um mapa** (*oong mah*-pah; a map) may be a good idea. It can show you the **ruas principais** (*hoo*-ahz pdeen-see-*pah*-eez; main streets) and **monumentos da cidade** (*moh*-noo-*mehn*-tohz dah see-*dah*-jee; city monuments), as well as the cardinal directions: **norte** (*noh*-chee; north), **sul** (soo; south), **oeste** (oh-*ehs*-chee; west), and **leste** (*lehs*-chee; east).

Of course, it can be fun to **se perder** (*see* peh-*deh;* get lost) in **um novo lugar** (*oong noh*-voo loo-*gah;* a new place). Just make sure you're not wandering into an area that's **periogoso** (*peh*-dee-*goh*-zoo; dangerous), and restrict your wandering to the daytime.

Onde? Where? The Question for Going Places

The word **onde** (*ohn*-jee; where) can be your best friend as you navigate any new place in Brazil. *Where is* . . . is expressed in three ways: **Onde é** (*ohn*-jee *eh*), **Onde fica** (*ohn*-jee *fee*-kah), and **Onde está** (*ohn*-jee eh-*stah*).

Onde é is used more for people and general locations, whereas **Onde fica** and **Onde está** are used to ask for the precise location of something. **Onde é o Macau?** (ohn-jee *ee* ooh mah-*kah*-ooh; Where is Macau?) someone asks. They expect to hear an answer like "in Asia," not the precise latitude and longitude of Macau. But by asking **Onde fica aquela loja?** (*ohn*-jee *fee*-kah ah-*keh*-lah *loh*-zhah; Where is that store?), you expect someone to explain the street, the cross street, and maybe the exact address so that you have no problems finding it. Generally speaking, **onde fica** is more commonly used than **onde está.**

Check out some common variations of phrases that use **onde:**

- ✔ **Para onde . . . ?** (*pah*-dah *ohn*-jee; To where . . . ?)

- ✔ **Onde que é . . . ?** (*ohn*-jee kee *eh;* Where is . . . ?)

- ✔ **Sabe onde fica . . . ?** (*sah*-bee *ohn*-jee *fee*-kah; Do you know where . . . is located?)

- ✔ **Sabe onde que tem . . . ?** (*sah*-bee *ohn*-jee kee *tang;* Do you know where there's a . . . ?)

- ✔ **De onde . . . ?** (*jee ohn*-jee; From where . . . ?)

Here are some sentences that use **onde** phrases:

- ✔ **Para onde vai esse ônibus?** (*pah*-dah *ohn*-jee *vah*-ee *eh*-see *oh*-nee-boos; Where does this bus go to?)

- ✔ **Onde que é a Rua Pedralbes?** (*ohn*-jee kee *eh* ah *hoo*-ah peh-*drah*-ooh-beez; Where is Pedralbes Street?)

- ✔ **Sabe onde fica o Citibank?** (*sah*-bee *ohn*-jee *fee*-kah ooh *see*-chee-*bahn*-kee; Do you know where the Citibank is located?)

- ✔ **Sabe onde que tem um supermercado?** (*sah*-bee *ohn*-jee kee *tang* oong *soo*-peh-meh-*kah*-doh; Do you know where there's a supermarket?)

- ✔ **De onde é o cantor?** (*jee ohn*-jee *eh* ooh kahn-*toh;* Where is the singer from?)

Another useful phrase is **Estou procurando . . .** (eh-*stoh* pdoh-koo-*dahn*-doh; I'm looking for . . .). The phrase uses the verb **procurar** (pdoh-koo-*dah;* to look/search for). The verb is related to the old-fashioned word *procure* in English. See Chapter 6 for more information on this phrase.

Talkin' the Talk

Silvio is in Rio, and she wants to visit the nearby city of **Petrópolis** (peh-*tdoh*-poh-leez) for the weekend. That's where the Brazilian Portuguese royalty lived, back when Brazil was an empire. (Check out Chapter 2 for more on numbers.)

Silvio:	**Por favor, sabe onde que passa o ônibus número sessenta e dois?** poh fah-*voh*, *sah*-bee *ohn*-jee kee *pah*-sah ooh *oh*-nee-boos *noo*-meh-doh seh-*sehn*-tah ee *doh*-eez? Excuse me, do you know where bus number 62 passes?
Passerby:	**Para onde quer ir?** pah-dah *ohn*-jee *keh ee*? Where would you like to go?
Silvio:	**Quero ir para Petrópolis.** *keh*-doo ee pah-dah peh-*tdoh*-poh-leez. I want to go to Petropolis.
Passerby:	**Não conheço o sessenta e dois, mas o quarenta e três vai para o Petrópolis.** *nah*-ooh kohn-*yeh*-soo ooh seh-*sehn*-tah ee *doh*-eez, *mah*-eez ooh kwah-*dehn*-tah ee *tdehz vah*-ee pah-dah ooh peh-*tdoh*-poh-leez. I don't know the number 62, but the 43 goes to Petropolis.
Silvio:	**Sabe onde que tem uma parada do quarenta e três?** *sah*-bee *ohn*-jee kee *tang* ooh-mah pah-*dah*-dah doo kwah-*dehn*-tah ee *tdehz?* Do you know where there's a bus stop for the 43?
Passerby:	**Tem uma do lado do Pão de Açúcar. Sabe onde que é?** *tang ooh*-mah doo *lah*-doo doo *pah*-ooh jee ah-*soo*-kah. *sah*-bee *ohn*-jee kee *eh?* There's one next to the Pão de Açúcar (the name of a supermarket chain). Do you know where it is?

Silvio: **Não, não sei.**
nah-ooh, *nah*-ooh *say.*
No, I don't.

Passerby: (Points to a nearby corner) **Fica naquela esquina. Tá vendo?**
fee-kah nah-*keh*-lah eh-*skee*-nah. tah *vehn*-doh?
It's on that corner. Do you see it?

Words to Know

passa	<u>pah</u>-sah	passes
ônibus	<u>oh</u>-nee-boos	bus
número	<u>noo</u>-meh-doh	number
conheço	kohn-<u>yeh</u>-soh	I know/I'm familiar with
vai	<u>vah</u>-ee	goes
parada	pah-<u>dah</u>-dah	bus stop
do lado	doo <u>lah</u>-doo	next to
naquela	nah-<u>keh</u>-lah	on that
esquina	eh-<u>skee</u>-nah	street corner
Tá vendo?	<u>tah</u> <u>vehn</u>-doh	Do you see it?

Understanding Spatial Directions

You can use the descriptions of space in Table 12-1 while asking for directions in a city, trying to **encontrar** (ehn-kohn-*tdah;* find) something in someone's **casa** (*kah*-zah; house), or even while taking an **axé** (ah-*sheh;* Brazilian-style aerobics) class.

Someone may explain that you can change your money at a travel agency that's **na frente** (nah *fdehn*-chee; in front of) a large bank that's a landmark in the city. Or that the museum you're looking for is **do lado** (doo *lah*-doh; next to) a subway station. And is the particular beach you're looking for **para a direita** (*pah*-dah ah jee-*day*-tah; to the right) or **para a esquerda** (*pah*-dah ah ehs-*keh*-dah; to the left) of the street you're on?

Table 12-1	Words That Describe Locations	
Term	*Pronunciation*	*Translation*
na frente	nah *fdehn*-chee	in front of
atrás	ah-*tdah*-eez	behind
para a direita	*pah*-dah ah jee-*day*-tah	to the right
para a esquerda	*pah*-dah ah ehs-*keh*-dah	to the left
abaixo	ah-*bah*-ee-shoh	below/underneath
acima	ah-*see*-mah	above/on top of
do lado	doo *lah*-doh	next to
dentro	*dehn*-tdoh	inside
fora	*foh*-dah	outside

Here are some sentences that use directional words and phrases:

- **Fica na frente do Corréios.** (*fee*-kah nah *fdehn*-chee doo koh-*hay*-ohz; It's in front of the post office.)

- **Está atrás da mesa.** (eh-*stah* ah-*tdah*-eez dah *meh*-zah; It's behind the table.)

- **Vá para a direita.** (*vah* pah-dah ah jee-*day*-tah; Go to the right.)

- **Fica para a esquerda da loja.** (*fee*-kah *pah*-dah ah ehs-*keh*-dah dah *loh*-zhah; It's to the left of the store.)

- **Olhe embaixo.** (*ohl*-yee em-*bah*-ee-shoh; Look underneath.)

- **Estão acima da geladeira.** (eh-*stah*-ooh ah-*see*-mah dah zheh-lah-*day*-dah; They're on top of the refrigerator.)

- **Está do lado da janela.** (eh-*stah* doo *lah*-doh dah zhah-*neh*-lah; It's next to the window.)

- **Está dentro da caixa.** (eh-*stah* *dehnt*-droh dah *kah*-ee-shah; It's inside the box.)

- **O carro está fora da garagem.** (ooh *kah*-hoh eh-*stah* *foh*-dah dah gah-*dah*-zhang; The car's outside of the garage.)

Straight ahead can be expressed a couple of ways: **direto** (jee-*deh*-too. *Literally:* direct) or **reto** (*heh*-too. *Literally:* straight). If you're driving, someone may tell you

- ✔ **Pode ir reto.** (*poh*-jee *ee heh*-too; You can go straight.)

- ✔ **Segue sempre direto.** (*seh*-gee *sehm*-pdee jee-*deh*-too; It's straight ahead, all the way. *Literally:* It's all straight.)

Navigating Cityscapes

Some Brazilian cities are harder to figure out than others. São Paulo, for example, is very confusing, even for longtime residents. It's gargantuan in size, yet it has only a small subway network — making having a car or taking a taxi essential to getting to know the city. I also didn't notice much of a real **centro da cidade** (*sent*-droh dah see-*dah*-jee; city center) like there is in most big cities.

A place to start your reconnaissance mission, however, is **Avenida Paulista** (*ah*-veh-*nee*-dah pah-ooh-*lees*-tah; Paulista Avenue), the most famous and busiest street in São Paulo. It's mainly famous for the number of banks, but it has many other attractions — at least four shopping centers with multiscreen cinema complexes, two music and arts centers, one of South America's most famous modern art museums (MASP), two of the city's largest hospitals, and at least five of the city's five-star hotels — all in an avenue no longer than two miles.

Rio and Brasilia, in contrast, are **fácil** (*fah*-seeh-ooh; easy) and **divertido** (jee-veh-*chee*-doo; fun) to figure out. They're much smaller, with just a few areas of major interest.

There are two main **bairros** (*bah*-ee-hooz; neighborhoods) in Rio to visit: **a zona sul** (ah *soh*-nah *soo;* the southern zone), where the famous beaches **Copacabana** (*koh*-pah-kah-*bah*-nah) and **Ipanema** (ee-pah-*neh*-mah) are, and the **centro histórico** (*sehn*-tdoh ee-*stoh*-dee-koh; historic center), where you can find the **museus** (moo-*zeh*-ooz; museums) and **galerias de arte** (gah-leh-*dee*-ahz jee *ah*-chee).

Brasilia (bdah-*zee*-lee-ah), the capital of Brazil, is a very new **cidade.** It was built mainly in the 1950s and '60s by Brazil's most famous architect, Oscar Niemeyer. The city is very well organized in large city **quarteirões** (kwah-tay-*doh*-eez; blocks).

Whichever the city, these terms should be helpful:

- **praça** (*pdah*-sah; plaza)
- **rua** (*hoo*-ah; street)
- **rio** (*hee*-ooh; river)
- **parque** (*pah*-kee; park)
- **centro comercial** (*sehn*-tdoh koh-meh-see-*ah*-ooh; shopping center)
- **jardim** (zhah-*jing;* garden)
- **mar** (mah; ocean)
- **beira-mar** (bay-dah-*mah;* shoreline/seafront)
- **morro** (*moh*-hoo; hill)
- **igreja** (ee-*gdeh*-zhah; church)
- **ponte** (*pohn*-chee; bridge)

Here are some words you can use to give directions:

- **vá** (vah; go)
- **cruza** (*kdoo*-zah; cross)
- **olha** (*ohl*-yah; look)
- **pega** (*peh*-gah; take)
- **segue** (*seh*-gee; follow)
- **sobe** (*soh*-bee; go up)
- **desce** (*deh*-see; go down)

When Brazilians give directions, they use what grammar books call a *command* or *imperative*. It's what people use in English, too. The word *command* sounds authoritarian, but in essence that's what you do — you tell people to take a certain street, cross on another, and so on.

In Portuguese, you can give commands to someone by using the **você** form of the verb. Simply use the –**a** ending for –**ar** verbs or the –**e** ending for –**er**/–**ir** verbs. The verb **ir** (ee; to go), however, is irregular; it takes the form **vá** (vah) for commands. Just like in English, the subject of the sentence (you/**você**) is implied, so you can start the sentence with the verb: **Cruza a ponte** (*kdoo*-zah ah *pohn*-chee; Cross the bridge).

Getting directions straight is hard enough in English — let alone in Portuguese! So here are sample sentences that put together some of the terms that have to do with location:

✔ **Está atrás da igreja.** (eh-*stah* ah-*tdah*-eez dah ee-*gdeh*-zhah; It's behind the church.)

✔ **Fica na beira-mar.** (*fee*-kah nah *bay*-dah *mah;* It's on the seafront.)

✔ **Olha para lá.** (*ohl*-yah *pah*-dah *lah;* Look over there.)

✔ **Pega a segunda direita.** (*peh*-gah ah seh-*goon*-dah jee-*day*-tah; Take the second right.)

✔ **Segue essa rua direto.** (*seh*-gee *eh*-sah *hoo*-ah jee-*deh*-toh; Follow this road all the way.)

You may want to use some of these handy connector words, which help tell you when to do something:

✔ **quando** (*kwahn*-doh; when)

✔ **antes** (*ahn*-cheez; before)

✔ **depois** (deh-*poh*-eez; after)

✔ **logo** (*loh*-goo; as soon as)

✔ **até** (ah-*teh;* until)

Just for fun, here are some more-complicated sentences that show you how you can use those connector words:

✔ **Vá até a praça, e depois pega a Rua Almirantes.** (*vah* ah-*teh* ah *pdah*-sah ee deh-*poh*-eez *peh*-gah ah *hoo*-ah ah-ooh-mee-*dahn*-cheez; Go until you reach the plaza, and then take Almirantes Street.)

✔ **Sobe a Faria Lima, e depois pega a Bandeirantes quando chegar no posto de gasolina.** (*soh*-bee ah fah-*dee*-ah *lee*-mah ee deh-*poh*-eez *peh*-gah ooh bahn-day-*dahn*-cheez *kwahn*-doh sheh-*gah* noo *poh*-stoo jee *gah*-zoh-*lee*-nah; Go up Faria Lima, and then take Bandeirantes when you get to the gas station.)

Talkin' the Talk

 Gilberto is trying to find the shopping mall nearest to his hotel, so he asks his waiter at breakfast.

Gilberto: **Oi, onde que tem um shopping por aqui?**
oh-ee, *ohn*-jee kee *tang* oong *shoh*-ping poh ah-*kee?*
Excuse me, where is there a shopping mall around here?

Waiter: **Quando sai da entrada, vai ver à sua direita a
            Avenida Espanha.**
            kwahn-doh *sah*-ee dah ehn-*tdah*-dah, *vah*-ee *veh* ah
            soo-ah jee-*day*-tah ah ah-veh-*nee*-dah eh-*spahn*-yah.
            When you go out the entrance, you will see Spain
            Avenue to your right.

Gilberto: **Okay . . .**
            oh-*keh*-ee . . .
            Okay . . .

Waiter: **Vai pegar a Espanha e seguir até uma ruazinha
            chamada Santa Maria.**
            vah-ee peh-*gah* ah eh-*spahn*-yah ee seh-*gee* ah-*teh*
            ooh-mah *hoo*-ah-*zing*-yah shah-*mah*-dah *sahn*-tah
            mah-*dee*-ah.
            You're going to take a right on Spain and follow it
            until a small street called Santa Maria.

Gilberto: **Tá bom . . .**
            tah *boh*-oong . . .
            All right . . .

Waiter: **Vá para a esquerda nessa ruazinha, e depois de mais
            dois quarteirões, vai ver um Bompreço.**
            vah pah-dah ah eh-*skeh*-dah *neh*-sah *hoo*-ah-*zing*-
            yah, ee deh-*poh*-eez jee *mah*-eez *doh*-eez *kwah*-tay-
            doh-eez, *vah*-ee *veh* oong *boh*-oong *pdeh*-soo.
            Go to the left on this little street, and after two
            blocks, you'll see a Bompreço (the name of a super-
            market chain).

Gilberto: **Muito obrigado.**
            moh-*ee*-toh oh-bdee-*gah*-doh.
            Thank you very much.

Waiter: **De nada. Não se preocupe, é fácil. Não vai se perder.**
            jee *nah*-dah. *nah*-ooh see pdeh-oh-*koo*-pee, eh *fah*-
            see-ooh. *nah*-ooh *vah*-ee see peh-*deh*.
            You're welcome. Don't worry, it's easy. You won't get
            lost.

Words to Know

por aqui	poh ah-<u>kee</u>	around here
sai	<u>sah</u>-ee	go out/leave
entrada	ehn-<u>tdah</u>-dah	entrance
vai	<u>vah</u>-ee	you will
ver	veh	see/to see
chamada	shah-<u>mah</u>-dah	called
nessa	<u>neh</u>-sah	on this
ruazinha	<u>hoo</u>-ah-<u>zing</u>-yah	little street
mais	<u>mah</u>-eez	another/more

Oi (*oh*-ee) normally means *Hi*. But it's also used to mean *Hey*, like when you want to get someone's attention in an informal situation. **Por favor** (poh fah-*voh*) can be used to say the same thing, in both informal and formal situations.

The Verbs That Take You Up and Down

Someone can tell you to go up or down a street by saying **Sobe** (*soh*-bee; Go up) or **Desce** (*deh*-see; Go down). Thinking about a related word in English, *descend*, may help you to remember **desce.**

The two terms come from the verbs **subir** (soo-*bee*; to go up) and **descer** (deh-*seh*; to go down). They're used in other situations, too, like going up and down in an **elevador** (eh-leh-vah-*doh*; elevator), coming up to see someone in his or her apartment, and going down to the street level of an apartment building. When you enter an **elevador,** you can say **Sobe?** to ask if it's going up or **Desce?** to ask if it's going down.

Imagine you're talking over an intercom system to someone who's in a **prédio de apartamentos** (*pdej*-yoh jee ah-pah-tah-*mehn*-tohz; apartment building). You may say or hear some of these phrases:

✔ **Vou subir.** (*voh* soo-*bee;* I'm coming up.)

✔ **Vou descer.** (*voh* deh-*seh;* I'm coming down.)

✔ **Ela vai subir agora.** (*eh*-lah *vah*-ee soo-*bee* ah-*goh*-dah; She's coming up now.)

✔ **Vou descer daqui a cinco minutos. Me espera?** (*voh* deh-*seh* dah-*kee* ah *sing*-koh mee-*noo*-tohz. mee eh-*speh*-dah; I'll come down in five minutes. Will you wait for me?)

Daqui a (dah-*kee* ah) plus a time reference is one of my favorite Brazilian expressions. **Daqui** is a shortened version of **de** and **aqui,** and it literally means *from here.* Use this phrase when you want to say how soon something's going to happen. When are you going to be ready? **Daqui a dois minutos** (dah-*kee* ah *doh*-eez mee-*noo*-tohz; In about two minutes). When will the TV program start? **Daqui a pouco** (dah-*kee* ah *poh*-koh). **Pouco** means *little,* so the program will start in very little time.

Over Here, Over There

Take a look at how you can say *here, there,* and *over there.* You can use these words in so many settings — when you're asking for directions, browsing in a shop, or pointing out a person on the street. These terms help you distinguish the physical position of the item or person in relation to your location.

✔ **aqui** (ah-*kee;* here)

✔ **ali** (ah-*lee;* there)

✔ **lá** (lah; over there)

In general, **lá** is reserved for places that are a few minutes' walk away or more. If you're talking about an object upstairs, use **ali.** If you're talking about your car parked on the other side of town, use **lá.** Also use **lá** to talk about stuff happening really far away, like in other countries. Here are some examples:

✔ **Estamos aqui.** (eh-*stah*-mohz ah-*kee;* We're here.)

✔ **Está ali, na mesa.** (eh-*stah* ah-*lee* nah *meh*-zah; It's there, on the table.)

✔ **Lá nos Estados Unidos, se come muita comida rápida.** (*lah* nohz eh-*stah*-dohz ooh-*nee*-dooz, see *koh*-mee moh-*ee*-tah koh-*mee*-dah *hah*-pee-dah; Over there in the United States, they eat a lot of fast food.)

✔ **Vá lá.** (*vah* lah; Go over there.)

Say you're in a taxi. You've told the driver the street where you're going, but now you're on that street and want to say *Let me off right here.* SAY **Aqui-o!** (ah-*kee*-ah; Right here!) to sound like a native Brazilian.

The one time you won't use **aqui** when you mean *here* is with the expression *Come here,* where **cá** replaces **aqui: Vem cá!** (vang *kah;* Come here!), a mother says to her child.

The Big Countdown: Ordinal Numbers

When people give directions, they often use ordinal numbers. Someone may tell you to take the **primeira** (pdee-*may*-dah; first) left and then the **terceira** (teh-*say*-dah; third) right. Or someone may say to take the elevator to the **sétimo** (*seh*-chee-moh; seventh) floor. Here's a handy list for all that (if you want to see the numbers you use to count, check out Chapter 2):

- **primeiro** (pdee-*may*-doh; first)
- **segundo** (seh-*goon*-doh; second)
- **terceiro** (teh-*say*-doh; third)
- **quarto** (*kwah*-toh; fourth)
- **quinto** (*keen*-toh; fifth)
- **sexto** (*sehs*-toh; sixth)
- **sétimo** (*seh*-chee-moh; seventh)
- **oitavo** (oh-ee-*tah*-voh; eighth)
- **nono** (*noh*-noh; ninth)

Try to remember to change the ending to **-a** instead of **-o** if the following word is feminine.

Here are some example sentences using the ordinal numbers:

- **Pega a primeira direita.** (*peh*-gah ah pdee-*may*-dah jee-*day*-tah; Take the first right.)
- **Moro no quarto andar.** (*moh*-doo noh *kwah*-toh ahn-*dah;* I live on the fourth floor.)
- **É a segunda porta.** (*eh* ah seh-*goon*-dah *poh*-tah; It's the second door.)

In any building in Brazil, the **primeiro andar** (pdee-*may*-doh ahn-*dah;* first floor) is what English-speakers call the *second floor.* That's because they have a special term for the first floor: **o térreo** (ooh *teh*-hee-oh; ground floor). The **basement,** where parking garages are often located, is called the **subsolo** (*soo*-bee-*soh*-loo).

How far? Perto ou Longe?

One question you may want to ask before hearing a complicated set of directions is **Fica longe?** (*fee*-kah *lohn*-zhee; Is it far?). Here are some handy words you can use for estimating distances:

- **longe** (*lohn*-zhee; far)
- **perto** (*peh*-too; close)
- **muito longe** (moh-*ee*-toh *lohn*-zhee; really far)
- **muito perto** (moh-*ee*-toh *peh*-too; really close)
- **pertinho** (peh-*cheen*-yoh; really close)

Talkin' the Talk

Taís is deciding how to spend her afternoon in **Vitória** (vee-toh-dee-ah), the capital of **Espirito Santo** (eh-*spee*-dee-toh *sahn*-too) state. Should she go to the shopping mall or the beach or both? She asks the hotel concierge how far away each place is from the hotel.

Taís:	**Por favor, qual fica mais perto, o shopping ou a praia?** poh fah-*voh*, *kwah*-ooh *fee*-kah *mah*-eez *peh*-too, ooh *shoh*-ping ooh ah *pdah*-ee-ah? Excuse me, which is closer, the shopping mall or the beach?
Concierge:	**A praia é bem mais perto. Fica aqui do lado.** ah *pdah*-ee-ah eh *bang* mah-eez *peh*-too. *fee*-kah ah-*kee* doo *lah*-doo. The beach is much closer. It's just on the other side of here.
Taís:	**E o shopping? Como se chega?** ee ooh *shoh*-ping? *koh*-moh see *sheh*-gah? And the mall? How do you get there?
Concierge:	**Olha, tem que pegar dois ônibus, ou pode ir em táxi.** *ohl*-yah, *tang* kee peh-*gah doh*-eez *oh*-nee-boos, oh *poh*-jee *eeh* ang *tahk*-see. Well, you have to take two buses, or you can take a taxi.

Taís:	**Tudo bem. O shopping para ir hoje parece longe demais.**
	too-doh *bang.* ooh *shoh*-ping pah-dah *eeh oh*-zhee pah-*deh*-see *lohn*-zhee jee-*mah*-eez.
	All right. The mall seems too far away to go to today.
Concierge:	**Melhor ficar tranqüila na praia.**
	mel-*yoh* fee-*kah* tdahn-*kwee*-lah nah *pdah*-ee-ah.
	It's better to relax on the beach.

Words to Know

mais perto	mah-eez peh-too	closer
bem mais perto	bang mah-eez peh-too	a lot closer
tem que pegar . . .	tang kee peh-gah	you have to take . . .
pode	poh-jee	you can
ir em táxi	eeh ang tahk-see	go by taxi
parece	pah-deh-see	it seems
longe demais	lohn-zhee jee-mah-eez	too far
ficar tranqüila	fee-kah tdahn-kwee-lah	to relax

Measuring Distances and Other Stuff

Brazilians' spatial sense is pretty common to all cultures. It's hard to imagine a language that doesn't have terms for *here, there,* and *over there,* for example.

Measuring things like volume and weight is just as universal. But if you happen to be an American, you'll find that the way Brazilians measure stuff is different: They use the metric system.

Check out Table 12-2 for the names of metric measurements and some U.S. equivalents.

Table 12-2		Brazilian Measurements		
Type of Measurement	*Term*	*Pronunciation*	*Translation*	*U.S. Equivalent*
distance	quilômetro	kee-*loh*-meh-tdoh	kilometer	0.62 miles
length	centímetro	sehn-*chee*-meh-tdoh	centimeter	0.4 inches
volume	litro	*lee*-tdoh	liter	1.06 quarts
weight/mass	quilo	*kee*-loh	kilogram	2.2 pounds
temperature	centígrados	sehn-*chee*-gdah-dohz	degrees Celsius	⅗ × Celsius temperature + 32

Fun & Games

Cláudio e Renata Alves (*klah*-ooh-jyoh ee heh-*nah*-tah *ah*-ooh veez) speak little English, and they're coming to your house for dinner. They've called you for directions — to your fabulous apartment in Rio that faces the beach. See whether you can translate the English directions given below into Portuguese. Then flip to Appendix C for the answers:

1. Go to the plaza.

2. Then take a left on Bela Cintra Ave.

3. Go straight all the way to the end.

4. On your right, you will see a church.

5. It's behind the church, on the beachfront.

Chapter 13

Staying at a Hotel or Guesthouse

. . . .

In This Chapter

▶ Checking out the accommodations before you check in

▶ Reserving a room

▶ Registering

▶ **Dormir** and **acordar:** Sleeping and waking up

▶ Being possessive: Whose stuff is whose?

. . . .

*I*n Brazil, there are two main types of **hospedagem** (oh-speh-*dah*-zhang; lodging). **Hotéis** (oh-*tay*-eez; hotels) are very large and impersonal, and **pousadas** (poh-*zah*-dahz; guesthouses) are small and friendly. Do I seem biased? Well, I really recommend staying at a **pousada,** because the close quarters and chatty **donos** (*doh*-nooz; owners) make for an excellent Portuguese classroom. The **donos** often work in the **pousada** themselves because it's their livelihood. Staying in a **pousada** sort of feels like staying in another family's home. They're similar to what North Americans refer to as a B&B ("bed and breakfast" — a small inn), except that **pousadas** can be larger. At a **pousada,** there can be anywhere from under 10 **quartos** (*kwah*-tooz; rooms) to maybe 20 at a large **pousada.**

Pousadas are generally **baratas** (bah-*dah*-tahz; inexpensive). A **simples** (*seem*-pleez; modest) one may cost only 30 reais (about $15, depending on the exchange rate) for two people **por noite** (*poh noh*-ee-chee; per night). As you get to desirable neighborhoods, say in **Olinda** (oh-*leen*-dah), a historic gem of a town in the northeast, **pousadas** can be pricier, at around 300 reais (about $135) **por noite** for **duas pessoas** (*doo*-ahz peh-*soh*-ahz; two people).

What you don't generally get with a **pousada** that you do get with a **hotel** (oh-*tay*-ooh) is an **academia** (ah-kah-deh-*mee*-ah; fitness room/gym) and full-service **restaurante** (*heh*-stah-ooh-*dahn*-chee; restaurant).

One nice thing about Brazilian **hospedagem** is that **o café da manhã** (ooh kah-*feh* dah mahn-*yah;* breakfast) almost always comes with the per-night rate. The term **o café da manhã** is often shortened to just **café,** so you can ask the receptionist **Vem incluído o café?** (*vang* een-kloo-*ee*-doh ooh kah-*feh;* Is breakfast included?). Brazilian breakfasts are ample and delicious — see Chapter 5 to get an idea of what's on the menu.

If you plan to visit Brazil for **Reveillón** (heh-vay-*yohn;* New Year's Eve) or for **Carnaval** (*kah*-nah-*vah*-ooh; Carnival), **Faz uma reserva com antecedência!** (*fah*-eez *ooh*-mah heh-*seh*-vah kohng ahn-teh-seh-*dehn*-see-ah; Make a reservation ahead of time!). In the case of **Carnaval,** it's best to book lodging and air travel about six months in advance. **Hotéis** and **pousadas** often offer a five-day **pacote** (pah-*koh*-chee; package) that covers Saturday through Ash Wednesday. For more on **Carnaval,** see Chapter 17.

Checking Out the Hotel or Pousada

Before you decide where to stay, you want to **revisar** (heh-vee-*zah;* check out) the **quartos** (*kwah*-tooz; rooms) and the place in general, **dentro** (*dehn*-tdoh; inside) and **fora** (*foh*-dah; outside). You'll want to ask some **perguntas** (peh-*goon*-tahz; questions), too.

You may have already seen the expression **Tem . . . ?** (tang; Does it have/Do you have . . . ?) in this book. Hotels are a great place to use it. Here are some **perguntas** you can use to ask about **o quarto:**

- ✔ **Tem agua quente?** (*tang* ah-gwah *kang*-chee; Does it have hot water?)

- ✔ **Tem banheira?** (*tang* bahn-*yay*-dah; Does it have a bathtub?)

- ✔ **Tem ar condicionado?** (tang *ah* kohn-*dee*-see-ooh-*nah*-doo; Does it have air conditioning?)

- ✔ **Tem ventilador?** (tang vehn-chee-lah-*doh;* Does it have a fan?)

- ✔ **Tem cofre?** (tang *koh*-fdee; Does it have a safe deposit box?)

- ✔ **Tem vista?** (tang *vee*-stah; Does it have a view?)

- ✔ **Tem acesso ao Internet?** (tang ahk-*seh*-soo *ah*-ooh een-teh-*neh*-chee; Does it have Internet access?)

- ✔ **Tem TV à cabo?** (tang teh-*veh* ah *kah*-boh; Does it have cable TV?)

- ✔ **Tem Jacuzzi?** (*tang* zhah-*koo*-zee; Does it have a Jacuzzi?)

And here's what you can ask about the **hotel** or **pousada** in general:

- ✔ **Tem piscina?** (tang pee-*see*-nah; Do you have a pool?)

- ✔ **Tem quarto para não fumantes?** (tang *kwah*-toh pah-dah *nah*-ooh foo-*mahn*-cheez; Do you have non-smoking rooms?)

- ✔ **Tem academia?** (tang ah-kah-deh-*mee*-ah; Do you have a gym?)

This phrase doesn't use **tem,** but you can use it to ask about one of the hotel services: **Ofereçam transporte do aeroporto?** (oh-feh-*deh*-sah-ooh tdahn-*spoh*-chee doo ah-eh-doh-*poh*-too; Do you offer a pick-up service from the airport?).

Making Reservations

You can use the preceding questions and phrases about **hospedagem** (oh-speh-*dah*-zhang; accomodations) either on the phone, when you're making a **reserva** (heh-*seh*-vah; reservation), or in person, at the **recepção do hotel** (heh-sep-*sah*-ooh doo oh-*teh*-ooh; hotel reception desk). (For more on talking on the phone, see Chapter 9.)

If you can do so, trying to **fazer uma reserva** (fah-*zeh* ooh-mah heh-*seh*-vah; make a reservation) before you **chegar** (sheh-*gah;* arrive) is always a good idea. But unless you're staying during a holiday or some special event's going on, you should be fine just showing up and scouting out the area.

The most important question, of course, is whether the place has a **vaga** (*vah*-gah; vacancy). Here are some helpful phrases:

- ✔ **Tem vaga para hoje à noite?** (tang *vah*-gah pah-dah *oh*-zhee ah *noh*-ee-chee; Do you have a vacancy for tonight?)

- ✔ **Tem vaga para o fim de semana?** (*tang vah*-gah pah-dah ooh *fing* jee seh-*mah*-nah; Do you have a vacancy for the weekend?)

- ✔ **Tem vaga para o mês que vem?** (tang *vah*-gah pah-dah ooh *mehz* kee *vang;* Do you have a vacancy for next month?)

- ✔ **Eu queria fazer uma reserva.** (*eh*-ooh kee-*dee*-ah fah-*zeh* ooh-mah heh-*seh*-vah; I wanted to make a reservation.)

- ✔ **É para duas pessoas.** (*eh* pah-dah *doo*-ahz peh-*soh*-ahz; It's for two people.)

- ✔ **Só para uma pessoa.** (*soh* pah-dah *ooh*-mah peh-*soh*-ah; Just for one person.)

These are some things the hotel clerk may ask or tell you:

- ✔ **Quantas pessoas?** (*kwahn*-tahz peh-*soh*-ahz; How many people?)
- ✔ **Por quantas noites?** (poh *kwahn*-tahz *noh*-ee-cheez; For how many nights?)
- ✔ **Cama de casal, ou duas camas solteiras?** (*kah*-mah jee kah-*zah*-ooh, ooh *doo*-ahz *kah*-mahz soh-ooh-*tay*-dahz; A double bed, or two twin beds?)

Checking In and Checking Out: Registration Procedures

Funnily enough, most Brazilians refer to *the check-in process* as **o check-in** (ooh sheh-*king*). **Fazer o check-in** (fah-*zeh* ooh sheh-*king*) means *to check in*.

Checking into a **hotel** (oh-*tay*-ooh; hotel) or **pousada** (poh-*zah*-dah; guest-house) in Brazil is the same process as you'd see in most places around the world. First, you give the desk clerk your **nome** (*noh*-mee; name). If you have a **reserva** (heh-*seh*-vah; reservation), the clerk will probably check the **detalhes** (deh-*tah*-leez; details) on file for you and then give you the **chaves** (*shah*-veez; keys) to the room. On the way to your **quarto** (*kwah*-too; room), a hotel worker will probably point out important places in the **prédio** (*pdehj*-ee-yoo; building), like where you'll be eating **café da manhã** (kah-*feh* dah mahn-*yah*; breakfast) and where the **academia** (ah-kah-deh-*mee*-ah; gym) and **piscina** (pee-*see*-nah; pool) are, if it's a large hotel.

By federal law, every **hotel** and **pousada** has to give every **hóspede** (*oh*-speh-jee; guest) a **ficha** (*fee*-shah; form) to fill out, which asks you to write down basic I.D. information, as well as which places you've visited in Brazil so far and which places you're headed to. This **ficha** helps **Embratur** (em-bdah-*too*; the federal tourism board) understand the activity of its tourists. The **ficha** uses the following terms:

- ✔ **nome** (*noh*-mee; first name)
- ✔ **sobrenome** (*soh*-bdee *noh*-mee; last name/surname)
- ✔ **pais de origem** (pah-*eez* jee oh-*dee*-zhang; country of origin)
- ✔ **data** (*dah*-tah; date)
- ✔ **próximo destino** (*pdoh*-see-moh dehs-*chee*-noo; next destination)
- ✔ **número de passaporte** (*noo*-meh-doh jee pah-sah-*poh*-chee; passport number)

The following are some phrases the hotel clerk may use:

- ✔ **Aqui tem duas chaves.** (ah-*kee* tang *doo*-ahz *shah*-veez; Here are two keys.)
- ✔ **Preenche essa ficha, por favor.** (*pdehn*-shee *eh*-sah *fee*-shah poh fah-*voh*; Fill out this form, please.)

Spending the Night

After doing some sightseeing around the city or town you're in, you'll want to settle in to your hotel for the night. You may want to talk to the **concierge** (kohn-see-*ezh;* concierge — yep, same as in English!) or hotel **equipe de funcionários** (eh-*kee*-pee jee *foon*-see-ooh-*nah*-dee-ooz; staff. *Literally:* team of workers) to help you **planejar** (*plahn*-eh-zhah; plan) what to do the next day.

You can then watch a little Brazilian **tevê** (teh-*veh;* TV) before going to sleep. At 8 p.m., tune in to Brazil's most popular TV station, **Globo** (*gloh*-boo), to watch the current hot **novela** (noh-*veh*-lah; soap opera). Some years, a different **canal** (kah-*nah*-ooh; channel) has the most popular **novela,** but nine times out of ten, the one to watch is on **Globo.** Watching the **novela** can tell you lots about Brazilian culture, as well as expose you to the **som** (*soh*-oong; sound) of Portuguese. And, hey, it's fun to know you're watching the show that probably 25 percent of the county is watching at the same time!

Using the sleeping verb: Dormir

If you want to **dormir bem** (doo-*mee bang;* sleep well) in Brazil, you should probably ask the **hotel** (oh-*tay*-ooh; hotel) or **pousada** (poh-zah-dah; guesthouse) receptionist whether to expect **barulho** (bah-*dool*-yoh; noise).

Brazilians' tolerance for **barulho** is generally higher than that of people from other cultures. So another question to ask may be to ask whether the place is close to any **bares** (*bah*-deez; bars) or **música ao vivo** (*moo*-zeeh-kah ah-ooh *vee*-voh; live music) — especially if you'll be there **no fim de semana** (noh *feeng* jee seh-*mah*-nah; on the weekend).

Hopefully, conjugating **dormir** will be a good luck charm for your sleeping soundly in the future:

Conjugation	*Pronunciation*
eu dormo	*eh*-ooh *doo*-moh
você dorme	voh-*seh doo*-mee
ele/ela dorme	*eh*-lee/*eh*-lah *doo*-mee
nós dormimos	*nohz* doo-*mee*-mooz
eles/elas dormem	*eh*-leez/*eh*-lahz *doo*-mang

And here's the past tense of **dormir** (see Chapter 9 for more on the simple past tense):

Conjugation	*Pronunciation*
eu dormi	*eh*-ooh doo-*mee*
você dormiu	voh-*seh* doo-*mee*-ooh
ele/ela dormiu	*eh*-lee/*eh*-lah doo-*mee*-ooh
nós dormimos	*nohz* doo-*mee*-mooz
eles/elas dormiram	*eh*-leez/*eh*-lahz doo-*mee*-dah-ooh

You can also practice some phrases that use both tenses, as well as the infinitive (unconjugated) form **dormir:**

- ✔ **Dormiu bem?** (doo-*mee*-ooh *bang;* Did you sleep well?)

- ✔ **Dormi muito máu.** (doo-*mee* moh-*ee*-toh *mah*-ooh; I slept really poorly.)

- ✔ **Dormi como uma pedra.** (doo-*mee* koh-moo *ooh*-mah *ped*-rah; I slept like a rock — Brazilian for *I slept like a log.*)

- ✔ **Dormimos só quatro horas.** (doo-*mee*-mooz *soh kwah*-tdoh *oh*-dahz; We slept only four hours.)

- ✔ **Eu preciso dormir oito horas.** (*eh*-ooh pdeh-*see*-zoo doo-*mee oh*-ee-toh *oh*-dahz; I need to sleep eight hours.)

- ✔ **Os gatos dormem no meu quarto.** (ooz *gah*-tohz *doo*-mang noh *meh*-ooh *kwah*-too; The cats sleep in my room.)

- ✔ **Adoro dormir na praia.** (ah-*doh*-doo doh-*mee* nah *pdah*-ee-ah; I love sleeping on the beach.)

- ✔ **Vou dormir. Boa noite.** (*voh* doo-*mee*. *boh*-ah *noh*-ee-chee; I'm going to bed. Good night.)

A useful sleep-related phrase is **estar com sono** (eh-*stah* kohng *soh*-noo; to be sleepy):

✔ **Está com sono?** (eh-*stah* kohng *soh*-noo; Are you sleepy?)

✔ **Estou com sono.** (eh-*stoh* kohng *soh*-noo; I'm sleepy.)

Hopefully, you'll never have **pesadelos** (*peh*-zah-*deh*-looz; nightmares) — only **sonhos doces** (*sohn*-yooz *doh*-seez; sweet dreams)!

Using the waking up verb: Acordar

Acorda! (ah-*koh*-dah; Wake up!) is what a Brazilian may say if you haven't set your **despertador** (deh-*speh*-tah-*doh;* alarm clock) properly. In **hotéis e pousadas** (oh-*tay*-eez ee poh-*zah*-dahz; hotels and guesthouses), you can always request to be woken up. Say **Poderia me acordar as . . .** (poh-deh-*dee*-ah mee ah-koh-*dah ahz* . . .) plus a time. (To find out more about telling time, see Chapter 8).

Here's how to conjugate **acordar**:

Conjugation	Pronunciation
eu acordo	*eh*-ooh ah-*koh*-doo
você acorda	voh-*seh* ah-*koh*-dah
ele/ela acorda	*eh*-lee/*eh*-lah ah-*koh*-dah
nós acordamos	*nohz* ah-koh-*dah*-mooz
eles/elas acordam	*eh*-leez/*eh*-lahz ah-*koh*-dah-ooh

And here's the past tense so you can say when you woke up:

Conjugation	Pronunciation
eu acordei	*eh*-ooh ah-koh-*day*
você acordou	voh-*seh* ah-koh-*doh*
ele/ela acordou	*eh*-lee/*eh*-lah *ah*-koh-*doh*
nós acordamos	*nohz* ah-koh-*dah*-mooz
eles/elas acordaram	*eh*-leez/*eh*-lahz ah-koh-*dah*-dah-ooh

And some practice using **acordar**:

✔ **Acordei cedo.** (ah-koh-*day* seh-doh; I woke up early.)

✔ **Acordei tarde.** (ah-koh-*day* tah-jee; I woke up late.)

✔ **Poderia me acordar as oito horas?** (poh-deh-*dee*-ah mee ah-koh-*dah* ahz *oh*-ee-toh *oh*-dahz; Could you wake me up at 8 o'clock?)

Talkin' the Talk

Two friends, **Marcos** and **Rodrigo**, are talking about sleep.

Marcos: **A que horas tem que acordar amanhã?**
ah *kee oh*-dahz *tang* kee ah-koh-*dah* ah-mahn-*yah?*
What time do you have to wake up tomorrow?

Rodrigo: **Às seis horas. Que mal, hein?**
ahz say-eez *oh*-dahz. kee *mah*-ooh, *ang?*
At six o'clock. How terrible, right?

Marcos: **Você deveria ir dormir cedo hoje.**
voh-*seh deh*-veh-*dee*-ah ee doo-*mee seh*-doo
oh-zhee.
You should go to sleep early today.

Rodrigo: **Vou. Não funciono se durmo menos de cinco horas.**
voh. nah-ooh foon-see-*oh*-noo see *doo*-moh *meh*-
nohz jee *seen*-koh *oh*-dahz.
I will. I can't function if I sleep less than five hours.

Words to Know

A que horas . . . ?	ah kee <u>oh</u>-dahz	At what time . . . ?
tem que acordar	<u>tang</u> kee ah-koh-<u>dah</u>	you have to wake up
Que mal!	kee <u>mah</u>-ooh	How terrible!
. . . hein?	ang	. . . right?
você deveria	voh-<u>seh</u> <u>deh</u>-veh-<u>dee</u>-ah	you should
ir a dormir	<u>eeh</u> ah doh-<u>mee</u>	to go to sleep
cedo	<u>seh</u>-doo	early
Não funciono.	<u>nah</u>-ooh foon-see-<u>oh</u>-noo	I can't function.
menos de	<u>meh</u>-nohz <u>jee</u>	less than

Getting Possessive

If you're traveling with a companion, you may want to tell hotel staff what your individual requests are. Or you may want to specify that there's a problem with **a sua cama** (*ah soo*-ah *kah*-mah; your bed) or that your friend Mary would like to put **as coisas dela** (*ahz koy*-zahz *deh*-lah; her things) in a safe deposit box, although you don't. And in some cases, you may want to denote sharing. Maybe your towels are missing and you want to ask about **as nossas toalhas** (*ahz noh*-sahz toe-*ahl*-yahz; our towels).

For all these situations, you want to use a *possessive* term. I go over these terms in the context of explaining who your relatives are in Chapter 4, but this section tells you how to use those words for objects.

If you want to express *It's mine*, say **É meu** (eh *meh*-ooh) while you're pointing to something. To say *it's yours*, use the phrase **É seu** (eh *seh*-ooh). To say *it's ours*, use the phrase **É nosso** (eh *noh*-soo). If you want to specify what exactly is yours, change the **meu, seu,** or **nosso** to match the thing that you're talking about. Just ask yourself: Is the name of that thing a masculine or feminine word? Is it singular or plural? Check out Table 13-1 for the possibilities of combinations for talking about *my* things, *your* things, and *our* things.

Table 13-1	Possessive Words — My, Your, and Our			
Meaning	*Singular Masculine Object*	*Singular Feminine Object*	*Plural Masculine Object*	*Plural Feminine Object*
my	o meu (*ooh meh*-ooh)	a minha (*ah ming*-yah)	os meus (*ooz meh*-ooz)	as minhas (*ahz ming*-yahz)
your	o seu (*ooh seh*-ooh)	a sua (*ah soo*-ah)	os seus (*ooz seh*-ooz)	as suas (*ahz soo*-ahz)
our	o nosso (*ooh noh*-soo)	a nossa (*ah noh*-sah)	os nossos (*ooz noh*-sooz)	as nossas (*ahz noh*-sahz)

Take a look at some examples that may come up in a **hotel** (oh-*tay*-ooh; hotels) or **pousada** (poh-*zah*-dah; guesthouses):

- **o meu passaporte** (ooh *meh*-ooh pah-sah-*poh*-chee; my passport)
- **o seu cartão de crédito** (ooh *seh*-ooh kah-*tah*-ooh jee *kdeh*-jee-toh; your credit card)
- **os nossos bagagens** (ooz *noh*-sooz bah-*gah*-zhangz; our baggage)
- **os nossos planos** (ooz *noh*-sooz *plah*-nohz; our plans)

When you want to talk about *his, her,* or *their* things, you have to switch the word order. Instead of putting the possessive word in front of the thing (**o meu quarto** [ooh *meh*-ooh *kwah*-too; my room]), first say what the thing is, and then say **de** (deh; of) plus the owner. The **de** gets attached to the **ele, ela,** or **eles/elas** (the *him, her,* or *them*), and the **e** between the words is dropped.

- **dele** (*deh*-lee; his. *Literally:* of him)
- **dela** (*deh*-lah; her. *Literally:* of her)
- **deles** (*deh*-leez; their — for all males or males and females. *Literally:* of them)
- **delas** (*deh*-lahz; their — for all females. *Literally:* of them)

Technically, when you say **o quarto dele** (ooh *kwah*-toh *deh*-lee; his room), you're saying *the room of him.* Remember, name the thing first, and then say whose it is:

- **o dinheiro dela** (ooh jing-*yay*-doh *deh*-lah; her money)
- **a comida deles** (ah koh-*mee*-dah *deh*-leez; their food — for all males or males and females)
- **as roupas delas** (ahz *hoh*-pahz *deh*-lahz; their clothes — for all females)

Using a specific name is the easiest situation. Just say the name of the thing plus **de** and the specific name. Also note that people's names always take an **o** or an **a** before them (depending on whether the person is male or female); when combined with **de**, these words become **do** or **da.** When you want to say *Lucia's house,* you can say **a casa da Lucia** (ah *kah*-zah dah loo-*see*-ah), which literally means *the house of Lucia.* Check out some other examples:

- **o carro do Mario** (ooh *kah*-hoh doo *mah*-dee-oh; Mario's car)
- **o cabelo da Ana Cristina** (ooh kah-*beh*-loh dah *ah*-nah kdee-*schee*-nah; Ana Cristina's hair)
- **as empresas do Petrobrás** (ahz ehm-*pdeh*-zahz doo peh-tdoh-*bdah*-eez; Petrobras' companies — Petrobrás is Brazil's largest oil company)
- **as praias do Pará** (ahz *pdah*-ee-ahz doo pah-*dah;* Para state's beaches)

Talkin' the Talk

 A mom is asking her son and daughter whose dirty socks are on the hotel room floor.

Mom: **De quem são essas meias sujas?**
jee *kang* sah-ooh *eh*-sahz *may*-ahz *soo*-zhahz?
Whose dirty socks are these?

Son: **São dela.**
sah-ooh *deh*-lah.
They're hers.

Daughter: **Não, são dele.**
nah-ooh, *sah*-ooh *deh*-lee.
No, they're his.

Mom: **Quem está mentindo?**
kang eh-*stah* mehn-*cheen*-doo?
Who's lying?

Words to Know

de quem	jee kang	whose
meias	may-ahz	socks
sujas	soo-zhahz	dirty
quem	kang	who
mentindo	mehn-cheen-doo	lying

Fun & Games

You're at an Amazonian lodge near Manaus, Brazil's biggest city in the Amazon rain forest. You're traveling with a man and a woman. To practice your Portuguese, you take a look at the things in your room and theirs and identify which objects belong to whom.

Translate the phrases in English into Portuguese. See Appendix C for the answers.

1. her hair dryer (*hair dryer* is **o secador de cabelo**)

2. his toothbrush (*toothbrush* is **a escova de dentes**)

3. their suitcases (*suitcases* is **as malas**)

4. my wallet (*wallet* is **a carteira**)

5. our guidebook (*guidebook* is **o guia**)

6. her purse (*purse* is **a bolsa**)

Chapter 14

Getting Around: Planes, Buses, Taxis, and More

*B*razil is a vast country, just about the same size as the U.S., and the best way to **viajar** (vee-ah-*zhah;* go. *Literally:* to voyage) from place to far-away place is by **ônibus** (*oh*-nee-boos; bus) or **avião** (ah-vee-*ah*-ooh; plane). **Trens** (tdangz; trains) are seldom used. You can also **alugar um carro** (ah-loo-*gah* oong *kah*-hoh; rent a car).

In Brazil's two biggest cities, Rio and São Paulo, you can find a **metrô** (meh-*tdoh;* subway). They are clean, punctual, and safe. **Táxis** (*talk*-seez) are safe, too, and inexpensive. City buses can also take you anywhere you need to go. But be cautious, especially in Rio, where buses are sometimes robbed.

Near beach areas, you can take joyrides on **buggys** (*boo*-geez; sand dune bug-gies) or on **jangadas** (zhan-*gah*-dahz; sailboats). And there are **barcos** (*bah*-kooz; boats) of all sizes that you can navigate in the **mar** (mah; ocean) or down a **río** (*hee*-ooh; river). Boats are the main mode of **transporte** (tdahn-*spoh*-chee; transport) in the Amazon. Of course, you can always see the coun-try by **bicicleta** (bee-see-*kleh*-tah; bicycle) or **a pé** (ah *peh;* on foot).

If you have cash to burn, you can also take a **helicóptero** (eh-lee-*kohp*-teh-doo; helicopter) ride. This option is particularly popular in São Paulo, supposedly the city with the second-highest helicopter air **tránsito** (*tdahn*-zee-toh; traffic) in the world!

This chapter tells you what you need to get around, from accessing **taxi** services to discussing whether buses are on schedule. Here are a few quick transportation-related phrases:

- ✔ **Vamos embora!** (*vah*-mooz em-*boh*-dah; Let's go!)
- ✔ **Como se chega?** (*koh*-moo see *sheh*-gah; How do you get there?)
- ✔ **Quanto tempo demora para chegar?** (*kwahn*-toh *tehm*-poh deh-*moh*-dah pah-dah sheh-*gah;* How long does it take to get there?)
- ✔ **Eu vou para . . .** (*eh*-ooh *voh* pah-dah; I'm going to . . .)
- ✔ **Vamos para . . .** (*vah*-mohz pah-dah; We're going to . . .)
- ✔ **Eu fui para . . .** (*eh*-ooh *fwee* pah-dah; I went to . . .)

Making a Plane Reservation

If you're in Brazil for longer than just a few days, you may decide to schedule a **viagem** (vee-*ah*-zhang; trip) somewhere within the country. There are **agências de viagens** (ah-*zhang*-see-ahz jee vee-*ah*-zhangz; travel agencies) all over the place in major cities, so finding one shouldn't be hard. This is where you **fazer uma reserva** (fah-*zeh* ooh-mah heh-*zeh*-vah; make a reservation) for your lodging (see Chapter 13) and transportation.

You usually have to **fazer fila** (fah-*zeh* *fee*-lah; wait in line) at the **agência de viagens.** You may have to pick up a **ficha** (*fee*-shah; ticket) with a number on it. After the **agente** (ah-*zhang*-chee; agent) says **Olá, posso ajudar?** (oh-*lah* poh-soo ah-zhoo-*dah;* Hello, can I help you?), he or she often asks some of the following questions:

- ✔ **Qual é o destino?** (*kwah*-ooh *eh* ooh dehs-*chee*-noo; What is the destination?)
- ✔ **Para quantos dias?** (pah-dah *kwahn*-tooz *jee*-ahz; For how many days?)
- ✔ **Quantos passageiros?** (*kwahn*-tohz pah-sah-*zhay*-dooz; How many passengers?)
- ✔ **Importa o horário do dia?** (eem-*poh*-tah ooh ooh-*dah*-dee-ooh doh *jee*-ah; Does the time of day matter?)

> ✔ **Quer reservar o vôo?** (*keh* heh-seh-*vah* ooh *voh;* Do you want to reserve the flight?)

> ✔ **Como vai pagar?** (*koh*-moo *vah*-ee pah-*gah;* How do you want to pay?)

You may want to ask which flight is **mais barato** (*mah*-eez bah-*dah*-toh; cheaper) or whether the agency can offer you a **pacote** (pah-*koh*-chee; package) that includes the hotel.

You can also make reservations online. Brazil's main airlines are Gol (`www.voegol.com.br`), Vasp (`www.vasp.com.br`), Varig (`www.varig.com.br`), Tam (`www.tam.com.br`), and BRA (`www.voebra.com.br`). BRA is normally the cheapest, but you have to buy the ticket at a BRA ticket agency in Brazil. It's worth checking out the Web site just for new vocabulary. Sometimes certain flights are cheaper online, too!

Here are some key terms Brazilian airlines have on their Web sites:

> ✔ **ida e volta** (*ee*-dah ee *voh*-ooh-tah; round trip)

> ✔ **somente ida** (soh-*mehn*-chee *ee*-dah; one way)

> ✔ **de** (jee; from)

> ✔ **para** (*pah*-dah; to)

> ✔ **data da ida** (*dah*-tah dah *ee*-dah; departure date)

> ✔ **data da volta** (*dah*-tah dah *voh*-ooh-tah; return date)

> ✔ **horário dos vôos** (ooh-*dah*-dee-ooh dooz *voh*-ooz; flight schedule)

> ✔ **formas de pagamento** (*foh*-mahz jee pah-gah-*mehn*-toh; method of payment)

> ✔ **cadastra-se** (kah-*dah*-stah-see; register)

Talkin' the Talk

It's Wednesday, and **Daniela** is in São Paulo and wants to visit her aunt in Rio for the weekend. The bus would take five hours. Not bad, but because she only has a couple of days, she decides to book a flight.

Travel agent: **Olá, posso ajudar?**
oh-*lah*, *poh*-soo ah-zhoo-*dah?*
Hello, can I help you?

Daniela: **Queria fazer uma reserva para ir para o Rio.**
kee-*dee*-ah fah-*zeh* ooh-mah heh-*zeh*-vah pah-dah *ee* pah-dah ooh *hee*-ooh.
I'd like to make a reservation to go to Rio.

Travel agent: **Que dia?**
kee *jee*-ah?
Which day?

Daniela: **Na sexta, retornando no domingo.**
nah *sehs*-tah, heh-toh-*nahn*-doh noh doh-*ming*-goh.
For Friday, coming back on Sunday.

Travel agent: **Olha, não sei se tem vaga. Mas vou checar.**
ohl-yah, nah-ooh *say* see tang *vah*-gah. mah-eez *voh* sheh-*kah.*
To be honest, I don't know if there are any seats. But I'll check.

Daniela: **Posso retornar também na segunda, de manhãzinha.**
poh-soo heh-toh-*nah* tahm-*bang* nah seh-*goon*-dah, jee mahn-yah-*zing*-yah.
I can also return on Monday, really early.

Travel agent: **Ai vai ser mais fácil.**
ah-*ee vah*-ee *seh* mah-eez *fah*-see-ooh.
Now that will be easier.

Daniela: **Fantástico.**
fahn-*tahs*-chee-koh.
Fantastic.

Travel agent: (After looking at her computer) **Tem duas opções — no Gol e na Vasp.**
tang *doo*-ahz ohp-*soh*-eez — noh *goh*-ooh ee nah *vah*-spee.
You have two options — on Gol and on Vasp.

Daniela: **Ótimo.**
oh-chee-moh.
Great.

Words to Know

retornando	heh-toh-<u>nahn</u>-doh	returning/coming back
vaga	<u>vah</u>-gah	seat/available spot
checar	sheh-<u>kah</u>	to check
retornar	heh-toh-<u>nah</u>	to return
de manhãzinha	jee mah-yah-<u>zing</u>-yah	really early in the morning
vai ser	<u>vah</u>-ee <u>seh</u>	it will be
opções	ohp-<u>soh</u>-eez	options

If you're successful in reserving the **bilhete** (beel-*yeh*-chee; ticket), you'll be assigned an **assento** (ah-*sehn*-too; seat). You may want to request an **assento** by a **janela** (zhah-*neh*-lah; window) or by a **corredor** (koh-heh-*doh;* aisle).

You may also want to travel by **primeira classe** (pdee-*may*-dah *klah*-see; first class). Otherwise, you'll be flying **classe econômico** (*klah*-see eh-koh-*noh*-mee-koh; economy class/coach).

In Brazil, there's usually a **taxa de embarque** (*tah*-shah jee em-*bah*-kee; boarding tax). It's significant for international flights, at around US$80 but only about US$3 for domestic flights. The **taxa** will be included in the quoted flight price.

Here are some useful words and phrases you can use when you travel internationally:

- ✔ **comprar um bilhete de avião** (kohm-*pdah* oong beel-*yeh*-chee jee ah-vee-*ah*-ooh; to buy an airline ticket)

- ✔ **levar o seu passaporte** (leh-*vah* ooh *seh*-ooh pah-sah-*poh*-chee; to bring your passport)

- ✔ **preencher as fichas** (pdehn-*sheh* ahz *fee*-shahz; to fill out forms)

✔ **a bagagem** (ah bah-*gah*-zhang; the baggage)

✔ **o visto** (ooh *vee*-stoh; the visa)

✔ **o consulado** (ooh kohn-soo-*lah*-doh; the consulate)

✔ **a embaixada** (ah *ehm*-bah-ee-*shah*-dah; the embassy)

✔ **o aeroporto** (ooh ah-*eh*-doh-*poh*-too; the airport)

✔ **a alfândega** (ah ah-ooh-*fahn*-deh-gah; customs)

✔ **a multa** (ah *mool*-tah; the fine)

✔ **os impostos** (oohz eem-*poh*-stooz; taxes)

✔ **a Loja Franca** (ah *loh*-zhah *fdahn*-kah; duty-free)

✔ **nada a declarar** (*nah*-dah ah deh-klah-*dah;* nothing to declare)

✔ **a segurança** (ah seh-goo-*dahn*-sah; security)

Check on the Web site of the Brazililan **embaixada** in your **pais** (pah-*eez;* country) to find out whether you need a **visto** to enter Brazil.

If you're coming to Brazil through another South American country, you'll probably be asked for proof of vaccination against **a febre amarela** (ah *feh*-bdee ah-mah-*deh*-lah; yellow fever). Airport vaccination officials are quite strict and often don't even tell your airline that you need it. I should know — I was stuck in Bolivia for a few days because Brazil wouldn't accept me without my vaccination papers! They were sitting in my apartment in São Paulo, but I had no idea I'd need them to reenter the country.

Taking Buses and Taxis

I generally recommend that you take an **ônibus** (*oh*-nee-boos; bus) for traveling long distances in Brazil and a taxi or the subway to get around cities. Taxis are cheap, and buses within a city can **demorar** (deh-moh-*dah;* take a long time).

The best way to get a **passagem de ônibus** (pah-*sah*-zhang jee *oh*-nee-boos; bus ticket) is to go to the **rodoviária** (hoh-doh-vee-*ah*-dee-ah; central bus station). They're gigantic places in Brazil, and you have many **companhias** (kohm-pahn-*yee*-ahz; companies) to choose from.

Try to buy the bus ticket the day before to make sure you get a **poltrona** (pohl-*tdoh*-nah; seat). Like at an airport, the competing bus companies have offices right next to each other. A sign above the ticket window tells you the name of the company and which **cidades** (see-*dah*-jeez; cities) the buses travel to.

Bring your **passaporte** (pah-sah-*poh*-chee; passport), because the bus company needs to write down the number. After you pay for the ticket, company employees issue you a seat number — seating isn't usually first-come, first-served. Keep the passport handy as you get on the bus. Employees of the bus company hand you a little paper form, which asks you for the **origem** (oh-*dee*-zhang; name of city you're traveling from/origin) and **destino** (dehs-*chee*-noo; destination), as well as your **nome** (*noh*-mee; name), your passport number, and the **data** (*dah*-tah; date).

Also keep in mind that Brazilians use military time for bus tickets. Eight o'clock at night becomes **às vinte horas** (ahz *veen*-chee *oh*-dahz; at 8 p.m./at 20:00 hours). See Chapter 8 for more on telling time.

Taking city buses is a good way to see how polite Brazilians are with each other. The buses are often crowded, and the people sitting down regularly offer to hold bags for the people who have to stand; it's an optional act of courtesy. Brazilians are also very good about giving up seats to the **idosos** (ee-*doh*-zooz; elderly), **deficientes** (deh-fee-see-*en*-cheez; disabled), and **mulheres grávidas** (mool-*yeh*-deez *gdah*-vee-dahz; pregnant women).

If you do plan to ride an **ônibus urbana** (*oh*-nee-boos ooh-*bah*-nah; city bus), check out some phrases you can use either with the **motorista** (moh-toh-*dee*-stah; driver) or another **passageiro** (pah-sah-*zhay*-doo; passenger):

- ✔ **Vai para . . . ?** (*vah*-ee *pah*-dah; Do you go to . . . ?)
- ✔ **Para na Rua . . . ?** (*pah*-dah nah *hoo*-ah; Do you stop on . . . Street?)
- ✔ **Quanto que é?** (*kwahn*-toh kee *eh;* How much?)

Táxis (*talk*-seez; taxis) are plentiful and cheap in Brazil. You can flag one down in the street, just like you would in big cities anywhere else in the world. If you're having trouble finding one, ask someone whether a **ponto de táxi** (*pohn*-toh jee *talk*-see; place where taxis line up to wait for passengers) is nearby.

The **ponto de táxi** consists of a bunch of taxi drivers sitting on a bench, sometimes watching a **novela** (noh-*veh*-lah; soap opera) or **jogo de futebol** (*zhoh*-goo jee foo-chee-*bah*-ooh; soccer match) on an overhead TV.

Here's some taxi talk:

- ✔ **Para . . . por favor.** (pah-dah . . . poh fah-*voh;* To . . . [location], please.)
- ✔ **Sabe como chegar em . . . ?** (*sah*-bee *koh*-moo sheh-*gah* ang; Do you know how to get to . . . ?)

✔ **Quanto seria para ir a . . . ?** (*kwahn*-toh seh-*dee*-ah pah-dah *ee* ah; How much would it be to go to . . . ?)

✔ **É perto?** (eh *peh*-too; Is it close?)

✔ **É longe?** (eh *lohn*-zhee; Is it far?)

Before you agree to ride, ask the **taxista** (tahk-*sees*-tah; taxi driver) whether he or she knows where your destination is. In big cities like São Paulo, taxi drivers often know only a part of the city well. They sometimes have to bring out a **mapa** (*mah*-pah; map) to help them figure out the way. You may want to bring a pen and paper with you to spell the name of your destination to prevent any miscommunication.

Talkin' the Talk

Ricardo and **Carolina** are visiting Rio for the first time. They're staying at a hotel near Ipanema (ee-pah-*neh*-mah) beach and are dying to see the city's world-famous soccer stadium **Maracanã** (mah-dah-kah-*nah*). They flag down a taxi.

Ricardo: **Olá, é longe o Maracanã?**
oh-*lah*, eh *lohn*-zhee ooh mah-dah-kah-*nah*?
Hi. Is Maracanã Stadium far?

Taxi driver: **Não, e pertinho.**
nah-ooh, eh peh-*ching*-yoo.
No, it's really close.

Carolina: **Quanto custaria?**
kwahn-toh koos-tah-*dee*-ah?
How much would it cost?

Taxi driver: **Uns dez reais.**
oonz *dez* hay-eyes.
About 10 reais.

Ricardo: **Tá bom.**
tah *boh*-oong.
Okay.

Taxi driver: **É a sua primeira vez no Rio de Janeiro?**
eh ah *soo*-ah pdee-*may*-dah *vez* noh *hee*-ooh jee zhah-*nay*-doh?
Is it your first time in Rio?

Ricardo:	**É. E nós estamos muito emocionados ao ver o famoso Maracanã.** eh. ee nohz eh-*stah*-mooz moh-ee-toh eh-moh-see-ooh-*nah*-dooz ah-ooh *veh* ooh fah-*moh*-zoo mah-dah-kah-*nah.* Yeah. And we're really excited to see the famous Maracanã.
Taxi driver:	**Não tem jogo hoje.** *nah*-ooh *tang zhoh*-goo *oh*-zhee. There's no game today.
Carolina:	**Tá bom, é só para ver.** tah *boh*-oong, eh *soh* pah-dah *veh.* That's okay. It's just to take a look.

Words to Know

pertinho	peh-<u>ching</u>-yoh	very close/ close by
uns	oonz	about/some
vez	vez	time
emocionados	eh-<u>moh</u>-see-ooh-<u>nah</u>-dooz	excited
famoso	fah-<u>moh</u>-zoo	famous

Renting a Car

If you're the adventurous type, you may decide to **alugar um carro** (ah-loo-*gah* oong *kah*-hoh; rent a car) from a **locadora de carros** (loh-kah-*doh*-dah jee *kah*-hohz; car rental agency) in Brazil. You're probably already familiar with several international rental agencies in Brazil, like Hertz and Avis.

You can use your **carteira de habilitação** (kah-*tay*-dah jee ah-*bee*-lee-tah-*sah*-ooh; driver's license) from home, although it's a good idea to get it translated by a **tradutor juramentado** (tdah-doo-*toh* zhoo-dah-men-*tah*-doo; official translator). The local consulate of your country or a local travel agency should be able to suggest where you can find one.

Cars tend to be smaller in Brazil. Be sure to first ask what **modelos** (moh-*deh*-lohz; types of cars) are available. And the roads can get pretty bad, too, so ask about road conditions. Also, Brazil doesn't have nearly the number of **postos de gasolina** (*poh*-stooz jee gah-zoo-*lee*-nah; gas stations) as North America, so keep your **tanque de gasolina** (*tan*-kee jee gah-zoh-*lee*-nah; gas tank) pretty full.

You may scratch your head when you first visit a **posto de gasolina** (gas station): In addition to **gasolina,** you sometimes have the option of choosing **álcool** (*ah*-ooh-koh-ooh; alcohol), a fuel made from **cana de açúcar** (*kah*-nah jee ah-*soo*-kah; sugarcane) that's cheaper than **gasolina.** The price difference is about US$2.30 per gallon of alcohol, compared with about US$4 per gallon of gasoline. Many cars made in Brazil use technology that converts the alcohol to car fuel. Ask your rental shop employees which you can use with your car.

Most international car rental companies have a flat rate and then charge per kilometer driven. Make sure to get a flat rate that includes **quilometragem livre** (*kee*-loo-meh-*tdah*-zhang *leev*-dee; unlimited mileage).

People at the rental agency refer to the checking-out and checking-in of the car as the **retirada** (heh-chee-*dah*-dah; check-out) and **devolução** (deh-voh-loo-*sah*-ooh; check-in).

Here are some questions to ask at a **locadora:**

- ✔ **Tem um carro disponível para hoje?** (*tang* oong *kah*-hoh jee-spoh-*nee*-veh-ooh pah-dah *oh*-zhee; Do you have a car available for today?)

- ✔ **Qual é a tarifa diária para esse modelo?** (*kwah*-ooh *eh* ah tah-*dee*-fah jee-*ah*-dee-ah pah-dah *eh*-see moh-*deh*-loo; What's the day rate for this [car] make?)

- ✔ **Tem assistência vinte-quatro horas?** (*tang* ah-see-*stehn*-see-ah *ving*-chee *kwah*-tdoh *oh*-dahz; Do you have 24-hour roadside assistance?)

- ✔ **Tem alguma promoção?** (*tang* ah-ooh-*goo*-mah pdoh-moh-*sah*-ooh; Do you have any deals/promotions going on?)

- ✔ **Oferece um plano de seguro?** (oh-feh-*deh*-see oong *plah*-noh jee seh-*goo*-doh; Do you offer an insurance plan?)

You may also want to get familiar with the names of the parts of a car in Portuguese — here are the basics: **volante** (voh-*lahn*-chee; steering wheel),

freios (*fday*-oohz; brakes), **rodas** (*hoh*-dahz; wheels), **párabrisa** (*pah*-dah-*bdee*-sah; windshield), **motor** (moh-*toh;* engine).

Here are another couple of questions you may need to ask about driving in general:

- ✔ **As estradas em . . . são boas ou ruins?** (ahz eh-*stdah*-dahz ang . . . *sah*-ooh *boh*-ahz oh hoo-*eenz;* Are the roads in . . . [location] good or bad?)

- ✔ **Tem um mecânico por aqui?** (*tang* oong meh-*kah*-nee-koh poh ah-*kee;* Is there a mechanic around here?)

The shapes and colors of the **placas** (*plah*-kahz; road signs) in Brazil are pretty much the same as in English-speaking countries.

Using the Arriving Verb: Chegar

Chegar (sheh-*gah;* Arriving/to arrive) someplace is what you're trying to do when you enter an **avião** (ah-vee-*ah*-ooh; plane), **ônibus** (*oh*-nee-boos; bus), or **táxi** (*talk*-see; taxi). Here are the basic conjugations:

Conjugation	*Pronunciation*
eu chego	*eh*-ooh *sheh*-goh
você chega	voh-*seh sheh*-gah
ele/ela chega	*eh*-lee/*eh*-lah *sheh*-gah
nós chegamos	nohz sheh-*gah*-mooz
eles/elas chegam	*eh*-leez/*eh*-lahz sheh-*gah*-ooh

The past tense of **chegar** looks like this (see Chapter 9 for more on forming the past tense):

Conjugation	*Pronunciation*
eu chegei	*eh*-ooh sheh-*gay*
você chegou	voh-*seh* sheh-*goh*
ele/ela chegou	*eh*-lee/*eh*-lah sheh-*goh*
nós chegamos	nohz sheh-*gah*-mooz
eles/elas chegaram	*eh*-leez/*eh*-lahz sheh-*gah*-dah-oong

Here are some example sentences that use both tenses:

- **Eles chegaram ontem.** (*eh*-leez sheh-*gah*-ah-oong *ohn*-tang; They arrived yesterday.)
- **Eu chegei tarde.** (*eh*-ooh sheh-*gay tah*-jee; I arrived late.)
- **Você sempre chega na hora certa.** (voh-*seh sem*-pdee *sheh*-gah nah *oh*-dah *seh*-tah; You always arrive at the right time.)
- **Chegou uma carta pelo correio.** (sheh-*goh* ooh-mah *kah*-tah peh-loh koh-*hay*-oh; A letter arrived in the mail.)

You can also use **chegar** in its infinitive form — that is, not conjugated. In this case, **chegar** stays **chegar**. Use the infinitive pretty much any time you'd use the words *to arrive* in English, as well as when you'd use *arriving* as a noun:

- **Chegar uma hora tarde é rude.** (sheh-*gah* ooh-mah *oh*-dah *tah*-jee *eh hoo*-jee; Arriving an hour late is rude.)
- **Tenta chegar cedo.** (*ten*-tah sheh-*gah seh*-doo; Try to arrive on time.)
- **Quando ela vai chegar?** (*kwahn*-doh *eh*-lah *vah*-ee sheh-*gah;* When is she going to arrive?)
- **Vou chegar logo.** (voh sheh-*gah loh*-goo; I'm going to arrive soon.)

If you'd like to find out more about how to use infinitives to help you talk about the future, see Chapter 15.

Chega! (*sheh*-gah) is a popular and useful expression that means *Stop it!* **Chegei!** (sheh-*gay*) is what you say when you arrive someplace — *I'm here!*

Using the Leaving Verb: Sair

Sair (sah-*ee;* to leave) is a verb Brazilians use to talk about *leaving.* If you read Chapter 8, you may already know that **sair** means *to go out,* as in *to go out and party.* **Sair** doesn't have that easy **-ar** ending. And it's a little weird that the word is so short; you have to conjugate based just on the root **sa.** But the rules ultimately follow what you know (see Chapter 2 for more on conjugations).

Here are the basic conjugations of **sair:**

Conjugation	Pronunciation
eu saio	*eh*-ooh *sah*-ee-oh
você sai	voh-*seh sah*-ee
ele/ela sai	*eh*-lee/*eh*-lah *sah*-ee
nós saimos	nohz sah-*ee*-mooz
eles/elas saem	*eh*-leez/*eh*-lahz *sah*-ang

And this is the past tense (more on the past tense is in Chapter 9):

Conjugations	Pronunciations
eu sai	*eh*-ooh sah-*ee*
você saiu	voh-*seh* sah-*ee*-ooh
ele/ela saiu	*eh*-lee/*eh*-lah sah-*ee*-ooh
nós saimos	nohz sah-*ee*-mooz
eles/elas sairam	*eh*-leez/*eh*-lahz sah-*ee*-dah-ooh

Here are some example sentences using **sair:**

- ✔ **Ela já saiu.** (*eh*-lah *zhah* sah-*ee*-ooh; She already left.)

- ✔ **O ônibus sai às onze e quarenta.** (ooh *oh*-nee-boos *sah*-ee ahz *ohn*-zee ee kwah-*den*-tah; The bus leaves at 11:40.)

- ✔ **A que horas sai o avião para Londres?** (ah *kee oh*-dahz *sah*-ee ooh ah-vee-*ah*-ooh pah-dah *lonh*-dreez; What time does the plane leave for London?)

Sair is also used to say *to come out:*

- ✔ **O relatório sai em breve.** (ooh heh-lah-*toh*-dee-ooh *sah*-ee ang *bdeh*-vee; The report will come out shortly.)

- ✔ **O novo disco da Madonna sai amanhã.** (ooh *noh*-voo *jees*-koh dah mah-*doh*-nah *sah*-ee ah-mah-*yah;* Madonna's new CD comes out tomorrow.)

- ✔ **O coelho está saindo de um buraco.** (ooh koh-*eh*-ooh-yoh eh-*stah* sah-*een*-doh jee *oong* boo-*dah*-koh; The rabbit is coming out of a hole.)

Asking about Timeliness: Early, Late, on Time

You may have noticed that some terms in this chapter express timeliness. The main terms to know are **cedo** (*seh*-doo; early) and **atrasado** (ah-tdah-*zah*-doo; late). **O atraso** (ooh ah-*tdah*-zoo) refers to *the delay*. (For information on telling time, check out Chapter 8.)

Chegar na hora certa (sheh-*gah* nah *oh*-dah *seh*-tah) means *to arrive on time*, and **chegar a tempo** (sheh-*gah* ah tem-*poo*) means *to arrive in time*. **Pontual** (*pon*-too-*ah*-ooh) means *punctual*. Here are some sentences that put these terms to use:

- ✔ **O avião está atrasado.** (ooh ah-vee-*ah*-ooh eh-*stah* ah-tdah-*zah*-doo; The plane is late.)

- ✔ **Está atrasado o ônibus?** (eh-*stah* ah-tdah-*zah*-doo ooh *oh*-nee-boos; Is the bus late?)

- ✔ **É sempre melhor chegar cedo.** (eh *sem*-pdee mel-*yoh* sheh-*gah seh*-doo; It's always better to arrive early.)

- ✔ **Acha que vamos poder chegar a tempo?** (*ah*-shah kee *vah*-mooz poh-*deh* sheh-*gah* ah *tem*-poh; Do you think we'll be able to arrive on time?)

- ✔ **O metrô de São Paulo é muito pontual.** (ooh meh-*tdoh* jee sah-ooh *pah*-ooh-loh eh moh-*ee*-toh pon-too-*ah*-ooh; The São Paulo subway system is very punctual.)

- ✔ **O atraso vai ser de uma hora.** (ooh ah-*tdah*-zoo *vah*-ee *seh* jee ooh-mah *oh*-dah; The delay will be an hour.)

- ✔ **Quase não chegamos a tempo.** (*kwah*-zee nah-ooh sheh-*gah*-mohz ah *tem*-poh; We almost didn't arrive in time.)

Using the Waiting Verb: Esperar

Unfortunately, if you're talking about transportation, you have to talk about waiting, too! But don't think of waiting at a Brazilian **rodoviária** (hoh-doh-vee-ah-dee-ah; central bus station) or **aeroporto** (ah-*eh*-doh-*poh*-too; airport) as a pain: Pick up a local **revista** (heh-*vee*-stah; magazine) to soak up Brazilian culture, or just watch the movement and listen to the people around you. Become an anthropologist.

This is how you conjugate **esperar** (eh-speh-*dah;* to wait/to wait for):

Conjugation	Pronunciation
eu espero	*eh*-ooh eh-*speh*-doo
você espera	voh-*seh* eh-*speh*-dah
ele/ela espera	*eh*-lee/*eh*-lah eh-*speh*-dah
nós esperamos	nohz eh-speh-*dah*-mooz
eles/elas esperam	*eh*-leez/*eh*-lahz eh-*speh*-dah-ooh

And the past tense (see Chapter 9 for more on talking about the past):

Conjugation	Pronunciation
eu esperei	*eh*-ooh eh-speh-*day*
você esperou	voh-*seh* eh-speh-*doh*
ele/ela esperou	*eh*-lee/*eh*-lah eh-speh-*doh*
nós esperamos	nohz eh-speh-*dah*-mooz
eles/elas esperaram	*eh*-leez/*eh*-lahz eh-speh-*dah*-dah-ooh

Here are some example sentences:

- ✔ **Eu esperei duas horas.** (*eh*-ooh eh-speh-*day* doo-ahz *oh*-dahz; I waited two hours.)

- ✔ **Espera aqui, por favor.** (eh-*speh*-dah ah-*kee,* poh fah-*voh;* Wait here, please.)

- ✔ **Esperaram a decisão do juiz.** (eh-speh-*dah*-dah-ooh ah deh-see-*zah*-ooh doh zhoo-*eez;* They waited for the judge's decision.)

Talkin' the Talk

Ofélia and **Sofia** are two elderly ladies waiting to see a doctor. They gossip about the waiting time.

Ofélia: **Meu deus do céu, não agüento esperar mais.**
meh-ooh *deh*-ooz doo *seh*-ooh, *nah*-ooh ah-*gwehn*-toh eh-speh-*dah mah*-eez.
My God in heaven, I can't stand waiting any longer.

Sofia: **Calma, tem que ser paciente. É bom para a saúde.**
kah-ooh-mah, tang kee *seh* pah-see-*ang*-shee. eh
boh-oong pah-dah ah sah-*oo*-jee.
Don't worry, you have to be patient. It's good for
your health.

Ofélia: **O que você diz? Está louca.**
ooh *kee* voh-*seh jeez*? eh-*stah loh*-kah.
What did you say? You're crazy.

Sofia: **Esperei no hospital ontem quatro horas.**
eh-speh-*day* noo oh-spee-*tah*-ooh *ohn*-tang *kwah*-
tdoh *oh*-dahz.
I waited in the hospital yesterday four hours.

Ofélia: **Sério?**
seh-dee-ooh?
Are you serious?

Sofia: **Sério. Mas fiz muitos amigos.**
seh-dee-ooh. maz *feez* moh-ee-tohz ah-*mee*-gooz.
Serious. But I made a lot of friends.

Words to Know

Meu deus do céu.	meh-ooh deh-ooz doo seh-ooh	My goodness. (Literally: My God in heaven.)
não aguento	nah-ooh ah-gwehn-toh	I can't stand
Calma.	kah-ooh-mah	Don't worry.
paciente	pah-see-ang-shee	patient
O que voce diz?	ooh kee voh-seh jeez	What did you say?
louca	loh-kah	crazy

Fun & Games

You've decided to do a heptathlon (you know, like a triathlon, except with seven types of activities) in Brazil. Okay, you'll just be sitting and enjoying the ride in most cases – not exerting your physical strength – but it'll be a challenge nonetheless.

Match the drawing of each of the modes of transportation you plan to use to its Portuguese equivalent. Then flip to Appendix C for the answers.

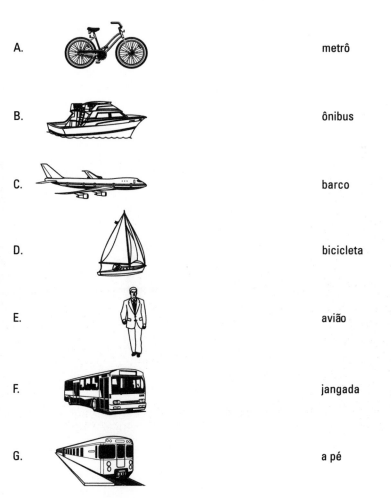

A.   metrô

B.   ônibus

C.   barco

D.   bicicleta

E.   avião

F.   jangada

G.   a pé

Chapter 15

Planning a Trip

. . . .

. . . .

1 don't know whether it's **verdade** (veh-*dah*-jee; true) that the **privada** (pdee-*vah*-dah; toilet) flushes in the opposite direction in the Southern Hemisphere, as it's said. I wanted to do an experiment before taking off to live in Brazil but somehow never got around to it. Maybe you can try it . . . .

What I do know firsthand, though, is how strange baking in the **sol** (*soh*-ooh; sun) in mid-January feels. That's right — wintertime in the Northern Hemisphere is summertime in Brazil. When you're planning a **viagem** (vee-*ah*-zhang; trip) to Brazil, this seasonal switcheroo is important to consider. This chapter tells you how to choose the best times to travel and lists a few places you may want to check out.

Picking the Best Time of Year for Your Trip

Prices are double, sometimes triple, for the Brazilian summer — **dezembro até março** (deh-*zehm*-bdoh ah-*teh mah*-soh; December to March). The summertime price hike is due more to the surge of Brazilian vacationers than foreign tourists. Foreign tourists flock to Brazil year-round, whereas most Brazilians go **de férias** (jee *feh*-dee-ahz; on vacation) in the **verão** (veh-*dah*-ooh; summer) only.

If you like crowds and **festas** (*feh*-stahz; parties) and want to meet lots of native Brazilians, visit Brazil during their **verão.** If you prefer to travel on the cheap, go during the Northern Hemisphere's summer months, the Brazilian equivalent of **inverno** (een-*veh*-noh; winter).

In Brazil's North and Northeast, the weather's **quente** (*kang*-chee; hot) year-round. In the North (Amazon), rain is likely at some point in the day all year round, so bring your **guarda-chuva** (*gwah*-dah *shoo*-vah; umbrella). And if you visit the Northeast from **abril até julho** (ah-*bdee*-ooh ah-*teh joo*-lyoh; April to July), the chance of **chuva** (*shoo*-vah; rain) is high. Brazilians call these three months **a época de chuva** (ah *eh*-poh-kah jee *shoo*-vah; the rainy season). On the other hand, the rain usually doesn't last all day. And having to wait out the tropical storms can be kind of relaxing.

In the South and Southeast (where Rio and São Paulo are located), weather patterns are a bit different; **dezembro até março** (deh-*zem*-bdoh ah-*teh mah*-soo) is hot and humid with a high probability of rainstorms, while **juno até setembro** (*zhoon*-yoh ah-*teh* seh-*tehm*-bdoh; June to September) is often sunny and dry.

Pull out a **mapa do Brasil** (*mah*-pah doh bdah-*zee*-ooh; map of Brazil). North of Rio is basically **quente** year round, but with considerable **chuva** from **abril até julho.** South of Rio has a real **inverno** from **abril até julho;** temperatures get pretty **frío** (*fdee*-oh; cold) the higher up you go in altitude. But the beaches there can still be a pleasant 70 degrees in July.

As you're thinking about the right time to visit Brazil, I'll give you the months of the year. Note that in Portuguese, the first letter of the name of each month isn't capitalized like it is in English:

- **janeiro** (zhah-*nay*-doh; January)
- **fevereiro** (feh-veh-*day*-doh; February)
- **março** (*mah*-soo; March)
- **abril** (ah-*bdee*-ooh; April)
- **maio** (*my*-oh; May)
- **junho** (*zhoon*-yoh; June)
- **julho** (*zhool*-yoh; July)
- **agosto** (ah-*goh*-stoh; August)
- **setembro** (seh-*tehm*-bdoh; September)
- **outubro** (oh-*too*-bdoh; October)
- **novembro** (noh-*vem*-bdoh; November)
- **dezembro** (deh-*zem*-bdoh; December)

To say *in* a certain month, use **em** (ang) plus the name of the month. Here are some example sentences:

✔ **Vou para o Brasil em maio.** (*voh pah*-dah ooh bdah-*zee*-ooh ang *my*-oh; I'm going to Brazil in May.)

✔ **Ela retornou do Canadá em novembro.** (*eh*-lah heh-toh-*noh* doo kah-nah-*dah* ang noh-*vehm*-bdoh; She returned from Canada in November.)

Talkin' the Talk

 Caio dreams about visiting the Amazon, but he only has vacation days off in June — right during the rainy season. He asks his friend **Fábio**, a biologist who's spent a lot of time in the Amazon, for advice.

Caio:	**Oi Fábio, já foi para o Amazonas no inverno?** *oh*-ee *fah*-bee-ooh, *zhah foh*-ee pah-dah ooh ah-mah-*zoh*-nahz noo een-*veh*-noh? Hey Fabio, have you been to the Amazon in the winter?
Fábio:	**Já. Por quê?** *zhah*. poh *keh?* Yeah. Why?
Caio:	**Qual mês foi?** *kwah*-ooh *mez foh*-ee? What month was it?
Fábio:	**Fui em junho.** fwee ang *zhoon*-yoh. I went in June.
Caio:	**Chovéu muito?** shoh-*veh*-ooh moh-ee-too? Did it rain a lot?
Fábio:	**Chovéu muito pela manhã, mas teve sol pela tarde.** shoh-*veh*-ooh moh-ee-too *peh*-lah mahn-*yah*, mah-eez *teh*-vee *soh*-ooh peh-lah *tah*-jee. It rained a lot in the morning, but it was sunny in the afternoon.
Caio:	**Ah é? Que bom.** ah *eh?* kee *boh*-oong. Really? Great.

Words to Know

Já foi . . . ?	zhah <u>foh</u>-ee	Have you been . . . ?
no inverno	noo een-<u>veh</u>-noh	in the winter
chovéu	shoh-<u>veh</u>-ooh	rained
pela manhã	<u>peh</u>-lah mahn-<u>yah</u>	in the morning
teve sol	<u>teh</u>-vee <u>soh</u>-ooh	it was sunny
pela tarde	<u>peh</u>-lah <u>tah</u>-jee	in the afternoon

Specifying Times and Dates

Está planejando uma viagem? (eh-*stah* plah-neh-*zhahn*-doh ooh-mah vee-*ah*-zhang; You're planning a trip?). You may want to talk about days of the month and time of day for your odyssey. (To find out how to pronounce numbers, see Chapter 2. The preceding section gives you months of the year, and you can read up on time of day in Chapter 8.)

Brazilians tend to use military time in formal situations, including when they're doing business; to convert to civilian time in the afternoon, you can subtract 12 from the time someone gives you. If you're at an **agência de viagens** (ah-*zhang*-see-ah jee vee-*ah*-zhangz; travel agency), the agent may offer several different travel times.

To say *on* a certain day, use **no** (noh) plus the date. Use **no dia . . .** (date) **de . . .** (month) (noo *jee*-ah . . . jee . . .) to say *on such-and-such day of such-and-such month*. For example, **no dia quinze de setembro** (noo *jee*-ah *keen*-zee jee seh-*tehm*-bdoh) is September 15.

Check out some phrases that give you dates and times:

- ✔ **no dia três de outubro, as oito e vinte e cinco da manhã** (noo *jee*-ah *tdehz* jee oh-*too*-bdoh ahz *oh*-ee-toh ee *veen*-chee ee *sing*-koh dah mahn-*yah*; on October 3, at 8:25 a.m.)

- ✔ **no dia vinte e dois de agosto, as vinte horas** (noo *jee*-ah *veen*-chee ee *doh*-eez jee ah-*goh*-stoh ahz *veen*-chee *oh*-dahz; on August 22, at 8:00 p.m. [2000 hours])

✔ **no dia dezessete de dezembro, as vinte e uma horas e cinquenta minutos** (noo *jee*-ah dehz-ee-*seh*-chee jee deh-*zem*-bdoh ahz *veen*-chee ee *ooh*-mah *oh*-dahz ee sing-*kwen*-tah mee-*noo*-tohz; on December 17, at 9:50 p.m. [2150 hours)

✔ **no dia quatorze de maio, as dez e quinze da manhã** (noo *jee*-ah kah-*toh*-zee jee *my*-oh ahz *dez* ee *keen*-zee dah mahn-*yah;* on May 14, at 10:15 a.m.)

Even though you usually don't need to express the **ano** (*ah*-noh; year) when you make travel plans, you may want to talk about past travels or trips you're planning years in advance. Most years people refer to start with either 19 or 20. If the year's in the 1900s, say **mil novescentos e . . .** (*mee*-ooh noh-vee *sehn*-tohz ee; Nineteen . . .) If the year's in the current **século** (*seh*-koo-loh; century), say **dois mil e . . .** (*doh*-eez *mee*-ooh ee; Two-thousand . . .).

When was the last time you went on a major trip? Check out some possible answers:

✔ **mil novescentos e cinquenta e dois** (*mee*-ooh noh-vee-*sehn*-tohz ee sing-*kwehn*-tah ee *doh*-eez; 1952)

✔ **mil novescentos e oitenta e três** (*mee*-ooh noh-vee-*sehn*-tohz ee oh-ee-*tehn*-tah ee *tdehz;* 1983)

✔ **mil novescentos e setenta e quatro** (*mee*-ooh noh-vee-*sehn*-tohz ee seh-*tehn*-tah ee *kwah*-tdoh; 1974)

✔ **dois mil e um** (*doh*-eez *mee*-ooh ee *oong;* 2001)

✔ **dois mil e seis** (*doh*-eez *mee*-ooh ee *say*-eez; 2006)

Talkin' the Talk

Daniela is planning a trip to **Londres** (*lone*-dreez; London). She's just checked a few airline Web sites, and asks her mom for her opinion on the best option.

Daniela: **Oi mãe, o que você acha? Escuta.**
            oh-ee *mah*-ee, ooh *kee* voh-seh *ah*-shah?
            eh-*skoo*-tah.
            Hey Mom, what do you think? Listen.

Mom: **Fala.**
            fah-lah.
            Tell me (*Literally:* Speak).

Daniela: **Tem duas opções que parecem boas.**
             tang *doo*-ahz op-*soh*-eez kee pah-*deh*-sang *boh*-ahz.
             There's two options that seem good.

Mom: **Ótimo.**
             oh-chee-moh.
             Great.

Daniela: **A Varig tem um vôo que sai no dia quinze, às sete da manhã, por mil e quinhentos reais.**
             ah *vah*-dee-gee *tang* oong *voh* kee *sah*-ee noo *jee*-ah *keen*-zee, ahz *seh*-chee dah mahn-*yah*, poh *mee*-ooh ee keen-*yehn*-tooz hay-*eyes*.
             Varig (a Brazilian airline) has a flight that leaves on the 15th, at 7:00 in the morning, for 1,500 reais.

Mom: **O preço não está mal.**
             ooh *pdeh*-soo *nah*-ooh eh-*stah mah-ooh*.
             The price isn't bad.

Daniela: **Só que sai muito cedo.**
             soh kee *sah*-ee moh-ee-toh *seh*-doo.
             It's just that it leaves really early.

Mom: **É claro . . .**
             eh *klah*-doh . . .
             Right . . .

Daniela: **Bom, e a British Airways tem um que sai no dia dezesseis, às dezessete horas, por mil e novecentos reais.**
             boh-oong, ee ah *bdee*-teesh ah-ehd-way-eez *tang* oong kee *sah*-ee noo *jee*-ah dez-ee-*say*-eez, ahz *dez*-ee-*seh*-chee *oh*-dahz, poh *mee*-ooh ee noh-vee-*sehn*-tooz hay-*eyes*.
             Okay, and British Airways has one that leaves on the 16th, at 5:00 p.m., for 1,900 reais.

Mom: **Acho melhor a primeira opção.**
             ah-shoo mehl-*yoh* ah pdee-*may*-dah op-*sah*-ooh.
             I think the first option's better.

Daniela: **E teria mais um dia também . . .**
             ee teh-*dee*-ah *mah*-eez oong *jee*-ah tahm-*bang* . . .
             And I'd have another day, too . . .

Mom:	**Filha, compre logo! As promoções na Internet não duram muito.**	
	feel-yah, *kohm*-pdee *loh*-goo! ahz *pdoh*-moh-*soh*-eez nah *een*-teh-*neh*-chee *nah*-ooh *doo*-dah-ooh moh-ee-toh.	
	Daughter, buy it ASAP! Good deals don't last long on the Internet.	

Words to Know

O que você acha?	ooh <u>kee</u> voh-seh <u>ah</u>-shah	What do you think?
Escuta.	eh-<u>skoo</u>-tah	Listen.
vôo	voh	flight
não está mal	<u>nah</u>-ooh eh-<u>stah</u> <u>mah</u>-ooh	it's not bad
Só que . . .	<u>soh</u> kee	It's just that . . .
cedo	<u>seh</u>-doo	early
teria	teh-<u>dee</u>-ah	would have
mais um dia	<u>mah</u>-eez <u>oong</u> <u>jee</u>-ah	another day
compre	<u>kohmp</u>-dee	buy
promoções	<u>pdoh</u>-moh-<u>soh</u>-eez	good deals/sales promotions
na Internet	<u>nah</u> <u>een</u>-teh-<u>neh</u>-chee	on the internet

Deciding Where to Go

In this section, I give you some highlights of places to go in Brazil, as well as a little bit about what you can expect from each one. I list the most popular tourist destinations in the country, for Brazilians and foreigners alike. These places feature some intriguing natural, urban, and historical wonders. But of course, veering off the beaten path is fun, too.

Brazil's airlines have daily flights to all parts of Brazil, so you can visit more than one region. The biggest companies are called **Varig** (*vah*-dee-gee), **Tam** (tah), **Vasp** (*vahs*-pee), and **Gol** (*goh*-ooh). Check out Chapter 14 for more on traveling by air.

The North

The North is not a very touristy area, which may delight those of you who like to make your own tracks.

Pará (pah-*dah*) state has beautiful beaches, and the **Lençois Maranhenses** (lehn-*soh*-eez mah-dahn-*yehn*-seez; turquoise lagoons amid white sand dunes) in **Maranhão** (mah-dahn-*yah*-ooh) state are like nothing else on Earth. **Belém** (beh-*lang*), the capital of **Pará** state, and **São Luis** (*sah*-ooh loo-*eez*), the capital of **Maranhão** state, are relaxed, culturally interesting cities to check out.

In the North, you can also find the world-famous Amazon rain forest. Most people fly into **Manáus** (mah-*nah*-ooz), the capital of **Amazonas** (ah-mah-*soh*-nahz) state and the biggest city in the Brazilian part of the Amazon. From **Manáus,** you can stay at several jungle lodges within a couple of hours of the city. You'll likely stay somewhere close to the **Rio Amazonas** (*hee*-ooh ah-mah-*soh*-nahz; Amazon River), because that's where most lodges and relative civilization are. You'll get a chance to see local indigenous culture, as well as see local fauna like **piranhas** (pee-*dahn*-yahz; piranas), **macacos** (mah-*kah*-kooz; monkeys), and **bicho-preguiças** (*bee*-shoo pdeh-*gee*-sahz; sloths). **Parintins** (pah-deen-*cheenz*), a town a few hours from **Manáus,** is famous for its Carnaval in July.

The Northeast

If you want to see what many people consider the country's best beaches, come here. Tourists often make a holiday in Brazil just by connecting the dots between the following places.

Bahia (bah-*ee*-ah) is the most popular destination in the Northeast. It's the place for relaxing and listening to music; many of Brazil's most famous musicians are from **Bahia. Salvador** (*sah*-ooh-vah-*doh*) is the capital, and it has beautiful old colonial architecture in the city center. **Bahia** is also the place to see **capoeira** (kah-poh-*ay*-dah), a world-famous martial arts form. Popular beach places to go in **Bahia** include **Morro de São Paulo** (*moh*-hoo jee sah-ooh *pah*-ooh-loo), **Itacaré** (ee-tah-kah-*deh*), and **Trancoso** (tdahn-*koh*-zoo), which are all rustic, and **Porto Seguro** (*poh*-too seh-*goo*-doo), which is urban and more expensive. In the interior of the state is a majestic plateau-filled area called **Chapada Diamantina** (shah-*pah*-dah jee-ah-mahn-*chee*-nah), which hikers can appreciate.

Besides Bahia, the Northeast has **Recife e Olinda** (heh-*see*-fee ee oh-*leen*-dah), two neighboring cities along the coast. **Recife** is very urban, while **Olinda** is maybe the most charming little town in Brazil, with its amazing views, narrow streets, colonial architecture, and emphasis on local art.

Rio Grande do Norte (hee-ooh *gdahn*-jee doo *noh*-chee), which boasts sand dunes and dolphins, and **Ceará** (see-ah-*dah*), which has turquoise water, are northeastern states famous for their beaches. My personal favorite beach is **Pipa** (*pee*-pah), in **Rio Grande do Norte**. It's pure magic, with its dolphins, views of turquoise waters from a bluff, rainbow-colored rocks, fun little town, and perfect mix of locals and tourists. And with just a few places to go out, you meet them all!

The Central-West

The Central-West region is historically where a lot of mining was done in Brazil. It's known today for its rock formations, mysticism, great food, and exotic animals in the plains and wetlands.

The **Pantanal** (pahn-tah-*nah*-ooh) is Brazil's Serengeti — its African plains. Here's the best place by far to see wild animals in Brazil. Spotting animals here is easier than in the Amazon simply because the **Pantanal** has a lot of open space. **Campo Grande** (*kahm*-poh *gdahn*-jee) and **Bonito** (boo-*nee*-too) are the two main towns in the **Pantanal;** both are located in **Mato Grosso do Sul** (*mah*-toh *gdoh*-soo doo *soo*) state. The area is huge, so going with a tour here, rather than just renting a car, is best. And the tour guides can lead you to all the magnificent flocks of rare **pássaros** (*pah*-sah-dohz; birds), giant **pintados** (peen-*tah*-dooz; catfish), gargantuan **tamuandá bandeiras** (tah-moo-ahn-*dah* bahn-*day*-dahz; anteaters), and fearsome **serpentes** (seh-*pen*-cheez; snakes)!

Minas Gerais (*mee*-nahz zheh-*dah*-eez; General Mines) state has no beaches, but it has some of the tastiest food in Brazil and some of the friendliest locals. It's full of historic towns with colonial Portuguese architecture, and it has lots of old mines to check out. The most famous town is called **Ouro Preto** (*oh*-ooh-doh *pdeh*-toh; Black Gold), named after the gold mines there. There's even a town in **Minas** (the state's nickname) that's famous for UFO sightings, called **São Tomé das Letras** (*sah*-ooh toh-*meh* dahz *leh*-tdahz).

The Southeast

This region is considered the most sophisticated in Brazil, with the country's two richest and most famous cities. Here you can find the best restaurants in the country, as well as all the cultural joys and the horrors stemming from poverty that are typical of any megalopolis in the world.

Rio (*hee*-ooh) is a gorgeous city, with its hills, fabulous urban beaches, **o Cristo** (ooh *kdees*-too; Christ the Redeemer statue), **Pão de Açúcar** (*pah*-ooh jee ah-*soo*-kah; Sugarloaf rock — with a cable car to get there), and lively locals. Popular beach places to go near **Rio** are **Ilha Grande** (*eel*-yah *gdahn*-jee), which is rustic, **Búzios** (*boo*-zee-oohz), which is sophisticated, and **Paraty** (pah-dah-*chee*), which is historic. Also worth a quick trip is **Petrópolis** (peh-*tdoh*-poh-leez), where the Portuguese royalty once lived.

Many foreigners are surprised to find out that most Brazilians refer to **Rio** by its full name, **Rio de Janeiro** (*hee*-ooh jee zhah-*nay*-doo). Brazilians don't generally nickname it *Rio*.

São Paulo (sah-ooh *pah*-ooh-loo) is great for anthropologists. This city has huge immigrant populations from Japan, Lebanon, and Italy, among other parts of the world. It's also one of the largest cities on Earth, with more than 18 million people. Art and restaurant buffs appreciate **São Paulo's** nightlife and cultural institutions — the best Brazil has to offer. But the heavy traffic makes transportation difficult, and the city isn't very pretty. **São Paulo** state beaches are at least two hours from the city of **São Paulo,** and they're gorgeous.

The South

Here the color of Brazilians' skin gets lighter, as you see a concentration of the descendants of German and Polish immigrants. The sea water also changes down here — it gets colder.

Rio Grande do Sul (*hee*-ooh *gdahn*-jee doo *soo*) state shares a border, as well as many cultural traditions, with Argentina. Here's where the famous Brazilian **churrasqueiras** (choo-hahs-*kay*-dahz; Brazilian all-you-can-eat steakhouses with a salad buffet) originate from. The capital, **Porto Alegre** (*poh*-too ah-*leh*-gdee), is a clean, safe, and pleasant city, and the people are polite but a bit more introverted compared to the rest of Brazil. The state hosts Brazil's most famous film festival in **Gramado** (gdah-*mah*-doo), a town in the interior. Hikers may like the **Serra Gaúcha** (*seh*-hah gah-*ooh*-shah) — the interior of the state, with its vast plains and plateaus reminiscent of the American West. By the way, this is the only Brazilian state on the Atlantic coast not known for its beaches!

Florianópolis (floh-dee-ah-*noh*-poh-lees) is the capital of Santa Catarina state and is known for its beautiful people, who often lounge on the beaches. It's on an island called **Santa Catarina** (*sahn*-tah kah-tah-*dee*-nah), with at least 32 stunning beaches — one for every day of the month, as the local tourism board would have you believe. This city's a modern place, without much emphasis on Brazilian culture and traditions. It attracts many Argentine tourists in the summer.

Iguaçu Falls is in southern Brazil, on the border of **Paraná** (pah-dah-*nah*) state and Argentina. The name in Portuguese is **Foz de Iguaçu** (*fohz* jee ee-gwah-*soo*). This attraction is a canyon filled with 250 breathtaking **cataratas** (*kah*-tah-*dah*-tahz; waterfalls). It was way more impressive and beautiful to me than Niagara, which has just two waterfalls.

Talking about Going: The Verb Ir

I'm excited to talk about this one. The verb **ir** (ee; to go/to be going) is so useful. You may feel like you've advanced by leaps and bounds in your Portuguese with this section. The verb **ir** is very common in Portuguese, just like all phrases that use *go* are so common in English.

First take a look at the present tense (the here and now) conjugations for **ir:**

Conjugation	Pronunciation
eu vou	*eh*-ooh *voh*
você vai	voh-*seh vah*-ee
ele/ela vai	*eh*-lee/*eh*-lah *vah*-ee
nós vamos	nohz *vah*-mohz
eles/elas vão	*eh*-leez/*eh*-lahz *vah*-ooh

Here are some sample sentences using **ir:**

- ✔ **Ela vai para a praia.** (*eh*-lah *vah*-ee *pah*-dah ah *pdah*-ee-ah; She's going to the beach.)

- ✔ **Você vai para o show?** (voh-*seh vah*-ee pah-dah ooh *shoh;* Are you going to the show?)

- ✔ **Eu vou para a minha casa.** (*eh*-ooh *voh* pah-dah ah ming-yah *kah*-zah; I'm going to my house.)

- ✔ **Nós vamos ao cinema.** (nohz *vah*-mooz *ah*-ooh see-*neh*-mah; We're going to the movies.)

- ✔ **Eles vão para o concerto.** (*eh*-leez *vah*-ooh *pah*-dah ooh kohn-*seh*-toh; They're going to the concert.)

Note that **ir** often goes with **para** (*pah*-dah). **Ir para** (*eeh pah*-dah) means *to go to.*

Now for the exciting part of the *going* verb. Use **ir** conjugated, add another verb, and voilá: You can talk about the future: *You're going to . . ., He's going to . . ., We're going to . . ..* For example, **Nós vamos dançar** (*nohz* vah-mohz dahn-*sah*) means *We're going to dance.*

Try the magic first with the verb **viajar** (vee-ah-*zhah*; to travel/to take a trip), because that's what this chapter's about. In each of these phrases, someone is *going to take a trip/going to travel:*

Conjugation	Pronunciation
eu vou viajar	*eh*-ooh *voh* vee-ah-*zhah*
você vai viajar	voh-*seh vah*-ee vee-ah-*zhah*
ele/ela vai viajar	*eh*-lee/*eh*-lah *vah*-ee vee-ah-*zhah*
nós vamos viajar	*nohz* vah-mohz vee-ah-*zhah*
eles/elas vão viajar	*eh*-leez/*eh*-lahz *vah*-ooh vee-ah-*zhah*

Take a glance at some examples that use the future tense:

 ✔ **Eu vou viajar de trem.** (*eh*-ooh *voh* vee-ah-*zhah* jee *tdang;* I'm going to travel by train.)

 ✔ **Você vai viajar de ônibus.** (voh-*seh vah*-ee vee-ah-*zhah* jee *oh*-nee-boos; You're going to travel by bus.)

 ✔ **Ela vai viajar de avião.** (*eh*-lah *vah*-ee vee-ah-*zhah* jee *ah*-vee-*ah*-ooh; She's going to travel by plane.)

Brazilians like to say *who's* going to do something except when they're talking about **nós** (nohz; we) and **eu** (*eh*-ooh; I). They often leave out the **nós** or the **eu** and just start the sentence with the verb, **vamos** or **vou.**

Now you can have fun using the formula **ir** plus a verb to talk about all kinds of things in the future:

 ✔ **Vamos fazer o jantar.** (*vah*-mohz fah-*zeh* ooh zhan-*tah;* We're going to make dinner.)

 ✔ **Você vai cantar para nós?** (voh-*seh vah*-ee kahn-*tah pah*-dah *nohz;* You're going to sing for us?)

 ✔ **Ele vai ligar para ela.** (*eh*-lee *vah*-ee lee-*gah pah*-dah *eh*-lah; He's going to call her.)

✔ **Vou fazer o trabalho.** (*voh* fah-*zeh* ooh tdah-*bahl*-yoh; I'm going to do the job.)

✔ **Você vai assistir aquela programa de TV?** (voh-*seh vah*-ee ah-sees-*chee* ah-*keh*-lah pdoh-*gdah*-mah jee teh-*veh;* Are you going to watch that TV show?)

✔ **Vamos sair?** (*vah*-mohz sah-*eeh;* Are we going to go out?)

✔ **Vou comer.** (*voh* koh-*meh;* I'm going to eat.)

✔ **Vou no supermercado.** (*voh* noh *soo*-peh-meh-*kah*-doh; I'm going to the supermarket.)

✔ **Vou para a Europa no mês que vem.** (*voh* pah-dah ah eh-ooh-*doh*-pah noh *mez* kee *vang;* I'm going to Europe next month.)

Talkin' the Talk

Today is **Pedro's** (*pehd*-roh) first day of school. His mom is asking him what he's promised to do and not do today. Pay attention to how they use the verb **ir.**

Mom:	**O que vai fazer hoje, meu filho?** ooh *keh vah*-ee fah-*zeh oh*-zhee, *meh*-ooh *feel*-yoh? What are you going to do today, my son?
Pedro:	**Vou ser um bom menino.** voh *seh* oong *boh*-oong meh-*nee*-noh. I'm going to be a good boy.
Mom:	**E o que mais?** ee ooh *keh mah*-eez? And what else?
Pedro:	**Vou comer tudo no almoço.** voh koh-*meh too*-doo noh ah-ooh-*moh*-soo. I'm going to eat everything at lunch.
Mom:	**Muito bem. E o que não vai fazer?** moh-ee-toh *bang.* eeh ooh *keh nah*-ooh *vah*-ee fah-*zeh?* Very good. And what are you not going to do?
Pedro:	**Não vou falar quando a professora está falando.** *nah*-ooh *voh* fah-*lah* kwahn-doh eh-*stah* fah-*lahn*-doh ah pdoh-feh-*soh*-dah. I'm not going to talk when the teacher is talking.

Mom: **E o que mais?**
         ee ooh *kee mah*-eez?
         And what else?

Pedro: **Vou te esperar na frente da escola no final
         do dia.**
         voh chee eh-speh-*dah* nah *fden*-chee dah eh-*skoh*-lah
         noh fee-*nah*-ooh doo *jee*-ah.
         I'm going to wait for you in front of the school at the
         end of the day.

Mom: **Muito bom, Pedro. Eu te amo.**
         moh-ee-toh *boh*-oong, *pehd*-roh. *eh*-ooh chee
         ah-moh.
         Very good, Pedro. I love you.

Pedro: **Eu te amo também, mamãe.**
         eh-ooh chee *ah*-moh tahm-*bang*, *mah*-ee.
         I love you too, Mommy.

Words to Know

O que vai fazer?	*ooh* <u>kee</u> <u>vah</u>-ee fah-<u>zeh</u>	What are you going to do?
meu filho	<u>meh</u>-ooh <u>feel</u>-yoh	my son
menino	meh-<u>nee</u>-noh	boy
está falando	eh-<u>stah</u> fah-<u>lahn</u>-doh	is talking
professora	<u>pdoh</u>-feh-<u>soh</u>-dah	teacher
esperar	<u>eh</u>-speh-<u>dah</u>	to wait
no final *do dia*	noh fee-<u>nah</u>-ooh doh <u>jee</u>-ah	at the end of the day
Eu te amo.	<u>eh</u>-ooh chee <u>ah</u>-moh	I love you.

Fun & Games

Choosing when you're going to travel is step number one. Unscramble the names of the 12 months in Portuguese. Then decide whether each month is mostly in Brazil's spring, summer, winter, or fall (remember, their seasons are the opposite of those in the Northern Hemisphere). Flip to Appendix C for the answers.

1. zdeobmer

2. liabr

3. otsmbeer

4. ieajnor

5. oima

6. vfeeiorr

7. çomar

8. goatso

9. lhjuo

10. vnoembor

11. ojnhu

12. tbuouro

Chapter 16

Me Ajuda! Help! Handling Emergencies

....

In This Chapter

▶ Shouting for help after a robbery or other incident

▶ Preventing illness and getting medical help

▶ Using the searching, looking, and helping verbs: **Procurar, olhar,** and **ajudar**

▶ Talking about legal problems

....

*E*mergencies can happen anywhere, and you can handle them best if you're prepared. This chapter tells you how to deal with life's unexpected adventures.

Despite what you may have read or heard, Brazil is pretty **tranquilo** (tdahn-*kwee*-loh; calm) for visitors in terms of **roubos** (*hoh*-booz; robberies). If you use **bom senso** (boh-oong *sen*-soo; common sense), you'll be fine.

If you get hurt in the country, you may be glad to know that there are state-of-the-art **hospitais** (oh-spee-*tah*-eez; hospitals) and **médicos** (*meh*-jee-kooz; doctors) in most parts of Brazil, especially in major urban areas. But before you go, you may want to consider buying a **plano de seguro saúde** (*plah*-noh jee seh-*goo*-doh sah-*ooh*-jee; health insurance plan) specifically for travelers.

Here are some basic emergency terms to start you out:

▸ **Cuidado!** (kwee-*dah*-doh; Watch out!)

▸ **Rápido!** (*hah*-pee-doh; Quick!)

▸ **Vamos!** (*vah*-mooz; Let's go!)

▸ **Me ajuda!** (mee ah-*zhoo*-dah; Help me!)

▸ **Fogo!** (*foh*-goo; Fire!)

Stick 'em Up: What to Say (and Do) If You're Robbed

The places in which you're most likely to have a bad experience are the most touristy parts of the country — the cities of Rio and Salvador. Small towns and beach towns tend to be **seguro** (seh-*goo*-doh; safe).

Use the same precautions you'd use in any **lugar que não conhece** (loo-*gah* kee *nah*-ooh kohn-*yeh*-see; place you don't know): Avoid being out in the street late at night, don't wear expensive jewelry or watches, and ask locals which areas you should avoid.

Be extra careful during festivals like **Carnaval** (kah-nah-*vah*-ooh). Consider sticking your **dinheiro** (jing-*yay*-doh; money) in your **sapatos** (sah-*pah*-tohz; shoes). Also consider buying a money belt you can wear close to your belly, under your clothes. The good news is that you don't need much **dinheiro** to enjoy yourself during the festivities.

Pegar táxi (peh-*gah talk*-see; taking taxis) is fine — Brazilian taxi cab drivers don't rob the passengers like drivers do in some other countries.

Brazil is actually much less **seguro** for locals, especially **os ricos** (oohz *hee*-kooz; the rich ones) with nice **carros** (*kah*-hooz; cars). These people are often **preocupados** (pdeh-oh-koo-*pah*-dooz; worried) about **seqüestros** (seh-*kwehs*-tdooz; kidnappings), in which the **seqüestradores** (seh-*kweh*-stdah-*doh*-deez; kidnappers) demand **dinheiro** from the **família** (fah-*mee*-lee-ah; family) of the **vítima** (*vee*-chee-mah; victim).

A more recent **problema** (pdoh-*bleh*-mah; problem) is **sequestros relâmpagos** (seh-*kweh*-stdros heh-*lahm*-pah-gohz; lightning-speed kidnappings). In this case, the kidnappers usually kidnap a driver in his or her car, take the victim to an ATM, and ask that person to withdraw a wad of cash. Then they leave him or her alone. At most, the person is held captive overnight.

Having a car in Brazil makes you more of a robbery target. People sometimes rob drivers at stoplights, which is why a lot of drivers go through red lights late at night.

Don't panic!

So what should you do if you're being robbed? The local refrain is **Não reage** (*nah*-ooh hee-*ah*-zhee; Don't react). That means: Don't shout, don't try to get away, don't punch the **ladrão** (lah-*drah*-ooh; robber/pickpocket).

Keeping things in perspective after a robbery

During my three years in the country, I was robbed only **uma vez** (*ooh*-mah *vehz;* once), and it happened in front of my apartment building in São Paulo. It was very late at night. I was upset at first but then realized that losing a little **dinheiro** isn't that big of a deal and that reordering credit cards is just a small annoyance. But after that, I was much more careful walking around **de noite** (jee *noh*-ee-chee; at night), that's for sure!

You may want to remember that **ladrões** (lah-droh-eez; robbers/pickpockets) in Brazil are sometimes just very poor people who need to feed a sick child. My Spanish friend Mario once resisted a **ladrão** at the back of a bus in Rio. The next day, he ran into the **ladrão** at a bus stop. They recognized each other, and the guy ended up explaining his sad life story to Mario!

Next, hand over your **carteira** (kah-*tay*-dah; wallet), **relógio** (heh-*loh*-zhee-ooh; watch), or **bolsa** (*boh*-ooh-sah; purse) — whatever the assailant wants. Nothing is worth getting hurt over.

Saying nothing during a robbery is generally best, but here are some classic phrases you may want to know:

- **Não tenho dinheiro.** (*nah*-ooh *tang*-yoh jing-*yay*-doh; I don't have any money.)
- **Não tenho nada.** (*nah*-ooh *tang*-yoh *nah*-dah; I don't have anything.)
- **Socorro!** (soh-*koh*-hoo; Help!)
- **É ladrão!** (*eh* lah-*drah*-ooh; He's a robber/pickpocket!)

Of course, you want to try to avoid having any problems in Brazil. Besides taking the same safety precautions you'd take back at home, it's always a good idea to ask locals whether a certain area is safe:

- **Essa região, é seguro?** (*eh*-sah heh-zhee-*ah*-ooh eh seh-*goo*-doo; Is this area safe?)
- **Quais os bairros que são perigosos?** (*kwah*-eez oohz *bah*-ee-hooz kee *sah*-ooh peh-dee-*goh*-zooz; Which neighborhoods are dangerous?)

Asking for and receiving help

Say you've just been robbed. You had only a little money on you, and the robber didn't get anything else. You now need to get back home or to your hotel.

For this situation, or any other time you need help for something that's not a major emergency, you can use these phrases:

- ✔ **Por favor, poderia me ajudar?** (poh fah-*voh* poh-deh-*dee*-ah mee ah-zhoo-*dah;* Excuse me, could you help me?)

- ✔ **Eu preciso de ajuda, por favor.** (*eh*-ooh pdeh-*see*-zoo jee ah-*zhoo*-dah, poh fah-*voh;* I need help, please.)

Conversely, what can you say if Brazilians offer you **ajuda** (ah-*zhoo*-dah; help)? Try these responses:

- ✔ **Obrigado/a, sim, eu preciso de ajuda.** (oh-bdee-*gah*-doh/dah sing *eh*-ooh pdeh-*see*-zoo jee ah-*zhoo*-dah; Thanks, yes, I need help.)

- ✔ **Estou bem, obrigado/a.** (*eh*-*stoh bang,* oh-bdee-*gah*-doh/dah; I'm fine, thanks.)

- ✔ **Não preciso de ajuda.** (*nah*-ooh pdeh-*see*-zoo jee ah-*zhoo*-dah; I don't need any help.)

- ✔ **Eu prefiro ficar sozinho/a.** (*eh*-ooh pdeh-*fee*-doo fee-*kah* soh-*zeen*-yoh/yah; I prefer to be alone.)

Talkin' the Talk

José, a tourist from **Moçambique** (moh-sahm-*bee*-kee; Mozambique), where Portuguese is the national language, has just gotten robbed. He goes to the nearest hotel and asks to use the phone.

José: **Por favor, poderia usar o seu telefone?**
poh fah-*voh*, poh-deh-*dee*-ah ooh-*zah* ooh seh-ooh teh-leh-*foh*-nee?
Excuse me, could I use your phone?

Hotel clerk: **Para o que precisa?**
pah-dah ooh *keh* pdeh-*see*-zah?
What do you need it for?

José: **Preciso ligar para o consulado moçambicano.**
pdeh-*see*-zoo lee-*gah* pah-dah ooh kohn-soo-*lah*-doo moh-sahm-bee-*kah*-noh.
I need to call the Mozambiquan consulate.

Hotel clerk: **É claro.** (Hands over the phone)
eh *klah*-doh.
Of course.

José:	**E tem o número da polícia local?**
	ee *tang* ooh *noo*-meh-doh dah poh-*lee*-see-ah loh-*kah*-ooh?
	And do you have the number for the local police?

Hotel clerk:	**Eu vou ver.**
	eeh-ooh voh *veh*.
	I'm going to see.

Words to Know

ligar para	lee-*gah* pah-dah	to call
consulado	kohn-soo-<u>lah</u>-doh	consulate
número	<u>noo</u>-meh-doh	phone number
polícia local	poh-<u>lee</u>-see-ah loh-<u>kah</u>-ooh	local police
delegacia	deh-leh-gah-<u>see</u>-ah	police station

Reporting a problem to the police

Most Brazilians will tell you they fear **a polícia** (ah poh-*lee*-see-ah; the police) more than they trust them. Police officers are generally fine with tourists, though, and they're good for filing insurance forms if you get robbed — especially in Rio, a city economically tied to its tourism trade.

Here's what you can tell the **polícia** if you want to report a robbery:

- **Fui roubado/a.** (*fwee* hoh-*bah*-doh/dah; I've been robbed.)

- **Eu preciso fazer um boletim de ocorrência.** (*eh*-ooh pdeh-*see*-zoo fah-*zeh* oong boh-leh-*ching* jee oh-koo-*hen*-see-ah; I need to report a robbery.)

- **É para a minha companhia de seguros.** (*eh pah*-dah ah *ming*-yah kom-pahn-*yee*-ah jee seh-*goo*-dohz; It's for my insurance company.)

The **policia** may ask you some of the following questions:

- **Quando aconteceu?** (*kwahn*-doh ah-kohn-teh-*seh*-ooh; When did it happen?)

- **Aonde aconteceu?** (ah-*ohn*-jee ah-kohn-teh-*seh*-ooh; Where did it happen?)

- **O que que foi roubado?** (ooh *kee* kee *foh*-ee hoh-*bah*-doh; What was stolen?)

- **Viu o assaltante?** (*vee*-ooh ooh ah-sah-ooh-*tahn*-chee; Did you see the assailant?)

- **Usou uma arma?** (ooh-*zoh* ooh-mah *ah*-mah; Did he use a weapon?)

Of course, the **policia** will probably ask you the regular questions outlined in earlier chapters, like **Qual é seu nome?** (*kwah*-ooh *eh* seh-ooh *noh*-mee; What's your name?) and **Você é de que país?** (voh-*seh* *eh* jee *kee* pah-*eez*; What country are you from?). (See especially Chapters 3 and 4.)

Using the Searching Verb: Procurar

Losing something or getting lost in an unfamiliar area can be an **emergência** (eh-meh-*zhang*-see-ah; emergency) sometimes. You may need to tell a police officer you're looking for a friend or tell a store clerk you're looking for something you left behind. No matter what you're looking for, use the verb **procurar** (pdoh-koo-*dah;* to look for). **Procurar** is related to the fancy English word *procure*.

Here are the basic conjugations of **procurar:**

Conjugation	Pronunciation
eu procuro	*eh*-ooh pdoh-*koo*-doh
você procura	voh-*seh* pdoh-*koo*-dah
ele/ela procura	*eh*-lee/*eh*-lah pdoh-*koo*-dah
nós procuramos	nohz pdoh-koo-*dah*-mohz
eles/elas procuram	*eh*-leez/*eh*-lahz pdoh-*koo*-dah-ooh

This is what **procurar** looks like in the past tense:

Conjugation	*Pronunciation*
eu procurei	*eh*-ooh pdoh-koo-*day*
você procurou	voh-*seh* pdoh-koo-*doh*
ele/ela procurou	*eh*-lee/*eh*-lah pdoh-koo-*doh*
nós procuramos	nohz pdoh-koo-*dah*-mohz
eles/elas procuraram	*eh*-leez/*eh*-lahz pdoh-koo-*dah*-dah-ooh

Here are some example sentences using both tenses:

- **Eles procuram os peixes maiores.** (eh-leez pdoh-*koo*-dah-ooh oohz *pay*-sheez mah-ee-*oh*-deez; They look for the biggest fish.)

- **Ela procurou umas rosas vermelhas.** (*eh*-lah pdoh-koo-*doh* ooh-mahz *hoh*-zahz veh-*mehl*-yahz; She looked for some red roses.)

- **Eu procuro as palavras novas.** (*eh*-ooh pdoh-*koo*-doh ahz pah-*lahv*-dahz *noh*-vahz; I look for the new words.)

Another common way of using **procurar** is **estar procurando** (eh-*stah* pdoh-koo-*dahn*-doh; to be looking for):

- **Estou procurando a minha mãe.** (eh-*stoh* pdoh-koo-*dahn*-doh ah *ming*-yah *mah*-ee; I'm looking for my mother.)

- **Nós estamos procurando a Avenida Paulista.** (nohz eh-*stah*-mohz pdoh-koo-*dahn*-doh ah ah-veh-*nee*-dah pah-ooh-*lee*-stah; We're looking for Paulista Avenue.)

- **Ela está procurando as chaves.** (eh-lah eh-*stah* pdoh-koo-*dahn*-doh ahz *shah*-veez; She's looking for the keys.)

Using the Looking Verb: Olhar

You can use the verb **olhar** (ohl-*yah;* to look) in an emergency situation, like when you need to tell a pharmacist to look at the ingredients in a medication so you can avoid a drug reaction. Or a **policial** (poh-*lee*-see-*ah*-ooh; police officer) may ask you to look in a certain direction to verify that the person standing before you is the one who just picked your pocket.

Olhar is most often used in combination with **para** (*pah*-dah; at): **olhar para** (ohl-*yah pah*-dah; to look at).

The conjugations for **olhar** have the same verb endings as **procurar** because it's an **-ar** verb (see Chapter 2):

Conjugation	Pronunciation
eu olho	*eh*-ooh *ohl*-yoh
você olha	voh-*seh ohl*-yah
ele/ela olha	*eh*-lee/*eh*-lah *ohl*-yah
nós olhamos	nohz ohl-*yah*-mohz
eles/elas olham	*eh*-leez/*eh*-lahz *ohl*-yah-ooh

Here are some practice sentences (see Chapter 9 for info on forming the past tense of **-ar** verbs):

- **Ele olha para ela.** (*eh*-lee *ohl*-yah pah-dah *eh*-lah; He looks at her.)

- **Eles olham para o mar.** (*eh*-leez *ohl*-yah-ooh pah-dah ooh *mah;* They look at the ocean.)

- **Eu olhei para a janela.** (*eh*-ooh ohl-*yay* pah-dah ah zhah-*neh*-lah; I looked at the window.)

- **Nós olhamos para a professora.** (nohz ohl-*yah*-mohz pah-dah ah pdoh-feh-*soh*-dah; We look at the teacher.)

- **O gato olhou para a comida.** (ooh *gah*-toh ohl-*yoh* pah-dah ah koh-*mee*-dah; The cat looked at the food.)

The most common use of **olhar** is probably when someone tells someone else to look at something:

- **Olha isso!** (*ohl*-yah *ee*-soh; Look at this!)

- **Olha para a frente.** (*ohl*-yah pah-dah ah *fdehn*-chee; Look forward.)

- **Olha aquele carro estranho.** (*ohl*-yah ah-keh-lee *kah*-hoh eh-*stdahn*-yoh; Look at that strange car.)

- **Olha para aquele homem.** (*ohl*-yah pah-dah ah-*keh*-lee *oh*-mang; Look at that man.)

- **Olha para os nuvens.** (*ohl*-yah pah-dah oohz *noo*-vangz; Look at the clouds.)

Just as English-speakers say *Look* . . . when they're ready to say something and want the listener to pay attention, or when they're about to explain something frankly, Brazilians say **Olha** . . .

Helping Out: Using Ajudar

Brazilians like to **ajudar** (ah-zhoo-*dah;* help). Their helpfulness may seem like an invasion of privacy at first if you're in an emergency situation, but just realize these are nice people wanting to offer some genuine warmth. Here's how to conjugate **ajudar:**

Conjugation	*Pronunciation*
eu ajudo	*eh*-ooh ah-*zhoo*-doh
você ajuda	voh-*seh* ah-*zhoo*-dah
ele/ela ajuda	*eh*-lee/*eh*-lah ah-*zhoo*-dah
nós ajudamos	nohz ah-zhoo-*dah*-mohz
eles/elas ajudam	*eh*-leez/*eh*-lahz ah-*zhoo*-dah-ooh

Here are some example sentences:

✔ **Quero te ajudar.** (*keh*-doo chee ah-zhoo-*dah;* I want to help you.)

✔ **Ele me ajuda muito.** (*eh*-lee mee ah-*zhoo*-dah moh-*ee*-toh; He helps me a lot.)

✔ **Você ajuda a sua mãe?** (voh-*seh* ah-*zhoo*-dah ah *soo*-ah *mah*-ee; Do you help your mother?)

✔ **Nós ajudamos as crianças de rua.** (nohz ah-zhoo-*dah*-mohz ahz kdee-*ahn*-sahz jee *hoo*-ah; We help street children.)

✔ **Ajuda.** (ah-*zhoo*-dah; That helps.)

Although **Socorro!** (soh-*koh*-hoo) means *Help!* Brazilians don't use the verb **socorrer** much. You can also shout **Ajuda!** if you're in trouble, though **Socorro!** is the classic plea for help.

Talkin' the Talk

Eliana and her friend **Cíntia** are at the beach. Eliana got hit by a huge wave and scratched her knee on a rock. She's bleeding.

Cíntia: **Eliana, você está bem?**
            eh-lee-*ah*-nah, voh-*seh* eh-*stah bang*?
            Eliana, are you okay?

Eliana: **Mais ou menos.**
            mah-eez ooh *meh*-nooz.
            More or less.

Cíntia: **Está sangrando muito!**
            eh-*stah* sahn-*gdahn*-doh moh-ee-toh!
            It's bleeding a lot!

Eliana: **Sim . . .**
            Sing . . .
            Yeah . . .

Cíntia: **Vou procurar o salva-vida.**
            voh pdoh-koo-*dah* ooh *sah*-ooh-vah *vee*-dah.
            I'm going to look for the lifeguard.

Eliana: **Acha que pode ajudar?**
            ah-shah kee *poh*-jee ah-zhoo-*dah?*
            Do you think he can help?

Cíntia: **Pode ter uma bandagem.**
            poh-jee teh ooh-mah bahn-*dah*-zhang.
            He could have a bandage.

Eliana: (Pointing) **Olha, lá — tem um.**
            ohl-yah, *lah* — *tang oong.*
            Look over there — there's one.

Cíntia: **Aguarde aqui e fique quieto, tá?**
            ah-*gwah*-jee ah-*kee* ee *fee*-kee kee-*eh*-too, *tah?*
            Stay here and stay still, okay?

Eliana: **Tá. Obrigada!**
            tah. oh-bdee-*gah*-dah!
            Okay. Thanks!

Words to Know

Você está bem?	voh-<u>seh</u> eh-<u>stah</u> <u>bang</u>	Are you okay?
Está sangrando.	eh-<u>stah</u> sahn-<u>gdahn</u>-doh	You're bleeding.
uma bandagem	<u>ooh</u>-mah bahn-<u>dah</u>-zhang	a bandage
Olha lá.	<u>ohl</u>-yah <u>lah</u>	Look over there.
Aguarde.	ah-<u>gwah</u>-jee	Wait.
Fique queto.	<u>fee</u>-kee <u>keh</u>-too	Stay still.

Handling Health Emergencies

In this section, I give you tips on what to do if you injure yourself or become ill in Brazil. Having to get medical treatment in another country can be scary, and it's never fun. You could scrape yourself badly at the beach, injure yourself while hiking, or come down with strange symptoms you need help interpreting. Knowing a few phrases that can help you communicate is bound to calm you down a bit!

Heading off illnesses

Think about your **saúde** (sah-*ooh*-jee; health) before you visit Brazil. You need certain vaccinations before you're even allowed to enter the country, and other vaccinations are highly recommended — I remember getting a 10-year shot for Hepatitis A, as well as a shot for **a febre amarela** (ah *feh*-bdee ah-mah-*deh*-lah; yellow fever). If you're still concerned about getting sick in Brazil, you can buy travel health insurance; rates are often more reasonable than you'd expect.

You may feel most comfortable talking with your local doctor or getting travel tips from a local health clinic. Most doctors' offices and hospitals have pamphlets and information sheets relating to disease prevention for international travelers.

For information about recommended vaccinations, you can visit the Web site of the World Health Organization (www.who.int) — the health arm of the United Nations. In the U.S., the Center for Disease Control (www.cdc.gov) has good information, particularly about malaria. At either site, just click on Travelers' Health. You can also contact a Brazilian consulate near you or your national health agency. Finally, you can also check the Brazilian government's Web site for vaccine recommendations (www.brasil.gov.br). Just click on In English to translate the site and then do a search for vaccinations.

If you've been in countries with a **febre amarela** alert within three months of your entry into Brazil, the Brazilian government won't let you in the country without a yellow fever proof-of-vaccination card. You may also want to keep in mind that a **febre amarela** vaccination takes ten days to take effect.

When deciding on vaccines, consider what part of the country you're going to. If it's the Amazon, ask a doctor whether you should take preventative medicine for **a malária** (ah mah-*lah*-dee-ah; malaria).

The most common tropical illness among locals and tourists in Brazil is one you may have never heard of — **a dengue** (ah *dehn*-gee; dengue fever). City subways in Brazil have ads to warn the public about dengue fever. Risk usually comes with stagnant water — breeding grounds for **mosquitos** (moh-*skee*-tohz; mosquitos) that carry the sickness. Having dengue fever usually just means you have a stomach ache and what feels like **a gripe** (ah *gdee*-pee; the flu) for a few days.

A dengue also has a much more serious variant called *hemorrhagic dengue,* which can be fatal if untreated. If your flu-like symptoms worsen and you begin to get restless, bleed easily, or go into shock, get medical help right away. **A dengue** is caused by one of four viruses, and your chances of getting hemorrhagic dengue increase if you've had a different strain of **dengue** before.

It's always a good idea to wear **repelente** (heh-peh-*len*-chee; insect repellent) while you're in Brazil. **Mosquitos** are thick in the Amazon, but the worst bites I ever got were in São Paulo! The climate in most of Brazil is humid at some point in the year, and mosquitos love it.

A diarréia (ah jee-ah-*hay*-ah; diarrhea) is very common among visitors to Brazil. The best way to avoid this is not to drink tap water or drinks with ice. Don't eat raw vegetables and unpeeled fruit, and avoid room-temperature sauces. Boiled, baked, or peeled foods are the safest. Taking a small dose of bismuth subsalicylate (like Pepto-Bismol) every day — provided your trip is less than ten days — can help to prevent diarrhea. Talk to your doctor about this and other preventative measures.

Getting sick

In addition to tropical diseases, you can develop the normal sicknesses, like a **resfriado** (hehs-fdee-*ah*-doo; cold), a **dor** (doh; pain), or even a **ressaca** (heh-*sah*-kah; hangover)! Brazil has plenty of **farmácias** (fah-*mah*-see-ahz; drug stores) around, so getting the **remédio** (heh-*meh*-jee-ooh; medicine) you need isn't hard.

Here are some helpful phrases to use, whether you're at the **médico** (*meh*-jee-koo; doctor) or the **farmácia:**

- **Estou com dor de cabeça.** (eh-*stoh* koh-oong *doh* jee kah-*beh*-sah; I have a headache.)

- **Estou com muita dor.** (eh-*stoh* koh-oong moh-*ee*-tah *doh;* I'm in a lot of pain.)

- **Tenho dores no corpo.** (*tang*-yoh *doh*-deez noh *koh*-poo; I have body aches.)

- **Tenho tosse.** (*tang*-yoh *toh*-see; I have a cough.)

- **Sou diabético.** (soh jee-ah-*beh*-chee-koh; I'm diabetic.)

- **Tenho asma.** (*tang*-yoh *ahz*-mah; I have asthma.)

- **Têm band-aids?** (*tang* bahn-*day*-ee-jeez; Do you have Band-Aids?)

- **Têm aspirina?** (*tang* ah-spee-*dee*-nah; Do you have aspirin?)

- **Têm algo para a diarréia?** (*tang ah*-ooh-goh *pah*-dah ah jee-ah-*hay*-ah; Do you have something for diarrhea?)

Here are some questions the pharmacist or doctor may ask you:

- **Dói?** (*doh*-ee; Does it hurt?)

- **Aonde dói?** (ah-*ohn*-jee *doh*-ee; Where does it hurt?)

- **Tem febre?** (*tang feh*-bdee; Do you have a fever?)

- **Tem náuseas?** (*tang nah*-ooh-zee-ahz; Are you nauseous?)

- **É alérgico?** (eh ah-*leh*-zhee-koh; Are you allergic?)

- **Tem alta pressão sanguínea?** (tang *ah*-ooh-tah pdeh-*sah*-ooh sahn-*gee*-neh-ah; Do you have high blood pressure?)

- **Já foi operado?** (*zhah* foh-ee oh-peh-*dah*-doh; Have you ever had surgery?)

- **Abre a boca, por favor.** (*ah*-bdee ah *boh*-kah, poh fah-*voh*; Open your mouth, please.)

- **Tome esses comprimidos.** (*toh*-mee *eh*-seez kohm-pdee-*mee*-dooz; Take these pills.)

Talkin' the Talk

Mauricio woke up in the morning with a swollen eye. He's worried but decides it's not an emergency, so he goes to a drug store and talks to a pharmacist.

Mauricio: **Por favor, estou com o olho inchado.**
poh fah-*voh*, eh-*stoh* koh-oong ooh *ohl*-yoh een-*shah*-doo.
Excuse me, I have a swollen eye.

Pharmacist: **Sabe por que está inchado?**
sah-bee poh *keh* eh-*stah* een-*shah*-doo?
Do you know why it's swollen?

Mauricio: **Não. Acordei hoje e já estava assim.**
nah-ooh. ah-koh-*day oh*-zhee ee *zhah* eh-*stah*-vah ah-*sing*.
No. I woke up this morning and it was already like that.

Pharmacist: **Não parece muito grave.**
nah-ooh pah-*deh*-see moh-ee-toh *gdah*-vee.
It doesn't look very serious.

Mauricio: **O que recomenda fazer?**
ooh *kee* heh-koh-*men*-dah fah-*zeh?*
What do you recommend I do?

Pharmacist: **Eu recomendo você colocar um saquinho de gelo em cima.**
eh-ooh heh-koh-*mehn*-doo voh-*seh* koh-loh-*kah* oong sah-*king*-yoh jee *zheh*-loh ang *see*-mah.
I recommend that you put a little bag of ice on it.

Mauricio: **Mas é normal o olho inchar, sem fazer nada?**
mah-eez eh noh-*mah*-ooh ooh *ohl*-yoh een-*shah*, *sang* fah-*zeh nah*-dah?
But is it normal for an eye to swell, without doing anything?

Pharmacist: **Poderia ser uma picada de inseto.**
poh-deh-*dee*-ah *seh* ooh-mah pee-*kah*-dah jee een-*seh*-toh.
It could be an insect bite.

Words to Know

olho inchado	<u>ohl</u>-yoh een-<u>shah</u>-doo	swollen eye
Sabe . . . ?	<u>sah</u>-bee	Do you know . . . ?
já	zhah	already
estava	eh-<u>stah</u>-vah	was
assim	ah-<u>sing</u>	like that
grave	<u>gdah</u>-vee	serious
colocar	koh-loh-<u>kah</u>	to put
saquinho	sah-<u>king</u>-yoh	little bag
gelo	<u>zheh</u>-loh	ice
inchar	een-<u>shah</u>	to swell
sem	sang	without
Poderia ser . . .	poh-deh-<u>dee</u>-ah <u>seh</u>	It could be . . .
picada	pee-<u>kah</u>-dah	bite
inseto	een-<u>seh</u>-too	insect

Handling broken bones and other injuries

Dealing with the misfortune of breaking a bone or suffering an immediate emergency in Brazil works much like it probably does in your home country. You can take a taxi to a local **sala de emergência** (*sah*-lah jee eh-meh-*zhang*-see-ah; emergency room), or you can call a three-digit number and request that an **ambulância** (ahm-boo-*lahn*-see-ah; ambulance) be sent to pick you up. The number in Brazil is 190.

Brazil's large cities have some very good **hospitais** (oh-spee-*tah*-eez; hospitals). You can get the same good care there that you'd get in the best **hospitais** in the world. The **salas de emergência** can no doubt be a little scary in small towns, especially the rural ones, but rest assured you'll get the basic care you need.

Brazilian research and politics regarding AIDS medicine is world-famous. The AIDS rate in Brazil is much lower than in other developing countries, thanks to effective local campaigns. Also, local scientists figured out how to make patented AIDS-related drugs and began offering them despite protests from multinational drug companies.

Whether you have a stomach virus or a broken leg, knowing what certain parts of the body are called in Portuguese is useful so you can more easily communicate with doctors in Brazil. I start with **a cabeça** (ah kah-*beh*-sah; the head) and work my way down **o corpo** (ooh *koh*-poo; the body):

- **olho** (*ohl*-yoh; eye)
- **boca** (*boh*-kah; mouth)
- **lingua** (*ling*-gwah; tongue)
- **orelha** (oh-*deh*-ooh-yah; ear)
- **nariz** (nah-*deez;* nose)
- **rosto** (*hoh*-stoo; face)
- **dentes** (*dang*-cheez; teeth)
- **sobrancelhas** (soh-bdan-*sel*-yahz; eyebrows)
- **pescoço** (peh-*skoh*-soo; neck)
- **costas** (*koh*-stahz; back)
- **peito** (*pay*-too; chest)
- **braços** (*bdah*-sooz; arms)
- **dedos** (*deh*-dooz; fingers)
- **bum-bum** (boong-*boong;* bottom)
- **barriga** (bah-*hee*-gah; belly)
- **pernas** (*peh*-nahz; legs)
- **joelho** (zhoh-*el*-yoh; knee)
- **pes** (pez; feet)
- **dedos do pé** (*deh*-dooz doo *peh;* toes)

And here are the names of some internal organs and useful medical terms:

- **coração** (koh-dah-*sah*-ooh; heart)
- **pulmões** (pool-*moh*-eez; lungs)

✔ **intestinos** (een-tehs-*chee*-nooz; intestines)

✔ **fígado** (*fee*-gah-doo; liver)

✔ **sangue** (*sahn*-gee; blood)

✔ **cirugia** (see-doo-*zhee*-ah; surgery)

Talkin' the Talk

João hurt his leg playing soccer. Here's the conversation he has with his doctor.

Doctor:	**Tem dores na perna?** tang *doh*-deez nah *peh*-nah? Your leg hurts?
João:	**Sim, dói muito.** *sing*, *doh*-ee moh-ee-toh. Yes, it hurts a lot.
Doctor:	**Vamos tomar uma radiografia.** *vah*-mohz toh-*mah* ooh-mah hah-jee-ooh-gdah-*fee*-ah. We're going to take an X-ray.
João:	**Acha que está quebrado?** *ah*-shah kee eh-*stah* keh-*bdah*-doo? Do you think it's broken?
Doctor:	**Não sei ainda.** *nah*-ooh *say* ah-*een*-dah. I don't know yet.
João:	**Vai ter que dar anestesia?** *vah*-ee *teh* kee *dah* ah-neh-*steh*-zee-ah? Are you going to have to give me anesthesia?
Doctor:	**Não, não é preciso.** *nah*-ooh, *nah*-ooh *eh* pdeh-*see*-zoo. No, that's not necessary.

Words to Know

uma radiografia	ooh-mah hah-jee-ooh-gdah-_fee_-ah	X-ray
quebrada	keh-_bdah_-dah	broken
ainda	ah-_een_-dah	yet/still
Vai ter que . . . ?	_vah_-ee _teh_ kee	Will you have to . . . ?
dar	dah	to give
anestesia	ah-neh-_steh_-zee-ah	anesthesia
Não é preciso.	_nah_-ooh _eh_ pdeh-_see_-zoo	That's not necessary.

Brazil is supposedly the number two country in the world, after the U.S., for **cirurgia plástica** (see-dooh-_zhee_-ah _plahs_-chee-kah; plastic surgery). And with Brazil's **cirurgiões** (see-dooh-_zhoh_-eez; surgeons) being some of the world's best — and the cost per operation being comparatively low — some people say there's a significant plastic surgery tourism trade.

Discussing Legal Problems

Most types of **atividades ilegais** (ah-_chee_-vee-_dah_-jeez ee-lay-_gah_-eez; illegal activities) in Brazil are also illegal in most countries of the Western world. But the enforcement and consequences of **a lei** (ah _lay;_ the law) can be different. For instance, in Brazil, possession of marijuana is treated much more seriously than in much of the West. Cultural norms are at play, too. For example, it's more normal in Brazil for lawbreakers to pay off a police officer or customs agent than it is in North America or Western Europe.

It's best to leave any borderline illegal activities — even speeding in your rental car — for when you're at home, where you understand the language perfectly and have familiar **recursos legais** (heh-_koo_-sohz leh-_gah_-eez; legal resources) at hand.

Misunderstandings with the police can occur. If the situation is at all **sério** (*seh*-dee-ooh; serious), the first thing to do is contact the nearest consulate for your country. You may also need to contact an **advogado** (*ahj*-voh-*gah*-doo; lawyer). In that case, ask for one who speaks English:

- ✔ **Tem um advogado que fala inglês?** (*tang* oong ahj-voh-*gah*-doh kee *fah*-lah een-*glehz;* Is there a lawyer who speaks English?)

- ✔ **Tem aqui um consulado americano?** (*tang* ah-*kee* oong kohn-soo-*lah*-doh ah-meh-dee-*kah*-noh; Is there an American consulate here?)

If you need to ask for another consulate, see Chapter 4 for a list of nationalities.

Hopefully, you won't ever have to say or hear these phrases:

- ✔ **Quero fazer uma queixa.** (*keh*-doo fah-*zeh* ooh-mah *kay*-shah; I want to register a complaint.)

- ✔ **Vamos ter que dar uma multa.** (*vah*-mohz *teh* kee *dah* ooh-mah *mool*-tah; We're going to have to give you a ticket.)

- ✔ **Vamos te levar para a delegacia de polícia.** (*vah*-mohz chee leh-*vah* pah-dah ah *deh*-leh-gah-*see*-ah jee poh-*lee*-see-ah; We're going to take you to the police station.)

You want to **evitar** (eh-vee-*tah;* avoid) a visit to **a cadéia** (ah kah-*day*-ah; jail) at all costs — jails in Brazil are notoriously overcrowded, scary places.

Fun & Games

Your new Brazilian friend **Caio** (*kah*-ee-oh) is a soccer fanatic. He's played the game for more than a decade and has experienced mild injuries to several parts of his body. During a break in a game, he sits down and points out his battle scars. Try to identify the Portuguese words for the places he's talking about. Then flip to Appendix C for the answers.

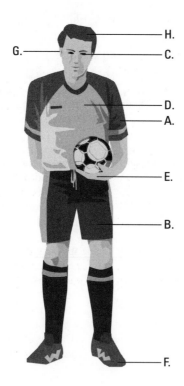

peito

dedos

dedos do pé

cabeça

perna

olho

orelha

braÁo

Chapter 17

O Carnaval!

Brazil is world-famous for its **Carnaval** (kah-nah-*vah*-ooh; Carnival). The festivities take place usually in **fevereiro** (feh-veh-*day*-doh; February) or **março** (*mah*-soo; March), when the weather is hot in Brazil, for the four days preceding **Quarta-feira de Cinzas** (*kwah*-tah-*fay*-dah jee *seen*-zahz; Ash Wednesday).

Other places famous for Carnaval are Venice, Italy, and New Orleans, in the U.S. The tradition dates back to the Middle Ages, and each place today celebrates the days of revelry a little bit differently. Venice is famous for people dressing up in costume and wearing masquerade masks, while New Orleans is known for people drinking in the street and wearing flashy beads for Mardi Gras.

If you can't get to Brazil during Carnaval (flights and hotels tend to be expensive), never fear: Brazilians hold unofficial Carnaval parties year-round. The most famous of all of these **Carnavais fora de época** (kah-nah-*vah*-eez foh-dah jee *eh*-poh-kah; out-of-season Carnavals) is **Fortal** (foh-*tah*-ooh), which takes place in the large northeastern city of Fortaleza in August. The name **Fortal** simply combines the words Fortaleza and Carnaval. This chapter gives you even more tips on how to discover and experience Carnaval, including information on how to samba and flirt with all those Brazilians you meet!

Exploring Carnaval in Brazil

The preparations for Carnaval — especially in Rio, where a ton of money is poured into the party — often take place year-round. Women from different **escolas de samba** (eh-*skoh*-lahz jee *sahm*-bah; samba schools) make the **fantasias** (fahn-tah-*zee*-ahz; costumes) months ahead of time. The **compositor** (kom-poh-zee-*toh;* composer) of the official song of a specific **escola de samba** starts humming ditties to himself as soon as the previous year's Carnaval ends.

Another surprising thing about Carnaval in Brazil is that Rio's is not necessarily the best. Rio certainly has the best **desfile** (des-*fee*-lee; parade) of **escolas de samba** over the four-day period, but it has little **carnaval de rua** (kah-nah-*vah*-ooh jee *hoo*-ah; street carnival) activity.

The other two less-publicized but equally fantastic **Carnavais** (kah-nah-*vah*-eez; Carnavals) — unique each in their own way — are those of Salvador and of the neighboring cities **Recife** (heh-*see*-fee) and **Olinda** (oh-*leen*-dah). Both locations are in the northeastern part of the country, and both are better for people-watching and partying in the streets than Rio.

Every Brazilian has a different opinion on which Carnaval best. Some don't like all the fuss and prefer to use their two vacation days (Monday and Tuesday before Ash Wednesday) to head to a secluded **praia** (*pdah*-ee-ah; beach).

Here are some questions you can ask a Brazilian to help you decide which Carnaval is right for you:

- **Qual Carnaval no Brasil você acha melhor?** (*kwah*-ooh kah-nah-*vah*-ooh noh bdah-*zee*-ooh *ah*-shah mel-*yoh;* Which Carnaval in Brazil do you think is best?)

- **Qual é o mais divertido?** (*kwah*-ooh *eh* ooh *mah*-eez jee-veh-*chee*-doo; Which one is the most fun?)

- **Qual tem o melhor show?** (*kwah*-ooh *tang* ah mel-*yoh* shoh; Which one has the best show?)

- **Qual tem a melhor carnaval de rua?** (*kwah*-ooh *tang* ah mel-*yoh* kah-nah-*vah*-ooh jee *hoo*-ah; Which one has the best street carnival?)

- **Já esteve no Carnaval de . . . ?** (*zhah* eh-*steh*-vee noo kah-nah-*vah*-ooh jee; Have you been to the Carnaval in . . . ?)

Rio's Carnaval

This is the one you want to go to if you want to see a huge **espetáculo** (eh-speh-*tah*-koo-loo; spectacle). Tickets can be relatively **caros** (*kah*-dooz; expensive) — say US$100 for a good seat. The entire four-day event takes place in Rio's **sambódromo** (sahm-*boh*-droh-moo; sambodrome), an open-air place with bleachers that looks like an oblong sports stadium. This venue is longer rather than wide because a **desfile** (dehs-*fee*-lee; parade) has to come through it.

CULTURAL WISDOM

Escola de samba: Carnaval as competition

I had thought that **uma escola de samba** (*ooh-mah eh-skoh-lah jee sahm-bah; a samba school*) was a place where people learned samba! In fact, they're not schools at all. They're just places where a group of people who want to compete in Carnaval meet up to plan and practice the moves and anthem they'll use that year. These people include the **músicos** (*moo-zee-kooz; musicians*), **passistas** (*pah-see-stahz; men and women in costume who parade with the school*), and people involved in the production of **fantasias** (*fahn-tah-zee-ahz; costumes*), as well as people who live nearby who just want to come and dance to the music. Because many **escolas de samba** in Rio are named after and originate in a specific **bairro** (*bah-ee-hoo; neighborhood*), the feel of visiting an **escola** is like hanging out at a community center. There are people of all ages enjoying themselves.

Each **escola** has a new anthem every year. Anthem **letras** (*leh-tdahz; lyrics*) often have socially progressive **temas** (*teh-mahz; themes*), like calling an end to racism or even encouraging water conservation. For this last Carnaval, I saw people dressed like water faucets! The **fantasias** (*fahn-tah-zee-ahz; costumes*) match the theme. What doesn't change from year to year, though, are a school's two official **cores** (*koh-deez; colors*).

Historically, the most famous **escolas de samba** in Rio are **Mangueira** (*mahn-gay-dah; the name of a neighborhood in Rio*), **Salgueiro** (*sah-ooh-gay-doh; a last name*), and **Beija-Flor** (*bay-zhah floh; Hummingbird*). One of these three schools usually wins first or second place each year.

You can check out the Web sites for these samba schools to see their colors and get a real feel for Brazilian Carnaval: **Mangueira** (www.mangueira.com.br), **Salgueiro** (www.salgueiro.com.br), and **Beija-Flor** (www.beija-flor.com.br).

On the Web sites, you can find information about **ensaios** (*en-sah-ee-ooz; rehearsals*). These can be great fun. **Ensaios** are held at each **escola de samba's** headquarters, usually a couple of times a week for the few months preceding Carnaval. The entrance fee is about **20 reais** (around US$8). Attending **ensaios** is a way to hear the **escola's** band practice and see some of its dancers in costume. And of course, you're allowed to **dançar** (*dahn-sah; dance*) with them!

Why is it called a *sambodrome?* Because people dance an extra-fast **samba** (*sahm-bah*) as they parade their way through. **Samba** is the most famous dance from Brazil. It's a three-beat step repeated over and over again. It can be fast- or medium-speed, but during Carnaval, it's very **rápido** (*hah-pee-doh; fast*). Check out the section on "Dancing the Samba!" for more information.

São Paulo also has a **sambódromo,** and everything I mention in this section holds for the Carnaval in São Paulo, too. The show in São Paulo keeps getting better every year, but it still doesn't draw the gigantic crowds that Rio does.

The entire Rio Carnaval is in fact a major **competição** (*kohm-peh-chee-sah-ooh; competition*). During the four days, each of the city's **escolas de samba** (*eh-skoh-lahz jee sahm-bah; samba schools*) has just one chance to move it, shake it, and show off the school's artistic talents and magnificently deco-rated floats. On Tuesday night, **os juízes** (ooz zhoo-*ee*-zeez; judges) decide who performed best.

Tourists (Brazilian and foreign) can actually parade with an **escola de samba.** I had a few daring friends who did (though they had their costumes on back-ward and only reversed them right before the show). They said they had a blast. Participation costs around US$80, and you don't have to know how to **sambar** (sahm-*bah;* dance samba) to get involved. It's more like jumping around when you're actually parading. Movement is key, not any actual **passos** (*pah*-sooz; steps). Have your travel agent or someone at a local tourist bureau make calls for you to figure out which **escolas** you can choose from. You can certainly impress friends back at home with the photos. And don't worry — the costumes for females are generally not skimpy.

Each **escola** has many floats decorated with the school's theme, and they take months to make. They are indeed works of art. On top of the floats are the famous samba-dancing babes with spectacular bodies, little clothing, and high heels. They often wear impressive feathery headdresses. On the ground, in front of and behind the float, are hundreds more **dançarinas** (dahn-sah-*dee*-nahz; dancers), all in costume. The parading of a single **escola** takes about an hour during the actual competition.

In terms of music, the most important part of any **escola** is the **batucada** (bah-too-*kah*-dah; drumming). There are up to 200 drummers in each **escola.** The beats of the drums is deafening, but the energy is contagious.

Talkin' the Talk

Susana and her friend **Lu** have decided to take the plunge. They want to join a samba school for the Rio Carnaval. They talk to their friend, **Clara**, who did it last year.

Clara: **Vocês estão pensando em desfilar?**
voh-*say*-eez eh-*stah*-ooh pen-*sahn*-doh ang des-fee-*lah?*
You guys are thinking about parading during Carnaval?

Susana: **Sim, é divertido?**
sing, eh jee-veh-*chee*-doo?
Yeah, is it fun?

Lu: **É demais . . .**
eh jee-*mah*-eez . . .
It's fabulous . . . (*Literally:* It's too much)

Susana: **Desfilou com que escola?**
des-fee-*loh* kohng *kee* eh-*skoh*-lah?
You paraded with which school?

Lu: **Com o Salgueiro.**
kohng ooh sah-ooh-*gay*-doh.
With Salgueiro.

Clara: **Custou caro?**
koos-*toh kah*-doh?
Was it expensive?

Susana: **Bom, duzentos reais. Mas valeu a pena.**
boh-oong, dooz-*en*-tooz hay-*eyes*. *mah*-eez vah-*leh*-
ooh ah *peh*-nah.
Well, 200 reais. But it was worth it.

Words to Know

estão pensando	eh-<u>stah</u>-ooh pen-<u>sahn</u>-doh	are thinking
desfilar	des-fee-<u>lah</u>	to parade during Carnaval
É demais.	eh jee-<u>mah</u>-eez	It's fabulous/great. (*Literally:* It's too much)
desfilou	des-fee-<u>loh</u>	you paraded
custou	koo-<u>stoh</u>	it cost
valeu a pena	vah-<u>leh</u>-ooh ah <u>peh</u>-nah	it was worth it

Carnaval in Salvador

Salvador's Carnaval is completely different from Rio's. Salvador doesn't have bleachers set up in a **sambódromo** (sahm-*boh*-droh-moo; sambodrome). Instead, a several-miles-long parade route winds its way through the city. The parade ends at Salvador's most famous landmark, **o farol** (ooh fah-*doh*-ooh; the lighthouse) — right on the beach. And instead of **escolas de samba** (eh-*skoh*-lahz jee *sahm*-bah), they have what are called **blocos** (*bloh*-kooz; bands that play on top of a truck with fans dancing below. *Literally:* blocks). The name of the **bloco** is usually that of a local or famous band. This is a different situation from the one in Rio, where the musicians aren't famous pop stars, though the traditional samba music composers often are some of the most famous in Brazil. But if you want to hear some of Brazil's most famed and beloved stars and musicians, **Salvador** is the place to go.

The **bloco** is made up of a **trio elétrico** (*tdee*-ooh eh-*leh*-tdee-koo; motorized truck with a platform on top, where people dance and a singer sings), with people who've paid to be a part of the specific **bloco** dancing on the ground and moving forward slowly with the truck, in front of and behind it. There are maybe about 40 different main **blocos** involved in the whole Carnaval.

If you're not in a **bloco,** you can either watch the parade from the sidelines or just roam the city. The parts near the parade route are filled with people, laughing and just generally hanging out. Some bars and restaurants remain open, but others close for the festivities.

Salvador's Carnaval is very hectic and crowded. That can be music to your ears if you're the adventurous, fun-loving type, or it can sound like a gigantic **dor de cabeça** (*doh* jee kah-*beh*-sah; headache) if you prefer low-key events. If you're the latter type, you'd probably like Carnaval in Recife/Olinda better than in Salvador.

Abadás and blocos

Most Brazilians and foreign tourists who go to Salvador for Carnaval buy T-shirts or tank tops called an **abadá** (ah-bah-*dah*) for a particular **bloco** months in advance. Unlike in Rio, if you choose to buy an **abadá** and participate in Salvador's Carnaval, there's no practicing involved. You can just show up, pick up the shirts, and meet your **bloco** at its scheduled time to begin the parade route.

Abadás can be expensive — they usually cost more than US$80. The price goes up for each of the four days you participate in Carnaval. For each day you pay for, you get a different T-shirt or tank top with a new design so you can prove you paid to be in the **bloco** for that specific day. Generally you have to pick up the **abadás** from each **bloco's** headquarters, but you may find street vendors with **abadás** to buy at the last minute.

Men usually wear an **abadá,** shorts, socks, and tennis shoes. Young women from Salvador take their **abadás** to a tailor months in advance. The tailors fashion the **abadás** into a unique top for each **garota** (gah-*doh*-tah; girl). This is the regimented clothing style of people parading in Salvador's Carnaval. On the sidelines, there's a huge crowd, where people wear whatever they feel like wearing.

After you buy a top with the name of your **bloco,** you can travel along the parade route with that **bloco,** participating — not spectating! If you prefer not to participate, you can sit and watch from the bleachers in some parts of the parade route. Or you can stand on the sidelines and watch the parade pass, though the crowd is thick.

Each **bloco** has a **trio elétrico** (*tdee*-ooh eh-*leh*-tdee-koo; motorized truck with a platform on top, where people dance and a singer sings). People with **abadás** dance in front of and behind the float. To separate the **bloco** from the crowd watching the parade, a group of people are paid to encircle each **bloco** with a **corda** (*koh*-dah; rope). They form a rectangle around each **bloco,** with the **trio elétrico** in the center. They slowly walk along. Though the music is fast-paced, the parade isn't.

Each **bloco** parades for about six hours a day. If you get tired, you can duck under the rope to escape. My friends and I had a lot of fun but decided before the end of the parade to leave our **bloco** and just walk around the city.

On the streets of Salvador, stands that sell all kinds of tropical cocktail concoctions are set up. These are generally the only vendors you'll find along the parade route, because the parade is the main focus.

Salvador Carnaval music

Some famous bands that play every year in Salvador are **Chiclete com Banana** (shee-*kleh*-chee kohng bah-*nah*-nah; Gum with Banana) and **Olodum** (oh-loh-*doong*), **Daniela Mercury** (dahn-ee-*eh*-lah *meh*-koo-dee) and **Ivete Sangalo** (ee-*veh*-chee sahn-*gah*-loo).

The general music genre of Salvador is different from that of Rio. In Rio, the music's a fast **samba,** whereas in Salvador, it's generally a music form known as **axé** (ah-*sheh*). The singing in **samba** is chorus-based. In **axé,** there's one singer. **Axé** also sounds more contemporary than **samba.** Music stores sell the CDs of hundreds of **axé** bands.

Sometimes the world-famous Brazilian singers **Gilberto Gil** (zhee-ooh-*beh*-too *zhee*-ooh) and **Caetano Veloso** (kah-eh-*tah*-noo veh-*loh*-zoo) perform, too.

The most unusual **bloco** in Salvador, in terms of Brazilian costume, is a group that dates back to 1949, called **os Filhos de Ghandi** (ooz *feel*-yooz jee gahn-*dee;* Sons of Ghandi). They wear white turbans.

As for dancing, it's mostly jumping around. No special moves required. Carnaval is so important in Brazil that there's even a verb that means enjoying Carnaval. It's **pular** (poo-*lah*), which also means *to jump*.

Talkin' the Talk

Zezé is a tourist from Rio who's at the Salvador Carnaval for the first time. He strikes up a conversation with **Teresa**, a woman in his **bloco**.

Zézé: **Oi, está gostando da festa?**
oh-ee, eh-*stah* goh-*stahn*-doh dah *feh*-stah?
Hi, are you enjoying the party?

Teresa: **Estou pulando muito.**
eh-*stoh* poo-*lahn*-doh moh-ee-toh.
I'm really enjoying myself.

Zezé: **Não tem tempo para a praia!**
nah-ooh *tang tehm*-poo pah-dah ah *pdah*-ee-ah!
There's no time for the beach!

Teresa: **Não, é só festa!**
nah-ooh, eh *soh feh*-stah!
No, it's all partying!

Zezé: **Você é da onde? Veio no ano passado?**
voh-*seh* eh dah *ohn*-jee? *vay*-oh noo *ah*-noo pah-*sah*-doo?
Where are you from? Did you come last year?

Teresa: **Sou de Minas. É a minha primeira vez no Carnaval de Salvador.**
soh jee *mee*-nahz. eh ah ming-yah pdee-*may*-dah *vehz* noo kah-nah-*vah*-ooh jee sah-ooh-vah-*doh*.
I'm from Minas (Minas Gerais state). It's my first time at the Salvador Carnaval.

Zezé: **É o melhor do Brasil, com certeza.**
eh ooh mel-*yoh* doo bdah-*zee*-ooh, kohng seh-*teh*-zah.
It's the best in Brazil, for sure.

Teresa: **Eu concordo!**
eh-ooh kohn-*koh*-doo!
I agree!

Words to Know

Estou pulando.	eh-<u>stoh</u> poo-<u>lahn</u>-doh	I'm enjoying myself (at Carnaval).
não tem tempo	<u>nah</u>-ooh tang <u>tehm</u>-poo	there's no time
veio	<u>vay</u>-oh	did you come/ you came
no ano passado	noo <u>ah</u>-noo pah-<u>sah</u>-doo	last year
com certeza	kohng seh-<u>teh</u>-zah	for sure
eu condordo	<u>eh</u>-ooh kohn-<u>koh</u>-doo	I agree

Carnaval in Recife/Olinda

Recife (heh-*see*-fee) and **Olinda** (oh-*leen*-dah) are two beachside cities in the northeastern state of **Pernambuco** (*peh*-nahm-*boo*-koh). They're right next to each other, with less than a mile separating them. The cities are close enough that you can spend time in both places in a single day. This is the place to see a bit more of a historic type of Brazilian Carnaval, and for me, it's the most **mágico** (*mah*-zhee-koo; magical).

Recife is a large city, with a population of about 2 million. Olinda is one of Brazil's most beautiful old colonial towns. It's very small, with narrow, winding streets, pastel-colored houses, and breathtaking views of the city and the ocean. Olinda is also home to many artists. The name of the town comes from **O, linda!** (Oh, beautiful!) — a Portuguese sailor was apparently smitten with the location.

Recife and Olinda

Carnaval takes place in the old section of Recife — **Recife antigo** (heh-*see*-fee ahn-*chee*-goo; old Recife) — and throughout the Olinda. Carnaval here feels less official than the ones in Rio and Salvador. There are no fees to pay (except for the hotels, which may be hard to book at this time), no T-shirts with logos.

And between the two, Recife is a little more **tranquilo** (tdahn-*kwee*-loo; low-key) than Olinda. Olinda's narrow streets make for a close-together crowd that's hard to walk through. But Olinda's parties are more energetic than Recife's.

The **Carnaval** in both places is the most colorful **carnaval de rua** (kah-nah-*vah*-ooh jee *hoo*-ah; street carnival) in Brazil. Most visitors don't wear a **fantasia** (fahn-tah-*zee*-ah; costume), but some do, and you certainly can. People tend not to dress in costume like during Halloween but rather wear flashy, colorful clothing or generally festive outfits.

People just mill about on the streets, **bebidas** (beh-*bee*-dahz; drinks) in hand, and stop to watch impromptu **blocos** (*bloh*-kooz; bands with fans dancing nearby. *Literally:* blocks) parade by. The "parade" in Recife is pretty disorganized, although there seems to be more timing involved in Olinda. But both places feature **blocos** of all sorts. A **bloco,** in either place, can simply be a group of co-workers who've picked a theme for themselves, dressed accordingly, and beat some makeshift percussion instruments. Little in either city feels "official." And the parading/roaming the streets lasts all day. There's also food you can buy on the street, as well as some plazas where you can hang out in the open air and eat a more substantial meal while you hear drumbeats in the distance (or parading by you).

In Olinda, what's famous and incredible are the **bonecos gigantes** (boo-*neh*-kooz zhee-*gahn*-cheez; gigantic dolls). They're handmade figures that stand about 20 feet tall — which is great, because they're visible no matter where you are in the crowd. The **bonecos** are sometimes of famous Brazilian people, like the 20th-century writer Jorge Amado.

The most famous **bonecos** are the **Homem da Meia-Noite** (*oh*-mang dah *may*-ah *noh*-ee-chee; Midnight Man) in Olinda and the **Galo da Madrugada** (*gah*-loo dah mah-droo-*gah*-dah; Sunrise Rooster) in Recife. Parading of the rooster kicks off the whole Carnaval in Recife on the first day. The **bonecos** are paraded through the **ruas,** along with informal **blocos.**

O frevo and o maracatu

The traditional Carnaval music from this part of northeastern Brazil by Recife/Olinda is **o frevo** (ooh *fdeh*-voo) and **o maracatu** (ooh mah-dah-kah-too). **Frevo** dancing is indeed strange and seemingly un-Brazilian when you first see it: Usually a small child or a grown man in a colorful, clownish outfit dances with a **guarda-chuva** (*gwah*-dah *shoo*-vah; umbrella). The name **frevo** comes from the verb **ferver** (feh-*veh;* to boil) — the dancing and footwork are so fast, the dancer seems to be on the boil. **Frevo** music sounds very traditional because the melodies hark back hundreds of years.

Maracatu has a fast, distinctive beat that really shows off Brazilians' talent for drumming. The drummers — all men — wear huge, shaggy, sparkling head-dresses. The tradition was brought to Brazil by African slaves, who used the music and dancing rituals for naming African royalty.

Talkin' the Talk

Fernando and **Roberta** are a couple from São Paulo. They're in Recife. They ask **Katia**, a local, where to go in Olinda to find the Carnaval action.

Fernando: **Por favor, você é daqui?**
poh fah-*voh*, voh-*seh eh* dah-*kee?*
Excuse me, are you from around here?

Katia: **Sou.**
soh.
I am.

Roberta: **Onde tem a festa na Olinda?**
ohn-jee *tang* ah *feh*-stah nah oh-*leen*-dah?
Where's the party in Olinda?

Katia: **Olha, a festa tem pela cidade toda, mas a rua principal é a Rua 15 de novembro.**
ohl-yah, ah *feh*-stah *tang* peh-lah see-*dah*-jee *toh*-dah, mah-eez ah *hoo*-ah pdeen-see-*pah*-ooh *eh* ah *hoo*-ah *keen*-zee jee noh-*vehm*-bdoh.
Well, the party is throughout the city, but the main street is 15 of November Street.

Fernando: **Acha que um táxi pode chegar até lá?**
ah-shah kee oong *talk*-see *poh*-jee sheh-*gah* ah-teh *lah?*
Do you think a taxi can get through to there?

Katia: **Têm muito movimento por ai; peça para o taxista te deixar ai perto daquela rua, e vai ver a festa.**
tang moh-*ee*-toh moh-vee-*men*-toh poh ah-*ee*; peh-sah pah-dah ooh talk-*see*-stah chee day-*shah* ah-*ee* peh-too dah-*keh*-lah *hoo*-ah, ee *vah*-ee *veh* ah *feh*-stah.
There's a lot of crowd activity over there; ask the taxi driver to leave you over there close to that street, and you'll see the party.

Roberta:	**Tá legal, obrigada!**
	tah lay-*gah*-ooh, oh-bdee-*gah*-dah!
	Cool, thanks!
Roberta:	**Não tem como errar.**
	nah-ooh *tang koh*-moo eh-*hah.*
	There's no way to make a mistake.

Words to Know

pela cidade toda	<u>peh</u>-lah see-<u>dah</u>-jee <u>toh</u>-dah	throughout the city
movimento	moh-vee-<u>men</u>-toh	crowd activity
peça	<u>peh</u>-sah	ask
deixar	day-<u>shah</u>	to drop off
daquela	dah-<u>keh</u>-lah	of that
errar	eh-<u>hah</u>	to make a mistake

Dancing the Samba!

If you visit Brazil, you can hear **samba** music and see people dancing **samba** (*sahm*-bah) regardless of where you go for Carnaval. So how is the famous **dança** (*dahn*-sah; dance) danced?

There are two basic **tipos** (*chee*-pooz; types) of samba: the step the women **sambistas** (sahm-*bee*-stahz; samba dancers) do during Carnaval while wearing high heels on top of a float and the type that everyone else does. The heels make the dance much more **difícil** (jee-*fee*-see-ooh; difficult). You can leave those moves to the talented women who remain a **mistério** (mee-*steh*-dee-ooh; mystery) to dazzled spectators.

It took me a good three years to **aprender** (ah-pdehn-*deh;* learn) to dance samba, and I still don't do it very well. The step is simple, but I'm convinced you need to have Brazilian **sangue** (*sahn*-gee; blood) in your veins to do it

muito bem (moh-*ee*-toh *bang;* very well). Nonetheless, for the mere mortals out there, here's what to do:

1. First, loosen those **joelhos** (zhoh-*ehl*-yooz; knees); **relaxe** (heh-*lah*-shee; relax) and bend them a little bit. Samba isn't danced with the **corpo** (*koh*-poo; body) straight up but rather like you're going to sit down.

2. Next, put your feet together. Shift your weight onto your **pé direito** (*peh* jee-*day*-too; right foot). Then shift the weight to your **pé esquerdo** (*peh* eh-*skeh*-doo; left foot). As you do this, fling your **pé direito** to the front, with your heel sliding on the ground, as if your heel is scuffing the floor — and at the end, fling your heel up, just slightly, off the floor.

3. As you do the scuff, point your right foot's toes slightly to the right, as if you're just starting to make an arc with the right foot. And your body faces forward the whole time, upper body moving as little as possible. Arms should be bent at the elbows, as if to balance yourself.

4. Now, bring that **pé direito** back to where it was and step on it. You're just moving in place — shifting your weight back to your right foot. Now do the same thing, starting with the **pé esquerdo!** It's a three-beat move, and the dance is subtle, not showy.

If you feel awkward trying it, don't worry. Here's a huge **segredo** (seh-*gdeh*-doo; secret): Many Brazilians can't samba. Either try it again, or just sit down, have a drink, and enjoy yourself. That's all that matters, anyway!

Falling in Love — in Portuguese

They say **o amor** (ooh ah-*moh;* love) is the international language. That's true, but why love without talking when saying lovey-dovey things in Portuguese is so much fun?

Brazilian Portuguese is an extremely romantic language — not only are the sounds beautiful and melodic, but Brazilians themselves are very **românticos** (hoh-*mahn*-chee-kooz; romantic). And you can't separate the **lingua** (*ling*-gwah; language) from its **cultura** (kool-*too*-dah; culture). The language **está cheia de poesía** (eh-*stah shay*-ah jee poh-eh-*zee*-ah; it's full of poetry).

In Brazil, most people are up-to-date on the television **novelas** (noh-*veh*-lahz; soap operas). And with 80 percent of Brazilian **novelas** dealing with **a paixão** (ah *pah*-ee-*shah*-ooh; passion), that means most Brazilians think about romance a lot. The stories are **alegres** (ah-*leh*-gdeez; happy) and **tristes** (*tdees*-cheez; sad), of course, and a touch of **tragédia** (tdah-*zheh*-jee-ah; tragedy) never hurts. In contrast, cop shows, talk shows, and sitcoms seem to top the ratings in the U.S.

Brazilians even have a specific verb to describe the act of smooching about town with your honey: **namorar** (*nah*-moh-*dah*). The root of the verb is **amor.** What did **Jaqueline** (*zhah*-keh-*lee*-nee) do Saturday? **Ela foi namorar** (*eh*-lah *foh*-ee *nah*-moh-*dah;* She hung out with her boyfriend).

Girlfriend, by the way, is **namorada** (nah-moh-*dah*-dah), and boyfriend is **namorado** (nah-moh-*dah*-doo). After things move along and the happy couple has a **casamento** (*kah*-zah-*men*-toh; wedding), they become husband and wife — **marido e mulher** (mah-*dee*-doo ee mool-*yeh*).

Check out some classic romantic phrases in Portuguese:

- **Eu te amo.** (*eh*-ooh chee *ah*-moo; I love you.)

- **Voce se casaria comigo?** (voh-*seh* see kah-zah-*dee*-ah koh-*mee*-goo; Will you marry me?)

- **Eu estou apaixionado/a.** (*eh*-ooh eh-*stoh* ah-pah-ee-shee-ooh-*nah*-doo/dah; I'm in love.)

- **Estou com muita saudade de você.** (eh-*stoh* kohng moh-*ee*-tah sah-ooh-*dah*-jee jee voh-*seh;* I miss you very much.)

- **Me da um beijo.** (mee *dah* oong *bay*-zhoh; Give me a kiss.)

- **Eu vou te amar por toda a minha vida.** (*eh*-ooh *voh* chee ah-*mah* poh *toh*-dah ah ming-yah *vee*-dah; I'm going to love you for the rest of my life.)

And here's how Brazilians say sweet nothings:

- **o meu amor** (ooh *meh*-ooh ah-*moh*; my love)

- **o meu querido/a minha querida** (ooh *meh*-ooh keh-*dee*-doo/ah *ming*-yah keh-*dee*-dah; my honey. *Literally:* my loved one)

- **o meu fofinho/a minha fofinha** (ooh *meh*-ooh foh-*fing*-yoh/ah *ming*-yah foh-*fing*-yah; my sweetie. *Literally:* my soft, fluffy one)

Here are some classic romantic phrases that Brazilians use to **paquerar** (pah-keh-*dah;* flirt):

- **Você é muito lindo/a.** (voh-*seh* eh moh-*ee*-toh *leen*-doh/dah; You're really handsome/beautiful.)

- **Você tem olhos muito bonitos.** (voh-*seh* tang *ohl*-yooz moh-*ee*-toh boo-*nee*-tooz; You have very pretty eyes.)

- **Gosto muito de você.** (*goh*-stoo moh-*ee*-toh jee voh-*seh;* I really like you.)

Here are some practical phrases, too, for when you meet someone you're interested in:

✔ **Me da o seu número de telefone?** (mee *dah* ooh *seh*-ooh *noo*-meh-doh jee teh-leh-*foh*-nee; Will you give me your phone number?)

✔ **O quê vai fazer amanhã?** (ooh *kee vah*-ee fah-*zeh* ah-mahn-*yah;* What are you doing tomorrow?)

✔ **Quer ir para o cinema comigo?** (*keh ee* pah-dah ooh see-*neh*-mah koh-*mee*-goo; Do you want to go to the movies with me?)

Of course, these are all things you say after the very first question: **Qual é seu nome?** (*kwah*-ooh *eh* seh-ooh *noh*-mee; What's your name?) or **Quer dançar?** (*keh* dahn-*sah;* Do you want to dance?)

Talkin' the Talk

Pay attention as **Jorge** and **Glória** flirt with each other.

Jorge: **Olá, quer dançar?**
oh-*lah*, *keh* dahn-*sah?*
Hi, do you want to dance?

Glória: **Tá bom.**
tah *boh*-oong.
Okay.

Jorge: **Você é muito linda. Qual é seu nome?**
voh-*seh* eh moh-ee-toh *leen*-dah. *kwah*-ooh *eh seh*-ooh *noh*-mee?
You're very pretty. What's your name?

Glória: **Obrigada. Sou a Glória. E você?**
oh-bdee-*gah*-dah. *soh* ah *gloh*-dee-ah. ee voh-*seh*?
Thanks. I'm Gloria. And you?

Jorge: **Jorge. Você vem aqui muito? Nunca te vi aqui.**
zhoh-zhee. voh-*seh vang* ah-*kee* moh-ee-toh? *noong*-kah chee *vee* ah-*kee*.
Jorge. Do you come here often? I've never seen you here.

Glória: **Só vim uma vez antes.**
soh *veeng ooh*-mah vehz *ahn*-cheez.
I only came once before.

Jorge: **Espero te ver mais por aqui.**
eh-*speh*-doo chee *veh mah*-eez poh ah-*kee*.
I hope to see you here more.

Glória: **Eu também.**
eh-ooh tahm-*bang*.
Me, too.

Words to Know

Você vem aqui muito?	voh-<u>seh</u> <u>vang</u> ah-<u>kee</u> moh-<u>ee</u>-toh	Do you come here often?
vim	ving	I came
uma vez	<u>ooh</u>-mah <u>vehz</u>	one time
Espero te ver mais.	eh-<u>speh</u>-doo chee veh <u>mah</u>-eez	I hope to see you more.

Talkin' the Talk

Two years after meeting, **Jorge** proposes to **Glória**.

Jorge: **Glória, eu te amo tanto.**
gloh-dee-ah, *eh*-ooh chee *ah*-moo *tahn*-toh.
Gloria, I love you so much.

Glória: **Eu te amo também.**
eh-ooh chee *ah*-moo tahm-*bang*.
I love you, too.

Jorge: **Você se casaria comigo?**
voh-*seh* see *kah*-zah-*dee*-ah koh-*mee*-goo?
Will you marry me?

Glória: **Oh, Jorge, sim!**
oh, *zhoh*-zhee, *sing*!
Oh, Jorge, yes!

Jorge: **Você é a mulher dos meus sonhos.**
voh-*seh eh* ah mool-*yeh* dooz *meh*-ooz *sohn*-yooz.
You're the woman of my dreams.

Glória: **Quero estar com você sempre.**
keh-doo eh-*stah* kohng voh-*seh sehm*-pdee.
I want to be with you always.

Fun & Games

You have a friend who's thinking about going to Brazil for Carnaval. You — now the expert on the topic — explain the three main options.

Match each term with the Carnaval they best describe — Rio, Salvador, or Recife/Olinda. See Appendix C for the answers.

1. frevo

2. sambódromo

3. abadá

4. samba

5. bonecos

6. farol

7. trio elétrico

8. maracatu

9. axé

Part IV
The Part of Tens

The 5th Wave — By Rich Tennant

"...and remember, no more Portuguese tongue twisters until you know the language better."

In this part . . .

*1*f you're looking for small, easily digestible pieces of information about Portuguese, this part is for you. Here, you can find ten ways to speak Portuguese quickly, ten useful Portuguese expressions to know, eleven common slang expressions, and eleven terms you can use to make people think you're fluent.

Chapter 18

Ten Ways to Get a Quick Handle on Brazilian Portuguese

*T*he real fun comes when you put this book down and listen to some live Brazilians talking. Even if you can't find any Brazilians or other Portuguese-speaking people near you, I give you some options for immersing yourself in their language. Take a peek at the following for some ideas.

Go to Brazil!

The absolute best way to learn Portuguese, or any foreign language, is to spend time in a country where the people speak the language. Brazil is a particularly great place to learn a new language, because locals are unbelievably friendly. They also don't speak English very fluently, so you'll be practically immersed in Portuguese.

You can meet waiters, new friends, people in shops. They'll probably speak a little English, and you'll speak a little Portuguese. That's the perfect language-learning situation — you can both have fun teaching each other some words.

Travel to Brazil can be a little pricey. But when you're there, the exchange rate means things are generally three or four times cheaper than they are in North America or Europe. The going rate for Brazil's **pousadas** (poh-*zah*-dahz; lovely small hotels) is only about US$20 a night for two people.

If you're interested in exploring several regions of Brazil (and hearing a few different accents within the country), look into buying a Brazil Air Pass. It allows you to make up to five one-way flights within Brazil for about US$560. Brazil Air Passes are offered by Varig and Tam — two Brazilian airlines — and you have to buy them outside Brazil (before you go).

Find Brazilians (or Other Portuguese-Speakers) Near You

To research whether you're in a Brazilian-immigration hot spot, look online for authentic Brazilian restaurants, Brazilian goods shops, or Brazilian live music in your area. If you get a hit, check it out. Ask one of the Brazilian workers (using a few Portuguese words if you can) where Brazilians in your area hang out. Or just make friends at the restaurant or venue. You can also try putting the name of your hometown in the Search box of Brazil's Google site (www.google.com.br) and see what comes up!

The majority of Brazilians in the United States live on the East Coast — in Miami, near Boston, or in New Jersey. You're in luck if you live near one of these places! But Brazilian immigration to the U.S. is increasing, and as soon as one cousin touches down in your town, more family members and friends are probably on the way.

If you're a sporty person, you can consider trying to meet people at a **capoeira** (kah-poh-*ey*-dah; Brazilian martial art/dance form) class. It's very trendy at the moment, and most metropolitan areas have classes.

You can also research whether any Portuguese restaurants (from Portugal) or neighborhoods with a known Portuguese district are near you (Newark's Ironbound District is one in New Jersey). The accent is very different, but any exposure to the language helps! Besides, written Portuguese (think restaurant menus) in both Portugal and Brazil is very standard.

Date a Brazilian

This option isn't for everyone, of course. But if you do find a place where Brazilians hang out near where you live and you're single, it's not a bad idea at all! Brazilians are a very affectionate and fun-to-date crowd. And they'll be more patient with your stuttered sentences and questions about Portuguese than any teacher you'll ever have.

Read the News in Portuguese

Your brain is constantly absorbing new information in ways that you don't even realize. By reading Portuguese news, you can familiarize yourself with the way Portuguese looks and the patterns its words make.

If you enjoy reading, you should consider browsing the day's top news online. First read the story in an English-language newspaper to get the facts. Then log on to a Brazilian newspaper's Web site and read the same story in Portuguese. It'll be easier to understand because you'll already know the context and most of the details. It's okay if you don't understand many of the words! But guaranteed, you'll notice a few words that look like English, and you may understand a few more given the context. Hopefully, you'll recognize some words that you've already picked up from this book.

The biggest newspapers in Brazil are *O Globo* (www.oglobo.com.br) in Rio and the politically left-leaning *Folha de São Paulo* (www.folha.com.br) and the politically right-leaning *O Estado de São Paulo* (www.estadao.com.br) in São Paulo. You can also check out *BBC Brazil* (www.bbc.co.uk/portuguese/).

Check Out Brazilian Web Sites

To research any topic in Brazilian Portuguese, try going to Google Brazil (www.google.com.br). **Pesquisa** (pehs-*kee*-zah) means *Search*. Below the Search box, you can select one of three options: **a web** (the Web), **páginas em português** (Portuguese-language Web sites), or **páginas do Brasil** (Brazilian Web pages). Click on the last option to limit your search to Web sites with a Brazilian domain name (.br). The button next to **Pesquisa Google** — **Estou com sorte** — means *I'm feeling lucky*. If you choose that, the search engine automatically takes you to the first Web page your search turns up.

You can try entering search terms on Brazilian Google in either Portuguese or English. Sometimes an English-language site comes up. Ignore it, and find one in Portuguese instead.

Try putting a hobby of yours in the Search box. Say you're a NASCAR fan. Or you like to knit. Or you love drinking Brazil's national drink, the **caipirinha** (kah-ee-pee-*deeng*-yah), which is made from lime, sugar, sugarcane liquor, and ice. Put **caipirinha** in the Search box, and you can discover how to make an authentic one.

Again, don't stress out when you see a ton of words you don't know. Your curiosity is your best learning aid. As you expose yourself to the language, you're taking sure but slow steps toward understanding and speaking Portuguese.

Here are some of Brazil's most popular sites and stores. Find out about Brazilian culture, and pick up a few new words, too:

- ✔ **Pão de Açucar** (www.paodeacucar.com.br): Supermarket goods
- ✔ **Mercado Livre** (www.mercadolivre.com.br): Brazil's main online auction site
- ✔ **UOL** (www.uol.com.br): Brazil's most popular online portal
- ✔ **Submarino** (www.submarino.com.br): Brazil's biggest online bookstore

Tourism sites are great, because they often have versions of the same text in English and Portuguese. Check out www.turismo.gov.br for general tourism information on Brazil. You can switch the language to Portuguese by clicking on the icon of Brazil's green, yellow, and blue flag; selecting an American or British flag changes the language back to English.

Listen to Brazilian Music

Absorb the sound of Brazilian Portuguese through its music. Take a look at the lyrics too, if they're included with the CD or are available online.

Brazil has many musical genres. The most famous ones are **bossa nova** (*boh*-sah *noh*-vah), slow, lyrical music from the 1960s; **música popular brasileira (MPB)** (*moo*-zee-kah poh-poo-*lah* bdah-zee-*lay*-dah [*eh*-mee *peh beh*]), which is mostly acoustic guitar and singing; **pagode** (pah-*goh*-jee), which is fun and has a light beat; **samba** (*sahm*-bah), call-and-response music with a medium beat; **chorinho** (shoh-*ding*-yoh), the precursor to samba, from the 1920s; and **axé** (ah-*sheh*), ultra-fast music typical of Carnival in Salvador.

Here are some popular artists:

- Gilberto Gil (MPB)
- Caetano Veloso (MPB)
- Marisa Monte (MPB)
- Jorge Ben Jor (MPB/funk)
- Tim Maia (funk)
- Gal Costa (bossa nova)
- Elis Regina (bossa nova)
- Vinicius de Moraes (bossa nova)
- Zeca Pagodinho (samba)
- Ivete Sangalo (axé)
- Revelação (pagode)
- Marcelo D2 (rap)
- DJ Patife (electronic)
- DJ Marky (hard electronic)

Rent a Brazilian Movie

Watching a Brazilian movie is another great way to learn about Brazilian culture and pick up some new words at the same time. The movie should have English subtitles. That allows your ear to absorb the new sounds as you read the translation in English.

Here are some famous Brazilian movies:

- *Deus É Brasileiro*/*God is Brazilian* (2003)
- *Carandirú*/*Carandiru* (2003)
- *Cidade de Deus*/*City of God* (2002)
- *Ônibus 174*/*Bus 174* (2002)
- *Eu, Tu, Eles*/*Me, You, Them* (2000)
- *Central do Brasil*/*Central Station* (1998)
- *Pixote* (1981)
- *Bye Bye Brazil* (1979)
- *Orfeu Negro*/*Black Orpheus* (1959)

Watch Globo on Cable or Satellite TV

Order **Rede Globo** (*heh*-jee *gloh*-boo; Globo Network), Brazil's best-known TV station. Watching Brazilian **novelas** (noh-*veh*-lahs; soap operas) is an excellent way to learn about Brazilian culture!

DISH Network (www.dishnetwork.com) offers **Rede Globo** anywhere in the U.S. for people who have a satellite dish. Otherwise, you can go to the following Web page on Rede Globo's international distribution partners: tvglobo internacional.globo.com/assinar.jsp. Click on the region of the world you're from, and a list of local companies appears.

Take a Portuguese Class

If you can't make it to Brazil, the next best thing may be to take a Portuguese class at a location near you. Make sure the teacher is a Brazilian if you're serious about learning Portuguese from Brazil and not Portuguese from Portugal. The accent and many common words are different.

"Say It Again, João!"

Talk to yourself on the street. If people think you're crazy, that's okay. Repetition is the only way to get new words to stick in your brain. Repeat words from this book and sound them out loud whenever you feel like it.

I talked to myself on the streets of Brazil, attempting to get that nasal sound so I could fake being a real Brazilian for a minute while I was alone. I found practicing my accent easier that way, because I'd get embarrassed trying to replicate all the new sounds in front of other people.

Chapter 19

Ten Favorite Brazilian Portuguese Expressions

Check out the phrases in this chapter. In using them, not only can you sound like a native Brazilian, but you may be able to recognize these commonplace expressions. Brazilian Portuguese is a fun language. It's humorous and full of spice and emotion.

Think of these phrases as clues to Brazilian culture. They start to paint a picture of a nation full of lively, friendly, and laid-back people.

Que saudade!

The word **saudade** (sah-ooh-*dah*-jee) has no direct translation in English, and it's a major source of linguistic pride for Brazilians. Use **Que saudade!** (kee sah-ooh-*dah*-jee) when you miss something so desperately, you have a heartache over it. People say **Que saudade!** when they remember their best friend who's now living far away, or their childhood beach. Brazilians also often say simply **Saudades!** at the end of e-mails to tell you they're missing you terribly.

Fala sério!

Say **Fala sério** (*fah*-lah *seh*-dee-oh) to mean *You're kidding!* or *You're joking!* or *No way!* Brazilians also say **Não acredito!** (*nah*-ooh ah-kdeh-*jee*-toh; I can't believe it!) in the same situations. But **Fala sério** has a funnier tone to it. It literally means *Talk seriously*.

. . . pra caramba!

Here's a great way to emphasize how off-the-charts something is. **Pra caramba** (pdah kah-*dahm*-bah) is most often used at the end of a sentence to exaggerate something. Use this phrase instead of putting **muito** (moh-*ee*-toh; very) or **bem** (bang; very) in front of these same words.

Take the classic phrase **É boa pra caramba** (eh *boh*-ah pdah kah-*dahm*-bah). **Boa** by itself means *good*. When **pra caramba** comes after *good*, it transforms *It's good* to *It's amazing*.

Engraçado means *funny*. **Engraçado pra caramba** (ang-gdah-*sah*-doo pdah kah-*dahm*-bah) means *hilarious*. **Muito frío** means very cold. So how cold was it? **Frío pra caramba!** (*fdee*-oh pdah kah-*dahm*-bah; Really, really cold!).

Lindo maravilhoso!

Lindo maravilhoso! (*leen*-doh mah-dah-veel-*yoh*-zoo) is a very Brazilian saying that literally translates to *Beautiful, marvelous!* Brazilians like to gush about beauty and how amazing things are.

The weather can be **lindo maravilhoso!** — **Hoje esteve um dia lindo maravihoso!** (*oh*-zhee eh-*steh*-vee oong *jee*-ah *leen*-doh mah-dah-veel-*yoh*-zoo; Today the weather was fantastic!). A place can be **lindo maravihoso!** — **O local é lindo maravihoso!** (ooh loh-*kah*-ooh eh *leen*-doh mah-dah-veel-*yoh*-zoo; The place is amazing!). If you admire someone's work, that can be **lindo maravilhoso!** too.

And try to remember to use an **-a** at the end of each word instead of the **-o** if the word you're talking about is feminine. A gorgeous woman is **linda maravilhosa!** And a handsome man is **lindo maravilhoso!**

É mesmo?

É mesmo? (eh *mehz*-moh) means *Really?* It's usually used to react to some interesting new fact.

You tell someone: Did you know that Portuguese is the fifth most-spoken language in the world? She answers back: **É mesmo?**

You tell someone: Did you know that Karla is dating Paulinho? He answers back: **É mesmo?**

You tell someone that you're learning Portuguese. What does she answer back? Sometimes it's an enthusiastic **É mesmo!** *Really!*

Um beijo! or Um abraço!

Brazilians are very affectionate people. They often end a conversation with a friend or acquaintance they feel friendly toward by saying **Um beijo!** (oong *bay*-zhoh; a kiss) or **Um abraço!** (oong ah-*bdah*-soh; a hug). In general, women use **Um beijo!** to male and female friends, and men use **Um beijo!** to women and **Um abraço!** to male friends. These expressions are also common ways to end an e-mail.

Imagina!

Brazilians are also very hospitable. After telling you *thank you* — **obrigado** (oh-bdee-*gah*-doh) if you're male and **obrigada** (oh-bdee-*gah*-dah) if you're female — a Brazilian often says **Imagina!** (mah-*zhee*-nah; *Literally:* Imagine!) to mean *It's no trouble at all!* The initial *i* is chopped off in spoken language. It sounds like **Magina!**

Pois não?

Here's a common phrase you may hear when you enter a shop or call a service-oriented company over the phone, like a restaurant. **Pois não?** (*poh*-eez *nah*-ooh) means *Can I help you?* It's a funny phrase, because it literally means *Because no?* It's pretty nonsensical, and Brazilians have a hard time saying where the phrase originated.

Com certeza!

This is another fun, common phrase. **Com certeza!** (koh-oong seh-*teh*-zah; *Literally:* With certainty!) translates to *Of course!* or *Definitely!*

If someone asks you **Vai para a festa?** (*vah*-ee pah-dah ah *fehs*-tah; Are you going to the party?), you can answer **Com certeza!**

Fique tranquilo

If Brazilians value any single trait, it's optimism; it's being able to solve problems. And if the problem can't be fixed, just relax and forget about it. At the first signs of someone's stress, a Brazilian often says **Fique tranquilo** (*fee*-kee kdang-*kwee*-loh; Don't worry). It has a very calming effect.

If the bus takes off just as you arrive to the bus stop, don't worry. **Fique tranquilo:** There'll be another one in ten minutes. And you can make friends while you wait.

Chapter 20

Eleven Common Portuguese Slang Words

In This Chapter
▶ Words you hear often in Brazil
▶ Words you can use to make you sound more like a native

*B*razilians use the words in this chapter on a day-to-day basis. It's okay if you don't feel comfortable stringing along whole sentences using these words. Being able to recognize real **jíria** (*zhee*-dee-ah; slang) when you hear it is fun enough!

Chato

This word is my personal favorite. What's interesting about **chato** (*shah*-toh) is that it doesn't really have a precise translation in English. It means *boring, annoying,* or *lame,* depending on the context. Here are some examples of how to use it:

✔ **Aquele filme é muito chato.** (ah-*keh*-lee *fee*-ooh-mee *eh moh*-ee-toh *shah*-toh; That movie is really boring.)

✔ **Que chato!** (kee *shah*-toh; How lame!)

Legal

Legal (lay-*gah*-ooh) is a very useful word. It means *cool*. **Legal** actually translates to *legal* in English, as in following the law. That usage may seem weird at first, but it's really how the word's used. Imagine shouting "Legal!" in English instead of saying "Cool!"

- ✔ **Que legal!** (kee lay-*gah*-ooh; How cool!)
- ✔ **Muito legal!** (moh-*ee*-toh lay-*gah*-ooh; Very cool!)

Cara

Cara (*kah*-dah) means *guy*. Here are some examples of how to use it:

- ✔ **Quem é aquele cara?** (*kang eh* ah-*keh*-lee *kah*-dah; Who is that guy?)
- ✔ **Lembra daquele cara?** (*lehm*-bdah dah-*keh*-lee *kah*-dah; Do you remember that guy?)

Gato and Gata

If a man is good-looking, Brazilian women call him a **gato** (*gah*-toh). A **gata** (*gah*-tah) is how a Brazilian refers to a beautiful woman. **Gato** and **gata** literally mean *cat*.

- ✔ **Ele é um gato.** (*eh*-lee *eh* oong *gah*-toh; He's gorgeous.)
- ✔ **Que gata!** (kee *gah*-tah; What a sexy woman!)

Grana

Grana (*gdah*-nah) is slang for *money;* it's like saying *dough* in English. Brazilians sometimes complain about their lack of **grana.** Here are some common ways to use the word:

- ✔ **Eu estou sem grana.** (*eh*-ooh eh-*stoh* sang *gdah*-nah; I don't have any money.)
- ✔ **Tem grana para me emprestar?** (tang *gdah*-nah *pah*-dah mee ehm-pdeh-*stah;* Do you have some money you can lend me?)

The real word for *money* in Portuguese is **dinheiro** (jing-*yay*-doh).

Chique

Chique (*shee*-kee) is a fun word. It's the Brazilianized version of the French word *chic*. **Chique** can replace **sofisticado** (soh-fee-stee-*kah*-doh; sophisticated) and **glamoroso** (glah-moh-*doh*-zoo; glamorous), but it can also be used for anything that is **caro** (*kah*-doh; expensive).

- ✔ **Que chique!** (kee *shee*-kee; How glamorous!)
- ✔ **O restaurante é muito chique.** (ooh heh-stah-ooh-*dahn*-chee eh moh-*ee*-toh *shee*-kee; It's a really nice restaurant.)

Valeu

Valeu (vah-*leh*-ooh) is an informal way of saying *Thanks* — instead of saying **obrigado** (oh-bdee-*gah*-doh) or **obrigada** (oh-bdee-*gah*-dah). **Valeu** tends to be used more by young people, especially surfers. It's like saying *Thanks, man* in English.

Valeu is most often used alone, but it can be part of a sentence:

- ✔ **Valeu pela dica!** (vah-*leh*-ooh peh-lah *jee*-kah; Thanks for the information/tip!)
- ✔ **Valeu pela carona!** (vah-*leh*-ooh peh-lah kah-*doh*-nah; Thanks for the ride!)

Esperto

Esperto (eh-*speh*-too) is a funny word because it looks like the word *expert* in English, and its meaning is very similar. You use it to say a person (or even an animal) is smart, street smart, or really good at something. Here's how it's used in conversation:

- ✔ **Ele é muito esperto.** (*eh*-lee eh moh-*ee*-toh eh-*speh*-too; He's really street smart.)
- ✔ **Os golfinhos são muito espertos.** (oohz goh-ooh-*feen*-yohz sah-ooh moh-*ee*-toh eh-*speh*-tooz; Dolphins are really smart.)
- ✔ **Ela é muito esperta na matemática.** (*eh*-lah eh moh-*ee*-toh eh-*speh*-tah nah mah-chee-*mah*-teh-kah; She's really good at math.)

Pinga

Pinga (*ping*-gah) is slang for **cachaça** (kah-*shah*-sah) — Brazil's most famous alcoholic spirit. It's made from sugar cane and tastes like a sweet tequila. The best **pinga** is made in the state of Minas Gerais. **Pinga** is also used to make **caipirinhas** (*kah*-ee-pee-*deen*-yah), Brazil's national drink, which is made by grinding lime and sugar in a mortar and pestle and then pouring the lime and sugar over ice and **pinga**.

Here are some sentences that use **pinga:**

- ✔ **Um copinho de pinga, por favor.** (oong koh-*ping*-yoh jee *ping*-gah poh-fah-*voh;* A small glass of cachaça, please.)

- ✔ **Que marcas de pinga tem ai?** (kee *mah*-kahz jee *ping*-gah tang ah-*ee;* What brands of cachaça do you have?)

Pinga com mel (*ping*-gah koh-oong *meh*-ooh; pinga with honey) is very popular. And in some places, you can find **pinga** that's been distilled with figs and other fruits.

Brega/Cafona

Maybe it's just me, but when I first got to Brazil, I found myself wanting to say *cheesy* in Portuguese. I discovered that Brazilians use two different words to express the concept. **Brega** (*bdeh*-gah) tends to mean *cheesy,* while **cafona** (kah-*foh*-nah) is more like *tacky.*

- ✔ **Essa música é muito brega.** (eh-sah *moo*-zee-kah eh moh-*ee*-toh *bdeh*-gah; This music is really cheesy.)

- ✔ **Viu o vestido dela? Que cafona!** (*vee*-ooh ooh vehs-*chee*-doo *deh*-lah kee kah-*foh*-nah; Did you see her dress? How tacky!)

Chapter 21

Eleven Terms That Make You Sound Fluent in Brazilian Portuguese

In This Chapter

▶ How Brazilian Portuguese really sounds

▶ The filler words and phonetic abbreviations that distinguish the way Brazilians speak

*P*eople often say that Brazilian Portuguese is lyrical. Following are some of the nuts and bolts of the language that help to give it its sound.

Some are "filler" words — think of how often most Americans say "like" when it adds no extra meaning to the sentence. And at the end of this chapter I give you some examples of how Brazilians often shorten certain words when they say them.

Relax — this stuff is here just to help you recognize the sound of the words so you have an idea of what they mean when you hear them. And if you're feeling up to using them, they can make you sound really fluent in Portuguese!

Né?

Brazilians probably say **né** (neh) more often than any other word or term. It means *Right?* They stick it at the end of sentences all the time: **Você vai para o aeroporto amanhã, né?** (voh-*seh vah*-ee pah-dah ooh ah-eh-doh-*poh*-too ah-mahn-*yah, neh;* You're going to the airport tomorrow, right?)

And you may also hear **né** in the middle of sentences, where it doesn't really have any use or meaning: **Eu vi o meu amigo, né, e depois não lembro mais nada** (*eh*-ooh *vee* ooh *meh*-ooh ah-*mee*-goh neh ee deh-*poh*-eez *nah*-ooh *lehm*-bdoh mah-eez *nah*-dah; I saw my friend, right, and then I don't remember anything else).

Né is the short way of saying **não é?** (*nah*-ooh *eh; Literally:* is it not?).

Ta

You know when you're listening to someone talking on the phone, and you hear them say *Oh . . . Yeah . . . Right . . . Uh-huh . . .*

Ta (tah) is the Brazilian equivalent of these words. If someone's giving you directions on how to get somewhere, for example, you can repeat **Ta . . . Ta . . . Ta . . .** and it'll sound like you're understanding and recording into memory everything he or she is saying.

Ta is the short way of saying **Está** (eh-*stah*).

Ah é?

Ah é (ah *eh*) is one of a few ways to say *Really?* It's also another of those phone conversation fillers. You can use it either to say *Really?* with real interest in what the person's saying or as a way to show the speaker you haven't fallen asleep.

My friend Jenny, an American who lived in Bahia state, said **Ah é?** was one of the first things she learned to say in Brazil.

Então

Então (eh-*tah*-ooh; so/then) is a major conversation filler in Brazil. People often say **então** to change the subject to something more interesting when there's a lull in a conversation. It also can be used to simply say *so* or *then*.

Sabe?

Here's a case where the translation and use of the word is exactly the same as in English. A Brazilian's saying **Sabe?** (*sah*-bee) is the equivalent of an American speaker's weaving the phrase *You know?* constantly throughout.

Imagine two people talking on the phone. Person A is telling a story to Person B. Person A says **Sabe?** about every 20 seconds as they talk. What does Person B say? (See previous entries for clues): **Ta . . . Ah é? . . . Ta . . .**

Meio

Meio (*may*-o; *sort of*) is an easy term for you to practice and wow native speakers with. Just remember — the pronunciation sounds like *mayo* in English. Yes, the short way of saying *mayonnaise*.

Use **meio** when you'd say *sort of:*

- ✔ **Ele é meio alto.** (*eh*-lee *eh may*-oh *ah*-ooh-*toh*-ooh; He's sort of tall.)

- ✔ **O vestido parece meio asiático.** (ooh vehs-*chee*-doo pah-*deh*-see *may*-oh ah-zee-*ah*-chee-koh; The dress looks sort of Asian.)

Ou seja/E tal

These two phrases are pure fillers. **Ou seja** (ooh *seh*-zhah) means *in other words* but is often used by speakers just to gather their thoughts for a few seconds. And **e tal** (ee *tah*-ooh) means *etc.* or *and stuff like that* or *and everything.*

Here is a real example of **e tal** I found on Google in Brazilian Portuguese (www.google.com.br): **O livro é sobre dragões e tal** (ooh *leev*-doh eh *sob*-dee drah-*goh*-eez ee *tah*-ooh; The book is about dragons and stuff like that).

Se Instead of Você

Here's an important one. People very often shorten **você** (voh-*seh;* you) to **se** when they speak. Instead of **Você entendeu? Você vai agora?** or **Você é da onde?** they say

✔ **Se entendeu?** (seh en-ten-*deh*-ooh; Did you understand?)

✔ **Se vai agora?** (seh *vah*-ee ah-*goh*-dah; Are you leaving now?)

✔ **Se é da onde?** (seh *eh* dah *ohn*-jee; Where are you from?)

A gente Instead of Nós

It's also common for people to say **a gente** (ah *jang*-chee) instead of **nós** (nohz) to mean *we* or *us*. **A gente** translates as *the people*.

At first, I felt very strange calling myself and my friends *the people,* as if I were talking about a group of people I didn't know.

But the weirdest aspect about this changeroo is the fact that **a gente** is conjugated like **ele/ela** (he/she):

✔ **A gente não é daqui.** (ah *jang*-chee *nah*-ooh *eh* dah-*kee;* We're not from around here.)

✔ **A gente trabalha muito.** (ah *jang*-chee tdah-*bahl*-yah moh-*ee*-toh; We work a lot.)

For more on verb conjugations, see Chapter 2.

Pra Instead of Para a

Para (*pah*-dah) means *for* or *in order to.* Sometimes Brazilians pronounce **para** as **pra** (pdah).

✔ **Vai pra praia?** (*vah*-ee *pdah pdah*-eeh-ah; Are you going to the beach?)

✔ **Pra fazer o quê?** (*pdah fah-zeh ooh keh;* To do what?)

Tô instead of Estou

Estou (eh-*stoh*; I am) is often shortened to **tô,** both in spoken speech and in e-mails.

✔ **Tô com fome.** (*toh* koh-oong *foh*-mee; I'm hungry.)

✔ **Hoje tô feliz.** (*oh*-zhee toh feh-*leez;* Today I'm happy.)

Part V

Appendixes

The 5th Wave By Rich Tennant

"My wife and I are taking the course together. I figure I only have to learn half as much, since she finishes all of my sentences anyway."

In this part . . .

This part of the book is a great reference guide. I lay out verb conjugation tables for the most common Brazilian Portuguese verbs. I also include two mini-dictionaries here — one from English to Portuguese, and the other from Portuguese to English. Another appendix lets you check out the answers to the Fun & Games activities. I also provide a listing of the tracks that appear on the audio CD that comes with this book (the disc is on the inside part of the last page). That's so you can listen and follow along while you're reading the dialogues. Finally, I list some countries where the official language is Portuguese.

Appendix A

Verb Tables

● ●

Portuguese Verbs

Regular Verbs Ending with -ar
For example: morar (to live)

	Present	Past	Future
eu (I)	moro	morei	vou morar
você (you)	mora	morou	vai morar
ele/ela (he/she)	mora	morou	vai morar
nós (we)	moramos	moramos	vamos morar
eles/elas (they)	moram	moraram	vão morar

Regular Verbs Ending with -er
For example: comer (to eat)

	Present	Past	Future
eu (I)	como	comi	vou comer
você (you)	come	comeu	vai comer
ele/ela (he/she)	come	comeu	vai comer
nós (we)	comemos	comemos	vamos comer
eles/elas (they)	comem	comeram	vão comer

Regular Verbs Ending with -ir
For example: abrir (to open)

	Present	Past	Future
eu (I)	abro	abri	vou abrir
você (you)	abre	abreu	vai abrir
ele/ela (he/she)	abre	abreu	vai abrir
nós (we)	abrimos	abrimos	vamos abrir
eles/elas (they)	abrem	abriram	vão abrir

Regular Portuguese Verbs

achar		Present	Past	Future
to find	eu	acho	achei	vou achar
	você	acha	achou	vai achar
	ele/ela	acha	achou	vai achar
	nós	achamos	achamos	vamos achar
	eles/elas	acham	acharam	vão achar

começar		Present	Past	Future
to start	eu	começo	comecei	vou começar
	você	começa	começou	vai começar
	ele/ela	começa	começou	vai começar
	nós	começamos	começamos	vamos começar
	eles/elas	começam	começaram	vão começar

comprar		Present	Past	Future
to buy	eu	compro	comprei	vou comprar
	você	compra	comprou	vai comprar
	ele/ela	compra	comprou	vai comprar
	nós	compramos	compramos	vamos comprar
	eles/elas	compram	compraram	vão comprar

		Present	**Past**	**Future**
conheçer	*eu*	conheço	conheçi	vou conheçer
to know	*você*	conheçe	conheçeu	vai conheçer
someone	*ele/ela*	conheçe	conheçeu	vai conheçer
	nós	conheçemos	conheçemos	vamos conheçer
	eles/elas	conheçem	conheçeram	vão conheçer

		Present	**Past**	**Future**
escutar	*eu*	escuto	escutei	vou escutar
to listen	*você*	escuta	escutou	vai escutar
	ele/ela	escuta	escutou	vai escutar
	nós	escutamos	escutamos	vamos escutar
	eles/elas	escutam	escutaram	vão escutar

		Present	**Past**	**Future**
falar	*eu*	falo	falei	vou falar
to speak	*você*	fala	falou	vai falar
	ele/ela	fala	falou	vai falar
	nós	falamos	falamos	vamos falar
	eles/elas	falam	falaram	vão falar

		Present	**Past**	**Future**
fechar	*eu*	fecho	fechei	vou fechar
to close	*você*	fecha	fechou	vai fechar
	ele/ela	fecha	fechou	vai fechar
	nós	fechamos	fechamos	vamos fechar
	eles/elas	fecham	fecharam	vão fechar

		Present	**Past**	**Future**
gostar	*eu*	gosto	gostei	vou gostar
to like	*você*	gosta	gostou	vai gostar
	ele/ela	gosta	gostou	vai gostar
	nós	gostamos	gostamos	vamos gostar
	eles/elas	gostam	gostaram	vão gostar

		Present	Past	Future
voltar	*eu*	volto	voltei	vou voltar
to come back	*você*	volta	voltou	vai voltar
	ele/ela	volta	voltou	vai voltar
	nós	voltamos	voltamos	vamos voltar
	eles/elas	voltam	voltaram	vão voltar

Irregular Portuguese Verbs

		Present	Past	Future
colocar	*eu*	coloco	coloquei	vou colocar
to put	*você*	coloca	colocou	vai colocar
	ele/ela	coloca	colocou	vai colocar
	nós	colocamos	coloquemos	vamos colocar
	eles/elas	colocam	colocaram	vão colocar

		Present	Past	Future
dar	*eu*	dou	dei	vou dar
to give	*você*	dá	deu	vai dar
	ele/ela	dá	deu	vai dar
	nós	damos	demos	vamos dar
	eles/elas	dão	deram	vão dar

		Present	Past	Future
estar	*eu*	estou	estive	vou estar
to be	*você*	está	esteve	vai estar
(temporarily)	*ele/ela*	está	esteve	vai estar
	nós	estamos	estivemos	vamos estar
	eles/elas	estão	estiveram	vão estar

fazer
to make/do

	Present	Past	Future
eu	faço	fiz	vou fazer
você	faz	fez	vai fazer
ele/ela	faz	fez	vai fazer
nós	fazemos	fizemos	vamos fazer
eles/elas	fazem	fizeram	vão fazer

ir
to go

	Present	Past	Future
eu	vou	fui	vou ir
você	vai	foi	vai ir
ele/ela	vai	foi	vai ir
nós	vamos	fomos	vamos ir
eles/elas	vão	foram	vão ir

peder
to lose

	Present	Past	Future
eu	perco	perdi	vou perder
você	perde	perdeu	vai perder
ele/ela	perde	perdeu	vai perder
nós	perdemos	perdemos	vamos perder
eles/elas	perdem	perderam	vão perder

pedir
to ask for

	Present	Past	Future
eu	peço	pedi	vou pedir
você	pede	pediu	vai pedir
ele/ela	pede	pediu	vai pedir
nós	pedimos	pedimos	vamos pedir
eles/elas	pedem	pediram	vão pedir

poder
to be able to

	Present	Past	Future
eu	posso	podia	vou poder
você	pode	podia	vai poder
ele/ela	pode	podia	vai poder
nós	podemos	podiamos	vamos poder
eles/elas	podem	podiam	vão poder

		Present	Past	Future
querer	*eu*	quero	quis	vou querer
to want	*você*	quer	quis	vai querer
	ele/ela	quer	quis	vai querer
	nós	queremos	quisemos	vamos querer
	eles/elas	querem	quiseram	vão querer

		Present	Past	Future
saber	*eu*	sei	sabia	vou saber
to know/	*você*	sabe	sabia	vai saber
understand	*ele/ela*	sabe	sabia	vai saber
	nós	sabemos	sabiamos	vamos saber
	eles/elas	sabem	sabiam	vão saber

		Present	Past	Future
sair	*eu*	saio	saí	vou sair
to leave/go out	*você*	sai	saiu	vai sair
	ele/ela	sai	saiu	vai sair
	nós	saimos	saímos	vamos sair
	eles/elas	saiam	saíram	vão sair

		Present	Past	Future
ser	*eu*	sou	fui	vou ser
to be	*você*	é	foi	vai ser
(permanently)	*ele/ela*	é	foi	vai ser
	nós	somos	fomos	vamos ser
	eles/elas	são	foram	vão ser

		Present	Past	Future
ter	*eu*	tenho	tive	vou ter
to have	*você*	tem	teve	vai ter
	ele/ela	tem	teve	vai ter
	nós	temos	tivemos	vamos ter
	eles/elas	têm	tiveram	vão ter

		Present	Past	Future
ver	*eu*	vejo	vi	vou ver
to see	*você*	vê	viu	vai ver
	ele/ela	vê	viu	vai ver
	nós	vemos	vimos	vamos ver
	eles/elas	vêem	viram	vão ver

		Present	Past	Future
vir	*eu*	venho	vim	vou vir
to come	*você*	vem	veio	vai vir
	ele/ela	vem	veio	vai vir
	nós	vemos	viemos	vamos vir
	eles/elas	vêm	vieram	vão vir

Portuguese-English Mini-Dictionary

A

a pé (ah *peh*): by foot
abacate (ah-bah-*koch*) m: avocado
abacaxi (ah-bah-kah-*shee*) m: pineapple
abraço (ah-*bdah*-soo) m: hug
abril (ah-*bdee*-ooh) m: April
abrir (ah-*bdee*): to open
advogada (ahj-voh-*gah*-dah) f: lawyer
advogado (ahj-voh-*gah*-doo) m: lawyer
agência (ah-*zhang*-see-ah) f: agency
agora (ah-*goh*-dah): now
agosto (ah-*goh*-stoo) m: August
água (*ah*-gwah) f: water
ajuda (ah-zhoo-*dah*) f: help
alface (ah-ooh-*fah*-see) m: lettuce
algodão (ah-ooh-goo-*dah*-ooh) m: cotton
algum (ah-ooh-*goong*): some
alho (*ahl*-yoh) m: garlic
almoço (ah-ooh-*moh*-soo) m: lunch
alto (*ah*-ooh-too): tall
amanhã (ah-mahng-*yah*): tomorrow
amarelo (ah-mah-*deh*-loo): yellow
andar (ahn-*dah*): floor of a building
antigo (ahn-*chee*-goo): old
apertado (ah-peh-*tah*-doo): tight
arroz (ah-*hohz*) m: rice

árvore (*ah*-voh-dee) f: tree
ator (ah-*toh*) m: actor
atum (ah-*toong*) m: tuna
avenida (ah-veh-*nee*-dah) f: avenue
avô (ah-*vah*) m: grandpa
avó (ah-*voh*) f: grandma
azul (ah-*zoo*): blue

B

bairro (*bah*-ee-hoo) m: neighborhood
banana (bah-*nah*-nah) f: banana
banco (*bahn*-koo) m: bank
banheiro (bahn-*yay*-doh) m: bathroom
barato (bah-*dah*-too): cheap
barco (*bah*-koo) m: boat
bastante (bah-*stahn*-ohee): a lot
beijo (*bay*-zhoo) m: kiss
bicicleta (bee-see-*kleh*-tah) f: bicycle
bife (*bee*-fee) m: skirt steak
bilhete (beel-*yeh*-chee) m: bill (as in dollar)
boate (boh-*ah*-chee) m: nightclub
boca (*boh*-kah) f: mouth
bom (*boh*-oong): good
braço (*bdah*-soo) m: arm
branco (*bdahn*-koh): white

C

cabeça (kah-*beh*-sah) f: head

cadeira (kah-*day*-dah) f: chair

café (kah-*feh*) m: coffee or a café

caixa eletrônica (*kah*-ee-shah eh-leh-*tdoh*-nee-kah) f: ATM

calça (*kah*-ooh-sah) f: pants

cama (*kah*-mah) f: bed

camarão (kah-mah-*dah*-ooh) m: shrimp

câmera (*kah*-meh-dah) f: camera

caminho (kah-*mee*-yoo) m: road

camiseta (kah-mee-*zeh*-tah) f: T-shirt

canção (kahn-*sah*-ooh) m: song

cancelar (kahn-seh-*lah*): to cancel

cantor (kahn-*toh*) m: singer

cantora (kahn-*toh*-dah) f: singer

caro (*kah*-doo): expensive

carro (*kah*-hoo) m: car

casa (*kah*-zah) f: house

cavalo (kah-*vah*-loo) m: horse

cebola (seh-*boh*-lah) f: onion

cem (sang): one hundred

cerveja (seh-*veh*-zhah) f: beer

céu (*seh*-ooh) m: sky

chocolate (shoh-koh-*lah*-chee) m: chocolate

chuva (*shoo*-vah) f: rain

cidade (see-*dah*-jee) f: city

cinco (*sing*-koh): five

cinema (see-*neh*-mah) m: movie theater

claro (*klah*-doo): light (in color)

coco (*koh*-koh) m: coconut

coisa (*koy*-zah) f: thing

colher (kool-*yeh*) m: spoon

com (kohng): with

comida (koh-*mee*-dah) f: food

computador (kohm-poo-tah-*doh*) m: computer

conta (*kohn*-tah) f: bill (at a restaurant)

contente (kohn-*ten*-chee): happy

copo (*koh*-poo) m: glass (cup)

correios (koh-*hay*-ooz) m: post office

cozinha (koh-*zing*-yah) f: kitchen

cunhada (koon-*yah*-dah) f: sister-in-law

cunhado (koon-*yah*-doo) m: brother-in-law

custar (koo-*stah*): to cost

D

data (*dah*-tah) f: date

dedo (*deh*-doo) m: finger

dedo do pé (*deh*-doo doo *peh*) m: toe

dela (*deh*-lah): her

dele (*deh*-lee): his

deles (*deh*-leez): their

dente (*den*-chee) m: tooth

dentista (den-*chee*-stah) m/f: dentist

devagar (deh-vah-*gah*): slowly

dez (dez): ten

dezembro (deh-*zem*-bdoo) m: December

dia (*jee*-ah) m: day

difícil (jee-*fee*-see-ooh): difficult

dinheiro (jing-*yay*-doo) m: money

direção (jee-deh-*sah*-ooh) f: direction

direita (jee-*day*-tah): right

disponível (jees-poh-*nee*-veh-ooh): available

divertido (jee-veh-*chee*-doo): fun

doce (*doh*-see): sweet

dois (*doh*-eez): two

domingo (doo-*ming*-goo) m: Sunday

dor (doh) m: pain

E

e (ee): and
encontrar (en-kohn-*tdah*): to find
escuro (eh-*skoo*-doo): dark
escutar (es-koo-*tah*): to listen
especial (eh-speh-see-*ah*-ooh): special
espinafre (es-pee-*nah*-fdee) m: spinach
esquerda (es-*keh*-dah): left
esquina (es-*kee*-nah) f: corner
estação (es-tah-*sah*-ooh) f: station
estado (eh-*stah*-doo) m: state
experimentar (eh-*speh*-dee-men-*tah*):
  to try

F

faca (*fah*-kah) f: knife
fácil (*fah*-see-ooh): easy
falar (fah-*lah*): to speak
farmácia (fah-*mah*-see-ah) f: drugstore
febre (*feh*-bdee) f: fever
fechar (feh-*shah*): to close
feijão (fay-*zhah*-ooh) m: beans
feliz (feh-*lees*): happy
feo (*fay*-ooh): ugly
fevereiro (feh-veh-*day*-doo) m: February
filha (*feel*-yah) f: daughter
filho (*feel*-yoo) m: son
flor (floh) f: flower
fome (*foh*-mee) m: hunger
fora (*foh*-dah): outside
foto (*foh*-too) f: photo
frango (*fdahn*-goo) m: chicken
fruta (*fdoo*-tah) f: fruit

G

garota (gah-*doh*-tah) f: girl
garoto (gah-*doh*-too) m: boy
gato (*gah*-too) m: cat
gerente (zheh-*dang*-chee) m: manager
goiaba (goy-*ah*-bah) f: guava
gostar (goh-*stah*): to like
grande (*gdahn*-jee): big
guerra (*geh*-hah) f: war
guia (*gee*-ah) m: guide

H

hoje (*oh*-zhee): today
homem (*oh*-mang) m: man
honesto (oh-*neh*-stoo): honest
hora (*oh*-dah) f: hour

I

identifição (ee-den-chee-fee-kah-*sah*-ooh)
  f: identification
idioma (ee-jee-*oh*-mah) m: language
ilha (*eel*-yah) f: island
imigração (ee-mee-gdah-*sah*-ooh)
  f: immigration
imprimir (eem-pdee-*meeh*): to print out
irmã (ee-*mah*) f: sister
irmão (ee-*mah*-ooh) m: brother

J

janeiro (zhah-*nay*-doo) m: January
jardim (zhah-*jing*) m: garden
jovem (*zhoh*-vang): young

julho (*zhool*-yoh) m: July
junho (*zhoon*-yoh) m: June
junto (*zhoon*-too): together

L

legal (lay-*goh*): cool (excellent)
leite (*lay*-chee) m: milk
leste (*lehs*-chee): east
ligar (lee-*gah*): to call
limão (lee-*mah*-ooh) m: lime
limpar (leem-*pah*): to clean
lingua (*ling*-gwah) f: language or tongue
livro (*leev*-doo) m: book
longe (*lohn*-zhee): far
longe (*lohn*-zhee): far away
lua (*loo*-ah) f: moon

M

maçã (mah-*sah*) f: apple
madeira (mah-*day*-dah) f: wood
mãe (*mah*-ee) f: mother
maio (*my*-oh) m: May
mais (*mah*-eez): more
manga (*mahn*-gah) f: mango
mapa (*mah*-pah) m: map
mar (mah) m: ocean
março (*mah*-soo) m: March
mariscos (mah-*dees*-kooz) m: shellfish
marrom (mah-*hohng*): brown
medicina (meh-jee-*see*-nah) f: medicine
médico (*meh*-jee-koo) m: doctor
melhor (mel-*yoh*): better
menina (meh-*nee*-nah) f: girl
menino (meh-*nee*-noo) m: boy
menos (*meh*-nooz): less

mesa (*meh*-zah) f: table
minuto (mee-*noo*-too) m: minute
moeda (moh-*eh*-dah) f: coin
montanha (mohn-*tahn*-yah) f: mountain
morar (moh-*dah*): to live
muito (moh-*ee*-toh): a lot
mulher (mool-*yeh*) f: woman
museu (moo-*zeh*-ooh) m: museum
música (*moo*-zee-kah) f: music

N

não (*nah*-ooh): no
nariz (nah-*deez*) m: nose
neta (*neh*-tah) f: granddaughter
neto (*neh*-too) m: grandson
noite (*noh*-ee-chee) f: night
norte (*noh*-chee) m: north
nove (*noh*-vee): nine
novela (noh-*veh*-lah) f: soap opera
novembro (noo-*vem*-bdoo) m: November
número (*noo*-meh-doh) m: number

O

ocupado (oh-koo-*pah*-doo): busy
oeste (oh-*es*-chee) m: west
oito (*oh*-ee-toh): eight
olho (*ohl*-yoo) m: eye
ônibus (*oh*-nee-boos) m: bus
orelha (oh-*dehl*-yah) f: ear
ou (ooh): or
ouro (*oh*-doo) m: gold
outro (*oh*-tdooh): another
outubro (ooh-*too*-bdoo) m: October
ovo (*oh*-voo) m: egg

P

pagar (pah-*gah*): to pay

pai (*pah*-ee) m: father

pais (pah-*eez*) m: country

pão (*pah*-ooh) m: bread

para (*pah*-dah): for/in order to

parque (*pah*-kee) m: park

passaporte (pah-sah-*poh*-chee) m: passport

paz (*pah*-eez) f: peace

pé (peh) m: foot

peito (*pay*-too) m: chest

peixe (*pay*-shee) m: fish

pequeno (peh-*keh*-noo): small

perguntar (peh-goon-*tah*): to ask

perna (*peh*-nah) f: leg

perto (*peh*-too): near

pessoa (peh-*soh*-ah) f: person

picante (pee-*kahn*-chee): spicy

pintar (peen-*tah*): to paint

pior (pee-*oh*): worse

piscina (pee-*see*-nah) f: pool

porta (*poh*-tah) f: door

pouco (*poh*-koo): little

praça (*pdah*-sah) f: plaza

praia (*pdah*-ee-ah) f: beach

preço (*pdeh*-soo) m: price

preto (*pdeh*-too): black

prima (*pdee*-mah) f: female cousin

primeiro (pdee-*may*-doo): first

primeiro nome (pdee-*may*-doo *noh*-mee): first name

primo (*pdee*-moo) m: male cousin

Q

quando (*kwahn*-doo): when

quanto (*kwahn*-too): how much

quarta-feira (*kwah*-tah *fay*-dah) f: Wednesday

quarteirão (kwah-tay-*dah*-ooh) m: city block

quatro (*kwah*-tdoo): four

que (kee): what

quem (kang): who

quinta-feira (*keen*-tah *fay*-dah) f: Thursday

R

rápido (*hah*-pee-doo): fast

recibo (heh-*see*-boo) m: receipt

reservar (heh-seh-*vah*): to reserve

responder (heh-spohn-*deh*): to answer

restaurante (heh-stah-ooh-*dahn*-chee) m: restaurant

reunião (hay-ooh-nee-*ah*-ooh) f: meeting

rio (*hee*-ooh) m: river

rosa (*hoh*-zah): pink

rua (*hoo*-ah) f: street

ruim (hoo-*eeng*): bad

S

sábado (*sah*-bah-doo) m: Saturday

sangue (*sahn*-gee) m: blood

seco (*seh*-koo): dry

seguinte (seh-*geen*-chee): next

segunda-feira (seh-*goon*-dah *fay*-dah) f: Monday

seis (*say*-eez): six

semana (seh-*mah*-nah) f: week

sete (*seh*-chee): seven

setembro (seh-*tem*-bdoo) m: September

sexta-feira (*ses*-tah *fay*-dah) f: Friday

sobrenome (soh-bdee-*noh*-mee) m: last name surname

sol (*soh*-ooh) m: sun

sul (soo) m: south

T

tamanho (tah-*mahn*-yoo) m: size

tarde (*tah*-jee): late

teatro (chee-*ah*-tdoo) m: theater

terça-feira (*teh*-sah *fay*-dah) f: Tuesday

terra (*teh*-hah) f: land

tia (*chee*-ah) f: aunt

tio (*chee*-ooh) m: uncle

tranquilo (tdahn-*kwee*-loo): calm or relaxed

tránsito (*tdahn*-zee-too) m: traffic

três (tdehz): three

U

um (oong): one

uva (*ooh*-vah) f: grape

V

velho (*vel*-yoo): old

verde (*veh*-jee): green

vermelho (veh-*mehl*-yoo): red

viagem (vee-*ah*-zhang) m: trip

vida (*vee*-dah) f: life

vidro (*vee*-droo) m: glass (material)

vinho (*ving*-yoo) m: wine

violão (vee-ooh-*lah*-ooh) m: guitar

vitamina (vee-tah-*mee*-nah) f: milkshake

voltar (vol-*tah*): to come back

English-Portuguese Mini-Dictionary

A

a lot: **muito** (moh-*ee*-toh)

actor: **ator** (ah-*toh*) m

agency: **agência** (ah-*zhang*-see-ah) f

and: **e** (ee)

another: **outro** (*oh*-tdooh)

to answer: **responder** (heh-spohn-*deh*)

apple: **maçã** (mah-*sah*) f

April: **abril** (ah-*bdee*-ooh) m

arm: **braço** (*bdah*-soo) m

to ask: **perguntar** (peh-goon-*tah*)

ATM: **caixa eletrônica** (*kah*-ee-shah eh-leh-*tdoh*-nee-kah) f

August: **agosto** (ah-*goh*-stoo) m

aunt: **tia** (*chee*-ah) f

available: **disponível** (jees-poh-*nee*-veh-ooh)

avenue: **avenida** (ah-veh-*nee*-dah) f

avocado: **abacate** (ah-bah-*koch*) m

B

bad: **ruim** (hoo-*eeng*)

banana: **banana** (bah-*nah*-nah) f

bank: **banco** (*bahn*-koh) m

bathroom: **banheiro** (bahn-*yay*-doh) m

beach: **praia** (*pdah*-ee-ah) f

beans: **feijão** (fay-*zhah*-ooh) m

bed: **cama** (*kah*-mah) f

beer: **cerveja** (seh-*veh*-zhah) f

better: **melhor** (mel-*yoh*)

bicycle: **bicicleta** (*bee*-see-*kleh*-tah) f

big: **grande** (*gdahn*-jee)

bill: **bilhete** (beel-*yeh*-chee) m

black: **preto** (*pdeh*-too)

blood: **sangue** (*sahn*-gee) m

blue: **azul** (ah-*zoo*)

boat: **barco** (*bah*-koo) m

book: **livro** (*leev*-doo) m

boy: **menino** (meh-*nee*-noo) m or **garoto** (gah-*doh*-too) m

bread: **pão** (*pah*-ooh) m

brother: **irmão** (ee-*mah*-ooh) m

brother-in-law: **cunhado** (koon-*yah*-doo) m

brown: **marrom** (mah-*hohng*)

bus: **ônibus** (*oh*-nee-boos) m

busy: **ocupado** (oh-koo-*pah*-doo)

by foot: **a pé** (ah *peh*)

C

to call: **ligar** (lee-*gah*)

calm, relaxed: **tranquilo** (tdahn-*kwee*-loo)

camera: **câmera** (*kah*-meh-dah) f

to cancel: **cancelar** (kahn-seh-*lah*)

car: **carro** (*kah*-hoo) m

cat: **gato** (*gah*-too) m

chair: **cadeira** (kah-*day*-dah) f

cheap: **barato** (bah-*dah*-too)

chest: **peito** (*pay*-too) m

chicken: **frango** (*fdahn*-goo) m

chocolate: **chocolate** (shoh-koh-*lah*-chee) m

city block: **quarteirão** (kwah-tay-*dah*-ooh) m

city: **cidade** (see-*dah*-jee) f

to clean: **limpar** (leem-*pah*)

to close: **fechar** (feh-*shah*)

coconut: **coco** (*koh*-koh) m

coffee: **café** (kah-*feh*) m

coin: **moeda** (moh-*eh*-dah) f

come back: **voltar** (vol-*tah*)

computer: **computador** (kohm-poo-tah-*doh*) m

cool (excellent): **legal** (lay-*goh*)

corner: **esquina** (es-*kee*-nah) f

cost: **custar** (koo-*stah*)

cotton: **algodão** (ah-ooh-goo-*dah*-ooh) m

country: **pais** (pah-*eez*) m

cousin: **primo** (*pdee*-moo) m or **prima** (*pdee*-mah) f

D

dark: **escuro** (eh-*skoo*-doo)

date: **data** (*dah*-tah) f

daughter: **filha** (*feel*-yah) f

day: **dia** (*jee*-ah) m

December: **dezembro** (deh-*zem*-bdoo) m

dentist: **dentista** (den-*chee*-stah) m/f

difficult: **difícil** (jee-*fee*-see-ooh)

direction: **direção** (jee-deh-*sah*-ooh) f

doctor: **médico** (*meh*-jee-koo) m

door: **porta** (*poh*-tah) f

drugstore: **farmácia** (fah-*mah*-see-ah) f

dry: **seco** (*seh*-koo)

E

ear: **orelha** (oh-*deh*-ooh-yah) f

east: **leste** (*lehs*-chee)

easy: **fácil** (*fah*-see-ooh)

egg: **ovo** (*oh*-voo) m

eight: **oito** (*oh*-ee-toh)

expensive: **caro** (*kah*-doo)

eye: **olho** (*ohl*-yoo) m

F

far away: **longe** (*lohn*-zhee)

fast: **rápido** (*hah*-pee-doo)

father: **pai** (*pah*-ee) m

February: **fevereiro** (feh-veh-*day*-doo) m

fever: **febre** (*feh*-bdee) f

to find: **encontrar** (en-kohn-*tdah*)

finger: **dedo** (*deh*-doo) m

first name: **primeiro nome** (pdee-*may*-doo *noh*-mee)

first: **primeiro** (pdee-*may*-doo)

fish: **peixe** (*pay*-shee) m

five: **cinco** (*sing*-koh)

floor: **andar** (ahn-*dah*) m

flower: **flor** (floh) f

food: **comida** (koh-*mee*-dah) f

foot: **pé** (peh) m

for/in order to: **para** (*pah*-dah)

four: **quatro** (*kwah*-tdoo)

Friday: **sexta-feira** (*ses*-tah *fay*-dah) f

fruit: **fruta** (*fdoo*-tah) f

fun: **divertido** (jee-veh-*chee*-doo)

G

garden: **jardim** (zhah-*jing*) m

garlic: **alho** (*ahl*-yoh) m

girl: **menina** (meh-*nee*-nah) f or **garota** (gah-*doh*-tah) f

glass (cup): **copo** (*koh*-poo) m

glass (material): **vidro** (vee-droo) m

gold: **ouro** (*oh*-doo) m

good: **bom** (*boh*-oong)

granddaughter: **neta** (*neh*-tah) f

grandma: **avó** (ah-*voh*) f

grandpa: **avô** (ah-*vah*) m

grandson: **neto** (*neh*-too) m

grape: **uva** (*ooh*-vah) f

green: **verde** (veh-jee)

guava: **goiaba** (goy-*ah*-bah) f

guide: **guia** (*gee*-ah) m

guitar: **violão** (vee-ooh-*lah*-ooh) m

H

happy: **feliz** (feh-*lees*) or **contente** (kohn-*ten*-chee)

head: **cabeça** (kah-*beh*-sah) f

help: **ajuda** (ah-zhoo-*dah*) f

her: **dela** (*deh*-lah)

his: **dele** (*deh*-lee)

honest: **honesto** (ooh-*neh*-stoo)

horse: **cavalo** (kah-*vah*-loo) m

hour: **hora** (*oh*-dah) f

house: **casa** (*kah*-zah) f

how much: **quanto** (*kwahn*-too)

hug: **abraço** (ah-*bdah*-soo) m

hunger: **fome** (*foh*-mee) m

I

identification: **identifição** (ee-den-chee-fee-kah-*sah*-ooh) f

immigration: **imigração** (ee-mee-gdah-*sah*-ooh) f

island: **ilha** (*eel*-yah) f

J

January: **janeiro** (zhah-*nay*-doo) m

July: **julho** (*zhool*-yoh) m

June: **junho** (*zhoon*-yoh) m

K

kiss: **beijo** (*bay*-zhoo) m

kitchen: **cozinha** (koh-*zing*-yah) f

knife: **faca** (*fah*-kah) f

L

land: **terra** (*teh*-hah) f

language: **lingua** (*ling*-gwah) f

last name: **sobrenome** (soh-bdee-*noh*-mee) m

late: **tarde** (*tah*-jee)

lawyer: **advogada** (ahj-voh-*gah*-dah) f or **advogado** (ahj-voh-*gah*-doo) m

left: **esquerda** (es-*keh*-dah)

leg: **perna** (*peh*-nah) f

less: **menos** (*meh*-nooz)

lettuce: **alface** (ah-ooh-*fah*-see) m

life: **vida** (*vee*-dah) f

light (in color): **claro** (*klah*-doo)

to like: **gostar** (goh-*stah*)

lime: **limão** (lee-*mah*-ooh) m
to listen: **escutar** (es-koo-*tah*)
little: **pouco** (*poh*-koo)
to live: **morar** (moh-*dah*)
lunch: **almoço** (ah-ooh-*moh*-soo) m

M

man: **homem** (*oh*-mang) m
manager: **gerente** (zheh-*dang*-chee) m
mango: **manga** (*mahn*-gah) f
map: **mapa** (*mah*-pah) m
March: **março** (*mah*-soo) m
May: **maio** (*my*-oh) m
medicine: **medicina** (meh-jee-*see*-nah) f
meeting: **reunião** (hay-ooh-nee-*ah*-ooh) f
milk: **leite** (*lay*-chee) m
milkshake: **vitamina** (vee-tah-*mee*-nah) f
minute: **minuto** (mee-*noo*-too) m
Monday: **segunda-feira** (seh-*goon*-dah *fay*-dah) f
money: **dinheiro** (jing-*yay*-doo) m
moon: **lua** (*loo*-ah) f
more: **mais** (*mah*-eez)
mother: **mãe** (*mah*-ee) f
mountain: **montanha** (mohn-*tahn*-yah) f
mouth: **boca** (*boh*-kah) f
movie theater: **cinema** (see-*neh*-mah) m
museum: **museu** (moo-*zeh*-ooh) m
music: **música** (*moo*-zee-kah) f

N

near: **perto** (*peh*-too)
neighborhood: **bairro** (*bah*-ee-hoo) m
next: **seguinte** (seh-*geen*-chee)

night: **noite** (*noh*-ee-chee) f
nightclub: **boate** (boh-*ah*-chee) m
nine: **nove** (*noh*-vee)
no: **não** (*nah*-ooh)
north: **norte** (*noh*-chee) m
nose: **nariz** (nah-*deez*) m
November: **novembro** (noo-*vem*-bdoo) m
now: **agora** (ah-*goh*-dah)
number: **número** (*noo*-meh-doh) m

O

ocean: **mar** (mah) m
October: **outubro** (ooh-*too*-bdoo) m
old: **velho** (*vel*-yoo)
one hundred: **cem** (sang)
one: **um** (oong)
onion: **cebola** (seh-*boh*-lah) f
or: **ou** (ooh)
outside: **fora** (*foh*-dah)
to open: **abrir** (ah-*bdeeh*)

P

pain: **dor** (doh) m
to paint: **pintar** (peen-*tah*)
pants: **calça** (*kah*-ooh-sah) f
park: **parque** (*pah*-kee) m
passport: **passaporte** (pah-sah-*poh*-chee) m
to pay: **pagar** (pah-*gah*)
peace: **paz** (*pah*-eez) f
person: **pessoa** (peh-*soh*-ah) f
photo: **foto** (*foh*-too) f
pineapple: **abacaxi** (ah-bah-kah-*shee*) m
pink: **rosa** (*hoh*-zah)

plaza: **praça** (*pdah*-sah) f
pool: **piscina** (pee-*see*-nah) f
post office: **correios** (koh-*hay*-ooz) m
price: **preço** (*pdeh*-soo)
to print out: **imprimir** (eem-pdee-*meeh*)

R

rain: **chuva** (*shoo*-vah) f
receipt: **recibo** (heh-*see*-boo) m
red: **vermelho** (veh-*mehl*-yoo)
to reserve: **reservar** (heh-seh-*vah*)
restaurant: **restaurante** (heh-stah-ooh-*dahn*-chee) m
rice: **arroz** (ah-*hohz*) m
right: **direita** (jee-*day*-tah)
river: **rio** (*hee*-ooh) m
road: **caminho** (kah-*mee*-yoo) m

S

Saturday: **sábado** (*sah*-bah-doo) m
September: **setembro** (seh-*tem*-bdoo) m
seven: **sete** (*seh*-chee)
shellfish: **mariscos** (mah-*dees*-kooz) m
shrimp: **camarão** (kah-mah-*dah*-ooh) m
singer: **cantor** (kahn-*toh*) m or **cantora** (kahn-*toh*-dah) f
sister: **irmã** (ee-*mah*) f
sister-in-law: **cunhada** (koon-*yah*-dah) f
six: **seis** (*say*-eez)
size: **tamanho** (tah-*mahn*-yoo) m
skirt steak: **bife** (*bee*-fee) m
sky: **céu** (*seh*-ooh) m
slowly: **devagar** (deh-vah-*gah*)
small: **pequeno** (peh-*keh*-noo)

soap opera: **novela** (noh-*veh*-lah) f
some: **algum** (ah-ooh-*goong*)
son: **filho** (*feel*-yoo) m
song: **canção** (kahn-*sah*-ooh) m
south: **sul** (soo) m
to speak: **falar** (fah-*lah*)
special: **especial** (eh-speh-see-*ah*-ooh)
spicy: **picante** (pee-*kahn*-chee)
spinach: **espinafre** (es-pee-*nah*-fdee) m
spoon: **colher** (kool-*yeh*) m
state: **estado** (eh-*stah*-doo) m
station: **estação** (es-tah-*sah*-ooh) f
street: **rua** (*hoo*-ah) f
sun: **sol** (*soh*-ooh) m
Sunday: **domingo** (doo-*ming*-goo) m
sweet: **doce** (*doh*-see)

T

table: **mesa** (*meh*-zah) f
tall: **alto** (*ah*-ooh-too)
ten: **dez** (dez)
theater: **teatro** (chee-*ah*-tdoo) m
theirs: **deles** (*deh*-leez)
thing: **coisa** (*koy*-zah) f
to think: **achar** (ah-*shah*)
three: **três** (tdehz)
Thursday: **quinta-feira** (*keen*-tah *fay*-dah) f
tight: **apertado** (ah-peh-*tah*-doo)
today: **hoje** (*oh*-zhee)
toe: **dedo do pé** (*deh*-doo doo *peh*) m
together: **junto** (*zhoon*-too)
tomorrow: **amanhã** (ah-mahng-*yah*)
tongue: **língua** (*ling*-gwah) f
tooth: **dente** (*den*-chee) m

traffic: **tránsito** (*tdahn*-zee-too) m

tree: **árvore** (*ah*-voh-dee) f

trip: **viagem** (vee-*ah*-zhang) m

to try: **experimentar** (eh-*speh*-dee-men-*tah*)

T-shirt: **camiseta** (kah-mee-*zeh*-tah) f

Tuesday: **terça-feira** (*teh*-sah *fay*-dah) f

tuna: **atum** (ah-*toong*) m

two: **dois** (*doh*-eez)

U

ugly: **feo** (*fay*-ooh)

uncle: **tio** (*chee*-ooh) m

W

war: **guerra** (*geh*-hah) f

water: **água** (*ah*-gwah) f

Wednesday: **quarta-feira** (*kwah*-tah *fay*-dah) f

week: **semana** (seh-*mah*-nah) f

west: **oeste** (oh-*es*-chee) m

what: **que** (kee)

when: **quando** (*kwahn*-doo)

white: **branco** (*bdahn*-koh)

who: **quem** (kang)

wine: **vinho** (*ving*-yoo) m

with: **com** (kohng)

woman: **mulher** (mool-*yeh*) f

wood: **madeira** (mah-*day*-dah) f

worse: **pior** (pee-*oh*)

Y

yellow: **amarelo** (ah-mah-*deh*-loo)

young: **jovem** (*zhoh*-vang)

Appendix C

Answer Key

Chapter 1: You Already Know a Little Portuguese!

1. e   2. c   3. b   4. a   5. d

Chapter 2: The Nitty-Gritty: Basic Portuguese Grammar and Numbers

1. Mauricio/Carolina   2. Mauricio   3. Carolina   4. Carolina
5. Mauricio   6. Mauricio/Carolina   7. Carolina   8. Mauricio

Chapter 3: Oi! Hello! Greetings and Introductions

1. **Oi, tudo bem?**   2. **Tudo bom.**   3. **Qual é seu nome?**
4. **O meu nome é . . .**   5. **Você fala bem o português!**   6. **Obrigado/a!**
7. **Adéus!**   8. **Tchau!**

(The last two lines can be switched.)

Chapter 4: Getting to Know You: Making Small Talk

1.f   2. i   3. a   4. h   5. b   6. c   7. g   8. d   9. e

Chapter 5: Dining Out and Going to Market

1. **frango**   2. **cerveja**   3. **água**   4. **cebolas**   5. **arroz**   6. **feijão**   7. **carne**
8. a light draft beer   9. sparkling mineral water   10. a sautéed beef and
cheese sandwich
without tomato

Chapter 6: Shopping Made Easy

1. e   2. c   3. d   4. a   5. b   6. **azul claro**   7. **lilás**

8. **preto**   9. **vermelho escuro**   10. **branco**

Chapter 7: At the Beach

1. j   2. g   3. f   4. a   5. c   6. b   7. e   8. d   9. h   10. i

Chapter 8: Going Out on the Town

The order's up to you, but here's a translation of what each activity is:

1. bar   2. movies   3. live music   4. modern art exhibition
5. rock music concert   6. *The Godfather*   7. *Gone with the Wind*
8. *The Wizard of Oz*   9. *Singing in the Rain*   10. *Star Wars*   11. *Jaws*

Chapter 9: Talking on the Phone

1. **nadei**   2. **tomei sol**   3. **cantei**   4. **falei**   5. **cozinhei**

Chapter 10: At the Office and around the House

1. **porta** (door)   2. **estacionamento** (parking)   3. **jardim** (garden)
4. **luz** (light)   5. **terraça** (balcony)   6. **piscina** (pool)
7. **geladeira** (refrigerator)   8. **cama** (bed)   9. **travesseira** (pillow)

Chapter 11: Money, Money, Money

1. **banco**   2. **retirar**   3. **dinheiro**   4. **conta**   5. **grana**
6. **caixa automática**   7. **duas notas**   8. **pagar**   9. **recibo**

Chapter 12: Onde Fica? (Where Is It?) Asking for Directions

1. **Vá para a praça.**   2. **Depois, pega esquerda na Avenida Bela Cintra.**
3. **Vá direto/reto até o final.**   4. **A sua direita, vai ver uma igreja.**
5. **Fica atrás da igreja, na beira-mar.**

Chapter 13: Staying at a Hotel or Guesthouse

1. **o secador de cabelo dela**   2. **a escova de dentes dele**   3. **as malas deles**
4. **a minha carteira**   5. **o nosso guia**   6. **a bolsa dela**

Chapter 14: Getting Around: Planes, Buses, Taxis, and More

A. **bicicleta**   B. **barco**   C. **avião**   D. **jangada**   E. **a pé**
F. **ônibus**   G. **metrô**

Chapter 15: Planning a Trip

1. **dezembro** (December); spring
2. **abril** (April); fall
3. **setembro** (September); winter
4. **janeiro** (January); summer
5. **maio** (May); fall
6. **fevereiro** (February); summer
7. **março** (March) summer
8. **agosto** (August); winter
9. **julho** (July); winter
10. **novembro** (November); spring
11. **junho** (June); fall
12. **outubro** (October); spring

Chapter 16: Me Ajuda! Help! Handling Emergencies

A. **braço** (arm)   B. **perna** (leg)   C. **olho** (eye)   D. **peito** (chest)
E. **dedos** (fingers)   F. **dedos do pé** (toes)   G. **ore ha** (ear)   H. **ca beça** (head)

Chapter 17: O Carnaval!

1. Recife/Olinda   2. Rio   3. Salvador   4. Rio   5. Recife/Olinda
6. Salvador   7. Salvador   8. Recife/Olinda   9. Salvador

Appendix D

On the CD

* *

*F*ollowing is a list of the tracks that appear on this book's audio CD, which you can find tucked into a sleeve inside the back cover. Please note that the CD is audio-only, and you can put it in your CD player or (with the right software) play it on your computer any time you please. It will help you with your pronunciations in Brazilian Portuguese.

Track 1: Introduction

Track 2: Pronunciation Guide (Chapter 1)

Track 3: Getting settled and chatting with a guide (Chapter 3)

Track 4: Conversation in a cafe (Chapter 3)

Track 5: Asking people where they're from (Chapter 4)

Track 6: Talking about the weather (Chapter 4)

Track 7: Discussing e-mail and music concerts (Chapter 4)

Track 8: Discussing the bill at a restaurant (Chapter 5)

Track 9: Going to market (Chapter 5)

Track 10: Shopping for sunglasses (Chapter 6)

Track 11: Shopping in a CD store (Chapter 6)

Track 12: Going to the beach (Chapter 7)

Track 13: Visiting the island of Ilha Grande (Chapter 7)

Track 14: Meeting a friend (Chapter 7)

Track 15: Planning to attend an event (Chapter 8)

Track 16: Planning to go to the movies (Chapter 8)

Track 17: Talking on the phone (Chapter 9)

Track 18: Discussing vacation over the phone (Chapter 9)

Track 19: Trading personal information (Chapter 10)

Track 20: Instant messaging over the Internet (Chapter 10)

Track 21: Getting change for $100 (Chapter 11)

Track 22: Making a big purchase (Chapter 11)

Track 23: Asking about bus routes (Chapter 12)

Track 24: Looking for a shopping mall (Chapter 12)

Track 25: Checking on distances (Chapter 12)

Track 26: Discussing sleep schedules (Chapter 13)

Track 27: Talking about who owns what (Chapter 13)

Track 28: Making travel reservations (Chapter 14)

Track 29: Hiring a taxi (Chapter 14)

Track 30: Discussing waiting times (Chapter 14)

Track 31: Asking vacation advice (Chapter 15)

Track 32: Checking and choosing airlines (Chapter 15)

Appendix E

Where in the World Is Portuguese Spoken?

● ●

*P*ortuguese explorers in the 15th and 16th centuries traveled the globe in search of adventure and riches and to spread the Catholic religion. Along the way, some countries adopted the Portuguese language. Today, Portuguese is the official language of five African countries — along with Portugal, Brazil, and East Timor, which is located in Asia. This part of the book explains a little about these countries.

In all cases except for Brazil and Portugal, many indigenous languages coexist with Portuguese. Though government officials and business people speak Portuguese, most regular people you'd encounter on the street use either a creole language to express themselves — Portuguese mixed with a local language — or a local indigenous language. That said, road signs and official information are in Portuguese, which can give you a great head start in learning about these countries.

Brasil (bdah-zee-ooh; Brazil)

Population: 186 million

Brazil is the largest country on the South American continent. It's also the world's fifth-largest country — in terms of both size and population. Geographically, Brazil is roughly the size of the U.S.

You may not know that this country is a world-class maker of commercial **aviões** (ah-vee-*oh*-eez; airplanes).

Brazil nuts originate in Brazil, but in Brazil, they're called **castanhas do Pará** (kah-*stan*-yooz doo pah-*dah;* Para nuts), after the northern Brazilian state where you can find many Brazil nut trees.

Moçambique (moh-sahm-bee-kee; Mozambique)

Population: 19.4 million

Mozambique is located in southeastern Africa. Opposite its shores is the island of Madagascar, and South Africa touches Mozambique to the south. This country is slightly less than twice the size of California.

Mozambique is home to a church that's considered the oldest European building in the Southern Hemisphere. The **Capela de Nossa Senhora do Baluarte** (kah-*peh*-lah jee *noh*-sah seen-*yoh*-yah doo bah-loo-*ah*-chee; Chapel of Our Lady of Baluarte) was built in 1522.

Although the **lingua oficial** (*ling*-gwah oh-*fee*-see-*ah*-ooh; official language) here is Portuguese, only 27 percent of the population actually speaks the language. But you'll be able to communicate in Portuguese for sure with government officials and business people.

Angola (ahn-goh-lah; Angola)

Population: 11.2 million

Angola is located on Africa's southwestern coast, with the Democratic Republic of Congo to the north, Zambia to the east, and Namibia to the south. It's a little less than twice the size of Texas.

One of the two types of **capoeira** (kay-poh-*ay*-dah) in Brazil is called **capoeira da Angola** (kah-poh-*ay*-dah dah ahn-*goh*-lah; capoeira from Angola) because this popular martial art originates in Angola. Slaves long ago brought the moves to Brazil. The moves themselves are slower and closer to the ground compared to **capoeira regional** (kah-poh-*ay*-dah *heh*-zhee-ooh-*nah*-ooh; *Literally:* regional capoeira), which was developed in Bahia state in Brazil.

Diamantes (jee-ah-*mahn*-cheez; diamonds) are a major export trade.

Portugal (poh-too-gah-ooh; Portugal)

Population: 10.6 million

Portugal is located on the Iberian Peninsula in Europe. It's about one-sixth the size of Spain, its neighbor to the north and east.

Vinho do Porto (*veen*-yoo doo *poh*-too; Port wine) originates in the northern Portuguese city of **Oporto** (ooh-*poh*-too).

Portuguese **escritor** (eh-skdee-*toh;* writer) José Saramago won the Nobel prize for literature in 1998.

Guiné Bissau (gee-neh bee-sah-ooh; Guinea-Bissau)

Population: 1.4 million

Guinea-Bissau is on the coast of northwestern Africa, and it's slightly less than three times larger than Connecticut. Its neighbors are the countries of Senegal to the north and Guinea to the south.

Guinea-Bissau is one of the world's ten poorest countries. Its economy is based on farming and fishing. Cashew exports have risen in recent years, however, and have made Guinea-Bissau the world's sixth in terms of cashew production.

This country gained independence from Portugal as recently as 1974.

In terms of religious beliefs, **Muçulmanos** (moo-sool-*mah*-nooz; Muslims) make up 45 percent of the population.

Timor Leste (tee-moo lehs-chee; East Timor)

Population: 1 million

East Timor lies to the northwest of Australia. It's part of the Lesser Sunda Islands, at the eastern end of Indonesia's island chain. East Timor is mostly on the eastern portion of an island called Timor. Indonesia controls the other side of the island, except for one small area that belongs to East Timor.

Along with a local language called Tetum, Portuguese shares the distinction of being East Timor's official national language. Sixteen other indigenous languages are also spoken here.

East Timor is the world's newest nation, having gained **independência** (een-deh-pen-*den*-see-ah; independence) from Indonesia in 1999.

Cabo Verde (kah-boo veh-jee; Cape Verde)

Population: 418,000

Cape Verde is a collection of islands off the northwestern coast of Africa. Together, the islands are smaller than Rhode Island. Nine are inhabited. The biggest island, Santiago, is only 55 km (34.3 miles) long and 29 km (18 miles) wide. The capital of Cape Verde is **Praia** (*pdah*-ee-ah; Beach).

The 12 major islands that make up this country were totally uninhabited in the 15th century, when they were **descobertos** (des-koo-*beh*-tooz; discovered) by the Portuguese.

Cape Verde's most famous artist is **Cesaria Evora** (seh-*zah*-dee-ah *eh*-voh-dah), whose lyrical interpretation of a local musical style called **mourna** (*moh*-nah) has won fans the world over.

São Tomé e Príncipe (sah-ooh toh-meh ee pdeen-see-pee; Sao Tome and Principe)

Population: 187,400

One of Africa's smallest countries, Sao Tome and Principe sits on the Equator, in the Gulf of Gabon, off Africa's western coast. The entire country is only five times the **tamanho** (tah-*mahn*-yoo; size) of Washington, D.C.

One of this country's few islands is called **Ilhéu Bom-Bom** (eel-*yeh*-ooh boh-oong *boh*-oong; Bon-Bon Island).

The country is known for its delicious coffee, stemming from its historic cash crop, coffee beans.

Recent discoveries of oil reserves within the country's domain are expected to boost the local economy.

Index

• T •

Notes

Notes

Notes

Notes

Notes

Notes

Notes

Notes

Notes

Notes

Notes

Notes

Notes

BUSINESS, CAREERS & PERSONAL FINANCE

Grant Writing FOR DUMMIES

0-7645-5307-0

Home Buying FOR DUMMIES

0-7645-5331-3 *†

Also available:

- Accounting For Dummies †
  0-7645-5314-3
- Business Plans Kit For Dummies †
  0-7645-5365-8
- Cover Letters For Dummies
  0-7645-5224-4
- Frugal Living For Dummies
  0-7645-5403-4
- Leadership For Dummies
  0-7645-5176-0
- Managing For Dummies
  0-7645-1771-6

- Marketing For Dummies
  0-7645-5600-2
- Personal Finance For Dummies *
  0-7645-2590-5
- Project Management For Dummies
  0-7645-5283-X
- Resumes For Dummies †
  0-7645-5471-9
- Selling For Dummies
  0-7645-5363-1
- Small Business Kit For Dummies *†
  0-7645-5093-4

HOME & BUSINESS COMPUTER BASICS

Windows XP FOR DUMMIES

0-7645-4074-2

Excel 2003 ALL-IN-ONE DESK REFERENCE FOR DUMMIES

0-7645-3758-X

Also available:

- ACT! 6 For Dummies
  0-7645-2645-6
- iLife '04 All-in-One Desk Reference
  For Dummies
  0-7645-7347-0
- iPAQ For Dummies
  0-7645-6769-1
- Mac OS X Panther Timesaving
  Techniques For Dummies
  0-7645-5812-9
- Macs For Dummies
  0-7645-5656-8

- Microsoft Money 2004 For Dummies
  0-7645-4195-1
- Office 2003 All-in-One Desk Reference
  For Dummies
  0-7645-3883-7
- Outlook 2003 For Dummies
  0-7645-3759-8
- PCs For Dummies
  0-7645-4074-2
- TiVo For Dummies
  0-7645-6923-6
- Upgrading and Fixing PCs For Dummies
  0-7645-1665-5
- Windows XP Timesaving Techniques
  For Dummies
  0-7645-3748-2

FOOD, HOME, GARDEN, HOBBIES, MUSIC & PETS

Feng Shui FOR DUMMIES

0-7645-5295-3

Poker FOR DUMMIES

0-7645-5232-5

Also available:

- Bass Guitar For Dummies
  0-7645-2487-9
- Diabetes Cookbook For Dummies
  0-7645-5230-9
- Gardening For Dummies *
  0-7645-5130-2
- Guitar For Dummies
  0-7645-5106-X
- Holiday Decorating For Dummies
  0-7645-2570-0
- Home Improvement All-in-One
  For Dummies
  0-7645-5680-0

- Knitting For Dummies
  0-7645-5395-X
- Piano For Dummies
  0-7645-5105-1
- Puppies For Dummies
  0-7645-5255-4
- Scrapbooking For Dummies
  0-7645-7208-3
- Senior Dogs For Dummies
  0-7645-5818-8
- Singing For Dummies
  0-7645-2475-5
- 30-Minute Meals For Dummies
  0-7645-2589-1

INTERNET & DIGITAL MEDIA

Digital Photography FOR DUMMIES

0-7645-1664-7

Starting an eBay Business FOR DUMMIES

0-7645-6924-4

Also available:

- 2005 Online Shopping Directory
  For Dummies
  0-7645-7495-7
- CD & DVD Recording For Dummies
  0-7645-5956-7
- eBay For Dummies
  0-7645-5654-1
- Fighting Spam For Dummies
  0-7645-5965-6
- Genealogy Online For Dummies
  0-7645-5964-8
- Google For Dummies
  0-7645-4420-9

- Home Recording For Musicians
  For Dummies
  0-7645-1634-5
- The Internet For Dummies
  0-7645-4173-0
- iPod & iTunes For Dummies
  0-7645-7772-7
- Preventing Identity Theft For Dummies
  0-7645-7336-5
- Pro Tools All-in-One Desk Reference
  For Dummies
  0-7645-5714-9
- Roxio Easy Media Creator For Dummies
  0-7645-7131-1

* Separate Canadian edition also available

† Separate U.K. edition also available

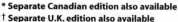

Available wherever books are sold. For more information or to order direct: U.S. customers visit www.dummies.com or call 1-877-762-2974.
U.K. customers visit www.wileyeurope.com or call 0800 243407. Canadian customers visit www.wiley.ca or call 1-800-567-4797.

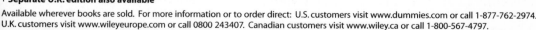

WILEY

SPORTS, FITNESS, PARENTING, RELIGION & SPIRITUALITY

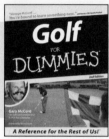

0-7645-5146-9

0-7645-5418-2

Also available:
- Adoption For Dummies
  0-7645-5488-3
- Basketball For Dummies
  0-7645-5248-1
- The Bible For Dummies
  0-7645-5296-1
- Buddhism For Dummies
  0-7645-5359-3
- Catholicism For Dummies
  0-7645-5391-7
- Hockey For Dummies
  0-7645-5228-7

- Judaism For Dummies
  0-7645-5299-6
- Martial Arts For Dummies
  0-7645-5358-5
- Pilates For Dummies
  0-7645-5397-6
- Religion For Dummies
  0-7645-5264-3
- Teaching Kids to Read For Dummies
  0-7645-4043-2
- Weight Training For Dummies
  0-7645-5168-X
- Yoga For Dummies
  0-7645-5117-5

TRAVEL

0-7645-5438-7

0-7645-5453-0

Also available:
- Alaska For Dummies
  0-7645-1761-9
- Arizona For Dummies
  0-7645-6938-4
- Cancún and the Yucatán For Dummies
  0-7645-2437-2
- Cruise Vacations For Dummies
  0-7645-6941-4
- Europe For Dummies
  0-7645-5456-5
- Ireland For Dummies
  0-7645-5455-7

- Las Vegas For Dummies
  0-7645-5448-4
- London For Dummies
  0-7645-4277-X
- New York City For Dummies
  0-7645-6945-7
- Paris For Dummies
  0-7645-5494-8
- RV Vacations For Dummies
  0-7645-5443-3
- Walt Disney World & Orlando For Dummies
  0-7645-6943-0

GRAPHICS, DESIGN & WEB DEVELOPMENT

0-7645-4345-8

0-7645-5589-8

Also available:
- Adobe Acrobat 6 PDF For Dummies
  0-7645-3760-1
- Building a Web Site For Dummies
  0-7645-7144-3
- Dreamweaver MX 2004 For Dummies
  0-7645-4342-3
- FrontPage 2003 For Dummies
  0-7645-3882-9
- HTML 4 For Dummies
  0-7645-1995-6
- Illustrator CS For Dummies
  0-7645-4084-X

- Macromedia Flash MX 2004 For Dummies
  0-7645-4358-X
- Photoshop 7 All-in-One Desk
  Reference For Dummies
  0-7645-1667-1
- Photoshop CS Timesaving Techniques
  For Dummies
  0-7645-6782-9
- PHP 5 For Dummies
  0-7645-4166-8
- PowerPoint 2003 For Dummies
  0-7645-3908-6
- QuarkXPress 6 For Dummies
  0-7645-2593-X

NETWORKING, SECURITY, PROGRAMMING & DATABASES

0-7645-6852-3

0-7645-5784-X

Also available:
- A+ Certification For Dummies
  0-7645-4187-0
- Access 2003 All-in-One Desk
  Reference For Dummies
  0-7645-3988-4
- Beginning Programming For Dummies
  0-7645-4997-9
- C For Dummies
  0-7645-7068-4
- Firewalls For Dummies
  0-7645-4048-3
- Home Networking For Dummies
  0-7645-42796

- Network Security For Dummies
  0-7645-1679-5
- Networking For Dummies
  0-7645-1677-9
- TCP/IP For Dummies
  0-7645-1760-0
- VBA For Dummies
  0-7645-3989-2
- Wireless All In-One Desk Reference
  For Dummies
  0-7645-7496-5
- Wireless Home Networking For Dummies
  0-7645-3910-8

HEALTH & SELF-HELP

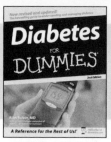

0-7645-6820-5 *†

0-7645-2566-2

Also available:
- Alzheimer's For Dummies
  0-7645-3899-3
- Asthma For Dummies
  0-7645-4233-8
- Controlling Cholesterol For Dummies
  0-7645-5440-9
- Depression For Dummies
  0-7645-3900-0
- Dieting For Dummies
  0-7645-4149-8
- Fertility For Dummies
  0-7645-2549-2

- Fibromyalgia For Dummies
  0-7645-5441-7
- Improving Your Memory For Dummies
  0-7645-5435-2
- Pregnancy For Dummies †
  0-7645-4483-7
- Quitting Smoking For Dummies
  0-7645-2629-4
- Relationships For Dummies
  0-7645-5384-4
- Thyroid For Dummies
  0-7645-5385-2

EDUCATION, HISTORY, REFERENCE & TEST PREPARATION

0-7645-5194-9

0-7645-4186-2

Also available:
- Algebra For Dummies
  0-7645-5325-9
- British History For Dummies
  0-7645-7021-8
- Calculus For Dummies
  0-7645-2498-4
- English Grammar For Dummies
  0-7645-5322-4
- Forensics For Dummies
  0-7645-5580-4
- The GMAT For Dummies
  0-7645-5251-1
- Inglés Para Dummies
  0-7645-5427-1

- Italian For Dummies
  0-7645-5196-5
- Latin For Dummies
  0-7645-5431-X
- Lewis & Clark For Dummies
  0-7645-2545-X
- Research Papers For Dummies
  0-7645-5426-3
- The SAT I For Dummies
  0-7645-7193-1
- Science Fair Projects For Dummies
  0-7645-5460-3
- U.S. History For Dummies
  0-7645-5249-X

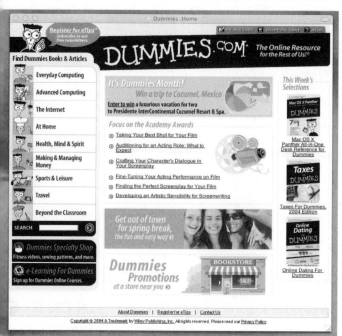

Get smart @ dummies.com®

- **Find a full list of Dummies titles**
- **Look into loads of FREE on-site articles**
- **Sign up for FREE eTips e-mailed to you weekly**
- **See what other products carry the Dummies name**
- **Shop directly from the Dummies bookstore**
- **Enter to win new prizes every month!**

* Separate Canadian edition also available

† Separate U.K. edition also available

Available wherever books are sold. For more information or to order direct: U.S. customers visit www.dummies.com or call 1-877-762-2974.
U.K. customers visit www.wileyeurope.com or call 0800 243407. Canadian customers visit www.wiley.ca or call 1-800-567-4797.